POVERTY——————
IN
——AMERICA

POVERTY—
IN
—AMERICA

The Welfare Dilemma

Ralph Segalman

Asoke Basu

CONTRIBUTIONS IN SOCIOLOGY, NUMBER 39

$\left(\dfrac{G}{P}\right)$ **Greenwood Press**
WESTPORT, CONNECTICUT • LONDON, ENGLAND

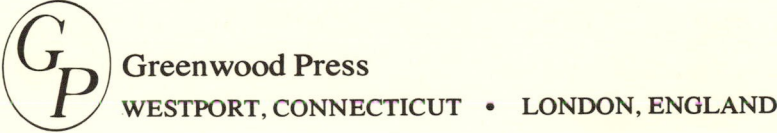

Copyright Acknowledgements

Portions of the material in the text have appeared previously in:

Ralph Segalman, *Social Legislation and the Constraints of Social Policy* (Northridge: California State University, Northridge Foundation, 1976). Copyright © Ralph Segalman.

Ralph Segalman, *Conflicting Rights: Social Legislation and Policy,* vol. 1 (Washington, D.C.: University Press of America, 1977). Copyright © Ralph Segalman.

Table 8.3 appeared in: Ralph Segalman, "The Cultural Chasm Reconsidered," *Rocky Mountain Social Science Journal* 6, no. 2 (1969): 143–45.

Library of Congress Cataloging in Publication Data

Segalman, Ralph.
   Poverty in America.

   (Contributions in sociology; no. 39 ISSN 0084–9278)
   Bibliography: p.
   Includes index.
   1. Public welfare—United States. 2. Poverty—
United States. I. Basu, Asoke, 1938–   joint author.
II. Title.
HV91.S33   362.5'0973   79–6568
ISBN 0–313–20751–8 lib. bdg.

Library of Congress Catalog Card Number: 79–6568
ISBN: 0–313–20751–8
ISSN: 0084–9278

First published in 1981

Greenwood Press
A division of Congressional Information Service, Inc.
88 Post Road West, Westport, Connecticut 06881

Printed in the United States of America

10 9 8 7 6 5 4 3 2 1

To
The Women of Valor
Anita and Mollie

CONTENTS

TABLES

PREFACE

Two different principles—equality of opportunity and delivered equality —define the crucial issue in the debate over America's social welfare proposals for alleviating poverty. Historically, equality of opportunity has meant that a democratic society is obligated to provide equal access to jobs, education, services, and, finally, improved life conditions. The tasks and duties of such an egalitarian society are to make a set of choices available to all. Viewed in this way, poverty is not a structural aberration. Welfare policies are therefore directed toward attracting the individual/ family upward from poverty and toward putting success within reach of anyone who seeks it. The viability of these policies requires that equal opportunity be made genuinely available to all.

The principle of delivered equality maintains that within the democratic order equality is a right and not an opportunity. Accordingly, society must provide every person with quality jobs, education, services, and comfortable life conditions.

The first position, equality of opportunity, assumes that each individual possesses free will. Given the appropriate availability of choices, then, man has the learned capacity to make critical decisions about his life at present and in the future. The democratic order can therefore provide only choices; in the final analysis, the willing, thinking person must choose and thus act.

The second position, delivered equality, is clearly deterministic for its premise is that man is shaped by factors beyond the individual's control. The current rhetoric emphasizes that man has become a mere object or, at best, an underclass citizen whose movements are controlled by forces beyond self. Thus, the state must ultimately be the dispenser of provisions.

In this book, we contend that social welfare policies based on the premise of delivered equality negates the norm of reciprocity under which each person is expected to supply a quid for each quo consumed. This position has become a self-fulfilling prophecy for those it claims to benefit because it frequently leads to the conclusion that man is indeed a victim.

The advocates of this position have created an atmosphere of failure for many who might otherwise have succeeded had they been stimulated to try. By its continued existence, the poverty population serves the interests of the delivered equality proponents by providing a raison d'être for their position. Thus, the proponents may be viewed, in part, as perpetuators of the poverty syndrome. The diagnosis perpetuates the disease to the benefit of the physician.

We must be aware of the implications and effects of such an advocacy on the client as person and on the society as provider and supporter. One pressing danger is that a social policy for the poor might evolve which, instead of providing for equality of choice, fosters a life-long delivered dependency that could seriously erode the democratic order.

In this work, we comprehensively explore the contours of social welfare and poverty in America. The opening chapter examines the definitions of poverty, its roots and social consequences. The second chapter traces the history of poor law—practices that originated in Britain and were adopted by the early settlers in America. Our purpose here is to pursue value transformations in the meaning of poverty over the past two centuries. Chapter 3 presents various types of programs of public assistance and social insurance in practice in America. Welfare legislation debated by the Ninety-fifth Congress (1978) has been incorporated. Chapter 4 deals with alternative social interventions against poverty. It discusses the increasing numbers on the welfare rolls and the costs of the Aid to Families with Dependent Children program. In addition, it underscores both the social basis and the social consequences of developing transgenerational poverty. Chapter 5 further explores some of the current income maintenance proposals, including the Carter welfare proposal and other alternatives. Chapter 6 articulates assumptions about medical services for the poor and outlines the Ninety-fifth Congress's proposals on national health insurance. Chapter 7 examines another key program—housing assistance for the poor. The literature on poverty and welfare has devoted very little space to employment and its concomitant relationship to educational programs and socioeconomic mobility. In postindustrial America, the amelioration of poverty depends on joining employment with educational experience. It is of primary importance that this relationship be understood, if we are to affirm and actualize a social structure based on achieved status. Chapter 8 and the postscript examine programs and policy alternatives in the light of this principle. (An earlier version of portions of the postscript was presented by Asoke Basu at the annual meeting of the Society for the Study of Social Problems in 1975.)

Finally, we attempt to demythologize the welfare rhetoric. Our fundamental assumption is that national resources are finite and that any policy governing poverty programs increasingly has to take the economic conditions (both from the public and client viewpoint) into account. Throughout our exploration, we have been influenced by the dictum of Auguste Comte—"Our analysis of the seen must be geared to the forseeable."

In many ways, this book has been a labor of collegiality. The principal author has benefited immensely from students' comments on an earlier draft. The California state universities at Hayward and Northridge have provided encouraging colleagues, students, library resources, and, however little, financial assistance to support this venture. To our institutions, we owe continuing gratitude. We specifically wish to thank Nathan Glazer, Alfred Himelson, Norman Jackman, S. M. Lipset, and Albert Pierce, as well as Professor Don Martindale, series editor, and Dr. James T. Sabin, editorial vice-president of Greenwood Press, for their helpful guidance. Finally, we express appreciation to Ruth Ancheta and James Scaminaci III for their research asssistance and to Randy Keith for his work in typing the final manuscript.

PROGRAMS AND BILLS

Aid to the Blind   (AB)
Aid to Families With Dependent Children   (AFDC)
    [AFDC-U = Unemployed Father]
Aid to the Totally Disabled   (ATD)
American Conservative Union   (ACU)
Basic Educational Opportunity Grant   (BEOG)
Better Jobs and Income Program (BJIP)
Charity Organization movement
Charity Organization Society   (COS)
Chicago Housing Authority   (CHA)
Child Saving movement
Civil Works Agency   (CWA)
Comprehensive Employment and Training Act   (CETA)
Elizabethan Poor Law
Emergency Employment Program   (EEP)
Family Assistance Plan proposal
Farmers Home Administration
Federal Emergency Relief Act
Federal Home Loan Bank
Federal Housing Administration   (FHA)
Federal National Mortgage Association
Food Stamp program
General Accounting Office   (GAO)
General Assistance   (GA)
Government National Mortgage Association   (GNMA)
Health Maintenance Organization   (HMO)
Health Services Agency   (HSA)

Home Owners Loan Corporation   (HOLC)
Housing Act of 1937
Housing Act of 1949
Housing Assistance Administration
Housing and Urban Development Act
Lanham Act of 1940
Law of Charitable Trusts
Law of Settlement and Removal
Medical Poor Law
Missionary Tract Society
National Home Mortgage Insurance   (NHMI)
National Housing Act
National Industrial Recovery Act   (NIRA)
National Insurance Act of 1911
New York Associates for Improving the Conditions of the
     Poor (NYAIP)
Nixon Family Assistance Plan
Old Age, Survivors and Disabled Insurance   (OASDI)
Old Age Assistance   (OAA)
Professional Standards Review Organization   (PSRO)
Public Employee Benefit Program
Public Housing Administration   (PHA)
Reconstruction Finance Corporation
Settlement house movement
State Vocational Rehabilitation Agency   (SVRA)
Sunday School Society
Supplementary Security Income Program   (SSI)
U.S. Department of Health, Education, and Welfare   (HEW)
U.S. Department of Housing and Urban Development   (HUD)
Widows, Orphans, and Old Age
Work Incentive program   (WIN)
Works Progress Administration   (WPA)

POVERTY
IN
——AMERICA

THE PARAMETERS OF POVERTY   1

HOULT (p. 245) defines poverty as (1) "a scarcity of the means of subsistence" and (2) "a level of living that is below a particular minimum standard." The Theodorsons (p. 307) define it as "a standard of living that lasts long enough to undermine the health, morale and self-respect of an individual or group of individuals. The term is relative to the general standard of living in society, the distribution of wealth, the status system and social expectations." If Hoult's definition is accepted, it becomes a fiscal exercise to determine who is poor. In his exploratory exercise *The Measurement of Poverty,* Watts provides one of many such economic conceptualizations of the condition. The Theodorsons' definition describes relative deprivation or affluence. In order to identify poverty, they say it is necessary to compare the subjects' wants—or needs—with those of nonpoverty population sectors (also see Theobald).

Milner's work makes it clear that inequality is an inevitable condition in an "equalitarian but striving" society (1972a). In such a society, everyone is given a chance to get ahead. Few people realize the corollary to this notion, which is that everyone has the opportunity to be gotten ahead of. In Milner's view, status insecurity is a necessary part of any society which affords both significant inequality and equal opportunity. In such a situation, a person's only defense is to stay ahead: "If others raise their income or education you must raise yours. If others get a new car, you must buy a bigger one" (1972b, p. 20). Milner terms this situation status inflation, which he states occurs "when there is a decrease in the social value attributed to a given level of absolute income." Thus, equality of opportunity, status insecurity, and status seeking combine to produce status inflation. Milner asserts that there is a paradoxical conflict between the belief that rights and respect are everyone's equal due, and the belief that there is virtue in individual achievement and that a person's rewards should closely correspond to his achievements. Thus, Milner portrays "equalitarian competition" as an unending relay race. "Whether you will be ahead when you finish your lap is strongly influenced by how far ahead

or behind your team was when you [began]." He shows that at the beginning of each lap, the society offers extra help to those who have to start
from behind.

According to Milner, our social justice assumes that a person's actions
are in large measure "determined by an inner will" and that everyone has
a "high degree of freedom to choose among the alternatives before him."
However, other people have come to the conclusion that man does not
always operate according to an inner-will. They increasingly attribute a
person's actions to his location in the social environment. Hence, our
ideals no longer condone the inequities of the "relay race" (1972b, p. 22).

Until now, when our society has focused on the issue of equality,
people have considered improving the conditions of those at the bottom.
"We have grown used to imagining that more can be given to those on the
bottom without taking anything away from those at the top [and] in the
middle." Milner states that the standard ideological assumption was that
"we can do much more for those at the bottom . . . if we concentrate on
expanding the size of the pie rather than on considering how it should be
divided [and] on starting everyone equally rather than on considering how
it should be divided" (Milner, 1972b, p. 25). Recently, we have begun to
realize that the size of the pie is not limitless and that the expansion of
goods and resources for one sector of the society must necessarily require
a change in priorities and distribution policies. The study of human development has caused us to realize that all are not born equal and that unless
we restructure our society into some grandiose kibbutz it will be impossible for all people to start life with the same opportunities. Hence, Milner's thesis is that "equal opportunity plus social equality leads to 'status
inflation' and thus there is ultimately 'no gain' for anyone" (1972b, p. 25).

If we accept Milner's logic, the relative deprivation definition of poverty becomes meaningless. If, in fact, we were to eliminate relative deprivation in the society, most economic operations would come to a standstill and qualified work of any kind would disappear from the market.

Ribich, in an examination of educational mechanisms for upgrading the
poor, supports Milner. He says that "mere equalizing of [educational]
expenditures will not get us very far in terms of equalizing 'life chances'
among different socio-economic classes and may in fact put us even further behind" (p. 525). We must therefore conclude that neither the economic nor the relative deprivation definition of poverty has much heuristic worth for a student of the subject. The economic definition is faulty
because it neglects conditions that are not measured by the family's income. It makes no distinction between the transitory poverty of the student or the temporarily laid-off worker and the chronic poverty of the
destitute. The relative deprivation definition allows for no solution except
that of an illusory utopia where people work without consideration of

reward. Similarly, relative deprivation is far from a suitable definition of poverty because the condition is found at all levels of the social strata when class comparisons are made. At what level of society can poverty be identified if it represents the condition of the lower-middle class in relation to the middle-middle class? Relative deprivation can also be faulted in that its corrections (aid to the affected level) merely lead to increased pressures from other levels for higher benefits and this in turn moves each population level above it to press for increased comparative benefits. Action to allay relative deprivation tends to become a momentary palliative, leaving the lower levels no better than they were before the action. It should be noted that the relative deprivation definition permits us to classify as poor a family that might be considered affluent in other nations. At best, relative deprivation merely describes a tenuous social condition; at worst, it provides a ludicrous view of a serious condition. The relative deprivation position of poverty is even more tenuous when one considers that only 10 percent of the families in the population (circa 1971) make $13,000 after taxes (see Passell and Ross).

Thus, "the dolce vita image of overabundance does not fit the facts. The importance of this preposterous minority . . . with lots of money to spend and little experience at spending it . . . has become magnified so that their possessions become the representation of American success and their failings the target of pop sociologists" (p. 7). In point of logic, if we assume the relative deprivation view of poverty, the entire lower and middle classes could probably be classified as deprived amidst considerable affluence.

Neither the economic nor the relative deprivation definition explains the differential life styles and value positions found between transitory poverty populations and residual poverty populations. These differential life styles (transitory versus chronic) can be found in the various levels as defined by relative deprivation poverty and economic poverty definitions, but pragmatic analysis of families will indicate that while there is great similarity among transitory poverty families, or residual poverty families, at all levels, there is a great variance between the life styles of the families found at each of the economic or relative deprivation levels. Thus neither the economic nor the relative deprivation definitions serve to provide adequate heuristic definitions of generic poverty populations.

Another widely held view of poverty is its conceptualization as a culture. This view holds that economic marginality, combined with patterns of social interaction, child-rearing practices, and values peculiar to such a culture, produces transgenerational poverty. Oscar Lewis presents the basic conceptualization and behavioral description of life in a culture of poverty (Lewis, 1956 and 1968). This form of analysis related to the culture of poverty has been related to American Aid to Families with

Dependent Children (AFDC) families by Glasser and Naverre, pp. 151–56; McCord and McCord, pp. 66–75; Battle and Rotter, pp. 482–90; Chilman, pp. 9–19; Stone and Schlamp, pp. 1–26; Miller, p. 287 and Pruitt and van de Castle, pp. 559–60.

According to the culture of poverty view, the granting of high status to males who engage in early sexual encounters produces more premarital pregnancies and earlier marriages among the lower class than among the middle class. Lower class marriages can be characterized by a high degree of separateness between the marital partners, a rigid division of family responsibility, an evaluation of the husband on his most vulnerable role (ability to support the family), a matrifocal structure of the family, and the *machismo* pattern of male counteractivity. All these factors disrupt family life among the poor. Couples often experience difficulties in settling down, and temporary separations are prevalent among the newly married poor. Separation is often followed by a mutual sense of depression, lowered energy, and lowered interest in the rewards of family life. Children are deeply affected by the interaction of lower class community and family dynamics. The child-rearing practices of the lower class place great emphasis on strictness, obedience, and staying out of trouble. In a community of marginal males, economic hardship, and family instability, control over children is weakened.

The role-model effects of a system and culture that interact must be considered. Often, the only significant women whom the welfare children see are welfare mothers who are tenuously holding together a "gray market" family. The only significant men they see are generally on again-off again visiting boyfriends, masculine street warriors, or both. It is obvious that in their adult lives the children will play out a version of the roles they learned in childhood, thereby almost geometrically increasing the chronic welfare population each generation. In Rainwater's opinion, the culture of poverty, along with economic marginality, makes the problems of chronic welfare something more than a matter of simple low-subsistence economics or relative deprivation.

For the poor, according to Rainwater, the basic barrier to well-being is the lack of resources or goods and services needed to carry out permissible, meaningful, and instrumental activities. Thus, part of the problem lies in the social psychology of materialism. In a materialist society, certain goods and services are essential to the performance of membership activities. These commodities are not provided without specific restraints. As societies move from primitive to technological stages, the living out of prescribed identities requires more material objects and services as a starting point for personal development. The starting line of the perpetual relay race is determined by a person's access to and control over such goods and services.

If one is to define the good society as one in which people have the life-experiences they need to regard themselves as members, then we can examine the goal of equality against our standards of justice. If people think they are what they know they should be and know they are generally accepted as such, then we presumably have what Rainwater believes to be a good society.

A study of comparative communities and collectivities shows that people can regard themselves as having a valid place in society without having equality of position and status. Many societies are highly egalitarian in the distribution of resources but are still highly stratified. The key to a content society is not necessarily equal status. A content society could be one in which individuals simply have a valid membership and a secure sense of place. Therefore, one way of abolishing poverty (in addition to providing adequate subsistence and the like) would be, as Rainwater puts it, "to make the poor content with their lot by convincing them that their status has meaning and purpose within the overall design of the society [and] that there are validated activities for which one does not need mainstream resources" (Rainwater, 1972, p. 35). This goal, however, would be impossible in a society that positions people principally by their relationship to the economy. A society's effective development of industrial capabilities requires considerable openness, fluid mobility of labor, and open competition. Definitions of self and others are also highly related to the degree of command over resources: "Where a group finds itself so removed from command over resources that it cannot participate in society . . . it adapts to its position by developing a lower class culture" (Rainwater, 1972, p. 36).

Conventional notions to the contrary, there is little solid empirical research to specify the extent and mechanisms by which low-income and badly designed welfare structures affect family stability and health. Traditionally, people have used situational theory or cultural theory to explain lower class behavior. A synthesis of the two theories is formulated by conceding that a lower class culture exists, although with a different set of values, beliefs, knowledge, and life-coping techniques. This configuration is adaptive to the socioeconomic marginality. The culture of poverty perspective is lacking because it does not take into account this adaptive nature. The situational perspective is faulty in that it fails to consider that the socioeconomic position does affect individuals' development and their techniques for controlling their environments.

Lower class values are not the only complex of culture that has an impact on the poverty populations. The residual poor, the working poor, the marginal middle class, and others generally agree on what constitutes the good life. They hold many conventional virtues in common, and these relate to the desirability of stable monogamous marriages, the legitimacy

of children, and intact families. There is a large difference between concepts of virtue and behavioral practices. The more economically marginal
a group is to the mainstream of the stable working class, the more lower
class adaptations the group develops. According to Rainwater, social
pathologies are products of these special adaptations. He postulates that
illegitimacy is not a distinctive cultural pattern deriving from the traditional culture of race. At least in the lower class, he observes, illegitimacy
is a product of a special adaptation of courtship institutions which places
boys and girls under strong pressure to engage in sexual relations without
regard to the possibility of marriage. Conditions of economic marginality
and involvement in street life as a way of salvaging self-esteem create
modified behavioral patterns which yield high rates of illegitimacy, marital disruption, and aversion to marriage.

From this viewpoint, it is logical to conclude that lower class behavior
will change only as the conditions underlying these special adaptive behaviors are changed. Thus, any structural change that reduces economic
marginality and increases validated earned life-careers will also cause
lower class behavior to become more like working-class behavior. The
degree to which such structural changes are feasible is dependent upon
the extent of mainstream resources, upon the ability to shift mainstream
priorities, and upon the extent to which changes in validated, earned life-
careers can be developed in the society. Rainwater questions the degree
to which a marriage can be brought about and kept intact if a given
increase in income is provided to a specified population. In this way, he
questions whether the culture of poverty is stronger than the intervention.

Rainwater observes that the central hypothesis of the welfare programs
is that grants provided to the poor will change their personal well-being.
From the volumes of hearings conducted in connection with the Family
Assistance Plan proposal (designed by Daniel P. Moynihan and offered by
President Richard M. Nixon in 1969 under the designation HR I), it is
obvious that welfare does not accomplish changes in personal well-being.
(See Hearings, Committee on Ways and Means, Ninety-first Congress,
1969.) Revisions of welfare to increase services have yielded no significant changes in either well-being or life-chances. Increased welfare grants
without structural and policy revisions provide no assurance of any significant change in the well-being and life-chances of the poor. Rainwater
concludes that a meaningful and guaranteed employment strategy must
accompany plans for an income floor, if such plans are to be effective
(1972, p. 72).

The best income guarantee is not the guarantee of an [income] transfer but the
guarantee of the capacity to work, to be productive, to return to society something of what one takes for personal and family maintenance [from that society].

A nation which cannot provide every [member] with a [meaningful] job at a decent wage is . . . telling too many of its members that they are superfluous.

It is useful to compare Rainwater's models of poverty with Valentine's three alternative models for the culture of poverty:
(1) A self-perpetuating subsociety with a defective, unhealthy subculture.
(2) An externally oppressed subsociety with an imposed exploited subculture.
(3) A heterogeneous subsociety with variable adaptive subcultures.
Valentine's description of model 1 is similar to Rainwater's except that he places greater emphasis upon its self-generating qualities and upon the consequent individual psychosocial inadequacies that block escape from poverty.

In this first model, the culture of poverty is seen as destructive to society and individuals, and the solution is to assimilate the poor into working-class and middle-class status and life-patterns. Without this change, poverty cannot be resolved. In an underdeveloped nation, this change occurs through revolution, whereas in an industrial Western country, it is effected through education, psychiatry, and social work.

In Valentine's second model, the poor are a structurally distinct subsociety, victims of a social pathology caused by their being denied cultural resources. The disadvantaged position of the poor is maintained primarily by the wealthier class's self-interest. This position reflects the Marxist view that the condition of the poor can be changed only through a radical redistribution of resources brought on by a revolutionary accession to power by agents of the poor.

Valentine's third model is a heterogeneous subsociety with variable adaptive subcultures. In this conceptualization, the poor are believed to possess some distinct subcultural patterns, even though they also subscribe to norms of the middle class or the mainstream. They are distinctive in some areas and not in others. Their distinctive patterns include not only pathogenic traits but also health and positive aspects. These are elements of creative adaptation to conditions of deprivation. In this model, the structural position and subcultural patterns of the poor stem from historical as well as contemporary sources that vary from one ethnic or regional group to another. The position of the poor derives from multicausal factors, often including those of models 1 and 2. For change to occur using this model, there would have to be simultaneous, mutually reinforcing innovations in all aspects, namely, increases in the resources available to the poor, alterations of the social structure, and changes in the subcultural patterns. Valentine believes that the agents for such innovations would have to be social movements involving both the whole society and the poor. The civil rights movement is a prototype for this kind of movement.

Although Rainwater accepts a synthesis of cultural and structural explanations for chronic poverty, his choice of resolution interventions involves a guaranteed employment mechanism combined with a continued income floor. In essence, his suggested approach is structural. Valentine also tends to explain chronic poverty using a synthesis of cultural and structural dynamics, but unlike Rainwater, his cultural explanations are cultural-historic in nature. This is an important distinction. Somehow, Valentine views chronic poverty, combined with a long history of cultural strengths, as more readily retrievable into mainstream involvement. His solutions involve not only structural interventions but also cultural interventions related to the ethnic and racial backgrounds of the chronic poor. Neither version of chronic poverty provides much of a basis for successfully reintegrating the transgenerational poor into mainstream activity.

Levels of Poverty in the United States

TRANSITIONAL POOR

The transitional poor are a population whose experience with poverty is only temporary, covering a relatively short period of time. In most cases

FIGURE 1.1 Levels of Poverty in the United States

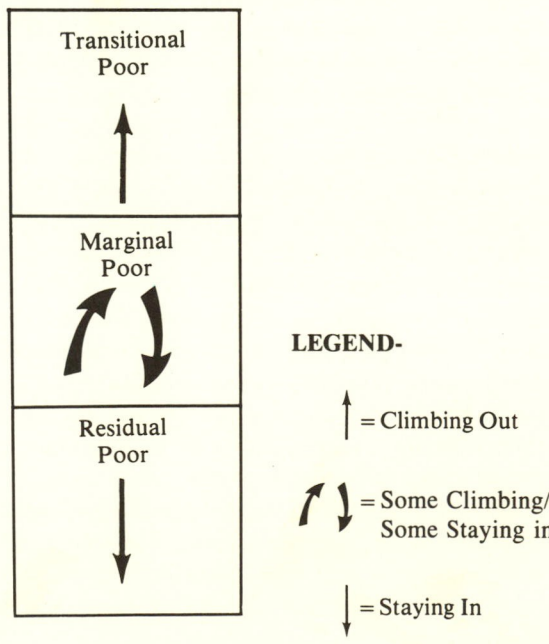

this population soon climbs out of poverty (see Figure 1.1). This condition is often precipitated by: a brief spell of unemployment with limited compensation, expensive medical problems, and legal litigations. This group consists of immigrants, both those of the early 1900s and the contemporary Vietnamese, Cuban, and other refugees, who, because of cultural, language, and other assimilative adjustments are currently provided with temporary aid (although aid to refugees by government is only a recent development for immigrants). College students, at times, interestingly enough, are also part of the transitional poverty. These students are unable to afford many basic necessities while financing their way through school.

It should be remembered that most of these populations, sooner or later, are able to become adequately self-sufficient themselves or are able to provide their children with a "head start" on the road to socioeconomic upward movement.

MARGINAL POOR

At various time periods, marginal poor may include the transitional poor. This population also contains many of the "working poor" who earn just enough to provide for their basic subsistence needs or sometimes, a bit better. From the daily subsistence point of view, this population is economically marginal. A down-turn in the national employment picture or a family mishap can tilt their situation toward a condition of dependency. Some climb out, while a proportion of the population may succumb to residual poverty (notice the flow of arrows in the diagram). It is with such families that a continued period of employment, a rising level of expectations, and a willingness to invest in themselves and in their children's education, will help them into secure self-sufficiency.

RESIDUAL POOR

Residual poverty is defined as the condition of a person/family who remains under poverty through a continued period of time. Most often, the poverty is transgenerational for this population. Their children, and even in some cases their grandchildren, are subsidized by welfare grants. Most of these transgenerational poor are governmentally supported under the welfare classification Aid to Families with Dependent Children (AFDC).

Policy-planning in the AFDC funding of the residual poor, in most part, has been guided by the concept of "relative deprivation." Samuel F. Stouffer et al. in their classic study of *The American Soldier* made one of the earliest operational uses of this concept (Stouffer et al., vol. 1, p. 250).

This concept suggests "that it is the comparison which an individual makes between his own situation and the situation of others which is critical in determining satisfaction, rather than the objective situation in which he finds himself (Glazer and Creedon, 1968, p. 4). Miller argues that beyond its original conceptualization, in the examination of poverty, it has acquired two additional meanings. First, absences resulting in deprivation are caused by both material and non-material conditions of life. Second, this deprivation is brought forth by an "active agent doing the depriving" (Miller, 1969, p. 272).

The net effect is a creation of incongruance of "relative status" (Merton, 1962, pp. 227-36) among the residual poor and the mainstream population of our society. In part, it may explain why AFDC families receive more in resources than many of the transitional poor.

THE RECORD

Recently, Rein and Rainwater (1977, pp. 20-23) report the transgenerational AFDC group to be nearly 20 percent of all persons on welfare. Previous national estimates of ten years ago, indicated that this clientele constituted only 10 percent. Mathematically, one may infer that the growth rate is geometric. In Los Angeles County, which maintains the second largest number of welfare clients, in 1960 the total AFDC case load was only 22,000. In 1978, it has jumped to 170,000. Included in this figure, are 37,000 second-generation families (Comrie, 1978, p. 1).

THE WORLD OF TRANSGENERATIONAL POOR

Residual poor, increasingly, are becoming welfare dependent. The welfare syndrome, furthermore, is being transferred to their children. A close examination of the institutional context of the transgenerational poor suggests that their world is one of social disorganization, which lacks mainstream societal norms and values. Faris has described "social disorganization" as "disruption of the fundamental relations among persons to a degree that interferes with the performance of the accepted tasks of the group." He argues that, primarily, such de-institutionalization is brought forth through the "disintegration of roles" where a member of the society no longer participates in stable social interactions within family, education, religion, economy, and politics (Faris, 1948, p. 19).

Oscar Lewis, in his development of the concept of "culture of poverty" stated that many of the residual poor live in an all-encompassing and self-reinforcing condition (Lewis, 1968, pp. 4-18). It is self-perpetuating (Lewis, 1966, pp. 19-25). He has listed some of the basic sociocultural traits of this level of poverty:(1) inability to plan for the future; (2) to seek immediate gratification; (3) an "oral" personality structure with weak impulse control; (4) an expressive life style; (5) to value acting-out more than thinking through a problem; (6) to self-expression more than self-constraint; (7) to pleasure more than productivity; (8) to spend more than save; and (9) to personal loyalty more than justice (Lewis, 1968, pp. 29, 58).

Such, then, is the world of the residual poor. It can be argued that these individuals/families are developing a culture of their own, contra-institutions whose way of life runs against the grain of the accepted designs of our society. Alternatively, the coping mechanisms by which the residual poor adjust to their state also serve to prevent them and their children from ever moving out of poverty.

Differential Models of American Poor

Many observers have suggested that the American image of the poor is a product of cultural lag rather than reality. To many Americans, the image of the poor gives rise to views of penniless immigrants to America. This disparity of images is a serious one, especially in light of the fact that immigration to America has long been at a plateau or decline, that the immigrants of yesteryear are largely members of today's middle class, and that the bulk of the current American poor are blacks, Mexican Americans, American Indians, Puerto Ricans, and others who are not "new" Americans. The disparity is made even more incongruous when one considers Glazer's observation that "the next wave of ethnic self-consciousness must reflect . . . the growing estrangement between European ethnic groups and the Negroes" (Glazer, p. 138).

The immigrant poor and the residual poor are historical contrasts in American poverty. The American public welfare system, which had its basic directional and policy development in the years 1929–1935, focused on the temporary poor, who at that time were primarily immigrants. Before that period, the public welfare system as we know it today was nonexistent. To a large part, various charitable organizations (see Chapter 2), coupled with the primary social ethos of self-dependence, played an important role in caring for the poor. In this situation, the client was left relatively free to allocate his resources. There were few external constraints. Since then, the American welfare system has changed radically. Social scientists and service agencies openly admit to a geometrically growing population (however small) of transgenerational poor. This is the category signified by the term *residual poor*. It does not include the transitional poor (such as people on welfare for a short period of time).

IMAGES OF THE POOR—HISTORICAL OVERVIEW

The purpose in developing this contrast is to underline both the socio-economic and value transformations in the current discussion of welfare policy premises in America. It is a painful study in social change. The term *residual poor* identifies a generation of men and women (mostly fatherless families) who are locked out of the mainstream socialization process. The culture of poverty envelops these welfare recipients (mostly AFDC) in a world of despair and normlessness. Furthermore, this bleak world is transmitted to their offspring. As Jimmy Breslin states, "The daughters of the poor regard pregnancy as the way to welfare and welfare as the way to lives of their own. There is not any other dream" (p. 36). The implications of this attitude from both a social and economic perspective are explored in forthcoming chapters.

In an analysis of the two images of the poor, it is useful to review the situational conditions of the early immigrants (those who came before 1930) and the refugee immigrants (those who fled from Germany, Austria, and other countries in the 1930s and 1940s fleeing Hitler). For a comparison of these two groups and the American Negro slave, see Table 1.1.

Whereas the immigrant poor had some limited specific resources at their disposal (such as mutual aid societies and railroad settlement schemes) and whereas the refugee poor had sectarian social work and private sector relief programs available to them, the blacks, on arrival, had only the slave market and the owner to direct them. The refugee poor arrived in the United States under immigration restrictions that precluded public assistance and dependency. Under the immigration laws, becoming a public charge put the refugee in jeopardy of deportation. Thus, both immigrants and refugees were motivated to develop life-patterns of self-sufficiency, rapid acculturation, and high levels of socioeconomic status improvement. In contrast, the slaves were punished for such patterns of behavior. Dependency upon the owner was a logical result of a social condition that viewed self-sufficiency as "uppity" or rebellious behavior for which a slave could easily lose his life.

The immigrant poor and the refugee poor were acculturated and absorbed into the American economic scene in due course (Decker; Briggs; Griffen; Yanis-McLauglin). The American black, the American Indian, and other minority groups, however, have often been held back by conditions and forces that have prevented meaningful access to many of the facilities readily offered the immigrants. These include effective education, consistent and fair wages, opportunities for upward economic mobility, and housing relatively free from restrictions.

A number of clear-cut facts about the blacks underscore the differences between the black poor and the immigrant poor. First, the Negro was torn from his culture in Africa and transferred to slave-breeding farms, where

TABLE 1.1 **Comparison of Earlier Immigrants, Refugee Immigrants, and Slave Negroes**

EARLIER IMMIGRANTS, PRE-WORLD WAR I	REFUGEE IMMIGRANTS, PRE-WORLD WAR II	SLAVES
Came primarily for economic reasons. Many planned to return to homeland.	Came primarily to escape persecution. Few planned to return to homeland.	Came under duress as slaves. Plans were not of their control and they knew it. No hope of return.
High proportion of unattached males but family life intact.	High proportion of women and young children; family life intact.	Proportion of male and female irrelevant because family life destroyed.
High sense of loyalty to community from which they emigrated. These ties were retained in social or religious organizations with close settlements of immigrants. Immigrant organizations maintained and retained.	High sense of loyalty to fellow emigrés with common newspapers, some organizations, and mutual aid programs. Joined American organizations.	Organizational and mutual aid approaches viewed as insurrection by their owners and the society. Only religious services permitted during slavery. Excluded from American organizations.
Primarily peasants, laborers, and artisans. Few intellectuals.	Primarily business, professional, and white collar groups, very large group of intellectuals.	Primarily unskilled, unlettered people. It was illegal to teach a black to read and write.
Majority had elementary education or less; few college or professional graduates.	Majority had high school education; many college and graduate degrees.	No Western education of any type (some tribal training which was not applicable to Western life).
Chiefly from rural areas and small towns.	Chiefly from large industrialized cities.	Chiefly from "undeveloped" hinterland.
Limited horizons, seldom traveled beyond their region or country. Knew only their own language.	Cosmopolitan outlook, traveled widely, familiar with more than one language.	Limited horizons, seldom traveled beyond their own region. Knew only their own one language, and this only orally.
Sometimes came with means, but always with personal possessions.	Rarely came with means but had basic clothing and the like for retention of personal self-respect and self-care.	Came without rudimentary clothing. Few items of self-identity retained.

Table 1.1—*Continued*

EARLIER IMMIGRANTS, PRE-WORLD WAR I	REFUGEE IMMIGRANTS, PRE-WORLD WAR II	SLAVES
Tended to concentrate in colonies and instant communities, based upon European home.	Widely distributed but often retained contact with one another despite distances.	Forcibly dispersed to distant plantations without contact of nuclear family, let alone extended family or tribe.
A low standard of living. Willing to work for low wages as long as hope for the future existed.	Usually came with a high standard of living. Worked for low wages only for a short period while retraining or seeking better positions.	A low standard of living and no hope of improving their lot.
Competed on lower occupational levels and aroused opposition of indigenous American workers.	Competed on higher occupational levels and aroused opposition of American business and professional groups.	Competed on lowest occupational levels and aroused opposition of earlier immigrants, poor white, and so forth.
Primarily concerned with making a living and surviving.	Concerned with raising themselves to a status equal to successful native Americans.	Few aspirations because of their circumstances. At best, the hope was for safety, security, and physical well-being for the immediate moment. This left its mark on their life-patterns.
Usually sought humble, unobtrusive, but productive, dignified participation in life.	Usually sought a place in life often without concern for visibility or obtrusiveness.	Usually sought to be unobtrusive for fear of punishment. Pattern was one of "simulation."
Acquired English slowly but didn't seek to master it in their generation.	Learned English rapidly and in depth, although they spoke with an accent.	Learned English only verbally and seldom in depth.
Placed little stress on children's education beyond basics.	Placed great stress on children's education without limitations.	Had no control over children's education; this education usually was rudimentary.
At first, their contribution to America mostly in brawn.	From the beginning, made contributions to America on intellectual levels.	Permitted only to contribute brawn and generally prevented from going beyond it.

Table 1.1—*Continued*

EARLIER IMMIGRANTS, PRE-WORLD WAR I	REFUGEE IMMIGRANTS, PRE-WORLD WAR II	SLAVES
Tended to delay naturalization. Many remained aliens, but their children grew up as Americans.	Rapidly became naturalized in high proportions. Made a conscious effort to adapt to America.	Generally prohibited from naturalization and later from use of civic potentialities (voting restraints and so forth).
Strain between generations relatively limited. Children held to parental controls,with exceptions.	Children infused with the child-centered American scene and with the democratic ethic. Strain between generations often apparent.	Children often deprived of contact with parents or parental controls. Some children controlled by mother. Father often absent, and as slaves, relations between child and parent tenuous and disrupted.

SOURCE: Davie, pp. 45-46, and Frazier.

the separation of mothers, fathers, and children was effected. Family life was destroyed, often purposefully, with concomitant psychological castration of the male as the head of the family. The whole southern slave system was designed to destroy any self-system held by the blacks. Second, the black has dwelt longer in poverty in America and in greater proportions than any other ethnic group. Though uneducated and poor, he has been continually beset with material desires, seen on the movies and television, toward which he can develop aspirations but seldom expectations. Such desires can only produce further hostility. Third, the "urban promised land" to which the black has come after great effort from a degrading life in the South has clearly brought him into a ghetto existence from which he can see no way of escape. Fourth, the urban black feels he is surrounded by hostile authority, in the form of police, officialdom, welfare authorities, and others, all of whom he believes continually exhibit harassment, harshness, contemptuousness, and distrust of the Negro poor. Angrow states that "to an oppressed, hurting people any expression of enforcement can be taken as harassment and quickly magnified into an insult" (p. 8). Finally, the black poor have no community to which to relate, and they have few real leaders. Many of those who have escaped the ghetto are regarded with suspicion.

The other elements in the residual poor group (such as Mexican Americans, American Indians, and Puerto Ricans) have experienced comparable conditions that have interfered with their absorption into the fabric of American life. According to Schmid and Nobbe:

The traditional method of assimilation process assumes that an immigrant group will acquire, within a matter of several years, the language, habits, customs, and values of the dominant, native-born Anglo-Saxon population, and as a consequence its members will eventually move up in the social and economic hierarchies. Assimilation is expected to be completed by the third generation (p. 921).

These investigators find that neither the black, the American Indian, nor the Filipino has been as successful in achieving this degree of upward economic movement as have the immigrant and refugee poor.

The family and marriage experience of the lower classes is quite different from that of many immigrant families, whose family patterns were middle class even before they arrived in America (see Table 1.2).

The ethics of marriage in the lower class are entirely different from the white middle class standards . . . entered upon much more casually . . . more tentative and more easily dissolved. The basic reason for the instability of the lower class marriage lies in the fact that it is generally entered upon for economic purposes by the female. (The wish to get away from an oppressive environment is a common inducement for the female to seek marriage precipitously, only to be disillusioned shortly after.) "Love" is not a predominant motive for marriage and companionship between mates is rare. Forced marriages because of pregnancy are quite frequent (Kardiner and Ovesey, pp. 70–71).

The position of the black male is also different from that of the earlier immigrant male.

He fears the female much more than is apparent for intrinsic genetic reasons and also, because his economic opportunities are worse than the females. Hence, he is not infrequently at the mercy of the woman. Masculinity is closely tied to power in every form of society. The male is much more vulnerable to socio-economic failure (Kardiner, p. 70).

A study of the relationship between the male and female among the black poor presents us with only a small aspect of the life patterns of some of the people in residual poverty. Many Americans tried to view the poor in the context of the past, when most of the poor were primarily recent immigrants. For many of the immigrant poor, poverty was a way station on the path toward self-dependence and security. Therefore, it is helpful to examine the differences between the immigrant poor and the residual poor. An analysis of these differences is also important in the examination of public welfare and its problems in light of the fact that the American public welfare system was originally designed to serve a population made up, in the main, of people who had immigrated to the United States in their lifetime.

TABLE 1.2   **The Nuclear Family—Patterns of the
Immigrant Poor and the Residual Poor**

IMMIGRANT POOR	RESIDUAL POOR
A patriarchy, but actually a partnership, with the mother in exclusive control over some family life functions. Mutual concern of all members of a family, one for another, but children show conflict of culture resulting from immigrant culture at home and New World culture at school. The result is lessened joint family activities, especially with regard to social activity and entertainment. Parental emphasis on child behavior requires strict adherence by children to school and community authorities. Despite cultural difference between parents and external society, parents enforce societal norms, particularly official norms, which are brought to their attention. Relatively stable marriages held together by internal bonds. Moderate discipline, appeal to reason with children and occasional appreciation for good behavior were often encountered among refugee and early immigrant families (Glazer and Moynihan, pp. 12, 18-19).	Often a matriarchy (in minority groups) within an outwardly patriarchal society. Father often missing or with an imparied self-esteem resulting from chronic unemployment, underemployment, and housework responsibility when wife is employed. Difficult housing conditions lead to less control of children, who are more numerous than in other models and whose playroom is often the street. Children are directed to help maintain the family economically as soon as they can. Early marriages, short courtship, and more prevalent divorce and desertion rates and lower remarriage rates. Identification of parents with children is often spotty within families, and variance is great within families. "He [the poor] sets great store by his family" and places great emphasis on his masculinity. "In the Negro sub-culture [even] the mother frequently plays a strong, masculine type of role and is prone to stress . . . physical force" (Riessman). Disciplinary treatment of children is inconsistent. Obedience is enforced toward ends not understood by child. High standards of behavior are required without an affectionate background as an offsetting incentive to child. Beatings without provocation are common, all mirroring the hardships and frustrations of parents (Kardiner).

The incidence of illegitimacy and unmarried motherhood is greater among the residual poor than among the immigrant poor. Moreover, unlike the case of the immigrant poor, where affection was reportedly a cohesive family force, the atmosphere among the residual poor is barren of love and affection. May reports a typical attitude of the residual poor woman:

I like a lot of attention and I like to feel that I'm appreciated. So I feel that you can't get this from a lot of men, you can only get it from one at a time. And this has been my way of livin' since I have been 18 years old . . . with three kids to educate and raise and you feel like if you associate with one person at a time they might be interested in you enough, they might want to help you . . . raise your children. . . . (pp. 51–52).

Moynihan presents a detailed picture of family life in black fatherless low-income groups. It is important to note that the members of a matriarchal minority in an officially patriarchal society easily fall victim to the self-hatred syndrome. Even the male's failure to practice birth control can be at least partially traced to a resulting sense of irresponsibility and a lack of a sense of living for the future. In a sense, the male experiences a kind of vicarious family life, often temporarily with the children of other men who are also missing from their families. This pattern is far different from that experienced among the immigrant poor.

Ornati, in exploring the differences between the immigrant poor and the residual poor, indicates that the residual poor are multiproblem families and that unemployment or poverty is only one of many interrelated problems that beset them. Among these difficulties are physical and emotional illness, low educational aspiration, expectation, and achievement, and shrinking occupational mobility. In contrast, most immigrant poor had only one or two problems, often less interrelated, namely, lack of employment and problems in adjusting to the American scene. These problems were soon overcome in an expanding economy that had need for the unskilled. The multiproblem immigrant case was rare, and in any event, the immigrant family had access to and made willing use of specialized social agencies, which were often created and designed to meet their special needs. The residual poor, on the other hand, with multiproblem families, have little or no readiness to surmount the class and communication barriers between them and the available social service resources.

For the immigrant family, the extended family was often their community, their social service agency, and their protectors. This has not been the case with many residual poor (see Table 1.3).

In the residual poor family, sibling relationships are generally hostile:

Sibling attitudes in the lower class show that animosity and hatred are the rule, with complete severance of relations . . . [where] friendly . . . ties are not currently maintained. In other cases, ties are maintained by a sense of duty, but attitudes are very hostile . . . in the struggle to obtain a share of these scarcities [of affection and material necessities] the ensuing rivalry is bitter and enormously exaggerated. (Kardiner and Ovesey, pp. 67–68).

Such a condition was not found among the immigrant poor during their period of adjustment and establishment on the American scene (see Table 1.4).

TABLE 1.3   **The Extended Family—Patterns of the Immigrant Poor and the Residual Poor**

IMMIGRANT POOR	RESIDUAL POOR
Members of the extended family were mutually responsible for one another. When older children emigrated to a new land, they first sent for their wives and children, then their parents, and then their brothers and sisters and their families (although not necessarily in that order). On arrival in the new land, they doubled up in their housing arrangements until the new arrivals could find employment and housing. Dependent elderly parents often stayed on in their children's home, but in any case, mutual aid continued, as did joint family activity. Often, housing locations were not distant from one another. Because the poor usually have more children than the general American family, the potential size of the extended family is thus larger. Among the immigrant poor, the cohesion of the extended family served as a strengthening force and as a built-in mutual aid society (Glazer and Moynihan, pp. 12, 18-19).	The extended family of the residual poor is often disintegrated or lost. The concerns of everyday living leave little opportunity for interfamilial contacts with extended family, except for rare holiday or family gatherings. Mutual aid of a practical nature (such as gifts of goods and used clothing), occurs only rarely because of the limited resources of the family and their own unmet needs. The residual poor family moves often, even though only within a local area. This mobility also cuts down on intensity of interfamilial contacts. Government functions are resorted to by members of extended family unable to provide their own means. The residual poor also have more children, and the size of the extended family, though often unassembled and dispersed, is larger than the general American family (Reissman and Haggstrom).

Adams, in his evaluation of Negro leadership prior to the civil rights movement, pinpointed three desirable qualities: knowledge of and ability for the job of leader; honesty of purpose in leadership; and ability to inspire the standards he felt were realistically required. He also found extreme divisiveness within the group. Silberman explains why such leadership is usually limited among blacks:

A terrible vacuum of leadership results (from the Black bourgeoise's distaste for Negro lower class and vice versa). . . . as soon as he [a leader] is able to move with ease among the whites, and raise money from them, he loses his rapport with the lower class Negroes, who resent his "going white" (p. 121). . . . The great mass of big-city Negroes trapped in the ghetto, become convinced that their "leaders," far from trying to help them, were merely trying to escape from being black.

In more recent years, with the increase of affirmative action programs and other actions for increased minority opportunities, there has been a recognizable tie between the large black middle class and the image of the ghetto poor. The black middle class has benefited from opportunities

TABLE 1.4 **Relationship of the Immigrant Poor and the Residual Poor to the Community**

IMMIGRANT POOR	RESIDUAL POOR
Immigrant parents brought with them a respect for their immediate community and sometimes a fear of the larger community. Parents were concerned to keep themselves and their children out of conflict with authorities. Immigrants rapidly gained citizenship and took up voting and other participatory activities in the community. Nevertheless, there was a feeling that one could not "fight city hall." When a mutual concern became important enough, however, they did act and they often won their point. Leadership readily arose within the immigrant groups, and in time, such leaders (and often pseudo-leaders, who accepted the support of the group but not its direction) found places for themselves within the power structure. Despite claims to the contrary, candidates for political office expend considerable campaign effort to appeal to and serve the expressed interests and needs of the established groups of ex-immigrants. When leaders of immigrant groups make the grade and secure political positions, estrangement between them and their group is often not as evident as is the case among the residual poor (Glazer and Moynihan, pp. 12, 18-19).	Mutual suspicion often exists between the residual poor and the community and its authorities. The community power structure often views the residual poor and their neighborhoods as the source of high costs of police, fire protection, and welfare, of crime and delinquency, and at times, of uncontrollable rioting. Informal community attitudes include fears of integration which may lower the standards of other community schools and lower property values. The participation of the poor in Johnson's War on Poverty programs in the 1960s led some political leaders to fear the conversion of poverty program participants into political challengers. The residual poor are usually fearful of community authorities. They believe, based on past experiences amended by personal perceptions, that any contact with them can only lead to trouble. Many have concluded that they cannot "fight city hall," either collectively or individually, and the usual reaction is to avoid such contacts. Many individuals even hold neighborhood associations suspect. Leaders of such groups are viewed with an unspoken question, "What's in it for them?" Participation in a community or neighborhood association requires energy and leisure, self-respect, understanding of operational procedures, and ability to communicate. These are often lacking, especially after an exhausting day's work (if employed). The residual poor generally lack a sense of personal worth (if unemployed), knowledge of what to do and how to participate, and necessary communication skills. A Latin American or black may occasionally show leadership, but all too often, "city hall" buys off such leadership with a political appointment, after which estrangement develops between the leader and the group (Riessman and Haggstrom).

developed under the pressures of the black poor upon the society, and in the process it is difficult to discern whether social distance between the social classes of blacks has changed. The position of the black middle class is hardly enviable. On the one hand, it must deemphasize its socio-economic improvement because of its economic tie to the poor in the societal image. On the other hand, it must seek to develop those aspects of middle-class behavior and associations which its children need if they are to continue to improve their lot. Obviously this pressure to promote one's own and one's children's progress can only increase the eventual separation of the black poor and the black middle class.

A similar condition exists among Latin Americans in the Southwest. Adams has found that the Latin American poor suspect those who seek leadership, either because the would-be leaders are better off than they or because they believe the would-be leaders want to use their positions for self-aggrandisement. "When they get a big car and a TV, they forget what it used to be like." Adams has also found that many Latin Americans are ready to work hard *against* a Chicano whom they think might try to claim a position as a representative of their group (Simmons, p. 389 and Gonzalez, pp. 77–78). Riessman refers to the willingness of the residual poor "to believe in the corruptness of leaders, and a generally antagonistic feeling toward 'big shots'." This condition is far different from that found among the immigrant groups during their days of arrival and hardship. There may have been cleavages between groups, but there was greater cohesion within groups than is currently found among the residual poor.

The immigrant poor and the residual poor also differ markedly in their attitudes toward official government bodies. Whereas immigrants usually held a respectful distance from officialdom, they did not hesitate to call on officials to meet a need, solve a problem, or undo a grave injustice facing their group. Among the residual poor, this is far from the case. Coles reports the residual poor's general suspicion of, withdrawal from, and rejection of any relationship with any type of authority. This attitude is also reported by Adams (p. 73), who quotes one respondent as follows: "The only thing the poor people can get from the government is trouble." When Adams discussed possible approaches to government to improve conditions, many asked him, "What good would it do? We can't change anything." With the experience of community action programs, model cities, and the like, this attitude has been altered to some degree. The residual poor now do take to the picket lines when leaders or would-be-leaders call attention to a perceived injustice. This kind of protest, however, buys small concessions over the short run compared to what the more powerful actions involving political and economic organizations can do. Participation in politics and local community activities won hope and gains for the early immigrants, but this has not as frequently been the case with the residual poor. The condition of personal group helplessness, powerlessness, suspicion of, fear of, and isolation from government and society is a clear indication of alienation as described by Seeman and others who consider this condition in terms of anomie (Merton; and MacIver).

Alienation among the Latin American poor is aggravated by an additional cultural factor: as a result of their previous Mexican experience, they fear all government and officialdom, for they fear being caught in a mesh of bureaucracy and required bribery. Lewis reports this factor in his various works, including *Five Families*. The residual poor are also alienated from community social agencies and public welfare. Coles indicates that this attitude is largely the result of the tendency of social and public welfare workers to try to instill their middle-class values into the poor. According to some of Coles' respondents, "they keep on telling us to do like them"; "they sure don't know what it is about" (p. 58). An additional factor in alienating the poor from the community is the relief program itself. Over the years, the restrictions of various relief programs have eroded the poor's freedom to act as autonomous individuals. While these programs have offered minimum provision for existence, they have given little opportunity for self-improvement and upward mobility. In recent years, legal services programs have been augmented and have somewhat offset this effect.

This condition was not found in the relationship between the immigrant poor and the social service agencies. In most instances, the immigrants were either middle class or aspired for middle-class status and had relatively little difficulty in relating to the agencies. In the case of the refugee group, the private agency relief standards were considerably above the public welfare budgets, and provision was made within the budget and in the agencies for opportunities for economic and occupational upgrading. The refugee client usually did not fear the agency, and for most of the clients, the period of dependency was shortlived. The goal of both the client and social worker was consistently to attain client self-sufficiency. This is not the case with most public welfare agency relationships, when of necessity workers are often investigators and recordkeepers rather than rehabilitators.

Cohen has noted that most private social agencies have concentrated on middle-class psychoanalytic services, a focus which has further increased the social distance between them and the poor. He states that "private social work has tended to disengage itself from the poor." Cloward and Epstein have arrived at the same conclusions. Thus, the residual poor, unlike their predecessors, the immigrant poor, have less contact with the community and lack sufficient leadership acceptable to it in building communication bridges with the community. Employment has always been the primary vehicle for socioeconomic upward mobility for the poor. It was also the key mechanism for improving one's lot, or, if not that, improving the life chances for one's children, and this was (and is) particularly so in the United States. Glazer and Moynihan (pp. 29–44) clearly indicate the differential orientations to work as viewed by the immigrant and residual poor populations. Table 1.5 presents some of these differences.

TABLE 1.5   **Relationship of the Immigrant Poor and the Residual Poor to Employment**

IMMIGRANT POOR	RESIDUAL POOR
The employer-employee relationship was generally not as personal as that in the Protestant Ethic pattern. Employer and employee had greater social distance between them. Employees worked hard in order to get ahead. In an expanding economy, employers valued work and increased skills. The immigrant employee did not often stay long with his employer; instead, he struck out for himself. When he did stay on, he participated in labor unions which gave him security in negotiating with his employer. Lesser job satisfaction (as compared to the Protestant Ethic pattern) was made up for in evening school, labor union activity, cultural activities, and the like.	For the residual poor, employment is often a tenuous, temporary condition. The employer-employee relationship is usually socially distant and impersonal. A mutual suspicion often exists between employer and employee and often follows the stereotype that the employee, because he is poor and unskilled, is ignorant and inherently lazy. Thus, the employer usually presses for optimum performance from employees. The employee, in turn, suspects the employer of seeking more from him than is the employer's due and helps to enforce the employer's self-validating prediction regarding his laziness and incompetence. The employee often suspects the employer's intention to lay him off and often simulates being busy on the job as well as a respect for the employer which he really does not feel.
Most immigrants were able to deal with objects both motorically and conceptually and thus learned from the usual teaching methods. The immigrant poor had communication with their employers, despite frequent language difficulties. In an expanding economy, workers with even little training but with good work habits were in demand and could seek improvements in work conditions either individually or through unions, in which they were willing to participate (Bailyn and Lockridge).	Generally, the work habits of the residual poor are productively negative, as are their work attitudes. They have little realization of the relationship between work habits and attitudes and possible avenues for upward economic mobility, for which they have often not learned to aspire.
	Communications with their employers are limited, and the need for unskilled workers is such that the residual poor are the last hired and the first fired. Because of the difficulties of unionization of this group (resulting from mutual suspicions, for example) and the few gains possible in such efforts, union organizations have, until now, done little with them. The residual poor tend to have greater physical and motoric abilities, and seem to need to manipulate objects physically in order to perform adequately (Riessman, Magnum, pp. 248, 250, Rose, pp. 28, 29, and Minuchin et al., pp. 24, 25, 28, 31-33, 36, and 219).

Riessman discusses the residual poor's preference for jobs that promise security, even at low wages, to jobs that pay greater wages but entail economic risks: "He does not want to become a foreman because of the economic insecurity resulting from the loss of job seniority." In contrast, the immigrant poor sought promotion and improvement, despite occasional risks to security for which they often provided for in advance with some limited savings (p. 75).

Finally, automation and cybernation have not only become established on the American scene but are also expanding. These processes eliminate unskilled jobs, while leaving a place for the skilled. The immigrant poor did not encounter this problem. If they had encountered it, they would probably have secured the necessary training to do the skilled job. For the residual poor, training opportunities to meet the problem have been relatively inadequate, inaccessible, and/or unacceptable within their framework and culture (Bagdikan).

Religion has been an important dimension of the lives of the immigrant poor and the residual poor. In the case of the former group, religion often served as an assembly point for people from the same countries and with similar backgrounds and cultures. Glazer and Moynihan point to the Synagogues (pp. 59 and 60) as rallying points for immigrant Jews for which the members went on to develop other self-help and mutual aid programs. Similar supports to immigrants were provided by churches, particularly in the case of Catholicism (Glazer and Moynihan, pp. 217–87). Religious institutions also provided the immigrant family with validation of its authority and thus strengthened its cohesion. The religious institutions of the immigrants served as a group conscience in its concern for the activities of its members, as a defense program against discrimination and as a mechanism for bridging the cultural gap between the mainstream society and the immigrant population. Thus the religious institutions served to provide the immigrant population with encouragement for interaction with the larger society while maintaining a pride in its cultural origins and values.

The religious institutions of the blacks were quite different (Moynihan, pp. 80–83). In the years of slavery only the churches were permitted as institutions and these were usually small and weak. After emancipation these were succeeded by institutions which continued to be generally separate from the mainstream society (see Table 1.6).

Minuchin et al. have made numerous references to the sense of identity of the residual poor (pp. 4, 6, 26, 133, 180, 183, 193, 194, 196–98, 201, 205, 209, 210, 212, 218, 220–23, 239, 260, 263, 363, 365, 366). They have shown that the sense of identity developed in children in the general population (p. 197) is quite different from that developed in the child in residual poverty. Haggstrom (p. 80) also presents the self-views of the residual

TABLE 1.6 Relationship of the Immigrant Poor and the Residual Poor to Religion

IMMIGRANT POOR	RESIDUAL POOR
The immigrant, like Protestant Ethic model, was religious, but his religion was less closely related to his work responsibilities. He had an intrinsic acceptance of religion and often accepted personal responsibility for his actions. To a lesser extent than the Protestant Ethic model, his religion reinforced his family sense of responsibility and cohesion. The immigrant often held to his religion as the nucleus of the culture he brought with him. The immigrant poor were quite dignified in their church performance. Religion was usually a total family matter and involved activity by all.	For the residual poor, religion may be an emotional escape, especially in the case of women who are heads of their families and are overladen with physical and emotional burdens. It may also be a necessary but meaningless procedure one needs to undergo to receive church aid (in the case of "rice-Christians"), who often gather around a growing number of religious missionary programs for the poor. In any case, it is not deeply related to one's worldly acts or activities. "The deprived individual is much more likely to enjoy physical manifestations of religious emotions such as handclapping and singing" (Riessman). "The deprived individual will most often leave religion to his wife" (Riessman).

TABLE 1.7 Concept of Self of the Immigrant Poor and the Residual Poor

IMMIGRANT POOR	RESIDUAL POOR
The immigrant knew who he was. He brought his own culture with him and infused into it those portions of American culture necessary for his assimilation into American society. His growth as a learning person and as a parent of learning, upwardly mobile children helped keep his sense of self-esteem secure. The immigrant's concept of self was strengthened not only by his employment, but also by his status and acceptance in a cohesive nuclear and extended family. Work often contributed to his sense of identity.	Except where religion may provide a cultural foundation, the residual poor individual usually has only a deprived sense of self, which makes learning, working, relating to others, and action (rather than being acted upon) difficult, and perhaps impossible, unless aided externally. This pattern is often tied in with a pattern of self-hatred, which sometimes leads the individual to withdraw from contact with other nonpoor (Silberman, 1964). This hatred has been directed not only against the individual, but also against others in society, especially the police, retailers, landlords, and even liberals, whom the individual often views as hypocritical (Silberman, 1964). Self-improvement is often linked with "Uncle-Tomism" and is avoided by those who are linked to the ghetto life.

poor. Throughout their descriptions of the Jews, Italians, and Irish, Glazer and Moynihan present a picture of immigrants and their descendants who generally believe in themselves and their life goals. Thus there is a discernable gap in the way the immigrant poor and the residual poor view themselves (see Table 1.7).

Critical to the concept of self and its utility in the functioning of the person in the family, in employment, and generally in interaction with others is the degree to which a person values himself and his qualities. Although the residual poor population is made up of many whites, Mexican Americans, Puerto Ricans, and others, the blacks represent a sizable proportion of the group. Many of the problems posed by the residual poor are particularly evident among blacks. Thus the question of self-acceptance among blacks provides us with an example of the problem among the residual poor. Silberman states that:

Self-hatred is manifested in the use of hair straighteners, skin bleaches . . . in the desperate but futile attempt to come close to the white ideal. [It is] evident also in the caste of color that still infects the Negro community. . . . It is expressed in apathy: there is no use trying anything, joining anything, doing anything, because you are just no damned good (1964, pp. 119–20).

Kardiner and Ovesey describe self-hatred, whether inwardly or outwardly directed, as "a slow but cumulative, fatal psychological poison" (p. 310).

Ellison describes the residual poor in their "desperate search for identity. . . . Not quite citizens and yet Americans, full of the tensions of modern man, but rejected as primitives . . . rejecting the second class status assigned them, their whole lives become a search for answers to questions: Who am I?, What am I? and Where?" (p. 54). Although self-hatred and devaluation of the self may have been a dominant pattern among many blacks before 1965, the situation since then has changed considerably. Many blacks are now middle-class, others are upwardly mobile. The self-hatred pattern, however, is one which cannot be disregarded among those blacks who are seemingly locked into residual poverty. The fact that other blacks have moved upward may in fact be an aggravating factor in relation to this condition among the residual poor. Significantly, in Harlem, the reply to the greeting "How are you?" is very often "Oh, man, I'm nowhere."

Wilhelm and Powell indicate that, despite attempts to help the black escape from his conditions, too often the effort is, in effect, an attempt to make the black into a "dark White man." "The Negro cannot establish his identity by erasing himself." Wilhelm and Powell believe that only a program which provides employment for all and which places a higher valuation on people than on machines and property will solve the problem of identity for the residual poor. Thus, for them the residual poor serve as only a symptom of a problem of total society. These authors seek a complete shift in societal values and priorities, which is obviously "not in the offing." Dolgoff, Kaplan, and Tausky, as well as Pavalko, support the critical role of work in the structure and process of a functional self-concept. For the residual poor the lack of remunerative work, the lack of an adequate work history, the lack of achievable career goals, and the lack of adequate work role models can all be related to a self-concept which is needed in working toward self reliance in the general society.

Related to work is the matter of remuneration. "Money" can be the product of one's work efforts or the proceeds of a dole related to dependency. For the immigrant poor there was no public welfare system prior to the depression years. The only assistance came from mutual self-help associations in the form of loans that had to be paid back and the episodic charity of voluntary agencies. The immigrant poor had no one to depend upon except themselves and they were accustomed to this reality. Kristol believes that if the present welfare system had been available in the years of the Irish immigration the contemporary residual poor would be made up of many persons of Irish extraction. It is probable that for some of that population not having to earn money would give money a different meaning than it does for others who have to earn it (see Table 1.8).

TABLE 1.8   **"Money" as a Value for the Immigrant Poor and the Residual Poor**

IMMIGRANT POOR	RESIDUAL POOR
The immigrant poor valued money for: 1. The security it could buy for periods of future difficulty. 2. Provision for one's immediate family needs and education for the children. 3. Opportunities for going into business and individual advancement. 4. Resources to aid overseas or newly arrived relatives. At first, the immigrant poor may have been short of money and ignorant of American methods of consumer purchasing, but they soon learned how to get their "money's worth."	The residual poor need money for daily bare subsistence. They buy on time because they are ignorant of the market or lack ready cash. The poor pay more. They view money as an escape from the present, as a means of getting some enjoyment in a deprived existence. They often use money to buy something which brings temporary color and show into a drab family life, but the object purchased quickly falls apart or into disuse. Generally, the residual poor lack ready cash, are ignorant of the basic principles of consumer purchasing, and are victimized (Stewart).

"Credit" has differential meanings for the residual poor and the immigrant poor in the same way that "money" is differentially valued (Stewart). Because of their inability to deal with the future many residual poor tend to accept credit obligations beyond their ability to repay. For the immigrant poor this was a different matter as shown in Table 1.9 (see Minuchin et al., pp. 135, 237, 321, 328 and Caplovitz, pp. 47–48, 190–91, 94–99, 116, 117, 120, 121).

TABLE 1.9   **Use of Credit by the Immigrant Poor and the Residual Poor**

IMMIGRANT POOR	RESIDUAL POOR
For the immigrant poor, credit was used sparingly and was acceptable only in a crisis. It was usually resorted to only within the extended family or immigrant association credit union. When credit was extended by a merchant, it was repaid on time, so that it would be available again.	For the residual poor, credit is necessary because there is never enough money for all of the immediate needs. The poor are often not concerned with keeping a good credit rating. Thus, they end up borrowing from marginal credit sources at exorbitant interest rates.

For the employed (or employable) immigrant family, time was an important value which could be converted into money, learning, or self-improvement (which included adult evening classes for English language and citizenship). This is touched on by many reporters of the immigrant experience including Karp and Glazer and Moynihan. For the residual poor time is used haphazardly (see Minuchin, pp. 30–33), Glazer, Moynihan, and Sheehan (see Table 1.10).

TABLE 1.10   **"Time as a Value" to the Immigrant Poor and the Residual Poor**

IMMIGRANT POOR	RESIDUAL POOR
While the immigrant was future oriented, his family's immediate needs came first. His plans were for upward mobility for his children and himself, and for the future aid of his relatives. The individual set a calendar and planned and acted accordingly.	The residual poor are present oriented: "Tomorrow cannot be expected to be any better than today, so let it take care of itself." Essentially, they view their existence as unplanned with the individual as object rather than as actor.
Time was less carefully hoarded than in the Protestant Ethic pattern, but because of pressure for upward mobility, many immigrants used it cautiously and purposefully.	Time is either plentiful (when unemployed) and a bore, or short (when employed).
	Less money means more difficult transportation and more time spent going to and coming from work.

When people consider what they have to be proud of, many respond with what they do (employment), what they have earned (money), what others think of them (which relates to credit), and where they live (housing). The immigrant poor have been known to move out of the inner city along with their upward climb on the economic ladder. The residual poor have remained, for the most part, in the inner city. We have dealt with the matter of housing for the poor in a subsequent chapter, but it is important to note here how housing is differentially viewed by the immigrant and residual poor (see Table 1.11).

TABLE 1.11   **Housing as a Style of Life-Pattern of the Immigrant Poor and the Residual Poor**

IMMIGRANT POOR	RESIDUAL POOR
The immigrant usually sought adequate housing within his needs, but housing expenditures had less priority than education. Generally, their limited means made for less than adequate housing.	Housing, especially that of the minority group poor, is inadequate and often overpriced. The poor are particularly victimized in housing rentals. They often use housing as a temporary camp. They express their resentment of the victimizing landlord and his authority by misusing the property.
When housing was overpriced, the immigrants would move elsewhere, and the only restriction usually encountered in housing was extent of ability to pay.	Housing costs and rents are artificially high for the residual poor because of de facto restrictive covenants, the unwillingness of many landlords to accept welfare tenants, and the like. This situation creates a double standard in American housing, with unkempt and badly maintained housing at high prices for some and not for others. The residual welfare poor, the most likely to have large families, heavy rents, and marginal housing thus become locked into a housing situation that feeds their grievances against landlords, welfare, and society in general.
For immigrants, housing was often a matter of status. Families would provide housing to satisfy their own needs and to indicate their position as self-respecting members of the community. Such housing would create an impression of neatness but seldom affluence.	

Associated with the way people value themselves is the idea of how they wish to appear to others in the community. Because this was less important to many of the immigrant poor than was the saving of money for future opportunities and familial goals, the immigrant poor tended to buy well-made, sturdy garments which were passed on from child to child as they "grew into them." Caplovitz states that "when they [the poor] move up even a short distance up the occupational ladder, they may be given to the almost exclusive emphasis on consumption" (p. 129). But for the residual poor, who stay on without a place on the ladder, these dynamics do not operate (see Table 1.12).

TABLE 1.12   **Clothing as a Style of Life-Pattern of the
Immigrant Poor and the Residual Poor**

IMMIGRANT POOR	RESIDUAL POOR
The immigrant sought adequate clothing for self and family but could seldom afford it. Thus, the special suit or dress was saved for occasions. Clothing was usually functional, not ostentatious. It was passed from older to younger children, who felt embarrassed or demeaned by the process of handing down clothing.	The clothing of the residual poor is often inadequate. Because the everyday clothing of both the poor and nonpoor often look alike, the poor may blend into the mass. Often, the poor will buy something garish to bring extra color into their lives. In many poor families, clothing wears out so quickly that it cannot be passed on from older to younger children even though the process is now culturally accepted in the American middle-class.

Education is a critical consideration for many remunerative high-status occupations. This was well known to the immigrant poor (see Glazer and Moynihan, pp. 115–59, 199, 201, 202, 276–81). For the residual poor education has an entirely different meaning. Deutsch believes that much of the difficulty encountered by the residual poor children in the schools derives from "stimulus deprivation" in the home. The restricted range of home experiences and available objects, Deutsch believes, leads to lessened learning readiness. Minuchin (pp. 29–30) disagrees with this indicating that it is not a lack of objects and perceptions but the more limited communicational, affective, and cognitive style of the family members, in addition to their more limited aspirations, goals, and values for the children, which makes for difficulty for the child in the school. Added to this is the more limited language preparation given the children of the residual poor by their families (Minuchin, p. 31). The lower levels of attentive ability skills and inappropriate behavioral styles provided to residual poor children by their families further aggravates the child's difficulties in school. In Minuchin's view, "the interpersonal and familial relationships in severely deprived homes contribute to the marked lack of skills essential in the early setting as well as life in general." This lack is evident in the lessened ability "to conceptualize, paying attention, being task-oriented and looking to adults for information, clarification and reality testing" (p. 31).

Perhaps the most important difference between the school readiness of immigrant poor and residual poor is the degree to which the parents view the schools as a "way station" on the children's path toward affluence and security and thus prepare their children for the experience. Similarly, the degree to which parents are equipped to provide such preparation and support can be critical to the child's success in school. "The child's early intensive training has a strong influence on his cognitive learning style"

(Minuchin, p. 216). The residual poor child tends to be unpredictable, overdeveloped in making quick maneuvers and underdeveloped in making sustained explorations. Thus, says Minuchin, the parental training of the residual poor prepares the child to clash with the school. Attempts by the child to resolve his inner conflict are often viewed by the school as aggression in need of control. Thus, says Minuchin, "the child's development of . . . a special coping repertoire (to deal with conflict) within the family is, in effect, preparation for failure in school (and in society generally)." Table 1.13 presents the differential views of education as a value by the two populations.

TABLE 1.13　**Education as a Value for the Immigrant Poor and the Residual Poor**

IMMIGRANT POOR	RESIDUAL POOR
The immigrant valued education for its usefulness in promoting upward mobility as well as for the sake of learning. Socialization for maximal utilization of educational resources began at an early age and continued. Children entering into public education had already absorbed behavioral patterns which maximized their readiness for schooling.	Many of the residual poor do not highly value education. They often suspect that education is a deadend and an arm of society's authority over their children and themselves, which they resent. For such parents, school keeps their children from going to work and from helping to support the family. Children are expected to earn money to help support the family as soon as they can. Many families cannot see any connection between school and "making it." Residual families believe that the school provides their children with a lesser education than is provided to others.

In the area of education, principals and teachers are usually not anti-poor, anti-Negro, or anti-American Indian. They are simply oriented to academic achievement. Because the parents of the immigrant poor sought educational achievement for their children, the teachers of immigrant children maintained a sense of hopefulness for achievement, and the self-fulfilling prophecy came true. Immigrant children were already literate in one language, which not only facilitated learning conceptualizations but also gave the child a sense of learning security which aided him in absorbing what the school offered. Such is not generally the case with the residual poor.

Kardiner and Ovesey examine the attitudes of the black impoverished child toward schooling:

School becomes a meaningless and unrewarding bore. Negro children understandably fail to see the relevance of education to their opportunities in life. Many are obliged to work half or full time; the competition of street life with school is too great and the street, with its imitation of the struggle for existence, with its sexual opportunities, and those for adventure, usually wins (p. 72).

The process often results in school failures. The deprived child enters school with a limited vocabulary, a limited self-concept, and limited external experience, so that he is approximately two years behind the child of the middle-class family in terms of readiness to learn what the school has to offer. He is also less prepared to conform to the discipline necessary for learning. For such children social promotion begins in first grade. The cumulative academic deficit makes the learning of the grade placement materials beyond him and, in turn, causes his teacher to have to decide whether the teacher or the student has failed. If the teacher concludes that it is hopeless, he or she, unwilling to engage in repeated attacks on the child's self-esteem by giving him failing grades, continues the cycle of social promotions until the child is legally permitted to drop from school into "limbo." It is thus understandable why teachers seek transfer to middle-class schools where such decisions and struggles with conscience can be avoided. In contrast, the immigrant poor have shown a remarkable educational record.

Just as the immigrant poor and the public schools had a common goal in the education of their children, so the immigrant poor and the society which they sought to join both espoused patterns of moral integrity. These standards were usually upheld by the immigrant poor, despite the fact that moral integrity was not always observable in the society. The residual poor however, whether because of the need to cope with an economically hostile world or because of a condition of isolation from the social mainstream, have not internalized the standards of behavior as generally espoused as the norm in the society. The divergent views on moral integrity are illustrated in Table 1.14.

One of the key factors named by Oscar Lewis (1968, p.29) in his description of the culture of poverty was the tendency of the residual poor not to plan for the future, whether that future involved career expectations for their children or budgeting the family resources for the next month. The inability to plan is of course tied to the tendency to seek immediate gratification which Lewis found in his studies. Thus one may indicate that the residual poor apparently live a day-to-day pattern of moment-to-moment existence, except where external realities create pressure for more ordered activity. Because of the lack of a future and a memorable past, life goals tend to be absent in the life of the residual poor. This, of course, is far different among the immigrant poor whose migration across the seas, the saving of passage money, the difficult gathering of necessary migration papers all indicate planning and careful life-goal design and implementation (see Table 1.15).

TABLE 1.14   **Moral Integrity in Relation to the
Immigrant Poor and the Residual Poor**

IMMIGRANT POOR	RESIDUAL POOR
Moral integrity was usually internalized in the immigrant. As people of considerable self-esteem, the immigrants could not afford to lose the respect of others because of lack of moral integrity. Nor could they face themselves or their extended family in such circumstances.	For the residual poor, moral integrity is a fluctuating matter. Truth and honesty, and moral virtues, depend on the relationship with others involved in the particular instance. Emotional identification with others and verifiability have much to do with the condition. An impaired self-concept makes moral integrity a real problem for the residual poor, especially in view of the hopelessness of seeking goals through legitimate means and in view of their continuing needs (Cloward and Epstein).

SOURCE: Davie, pp. 45-46, and Frazier.

TABLE 1.15   **The Life-Goals of the Immigrant Poor and the Residual Poor**

IMMIGRANT POOR	RESIDUAL POOR
The immigrant sought security and economic mobility for himself and his family. Thus, he sought self-dependence. Saving had nothing to do with religion as was the case with the Protestant Ethic model. It was purely a rational act toward the individual's life-goals.	The residual poor's life-goal is to get by for the moment in order to enjoy a momentary satisfaction, within an atmosphere of hopelessness and helplessness which prevents goal orientation. To be an actor for the moment instead of always being acted upon may be another way of expressing this orientation.

The life pattern of the immigrant poor and the residual poor have little in common. The immigrant poor lived a life-style related to making their way in the society, to preparing their children for something better than their lives could provide and to becoming integrated in the society (see Gordon, pp. 60-83). The residual poor are neither motivated to join nor attracted by the larger society. Whether it is a matter of being ill-equipped to assimilate or a matter of not perceiving the opportunities to become a part of that society or a matter of being structurally prevented from moving into that society or a combination of these factors, is not an issue in the conclusion that the residual poor live out their lives in a manner which is far different from that of the immigrant poor. Similarly it should be noted (Table 1.16) that the general life-style of the immigrant is not in great divergence from most of the mainstream society.

TABLE 1.16   **General Life-Style of the Immigrant Poor
and the Residual Poor**

IMMIGRANT POOR	RESIDUAL POOR
The life of the immigrant was characterized by hard work and careful living to prevent difficulties and to save money. Violence was rare among them, and most differences were resolved by discussion. Many minorities set up special internal arbitration structures for the purpose of resolving conflict. Limited geographical mobility was apparent once the immigrant got settled.	Before those in authority, the residual poor often play the role expected of them (a simulation for the occasion). They work only as hard as the "boss" requires, and the "boss" usually watches carefully. There is very little leisure time for employed women and until free time does become available, neither the mother in chronic poverty nor the chronically unemployed man have much interest in political action. Thus, the poor often resort to general avoidance or temporary violence to resolve frustration or conflict. The residual poor are locally mobile—just a few steps ahead of the landlord and installment bill collectors. Thus, they go from inadequate housing, often leaving their inadequate furnishings behind.

The motivation behind the divergent coping mechanisms of the immigrant poor and the residual poor becomes more clear when patterns of behavior and attitude are examined. The immigrant poor had no alternative but to seek to make their way in the new world. This was based upon the external pressures of being able to depend upon no one other than themselves and on their ethos which placed high valuation on self-reliance and self-sufficiency (Handlin). The residual poor, on the other hand, also have external and internal pressures but in the opposite direction. The external pressures apparently consist of the limited but dependable rewards of welfare and the constraints of a society which is perceived as antagonistic. The inner pressures relate to impaired self-esteem and alienation (see Haggstrom, 1964; Foreman and Kornbluth, 1965; Herbert Hyman, 1953; Sheehan, 1976; and Waxman, 1977). Although the poor pay lip service to the values of the dominant society and the work ethic, Scarpatti, 1977, indicates that these values are largely irrelevant in their lives. (For divergent social-psychological dynamics of the immigrant and residual poor see Table 1.17.)

The social-psychological dynamics of the residual poor have been exemplified by materials from reports of black and Mexican-American studies. The adjustment of those blacks, who make up a sizable proportion of the residual poor, has been aggravated by a long history of being dealt with as objects rather than self-determining persons and actors.

TABLE 1.17 **General Social-Psychological Dynamics of the Immigrant Poor and the Residual Poor**

IMMIGRANT POOR	RESIDUAL POOR
The immigrant poor were a self-reliant group. In the New World, where their only aid came from a few relatives and countrymen, the immigrants had to work hard and stay out of trouble if they were to survive and progress. In an expanding economy, there was need for the immigrant's "hands," and there was hopefulness for the future.	The residual poor usually have more children than other people, but with a number of mates. They are alienated from and suspicious of the greater society. With impaired self-esteem, which often prevents learning and upward mobility, continued routinized treatment by society reinforces their socio-economic immobility.
The immigrant poor were relatively temperate in their emotional expression because they had means of communication other than violence and because they could look ahead to moving up and out.	The residual poor are often beset with emotional upset, which is a major form of the impoverishment cycle (Macdonald).
	Their inability to move up and to communicate their sense of hoplessness and powerlessness often leads to a self-defeating dynamics.

The psychological effects of the slave status on the individual [included]

(1) Degradation of self-esteem.
(2) Destruction of cultural forms and forced adoption of foreign culture traits.
(3) Destruction of family unit, with particular disparagement of the male.
(4) Relative enhancement of the female status, thus making her the central figure in the culture, by virtue of her value to the white male for sexual ends and "mammy" to the white children.
(5) The destruction of social cohesion among Blacks by the inability to have their own culture.
(6) The idealization of the white master; but with this ideal was incorporated an object which was at once revered and hated.

These became incompatible constituents of the Negro personality. Kardiner and Ovesey add that "what to do about the Negro was subject to violent oscillation and was the pawn in conflicts that had deep economic roots." Consequently, the Negro was never secure; he was always in fear of a shift.

Another compensatory feature of slavery was the vicarious participation in the culture through identification with the master. The slave could get some prestige by belonging to a wealthy or influential household. (Usually these were mulattos, and thus the seeds of self-hatred, the hatred of that which made one less than "fully white" were sown.)

There was an absence of strong pressure [in slavery] on the individual to achieve status, a feature that was very conspicuous in the white man's culture.

When status is frozen, one cannot successfully direct one's aspirations toward goals that are beyond possibility of attainment. Some inner peace can be achieved by ceasing to struggle for it (p. 47).

Thus slavery explains some of the motivation of "nonstriving" among blacks.

Unlike the immigrant poor and the refugees, the residual poor are not the beneficiaries of a long heritage of experience up from serfdom. Unlike the immigrant poor, many of the residual poor have not had the opportunity to make efforts in their own behalf. Unlike the immigrant poor, the residual poor do not have achievement experience. Unlike the immigrant poor, the residual poor have few institutions. Unlike the immigrant poor, the residual poor have a problem in finding employment for their men during a period of shrinking opportunities for unskilled workers. Unlike the immigrant poor, the residual poor are not supported by cultural bridges to the mainstream of the society. It is thus obvious that the residual poor are alienated from their world because it is a world they never made or chose to live in. The immigrant poor, on the other hand, chose the New World.

The residual poor meet all the conditions of alienation as set out by Scott, and they are motivated to self-perpetuating and defeating patterns.

From a sociological point of view . . . sources of alienation are to be found in the lack of:
    (a) commitment to values.
    (b) conformity to values.
    (c) responsibility in roles.
    (d) control of faculties.
The psychological states of alienation . . . powerlessness, meaninglessness, isolation, normlessness, and self-estrangement.

The flight of the Negro father from family responsibility after unemployment and failure is a continuation of the "flight from problems" pattern. Kardiner and Ovesey state that under slavery:

There was no possibility for emotional interchange [between master and slave]. If a slave was sick, he would be treated like a sick horse, to restore his utility. The rage or protest of the slave could be ignored or treated with violence. The only really effective form of protest was flight (p. 43).

Perhaps a key to the entire problem of life-patterns can be found in the "actor acted upon" concepts as described by Roach, Howe, Harrington, Scott, and others. Roach, for example, presents a dynamic system which can promote understanding of the dynamics of the poor as well as the motivation of the society's relations with the poverty group. His system is based on the Parsonian "actor acted upon" concepts which define the actor (the autonomous person) as one who has a complex inner life, is future oriented, and can evaluate, choose, and plan. Roach states that an actor must have the following properties:

1. The actor has internalized the common value standards of society (the residual poor have not; the immigrant poor had).
2. The actor has a stable set of motives. (The residual poor perhaps not; the immigrant poor had.)
3. The actor has an elaborate repertory of roles. (The residual poor are culturally deprived and do not; the immigrant poor had many roles.)
4. The actor has sophisticated role skills. (The residual poor are culturally deprived and do not; the immigrant poor had such skills.)
5. The actor has a developed self-system. (The definition of the culturally deprived poor carries with it implications of a deprived or impaired ego system; the immigrant poor knew who he was.)
6. The actor is capable of complex mental functioning. (The residual poor have trouble handling conceptual thinking; the immigrant poor had the ability soon after, if not on arrival.) (p. 71)

The immigrant poor and the refugee poor were "actors" in their life space, even when they were temporarily dependent upon public or private welfare. This conceptualization of the immigrant poor was apparently the model used in the design of public welfare programs in the 1930s. Many of these principles were retained into the 1960s and 1970s, despite the fact that they are no longer appropriate to a sizable proportion of the clientele. This model is also important in understanding public criticisms of the residual poor whose experience with public welfare differs so radically from that of the immigrant poor. This description of the residual poor explains why a mechanistic single-policy public assistance system is an inadequate means of rehabilitation for this population. The immigrant poor were once the majority of the poor in the United States or were the parents of those who were dependent during the Great Depression. Unlike the residual poor, the immigrant poor population and their descendants probably retained their own rehabilitative dynamics. Only by restructuring the conceptualizations of public welfare models and the related opportunities (of employment, advancement, and so forth) can the residual poor become actors and in the process become productive.

Social Theory and Poverty

We have dealt with poverty as defined by historical considerations, by a lack of resources, by a low position on the socioeconomic ladder, and by differential theoretical causative explanations. Clearly, before a social problem such as poverty can be identified, it must first be defined. The definition of a social problem is in turn dependent upon the values of the definer. Hoult indicates that a social problem is "any situation which is regarded by a significant number of the members of a group as a threat to one or more of a group's basic values and which is believed to be remediable by collective action" (p. 301). In the context of social legislation and policy, social problems are viewed as target conditions to be prevented or resolved. The definition of a social problem in the context of legislation is whatever the society and its agents (the legislature and official implementers of law) define it to be.

Poverty has been described as a condition originating from sinfulness, ignorance, laziness, misfortune, powerlessness, and various other personal defects, cultural patterns, or societal conditions. Whether poverty is the result of a personal defect or the workings of the social system or subsystem is a factor not only of the specifics of the individual condition but also of the parameters of the definition utilized and of the value systems underlying the definition. Thus, the definition sets out what the problem is and indicates the upper and lower limits of the norm by which the problem is identified. Included in the value system of the definer (and usually apparent in the results of the definitional process) is the basic conceptualization of the structure of society as held by the definer.

Social legislation in the United States has been conducted within the framework of various behavioral conceptualizations which, in turn, have been derived from intellectual movements within the larger society. Until the Great Depression, such legislation strongly reflected the Protestant Ethic, and beneficiaries were redirected, guided, controlled, or advised. In the 1930s, temporary assistance and the creation of opportunities in the social structure were emphasized. In recent years, the focus has shifted to the creation of increased opportunities, egalitarian access, and advocacy.

Each of these theoretical frameworks is directly related to one of a number of societal conceptualizations, which is probably not considered in the policy design of social legislation. Each of these models of society, however, is the unrecognized starting point from which the policy-maker begins in planning and implementing various social legislative interventions. The model of society held by the designer determines his definitions of problems and his choice of interventions. These unrecognized societal conceptualizations held by designers place upon each intervention values that correspond to these models.

At this point, it is helpful to present the major societal formulations and then to indicate how each determines the view of the legislative beneficiary, the role and definition of social legislation, the methodological emphasis, and even the expected degree of success of each methodology. The sociological literature indicates four major theories of macrosociety:

structural-functional (consensus) theory, exchange theory, conflict theory, and interaction theory.

The structural-functional theory holds that society is self-balancing, self-regulating, and boundary-maintaining. Society is a self-sufficient, self-perpetuating unit which strives to maintain a homeostasis of relationships among its systems, subsystems, and individuals within these components. Consensus theory carries an unspoken devaluation of factors which interfere with smooth retention of homeostatic balance and boundary-maintenance. Spokesmen for the consensual society consider as deviants: outsiders, troublemakers, persons unwilling to undertake the efforts needed to enter the system, persons unwilling to undergo the metamorphosis of the melting pot, "poor unfortunates" (those who fall through the cracks of the system), the lazy, the sick, the neurotic, the weak, the selfish, the childish, the unadjusted, the unsaved, the evil, the uneducated, the uncultured, and the ignorant. (See Parsons; Parsons and Shils; Blau, 1963; Buckley; Merton; and McIntosh.)

The exchange theory holds that social transactions occur because each actor hopes to gain something from the other. The transactional episode is completed only if the persons to whom the act is directed perceive that some desired benefit will accrue to them. Once an exchange process is initiated, an emergent form of social organization is evident. The continuation of the initial relationship presumes that norms are established which structure relationships. In turn, the conditions of social exchange become crystalized, and the prerequisites of social organization are met.

The exchange theory requires that the initiators of a transactional relationship want a commodity or service which the others can provide and must have confidence that the others will want what they have to offer as exchange. The theory also requires that that which is desired by the initiator must be obtained from others. Without an exchange, no bonds can be established to relate one actor to another. Exchange, by definition, denotes a fair and meaningful exchange. This is not the case where one actor seeks to provide less than a just trade.

The proponents of exchange theory view as functional those societal components and individuals who can and do enter into and complete meaningful exchanges. Deviants, according to the exchange theory, lack tradable skills, knowledge of how to effect exchanges, and information on the location of potential exchanges, or they otherwise lack opportunity to effect meaningful exchanges. Because of their inactivity on the exchange marketplace, they may be viewed not only as untrained, uninformed, lost, or unfortunate, but also as slackers in the structuring and support of society. (See Blau, 1964; Levine and White; and Storer.)

The conflict theory assumes that all individuals have interests that can be served only by an encroachment on the interests of others, which, in

turn, forces the occurrence of transactions that are not mutually benefi-
cial. Thus, persons with more power, as part of the natural scheme of
things, will coerce those with less power into accepting bargains that are
not a fair trade of goods or services. Once control is secured over others,
rules of behavior (laws and norms) are imposed; these rules define the
social structure. This theory differs from consensus theory in that transactions are inspired by selfish interests and implemented by implied or
direct force. It also differs from the consensus theory in the view that
underlying values or desired societal consequences have little or no meaningful effect. Conflict theory differs from exchange theory in that inducement and coercion rather than fair exchange are the dynamic factors.
Conflict theory emphasizes change in social structure rather than equilibrium and boundary-maintenance. The structural origin of conflict is inherent in the dominant relationships that develop in social organizations and
systems in confrontation. Regulations represent the will of those in su-
perordinate or power positions, regardless of how these positions were
obtained. Conflict theory views society as a jungle, or at best a genteel
jungle, where rules of courtesy mask the powerful's carniverous stalking
of the weak. Social structure is viewed as a byproduct of the powerful
seeking to keep others under control but attempting to gain control. If
they succeed, they set up their own social structure of expected and
acceptable behaviors. From a conflict view, those who are not powerful
need to learn how to accumulate power and to learn the skills necessary to
exert power purposefully. Those who fall to the jungle floor are fair game
for scavengers.

According to the conflict theory, the alternatives for members are limited to becoming powerful, joining with others for more effective use of
power, escaping from the power of others, or becoming a willful victim.
(See Bertrand; Coser, 1956; Coser, 1967; Dahl; Dahrendorf; Horowitz;
Horton; Loomis; Mack and Snyder; Simmel; and Warren.)

The interactionist societal theory holds that the nature of the transaction or confrontation is not as important as the meaning people attach to
their own actions and to the actions of others. A person does not act in a
predeterminable way; his actions are purposeful and voluntaristic. Reactions are in terms of interpretations and implications derived from a personal definition of the situation. Actions are products of assessments of
what is right and proper at the moment. Thus, actions are not as much the
result of exchange or coercions as they are the interactions of differential
complexes of personally perceived situational definitions. These situational definitions may or may not be congruent. From the viewpoint of the
interactionist, social organization is the end-product of behavior patterns
that evolve from attempts to achieve goals that are perceived as desirable.
Situational definitions are never completely identical. These definitions

are continually reinterpreted and reappraised, and behavior is readjusted accordingly.

Interactional stabilities provide a behavioral referrent and derive from a shared culture of the actors. As people interpret situations and make decisions regarding the propriety of behaviors, they make known their ideas and evaluations. To the degree that these patterns are accepted, a common culture develops. The symbols that are shared, interpreted, and given a common meaning find their origin in social organization even as they are derived from the social organizations.

From the interactionist viewpoint, a fully functional person would have a broad spectrum of well-understood roles, role behaviors, norms, symbols, and role equipment. He would have adequately tested and used these roles, and related equipment and scripts in the mainstream of societal interaction. The meanings, value ladings, and related feelings of this repertoire generally would be congruent with those of most mainstream people. Because of this role and symbol competence, such an actor would be secure enough in his interactions to go beyond the scripts. Thus, he would be able to balance personal autonomy within the constraints of social responsibility.

According to the interactionist theory, the deviant is someone with problems of communication and understanding. Among the various societal theories, interactionism is probably singular in its emphasis upon the mutual causality of communication difficulty and deviance. It takes two or more persons to create communication ineffectiveness. Functional deviance is a product of ineffective communication. In this view, causality of such problems as nonsomatic mental illness, mental retardation, neurosis, character disorders, and difficult interpersonal relations can be traced to misperception, misinterpretation, misorientation, and inadequately provided and perceived socialization. (See Blumer, 1967; Blumer, 1969; Scheff; Gilsinian; Hurvitz; Rose; Manis and Meltzer; Dreitzel; Gordon and Gergen; Kuhn; Thomas; Berger and Luckmann; Shibutani, 1961; and Shibutani, 1970.)

Theory and Social Legislation

All four theories of macrosociety can be found in contemporary life. A synthesis view can be considered: the consensual society is intermittently in balance; at times it is attacked by groups from outside the consensus; conflict occurs and finally exchanges are sought between the challengers and the consensus; stability is achieved and the contenders become part of the new consensus. The negotiations for exchanges which occur regularly within the consensus'and between the consensus and the exterior are based on a condition of relative congruence of the meanings, values, and norms. Without such congruency, consensus or conflict might be based upon interactive confusion.

In the study of social legislation, it is important to understand that the societal model utilized (or inferred) not only sets the stage for the choices of alternative legislative interventions, but, in practice, also sets up a series of definitions that are critically decisive for the beneficiaries of social legislation.

The model of society utilized by the social policy formulator has a number of key parameters: Definition of the populations to be served and why it is necessary they be served; definition of the most effective service and interventions; definition of the legislative task and its parameters; definition of the nature of the social problem; definition of the structure to implement the planned intervention; definition of the roles of the beneficiaries and administrators of the program; definition of the sanctioning authority and its degree of legitimization; location of responsibility for the service in the society; priorities for clienteles to be served, problems to be addressed, services to be rendered; and choice of the theoretical frameworks to be utilized.

Because the model of society used has import for the definition of the implementive task, it is easy to understand the difficulty administrators have in arriving at a definition of what is effective service. Programs can be viewed as effective, from a legal-realist orientation, if the social problems focused upon are resolved or prevented. Administrators of programs, however, tend to view as effective programs that provide the services specified regardless of whether the basic social problem is resolved or prevented.

It is helpful to examine some of the differential definitions listed above as they relate to each of the four societal models. The structural-functional (consensus) society presents us with a view of the beneficiary group as either recalcitrant, maladjusted, sick patients, ignorant, or outsiders who resist the processes of organized life in society. Because of this typification, society's role becomes one of treatment (along the medical format), reeducation (in regard to interpersonal behavior and personal adjustment), controlled custodial care (for those who cannot fit into the system), or aid in kind for those who cannot be refitted into the system. In this model we find a justification for corrections work, involuntary treatment in mental hospitals, adoption and foster home programs authorized by legislation, and (Aid to Families with Dependent Children) AFDC. In each of these services, the onus of responsibility for change is placed primarily on the beneficiary. As long as the client does not fit into some accepted subsystem of the consensus, it is up to him to work to achieve change in himself until he does. Society accepts a role of helping the client change himself so that he may, in time, become acceptable to the consensus.

The standards of comparison by which the client is judged to be deviant are derived from the interpretations presented by the consensus. In its role as a helper to deviants, society clearly adopts a social control assignment for which sanction is provided by the consensus. In its service to the consensus, agents of the society, qua social legislation, play the role of an immigration and naturalization service, guarding the consensus boundary and retraining deviants for reentry into the consensus. In this way, social legislation protects the consensual homeostatic balance which might otherwise be seriously disturbed by deviance. In the process, social legislation helps prevent norm violations, restrains the development of disturbers and dependents, provides a holding action for those who have fallen out of the machinery, conserves human resources for the consensus, and works to minimize social strains.

The exchange model of society presents us with a view of deviants as persons who cannot or do not perform meaningful exchanges with others. Deviants cannot exchange because they lack training and experience in acquiring tradable skills, knowledge and skill in tradable relationships, opportunity to trade, and information on trades and trading. The exchange theory provides an added analytical approach to deviants as victims. If the victim serves the society by being a victim and if the establishment serves the victim with financial aid, it may be considered that the victim and the establishment are engaged in a meaningful exchange and thus are symbiotic. If this view is accepted, then it might be judged that the victim cooperates with the establishment in structuring society. It is quite possible that the victim does serve society in the same sense as the criminal serves society as described by Kai Erikson in *Wayward Puritans.* This view is that the victim helps define the norms of the society in exchange for the limited support provided to him. In this sense, if society did not have victims it would have to invent them. If this view is accepted, then the role of social work becomes very limited in that it provides a fated view of the victim and social change.

A corollary view of the victim (or social legislative beneficiary) is one which portrays social stratification as inevitable. If we are to have social classes, someone will always be less adept at exchanges that are contemporaneously valued at different times. Thus, there will always be the less competent exchangers who help define the more competent. By the very process of being labeled, they provide a service to the society for which they are provided, in turn, with a marginal exchange account which they may use in the marketplace. Such exchange accounts may be the less stigmatized, public-subsidized surrogate social insurances such as the Supplementary Security Income program which is currently available to the aged, blind, and disabled in need, or food stamps, or financial aid programs such as AFDC. Financial aid represents a subsidy to provide exchange mechanisms for those who cannot or will not develop their own resources for exchanges. A surrogate social insurance is a subsidized program which provides exchange mechanisms for those at the bottom who are viewed to be more deserving. These beneficiaries, according to the Protestant Ethic, include the aged, blind, and disabled. Others at the bottom are provided with the less valued programs of financial aids which they utilize in their exchanges. In other words, those who pay into their social insurance accounts can expect to exchange their accrued payments of the past in the form of currently exchangeable benefits in the present. Those who have not made payments and have no resources for exchange, but who have a higher valuation among the nonexchanger category, are provided with surrogate benefits to exchange. Those who are nonexchangers and who have less valuation are served for purposes of the society by direct, uncamouflaged financial aid grants.

Alternatively, for those who can be retrained as exchangers, the task for social legislation becomes that of helping them to become better equipped for exchanges and of finding a more favorable location for them in the social structure. Another aspect of this process, where appropriate, would be one of working for client change with the goal of helping the client become better equipped to enter into and complete meaningful exchanges.

Under the exchange model, society is served by promoting meaningful exchanges that further the structuring of society. To the extent that social legislation reduces the size of the population left out of exchange processes, it strengthens the exchange society.

The conflict model of society depicts the client as a generally powerless victim of elements around him. The client is seen as an object of others and unable to participate as an actor in society. The role of social policy thus becomes one of serving as an advocate of the client, a position which carries the assumption that a society would be willing to provide a mechanism that would joust with other societal mechanisms. Such advocacy mechanisms also include a responsibility to teach its clients how to gain and use power so that they can function as independent members in the society. Within the conflict model of society, social legislative roles also include functions of proposing regulation of conditions of unequal power. As such, the social legislation function includes an attack on those rules of society that create unneeded or unjust disparities in power.

Sanctions for the conflict model differ from those in the consensus or exchange models. In the conflict model, the legislator-intervenor not only secures its authority from the society but also operates as according to some higher sense of authority. Advocacy programs and power-balancing programs can be found in many contemporary and historical settings. These include the original thrust of the National Labor Relations Act, child protection programs, consumer protection programs, minimum wage laws, legal aid actions, public defender programs, and monopoly control commissions.

Under the interactionist model, the deviant is one who is out of communication with society and its subsystems. The client is therefore someone who attaches meanings and value ladings to his own actions and the actions of others which are not in congruence with accepted meanings and value ladings. He is unable or has no desire to perceive value in interactive processes within the mainstream of society. Thus, social conflict or social dysfunctionality occurs. When the client presents a problem in his own functioning, the dysfunctionality can be viewed as deriving from inadequate interactional socialization and understanding. Inadequate interactional socialization and understanding can be used as an explanation for problems of interpersonal difficulty, nonsomatic mental retardation, or other malfunctions. Where interactional dysfunctionality occurs in groups, it can be related to incongruities of understanding of role functions. Where it occurs between marginal groups and society, it can be laid to deviant cultures and to the gap in communication between them and the mainstream.

A utopian model for social legislation under the interactionist theory would focus on effecting or re-effecting communication and relative congruence of meaning between participants in social conflict, between the deviant cultures and the mainstream, and between individuals and groups who create or perpetuate social problems by their differential understandings of symbols at issue. Consequently, service to those who are alienated would address itself to their understanding of realities and to the definitions of realities held by the mainstream in efforts to achieve some congruency of comprehension.

Under the interactionist theory, social problems are defined differently than under other theories. The "consensualist" might label distorted inappropriate behavior (and explanations of such behavior) as mental illness of the individual; the exchange theorist, as inadequate preparation for meaningful exchanges; and the conflict theorist, as coping mechanisms resorted to by a loser in what Laing has designated family politics. Under the interactionist theory, such behavior (and the counterpart behavior of other members of the family) would be viewed as mutually aberrant distortions of reality involving a complex of interacting persons. In this sense, the interactionist view is parallel to that of Szasz and Rycroft.

Under interactionism, the task of society is to achieve a common set of meanings and valuations of symbols (and the feelings related to these meanings and valuations) for the purpose of permitting as many as possible to retain symbiotic and functionally interactive life activities. This achievement is to be sought not only between existent cultures but also from generation to generation and from person to person. In the process of reducing incongruity of meanings to a minimum and of seeking to reduce communication entropy, a commonly acceptable civilization and a minimization of societal strain are gained. It should be noted that social structure, under the interactionist theory, is founded upon the commonality of meanings and value systems. Community and human welfare is unattainable in both a semantic and emotional "tower of babel." When one person has meanings, values, and associated feelings that are different from those held by others, he obviously cannot live and interact with others without severe strain. When almost everyone has such distortions or blunting of meanings, because of an inexact communication process, it is reasonable to expect that strains and problems will proliferate in the society.

Thus, the consensualist orientation seeks to use the governmental thrust to treat, control, or at least hold the deviant; the exchange orientation, to provide the deviant with a mechanism by which he can participate in exchanges; the conflict theorist, to defend him and to teach him self-defense; and the interactionist, to educate him and others for unitary purposes. The consensualist policy promotes corrections, psychotherapy, and social control personnel; the exchange theory orientation, vocational rehabilitation and rehabilitative welfare workers; the conflict theorist, defenders and trainers of self-defense; and the interactionist, education to prevent confusion and misunderstanding. The social policy designer therefore needs to carefully examine his own definition of the society before he designs programs. In each design, the definition of villain and hero is implicit, and the scenario is contained in the societal model used.

References

Adams, Julius J. *The Challenge: A Study in Negro Leadership.* New York: Malliet, 1949.

Allen, Vernon. "Introduction" in Vernon Allen (ed.), *Psychological Factors in Poverty.* Chicago: Markham Publishing, 1970.

Angrow, Webster. "Formula for Explosion," *Frontier,* 16(12): 7–9, October 1965.

Bagdikan, Ben H. "The Invisible Americans," *Saturday Evening Post,* 236(45):28–33, 37–38, 1963.

Bailyn, Bernard. *The Ideological Origins of the American Revolution.* Cambridge, Mass.: Harvard University Press, 1967.

Bandler, Louise S. *Casework with Multi-Problem Families.* New York: Columbia University Press, 1964.

Battle, Esther S., and Julian B. Rotter. "Children's Feelings of Personal Control as Related to Social Class and Ethnic Group," *Journal of Personality*, 31:482–90, 1963.

Berger, Peter, and Thomas Luckmann. *The Social Construction of Reality*. New York: Doubleday, 1966.

Bertrand, Alvin L. "The Stress-Strain Element of Social Systems: A Micro-Theory of Conflict and Change," *Social Forces*, 42(1):1–9, 1963.

Blau, Peter M. "Critical Remarks on Weber's Theory of Authority," *American Political Science Review*, 57(2):305–16, 1963.

———. *Exchange and Power in Social Life*. New York: Wiley, 1964.

Blumer, Herbert. "Society as Symbolic Interaction." Pp. 139–48, in Jerome G. Manis and Bernard N. Meltzer (eds.), *Symbolic Interaction: A Reader in Social Psychology*. Boston: Bacon, 1967.

———. *Symbolic Interactionism: Perspectives and Methods*. Englewood Cliffs, N.J.: Prentice-Hall, 1969.

Breslin, Jimmy. "Why a 15 Year-old Girl Wants to Have a Baby," *San Francisco Chronicle*, April 27, 1978, p. 36.

Briggs, John Walker. *An Italian Passage: Immigrants to Three American Cities, 1890–1930*. New Haven, Conn.: Yale Press, 1978.

Buckley, Walter. *Sociology and Modern Systems Theory*. Englewood Cliffs, N.J.: Prentice-Hall, 1967.

Caplovitz, David. *The Poor Pay More*. New York: Free Press, 1967.

Chilman, Catherine S. "Child-rearing and Family Relations: Patterns of the Very Poor," *Welfare in Review*, 3:9–19, 1965.

Cloward, Richard, and Irwin Epstein. "Private Social Welfare's Disengagement from the Poor." Mimeographed, n.d.

Cohen, Nathan E. "Reduction of Welfare Dependency." Pp. 292–93, in Margaret S. Gordon (ed.), *Poverty in America*. San Francisco: Chandler, 1965.

Coles, Robert. "The Poor Don't Want to Be Middle Class," *New York Times Magazine*, December 19, 1965, pp. 7, 54–56, 58.

Comrie, Keith. "Statement by Keith Comrie, Director, Los Angeles County, Department of Public Social Services," Testimony to the Subcommittee on Social Services and Welfare, California Legislature, December 11, 1978, Mimeographed.

Coser, Lewis. *Functions of Social Conflict*. Glencoe, Ill.: Free Press, 1956.

———. *Political Sociology: Selected Essays*. New York: Harper, 1967.

Dahl, Robert A. "The Concept of Power," *Behavioral Science*, 2: 201–15, 1957.

Dahrendorf, Rolf. "Toward a Theory of Social Conflict," *Journal of Conflict Resolution*, 2(1):170–83, 1958a.

————. *Essays in the Theory of Society*. Stanford, Calif.: University Press, 1958b.

Davie, Maurice R. *Refugees in America*. New York: Harper, 1947.

Decker, Peter R. *Fortunes and Failures: White Collar Mobility in Nineteenth Century San Francisco*. Cambridge, Mass.: Harvard Press, 1978.

Deutsch, M. "The Disadvantaged Child and the Learning Process." Pp. 163–79, in A. H. Passow (ed.), *Education in Depressed Areas*. New York: Bureau of Publications, Teachers College, Columbia University, 1963.

Dolgoff, Thomas "The Psychological Meaning of Work," *Menninger Perspective*, pp. 5–9, Summer 1976.

Dreitzel, Hans Peter. *Recent Sociology, Patterns of Communicative Behavior*. New York: Macmillan, 1970.

Dugan, Dennis and William H. Leaky. "Poverty Reconsidered," in Dennis Dugan and William H. Leaky (eds.), *Perspectives on Poverty*. New York: Praeger, 1973.

Ellison, Ralph. "Harlem Is Nowhere," *Harpers*, 229(1371):53–57, 1964.

Erikson, Kai Ti. *Wayward Puritans: A Study in the Sociology of Deviance*. New York: Wiley, 1966.

Faris, Robert E. L. *Social Disorganization*. New York: The Ronald Press, 1948.

Forman, Lewis, Joyce Kornbluth, and Alan Forman. *Poverty in America*. Ann Arbor: University of Michigan Press, 1965.

Frazier, E. Franklin. *The Negro Family in the United States*. Chicago: The University of Chicago Press, 1937.

Gilsinian, James F. "Symbolic Interaction and Ethnomethodology: A Comparison." Paper presented at Rocky Mountain Social Sciences Association, Salt Lake City, Utah, 1972.

Glasser, Paul H., and Elizabeth L. Navarre. "The Problems of Families in the AFDC Program," *Children*, 12:151-56, July /August 1965.

————. "Structural Problems of the One Parent Family," *Journal of Social Issues*, 21:98–109, 1965.

Glazer, Nathan. "The Peoples of America," *The Nation*, 201(8):137–41, 1965.

Glazer, Nathan, and Daniel P. Moynihan. *Beyond the Melting Pot: The Negroes, Puerto Ricans, Jews, Italians, and Irish of New York City*. Cambridge, Mass.: MIT Press, 1963.

Glazer, Nona, and Carol Creedon. *Children and Poverty: Some Sociological and Psychological Perspectives*. Chicago: Rand McNally, 1968.

Gonzalez, Nancie L. *The Spanish-Americans of New Mexico*. Albuquerque: University of New Mexico Press, 1967.

Gordon, Chad, and Kenneth J. Gergen. *The Self in Social Interaction*. New York: Wiley, 1968.

Gordon, Milton M. *Assimilation in American Life.* New York: Oxford University Press, 1964.

Griffen, Clyde, and Sally Griffen. *Natives and Newcomers: The Ordering of Opportunity in Mid-Nineteenth-Century Poughkeepsie.* Cambridge, Mass.: Harvard Press, 1977.

Haggstrom, Warren C. "The Power of the Poor," in Frank Riessman, J. Cohen, and Arthur Pearl (eds.) *Mental Health of the Poor.* Glencoe, Ill.: Free Press, 1954.

Handlin, Oscar. *The Uprooted.* New York: Brown, 1951.

Harrington, Michael. *The Other America.* Baltimore: Penguin, 1963.

————. "Is There a Culture of Poverty?" New York: National Social Welfare Assembly, Occasional Papers, Poverty No. 1, May 12, 1964.

————. "Introduction," in Susan Sheehan, *A Welfare Mother.* New York: Mentor-New American Library, 1976.

Hearings before the Committee on Ways and Means of the House of Representatives, Ninety-First Congress on the Subject of Social Security and Welfare Proposals. Washington D.C.: U.S. Government Printing Office, 1969.

Horowitz, Irving Louis. "Consensus, Conflict and Cooperation: A Sociological Inventory," *Social Forces*, 41(2):177–88, 1962.

Horton, John. "Order and Conflict Theories of Social Problems as Competing Ideologies," *American Journal of Sociology*, 71(6):701–13, 1966.

Hoult, Thomas Ford. *Dictionary of Modern Sociology.* Totowa, N.J.: Littlefield, 1969.

Howe, Louisa P. "Some Sociological Aspects of Identification." Pp. 61–79, in Warner Muensterberger and Sidney Axelrad (eds.), *Psycho-Analysis and the Social Sciences*, Vol. 4. New York: International Universities Press, 1955.

Hurvitz, Nathan. "Symbolic Interactionism: A Social Psychological Theory for Marriage and Family Counseling." Pp. 853–54, in Proceedings of the Eightieth Annual American Psychological Association. Washington, D.C.: American Psychological Association, 1972.

Hyman, Herbert H. "The Value Systems of Different Classes," in Rheinhard Bendix and Seymour Martin Lipset (eds.), *Class, Status and Power.* Glencoe, Ill.: Free Press, 1953.

Jordan, Bill. *Poor Parents: Social Policy and The Cycle of Deprivation.* London: Routledge and Kegan Paul, 1974.

Kaplan, Roy H. and Curt Tausky. "The Meaning of Work Among the Hard Core Employed," *Pacific Sociological Review*, 17(2):185–98, 1974.

Kardiner, Abram. *The Individual and His Society.* New York: Columbia Press, 1974.

————, and Lionel Ovesey. *The Mark of Oppression: Explorations in the*

Personality of the American Negro. New York: Meridian, 1964.

Karp, Abraham J. *Golden Door to America: The Jewish Immigrant Experience.* New York: Penguin, 1977.

Kluckhorn, Florence. "Family Diagnosis: Variations in the Basic Values of Family Systems," *Social Casework,* 1958.

Kristol, Irving. "Welfare: The Best of Intentions, The Worst of Results," *Atlantic Monthly,* 228(2):45–47, 1971.

Kuhn, Manford H. "Major Trends in Symbolic Interaction Theory in the Past 25 Years," *Sociological Quarterly,* 5(1):61–84, 1964.

Laing, R. D. *The Politics of Experience.* New York: Pantheon, 1967.

Levine, Sol, and Paul E. White. "Exchange as a Conceptual Framework for Study of Interorganizational Relationships." Pp. 117–32, in Amatai Etzioni (ed.), *A Sociological Reader on Complex Organizations.* New York: Holt, 1969.

Levy, Frank. "Poverty by the Numbers," *The American Spectator,* 2(7):24–26, May 1978.

Lewis, Oscar. *La Vida: A Puerto Rican Family in the Culture of Poverty: San Juan and New York.* New York: Random House, 1956.

———. *Five Families.* New York: Basic Books, 1959.

———. "The Culture of Poverty," *Scientific American,* 215(4):19–25, October 1966.

———. *A Study of Slum Culture: Backgrounds for La Vida.* New York: Random House, 1968.

Lockridge, Kenneth A. *A New England Town: The First Hundred Years.* New York: W. W. Norton, 1970.

Loomis, Charles P. "In Praise of Conflict and Its Resolution," *American Sociological Review,* 32(6):875–90, 1967.

McCord, Joan, and William McCord. "The Effects of Parental Role on Criminality," *Journal of Social Issues,* 14:66–75, 1958.

Macdonald, Dwight. *Our Invisible Poor.* New York: Sidney Hillman Foundation, n.d.

McIntosh, Donald. "Weber and Freud: On the Nature and Sources of Authority," *American Sociological Review,* 35(5):901–11, 1970.

MacIver, R. M. *The Ramparts We Watch.* New York: Macmillan, 1950.

Mack, Raymond W., and Richard C. Snyder. "The Analysis of Social Conflict—Toward an Overview and Synthesis," *Journal of Conflict Resolution,* 1(1):212–48, 1957.

Magnum, Garth L. "The Why, How and Whence of Manpower Programs," in Lawrence F. Sneden, II (ed.), *Poverty: A Psychosocial Analysis.* Berkeley: McCutchan, 1970.

Manis, Jerome, and Bernard Meltzer (eds.). *Symbolic Interaction: A Reader in Social Psychology.* Boston: Bacon, 1967.

May, Edgar. *The Wasted Americans*. New York: Signet, 1964.

Meltzer, Bernard N., John W. Peters, and Larry T. Reynolds. *Symbolic Interaction: Genesis, Varieties, and Criticism*. Boston: Routledge, 1975.

Merton, Robert K. "Social Structure and Anomie," *American Sociological Review*, 3(5):672–82, 1938.

———. *Social Theory and Social Structure*. Glencoe, Ill.: Free Press, 1957.

Miller, Walter B. "The Elimination of the American Lower Class as National Policy: A Critique of the Ideology of the Poverty Movement of the 1960's." Pp. 260–316, in Daniel P. Moynihan (ed.), *On Understanding Poverty: Perspectives in the Social Sciences*. New York: Basic Books, 1968.

Milner, Murray, Jr. *The Illusion of Equality*. San Francisco: Josey Bass, 1972a.

———. "On Getting Somewhere: Notes On 'Equal Opportunity' and Other Convenient Delusions," *Columbia Forum*, 1(2):19–25, 1972b.

Minuchin, Salvador, Broulio Montalvo, Bernard G. Guerney, Jr., Bernice L. Rosman, and Florence Schumer. *Families of the Slums: An Exploration of Their Structure and Treatment*. New York: Basic Books, 1967, pp. 192–243.

Moynihan, Daniel P. *The Negro Family: The Case for National Action*. Washington, D.C.: U.S. Government Printing Office, 1965.

Ornati, Oscar. *Poverty in America*. National Policy Committee on Pockets of Poverty on the Farmers Educational Foundation. Washington, D.C., 1964.

Parsons, Talcott. *The Social System*. Glencoe, Ill.: Free Press, 1951.

———. *Societies: Evolutionary and Comparative Purposes*. Englewood Cliffs, N.J.: Prentice-Hall, 1966.

———, and Edward A. Shils. *Toward a General Theory of Action*. Cambridge, Mass.: Harvard Press, 1951.

Passell, Peter, and Leonard Ross. *The Retreat from Riches. Affluence and Its Enemies*. New York: Viking Press, 1973.

Pavalko, Ronald M. *Sociology of Occupations and Professions*. Itaska, N.Y.: Peacock, 1971.

Pruitt, Walter A., and H. van de Castle. "Dependency Measures and Welfare Chronicity," *Journal of Consulting Psychology*, 26:559–60, 1962.

Rainwater, Lee. "Poverty, Living Standards and Family Well Being," Working Paper No. 10, Joint Center for Urban Studies of the Massachusetts Institute of Technology and Harvard University, 1972.

Rein, Martin and Lee Rainwater, "How Large is the Welfare Class?"

Challenge, pp. 20–23, September/October 1977.

Ribich, Thomas I. "The Problem of Equal Opportunity: A Review Article," *Journal of Human Resources*, 7(4):518–26, 1972.

Riessman, Frank. *The Culturally Deprived Child*. New York: Harper and Row, 1962.

———. "A Portrait of the Underprivileged." Pp. 74–77, in Robert E. Will and Harold G. Vatler (eds.), *Poverty in Affluence: The Social, Political and Economic Dimensions in the U.S.* New York: Harcourt, 1965.

Roach, Jack L. "Sociological Analysis and Poverty," *American Journal of Sociology*, 71(1):68–77, 1965.

Rose, Arnold. *Human Behavior and Social Processes*. Boston: Houghton Mifflin, 1962.

———. "Law and the Causation of Social Problems," *Social Problems*, 16(1):33–43, 1968.

———. "The Unemployables," in Irwin Deutscher and Elizabeth J. Thompson, *Among the People: Encounters with the Poor*. New York: Basic Books, 1968.

Rycroft, Charles. *A Critical Dictionary of Psychoanalysis*. New York: Basic Books, 1968.

Sarbin, Theodore R. "The Culture of Poverty, Social Identity and Cognitive Outcomes," in Vernon Allen (ed.), *Psychological Factors in Poverty*. Chicago: Markham Publishing, 1970.

Scheff, Thomas J. *Being Mentally Ill: A Sociological Theory*. Chicago: Aldine, 1966.

———. "Toward a Sociological Model of Consensus," *American Sociological Review*, 32(1):32–46, 1967.

Schmid, Calvin F., and Charles E. Nobbe. "Socio-economic Differentials Among Non-white Races," *American Sociological Review*, 30(6):909–22, 1965.

Scott, Marvin B. "The Social Sources of Alienation." Pp. 239–52, in I. L. Horowitz (ed.), *The New Sociology: Essays in Social Science and Social Theory in Honor of C. Wright Mills*. New York: Oxford Press, 1965.

Seeman, Melvin. "On the Meaning of Alienation." Pp. 525–39, in Lewis A. Coser and Bernard Rosenberg (eds.), *Sociological Theory: A Book of Readings*. New York: Macmillan, 1964.

Sheehan, Dorothy. *A Welfare Mother*. New York: Mentor-New American Library, 1976.

Shibutani, Tamotsu. *Society and Personality: An Interactionist Approach to Social Psychology*. Englewood Cliffs, N.J.: Prentice-Hall, 1961.

———. *Human Native and Collective Behavior: Papers in Honor of Herbert Blumer*. Englewood Cliffs, N.J.: Prentice-Hall, 1970.

Silberman, Charles E. *Crisis in Black and White.* New York: Random House, 1964.

———. "Beware the Day They Change Their Minds," *Fortune:* 150–53, 255, 258, 262, 267, November 1965.

Simmel, Georg. *Conflict and the Web of Group Affiliations.* Glencoe, Ill.: Free Press, 1955.

Simmons, Ozzie G. "The Mutual Images and Expectations of Anglo-Americans and Mexican Americans," in John H. Burma (ed.), *Mexican Americans in the United States.* New York: Schenkman, 1970, pp. 383–95.

Stewart, Maxwell S. *The Poor Among Us: Challenge and Opportunity.* New York: Public Affairs Pamphlet No. 22, 1972.

Stone, Robert C., and Frederic T. Schlamp. "Characteristics Associated with Receipt and Non-Receipt of Financial Aid from Welfare Agencies," *Welfare in Review,* 3:1–11, 1965.

———. *Family Life Styles Below the Poverty Line.* Institute for Social Science Research, San Francisco State University, 1967

Storer, Norman W. *The Social System of Science.* New York: Holt, 1966.

Stouffer, Samuel F. et al. *Studies in Social Psychology in World War II.* Volume 1, *The American Soldier: Adjustment During Army Life.* Princeton, N. J.: Princeton University Press, 1949.

Szasz, Thomas S. *The Myth of Mental Illness.* New York: Harper, 1961a.

———. *The Myth of Mental Illness: Foundations of a Theory of Personal Conduct.* New York: Dell, 1961b.

Theobald, Robert. *The Rich and the Poor.* New York: Mentor, 1961.

Theodorson, George A., and Achilles G. Theodorson. *Modern Dictionary of Sociology.* New York: Crowell, 1969.

Thomas, E. J., and R. D. Carter. "Social Psychological Factors in Poverty," in M. N. Zald (ed.), *Organizing for Community Welfare.* Chicago: Quadrangle Books, 1967.

Thomas, W. I. *The Unadjusted Girl.* Boston: Little, Brown, 1931.

Thurz, Daniel. "Social Aspects of Poverty," *Public Welfare* 25(3):179–86, July 1967.

U.S. Bureau of the Census, *Current Population Reports,* Series P-60, No. 115, "Characteristics of the Population below the Poverty Level: 1976." U.S. Government Printing Office: Washington, D.C., 1978.

Valentine, Charles A. *Culture and Poverty: Critique and Counter-Proposals.* Chicago: University Press, 1968.

Warren, R. L. "The Conflict Intersystem and the Change Agent," *Journal of Conflict Resolution,* 8(3):231–41, 1964.

Watts, Harold W. "The Measurement of Poverty: An Exploratory Exercise," Institute for Research on Poverty, University of Wisconsin at

Madison, Reprint No. 42, 1969.

Waxman, Chaim. *The Stigma of Poverty: A Critique of Poverty Theories and Policies.* New York: Pergamon, 1977.

Wilhelm, Sidney M., and Edwin H. Powell. "Who Needs the Negro?" *Transaction,* 1(6):3–6, 1964.

Yanis-McLaughlin, Virginia. *Family and Community: Italian Immigrants in Buffalo, 1880–1930.* Ithaca, N.Y.: Cornell Press, 1978.

POOR LAW AND THE POOR   **2**

Community (Gemeinschaft) and Society (Gesellschaft)*

AS THE POPULATION moved from the *gemeinschaft* to the *gesellschaft* pattern of community (Tonnies), it became necessary to service and control the poor. In the *gemeinschaft* there were no poor. All members of the community or tribe were provided for, usually as equals, either through the family or through the feudal social structure of which the family was a part. Table 2.1 shows how the social structure of the *gemeinschaft* lent itself to caring for the poor.

TABLE 2.1   **Aspects of *Gemeinschaft* Society and Aid for the Poor**

GEMEINSCHAFT SOCIETY (ASPECTS OF)	RELATED AID
1. Inherited statuses	1. *Noblesse oblige* on the part of upper echelons.
2. Occupations static	2. No unemployment unless all unemployed.
3. Agricultural, manual or primitive manufacture	3. In-kind aid predominant
4. Closeness of members, affective relationships	4. Mutual Aid (little or no stigma)
5. Social control by kinship relations	5. Social responsibility for those aided by donors
6. Local production of most local consumption and vice versa	6. Sharing by all of production and consumption
7. Subsistence economy	7. Periodic feast and famine
8. Strong boundary control	8. Xenophobic reaction to nonmembers and little or no aid to nonresidents
9. Sentiments expressed spontaneously and not for ulterior effect	9. Aid provided with little or no associated control of these aids

SOURCE: Gould and Kolb, pp. 281-82.

*Hoult (p. 142) says that the gemeinschaft denotes social situations "wherein those involved treat one another as ends rather than means." He lists the gesellschaft (p. 144) as social conditions "wherein those involved treat one another as means rather than ends."

Each individual's status provided roles and role-related constraints for the individual from the cradle to the grave. There was little or no loneliness, but for the intellectual there was often boredom. *Gemeinschaft* societies often tolerated deviance, as long as the deviant was one of their own. There were mutual obligations between the holders of interacting statuses and roles. An example of such structural interactions was *noblesse oblige* by which the nobleman was responsible for the care and protection of his serfs. A corresponding structural interaction was fealty, which the serf was required to pay to the nobleman in return for care and protection. The *gemeinschaft* was both small and functional. All elements in the community were symbiotic and had a mutual fate. Each was dependent upon the other for participation and support of the community. Roles and occupations were available to both the able-bodied and high-born and the handicapped and low-born; no special stigma was attached to occupations in the latter category.

In some *gemeinschaft* communities, of course, the model presented above was not valid. The quid pro quo arrangement did not always operate, and coercion, rather than mutual benefit or concern, was sometimes the cohesive community bond. It is obvious, however, that where coercion occurred it was eventually self-defeating for those in control. Not all *gemeinschaft* communities followed the feudal model. Many such communities followed tribal models, in which familial bonds were the cohesive mechanisms. Tribal loyalty and traditions were often supported at the expense of logical community purposes. Tribal or community loyalty also supported many members who were unable to participate in productive enterprises. The *gemeinschaft* community required no old age homes, mental hospitals, or public welfare programs. The community provided for all, regardless of degree of productivity or deviance. The thrust of the *gemeinschaft* was mutual protection, concern, aid, and survival. Because the community did not need and did not provide special institutions for the deviant, the handicapped, and the incompetent, there were no legislative provisions for these people.

With the development of the economic marketplace, the *gemeinschaft* pattern of communities declined. Entire populations moved to communities where they hoped to find work and economic survival. It was in the economic community that the *gesellschaft* developed. This community model differed in a number of ways from the *gemeinshaft* (Gould and Kolb, pp. 286–87). The *gesellschaft* included the following features:

1. Status in the community was primarily by savings, achievement, entrepreneurship, and training. Persons with a high degree of social stigma had either a low or no status in society. Recipients of aid were assigned a high degree of stigma and a low status. This pattern of relationships fitted in with community emphasis on employee productivity and on conservation of resources. The diversion of sizable amounts of resources

to public aid would be counterproductive for the economy of a market-place community.

2. Occupations were established and retained on the basis of market needs and not family tradition. Employability and wages in the market-place community were related not to who one was but to what work one could perform and how much demand there was for that type and quality of work. Thus, there was a continuous fluctuation in statuses and societal supports based upon one's revealed and paid-for work contributions, as determined by the current market.

3. Complicated, comprehensive, and specialized manufacturing and distribution mechanisms proliferated in the *gesellschaft*. Consequently, a productivity and commodity orientation was emphasized in the *gesellschaft* community. People who could not fit the needs of the comprehensive, specialized labor market were excluded from the economic mainstream either temporarily or permanently. Among these people were the aged, the handicapped, and the deviant.

4. Because of the emphasis upon the business contract and commercial performance, relationships were formal, functional, and oriented to socioeconomic purposes. The formalistic and functionally oriented relationships provided little basis for mutual concern. The emphasis was on competition rather than on cooperation and helpfulness to others. Because of the great social distance between persons, there was little or no affective base of concern for others.

5. Social control was vested more in the marketplace and the government than in kinship groups. Social control rested upon the interests of the marketplace rather than upon a community of people. Aid to the aged, handicapped, and deviant was a means not only of support but also of social control. In the bustling marketplace with new faces appearing every day, and the constant threat of theft, aid programs provided ways to control persons not tied to marketplace employment.

6. Production was related to the needs of distant markets rather than to local consumption needs alone. Aid was viewed in relation to comparable costs rather than to the degree of individual need and community membership alone. That is why the principle of lesser eligibility came into use. According to this principle, no welfare would amount to more than the potential earnings of the lowest paid worker in the marketplace. Thus, the cost of welfare was considered not only in terms of the direct expenditures involved, but also in terms of its effect on the economic marketplace and on the availability of marginal labor. When deciding what kind of aid to give, the community compared the costs of in-kind assistance, in-house assistance (the poor house), and outdoor relief (financial grants). The type of assistance chosen was based not on the best interests of the client, but on the comparative direct costs to the community.

7. The *gesellschaft* operated on the basis of a savings economy and

eventually on the basis of an economy of abundance, but with unequal distribution of products to the members of the society. An economy of savings and abundance provides differential access to honors and stigma, based upon their differential access to ready supply. In turn, the economy perpetuates high aspirations for more individuals and limited achievement and access to many. Accompanying these is a highly disparate relationship between marketplace-fostered wants and reality supplies.

In the *gemeinschaft* community, aid was almost egalitarian for members and less than generous for nonmembers and strangers. Thus, in the *gemeinschaft,* aid was based on the relationship to members and in the *gesellschaft,* on the relationship of the individual's value to the marketplace.

History of the Poor Law

In the early period (the twelfth, thirteenth, and fourteenth centuries), various transitional aid mechanisms supplemented the mutual aid services of the *gemeinschaft.* These were programs made necessary by the lack of facilities to care for detached outsiders who because of migrations to the cities were no longer members of a *gemeinschaft.* These programs were motivated by religion and directed by the church. The church held that "the destitute have a right to assistance [and those who are] better off [have] a duty to provide charity" (de Schweinitz, Kurzman, and Loch). Under these programs, a comprehensive network of services was developed with special attention to the needs of the aged, sick, widows, and orphans. Thus, Coll (p. 2) describes the two pictures of medieval charity: one of a wealthy lord giving alms to ragged beggars and one of hordes of importuners crowding at the gates of monasteries.

The church operated its services according to Medieval Poor Law, which was a set of policies designed by church lawyers and designated as part of canon law. A poor man was considered an honorable man, and the only test for aid was need. "In case of doubt, [it is] better to do too much than to do nothing at all" (Coll, p. 3). Under canon law, a man's first responsibility was to his family. Then came his neighbors and finally strangers. Canon law placed heavy pressure on men who had more than they needed to contribute to the poor, particularly through the vehicle of church charities. In the twelfth, thirteenth, and fourteenth centuries, a great deal of thought was given to the distribution of alms. The canonists believed that poverty was not a crime and that one could be poor and yet honorable. According to medieval thought, the poor had a right to assistance, and those who were better off had a duty to give help. Both the Jewish view of aid—"not charity but justice (Tzodakah)"—and the Christian concern for personal salvation were upheld in church policy.

Church property and income were very much involved in the care and support of the poor.

Canonist altruism was extended to the poor and the ill; particular attention was focused on widows and orphans. The able-bodied nonworker was "corrected" rather than aided. (This view was a reasonable one in light of the employment opportunities and economic prosperity of the times. The only test for eligibility for aid was evidence of need.) Much of this aid was distributed through local, often rural, parishes. Priests were responsible to their bishops for the care of the poor, but by the fourteenth century, many individuals in addition to the priests became involved in this aid effort.

These medieval men were concerned with doing good works more because of a personal interest in their own salvation than because of the needs of the poor. For this reason, they were not greatly concerned about the effect of their benefactions; the pattern was generally one of indiscriminate almsgiving. Begging and unnecessary dependency on alms for support, especially among transient populations, soon became a concern of the communities.

Canon law originally dealt with welfare from the point of view of natural law. As its arrangements for welfare became codified, increasingly formal laws were enacted. According to the statutes, poverty was not a crime, the poor man was honorable, and the destitute had a right to assistance. Only able-bodied beggars, fortune-tellers, and others seeking to avoid work were categorized as unworthy. Great social pressure was placed upon the wealthy to give to church charities, and it was usually quite effective, as could be expected in a *gemeinschaft* type of community.

The pressure for welfare in England during the twelfth and thirteenth centuries was not so great that the church parish system could not effectively deal with it. The communities were still strongly *gemeinschaft*. The extended family and community infrastructure had not yet been attacked by industrial developments. The serfs were still strongly tied to the land by law, custom, and value system. The traveling poor were not warmly welcomed in communities, and this public attitude served as a deterrent to travel by the destitute. One had to make it on one's own in a town for a year and a day to be considered free of the land to which one had previously been tied. Thus, a destitute stranger would be served for a time by a church or monastery and would usually be refused aid by others. The church provided care for those for whom there were no other resources. With the ensuing social transformations, however, this welfare system had to change. In response to social change, a series of laws that followed the events and needs of the time was enacted.

In 1348, with the outbreak of the Black Death, the population of En-

gland and other European countries dropped sharply. Because of the fear
that the disease would spread and because of the shortage of laborers,
unnecessary travel was discouraged. Edward III proclaimed the Statute
of Laborers under which able-bodied men without means of support were
required to accept employment offered to them. Laborers were forbidden
to leave their parishes, and alms to able-bodied beggars were prohibited.
This statute was the forerunner of the vagrancy laws that proliferated in
England, Europe, and the United States in later centuries. To this day,
many communities permit the police to request that strangers show proof
of a visible means of support or risk almost indefinite imprisonment. The
Statute of Laborers was an incursion by the state into church administration of welfare. It prohibited alms for a category of clients, and it contravened many canonical precepts of charity. This law was the first legislative constraint on church welfare administration.

Numerous societal changes, in addition to the plague, helped set the
stage for the Statute of Laborers. The displacement of many farmers
produced massive dislocations. Landlords, who gained control of land
from the extended farming families, secured acts of enclosure which
closed the commons. These grounds were open for community grazing,
wood gathering, hunting, and farming. The landlords now fenced these
grounds, and many farmers were no longer able to earn a livelihood on the
land. Feudal communities broke up as people moved to towns and cities
in search of employment.

The Statute of Laborers was the first of a series of punitive acts designed to keep the laborer on the land or near employment or fealty. In
terms of legal realism, poverty became equivalent to a crime. Alms-giving
and begging were outlawed. Laborers' movements were subject to strict
control based upon labor market needs (see Booth; Coll, 1966; Coll, 1969;
Kurzman; Leonard; Loch; Mencher; Notestein; Rodgers, 1968; Rowntree; Woodroofe). Hence, the Statute of Laborers could be viewed as an
attempt to tie the individual to his assigned marketing society.

In 1536, a law was passed stating that alms collected by the churches
and others were to be used by the mayor and the church wardens for the
needy. Thus, the influence of the church in welfare matters was diluted by
city and local governmental involvement. This law marked a shift from
church-administered welfare to a secular system. Similar developments
occurred elsewhere on the European scene. In Lyon, France, in 1534, the
Aumône General was established. Churches, monasteries, and donors
were permitted to give only to the Aumône and not directly to the poor.
The needy people were recorded in a census and then were given tickets
for food and money. A followup of the results of alms given was arranged
for. Another legal move that reduced church control was the Act of
Enclosure promulgated in 1531 by Henry VIII. This law was the first

national government effort to control welfare and relieve economic distress. It was also a feudal measure to increase the king's revenue and thwart the ever-increasing power of the church. This act restricted begging to designated areas and imposed fines on those who gave food or lodging to beggars outside of designated areas. Able-bodied beggars were whipped and returned to their place of birth.

Next, the Crown expropriated monasteries which had formerly housed many of the poor. Instead, the able-bodied poor were to be given allowances if their income was insufficient for survival, with the government paying the difference between the income and the amount needed. This wage subsidy depressed wages generally and further pauperized the poor because employers counted on the subsidy in determining the wage they would be willing to pay.

By 1572, the position of overseer of the poor was increasingly secular with no church involvement. As a result, public control of welfare had the following concomitant effects: able-bodied beggars were made subject to punishment; begging was permitted only by locals who were not able-bodied; and it became a crime to change one's place of residence in a search for rising wages. In this way, vagrancy, poverty, and crime were linked under the law (Coll, 1969: 5–8).

Despite the settlement law, "men and youth by the thousands and tens of thousands [moved] into the inexhaustible maw of the London employment market—but always faster than London could absorb them" (Coll, 1969, p. 5). (The impact of this population shift was similar to that of the move of rural and southern Americans to the urban centers beginning in the early twentieth century.) This shift resulted in a more skilled labor force; seasonal and cyclical unemployment in locations where employment conditions were variable; considerable urban inflation and depression; and, in the cities, a crowded population, and famine, bread riots, and unrest. The settlement laws reflected a shift in attitudes toward the able-bodied poor. For over 200 years, the problem of poverty was intricately linked to the problems of vagrancy, and the link was formalized into law.

The period between the late fifteenth century and the early seventeenth century was generally prosperous, and employment opportunities expanded, but not so fast as to be able to absorb the steady influx of rural populations into the towns. This constant labor surplus had to be fed and controlled, and it created a situation in the towns which was often beyond their ingenuity and resources. In a sense, the prosperous towns viewed the influx of unskilled laborers not as a blessing which kept their labor costs low and their profits high, but rather as a nuisance and unnecessary expense. The image of the wandering poor as "ne'r-do-wells" and criminals was, to some extent, reinforced by the fact that thieves, highwaymen, and purse snatchers found it easy to hide themselves among the masses of the itinerant poor.

Over and beyond the decisive effect of legal statutes on church welfare administration was the Protestant Reformation which further changed church attitudes toward poverty and charity. Martin Luther (born 1483) expressed the new view that the church had used charity to corrupt men. For the Protestants, industry, sobriety, and thrift were the saving virtues. Poverty was seen as a failure of character, and it was the duty of the pious to lead others into the path of industry, sobriety, and thrift. Later, John Calvin led in the acceptance of these Protestant views of welfare. Luther and Calvin would have preferred voluntary charity (rather than government aid) if it could have been effective and logically managed, but this was considered impossible. Calvin, in Geneva, worked to found the first free comprehensive public school, presumably because he believed that schooling was related to employability. He founded the first poor peoples' industry under government auspices, arranging for cloth manufacture to provide a livelihood for the unemployed poor. He set up government-sponsored hospitals, houses for travelers, and "pest houses" for people with contagious diseases. He established medical care for the poor in their own homes. The Lutheran-Calvinist emphasis on work as a path to salvation made productivity a substitute for birth and class as the only basis for socioeconomic status. This influence made the society more permeable and more democratic, providing opportunity for those able to use it.

By the 1650s, the church's views on alms-giving had shifted. Calvinists and Lutherans saw the giving of alms or aid as a corruption of individuals who already had a vicious nature. Idleness was considered evil, and the poor were dealt with severely. It was a duty (not a sin) to deal severely with people who were destitute through their own inaction or lack of planning for their futures.

During the church-administered welfare era, there had been some secular assistance organizations in the growing towns and cities, a few of which were mutual aid societies organized on a craft or guild basis. These work associations formed the basis for many of today's voluntary aid and service programs. Many of these programs were utilized as the chosen instruments of government to carry out public aid responsibilities under a variety of laws and regulations. After a century of patchwork lawmaking and revisions, poor law was codified into the Elizabethan Poor Law which legitimated and arranged for the resident helpless poor to receive aid. The government accepted responsibility for the relief of poverty. Funds for relief were to be raised by taxation or by assessed poor rates which were levied upon the newly affluent segment of the society—the businessmen and entrepreneurs. All welfare would be locally financed and administered.

The Elizabethan Poor Law also stipulated that responsibility for aid was secular rather than religious. This provision was probably as much a result of Henry VIII's expropriation of church lands as it was a conscious policy choice. The local parish was established as the unit of settlement, residence, and aid administration. The parish officials and entrepreneurs saw to the appointment or election of an overseer of the poor, who was held responsible for public aid and control of the indigent. Family responsibility was legitimated and required under public aid. Parents were required to provide for children and grandchildren, and grown children were held responsible for elderly parents and handicapped family members.

The poor were categorized according to their degree of personal responsibility for their condition of indigency. The helpless, the aged, and the handicapped were scheduled for aid in their own homes or almshouses. The involuntarily unemployed were scheduled for made-work programs and community work opportunities during their period under assistance. The vagrant, able-bodied persons who refused or avoided work were scheduled for commitment to a workhouse or jail. Children who were unattached were bound out as apprentices or set to work in order to learn a trade. Although some historians believe that the Elizabethan Poor Law established the right to assistance, one might better define it as a broadening of eligibility to proof of need and acceptability.

Elizabethan Poor Law

The philosophical foundations for the Elizabethan Poor Law reflected Protestant Ethic views. Key elements of the Protestant Ethic as it related to social welfare (Segalman) were as follows. Since work was not connected with religious purposes, idleness, drunkenness, waste, and other nonproductive acts became irreligious activities. Wealth was viewed as stewardship and was supposed to be used responsibly for the creation of employment and production. Employability was also viewed as stewardship and was not to be wasted. Finally, parenthood was considered to be a responsibility for the wise use and development of children's opportunities and abilities. Thus, under the Protestant Ethic hard work was seen as a service to God. Work was holy if undistracted by activities unrelated to work. The honored person was one who deferred all immediate rewards for the sake of prestige and economic success to be achieved later. Such a person conserved assets for a time of need. An honorable person saved surplus wealth to be used in extended economic enterprise, even to the point of self-denial.

According to the Protestant Ethic, success was a sign of recognition of one's morality and of accepted membership in the religious elite. Similarly, hard work and honesty were considered religious duties. To turn a profit was considered a moral good, and to incur an unnecessary debt was a moral wrong. Not to seek economic upgrading by increasing one's skill, devotion to work, and work hours was considered sinful and immoral. Under the Protestant Ethic, man was responsible for his own deeds, and he who did not take responsibility for himself and his own was subject to social stigma and religious damnation.

The Elizabethan Poor Law of 1597-1661 (see Table 2.2) firmly vested all responsibility for aid to the poor in the secular agencies with the parish as the administrative unit. This law distinguished three major categories of dependents: the vagrant, the involuntarily unemployed, and the helpless, each with a prescribed form of aid to be rendered. The parish was empowered to raise taxes, to operate, build, and sustain almshouses, and to provide aid to selected persons in their own homes (the aged, the handicapped, and the helpless). Parents were required within their means to support their children and grandchildren, grown children were required to care for their parents and grandparents in need. Able-bodied persons refusing to work were to be committed to a corrections unit or pilloried (see Coll, pp. 5–6). The administrative official required to carry out the poor law was the overseer of the poor, appointed annually by the justices of the peace (see Trattner, p. 11).

Another law enacted in 1601 was the Law of Charitable Trusts, which provided a framework for private or voluntary charity. It provided for the protection of funds left for charitable purposes, for educational programs, for assistance of persons in their own homes, and for the building of almshouses. Later, the Elizabethan Poor Law and the Law of Charitable Trusts became models for similar poverty legislation in most of the American states. The general design of the Elizabethan Poor Law can be found in the provisions of many contemporary public aid programs (McClure, 1968, p. 1).

In 1662, the revised Law of Settlement and Removal authorized the ejection of persons and families from the parish when local authorities believed those persons were likely to become public dependents. This law included a scheme for the enforced workhouse confinement of vagrants. It sought a plan for the profitable return of vagrants and enforced employment of the idle. This law was not rigidly enforced. It proved easier and cheaper to grant temporary public assistance than to confine sizable numbers of vagrants or traveling workers to the workhouse. After a short period of limited assistance, the poor person was usually escorted to the parish boundary. This pattern would often result in the person's being passed from parish to parish until the home parish was reached. Many American states adopted a similar procedure for "warning out" such persons. (This process is described more fully later in this chapter.)

TABLE 2.2   **Common Provisions for the Poor under English Poor Law Administration**

CATEGORY	AID OFFERED
Widow of resident of the parish with minor children.	Outdoor relief, in-kind commodities and cottage, and in some instances cash.
Widow of nonresident of the parish with minor children or abandoned or deserted woman with minor children.	Indoor relief in the parish almshouse, with work assignments usually within the almshouse.
Minor children who were orphaned.	Placement with farmers and others who could rear them and put them to work (sometimes fee paid by parish), or placement in apprenticeship with promise of livelihood after term of apprenticeship was over (sometimes fee paid to craftsman by parish). Often the livelihood did not become a reality because of the marginal nature of the craft.
Able-bodied unemployed for whom employment was available (local resident).	Workhouse confinement with assigned work contracted for by the workhouse superintendent or the overseer of the poor.
Able-bodied unemployed (nonresident).	Legal notice to leave the parish, plus formal, accompanied dispatch to the parish border.
Disabled persons, unemployed, and legal residents.	Indoor relief in the parish almshouse, with work assignments sometimes in house. In exceptional circumstances and in the later period, outdoor relief was given.

The welfare system under the Elizabethan Poor Law did not constitute a great expense for the government. Because many successful business leaders made contributions, over 97 percent of the costs came from non-tax funds. Later, as contributions declined, funds were derived from the poor tax levied on parish landowners.

In 1697, the workhouse test for public assistance was established. It was first used in Bristol, England, and was found to reduce the costs of welfare by the institution of work relief. The test was to offer work to the applicant; to refuse employment was to court rejection as a welfare client. Under this law, parishes were permitted to farm out their poor on contract. Parishes were also enabled to join forces in establishing workhouses. The farming-out provision became a common mechanism for securing cheap, exploitable labor. It developed into so inhumane a practice that it was abolished by Parliament in 1782.

During the Elizabethan Poor Law period, the obligation of the landowner to the tenant became diluted, and the bonds between master and

servant were severed. Along with the Elizabethan Poor Law were enacted measures to prevent evictions, to stabilize employment, and to
prevent worker dismissal. There was also a prolific development of private almshouses, hospitals, and fund organizations to provide employment and aid treatment. Almshouses under the Elizabethan Poor Law
were not so much a matter of humaneness as a means of removing the
embarrassing and inconvenient poor from the body politic. The Settlement Act of 1662 operated on the belief that a community should not have
to provide for those who did not belong to it (xenophobia of the non-
gemeinschaft member). This law was an attempt to prevent squatters
from taking over untilled land and to prevent movement to the cities,
which by then had become a real problem.

Thus, the Elizabethan Poor Law, along with other related legislation,
was a utilitarian attempt to control the population for the good of the
many. The mechanism of these laws was to use rewards and, more often,
punishments to control the movements from the land to the towns. Many
found that the Elizabethan Poor Law and related legislation did seek to
encourage initiative and to provide for the helpless. For its time, it was a
democratic move to extend protection to all and to promote order, without which progress would have been possible for no one.

The Elizabethan Poor Law and related enactments sought to sustain
family and community ties at a time when the Industrial Revolution had
begun to threaten the stability of social institutions generally. These statutes can also be seen as an attempt at cultural historical law in that they
tried to legislate the cultural views of the people of that era. They were
also an attempt at sociological jurisprudence because they were designed
to deal with the social changes brought on by the Industrial Revolution
and the economic conditions of the time.

In 1796, an attempt was made to experiment with the liberalization of
the poor law. In Speenhamland, the parish provided supplementary aid in
case wages fell below a specified standard of subsistance as measured by
the price of wheat. This "bread scale" took into account the size of the
family, and small amounts were granted to families after the birth of the
third or fourth child. The Speenhamland system was so abused and had
such a depressive effect on the economy that it has become the traditional
example of the problems caused by substituting wage supplements for
public aid.

As a result of the public outcry against the Speenhamland system and
against the rising costs of public welfare in general, the Royal Commission on Poor Relief was established. This commission recommended the
abolition of the Speenhamland system; the reestablishment of the workhouse test and denial of aid to able-bodied persons and their families; the
reinforcement of the principle of lesser eligibility, a mechanism that pre-

vented unnecessary expansion of welfare, shortage of labor occasioned by the availability of public welfare, and inflation of wage levels; continuation of categorical relief, with various amounts of aid allotted according to recipients' degree of irresponsibility for being in need; and continuing responsibility of the parish for administering aid. Under the Royal Commission recommendations, local residence continued to be a prerequisite for eligibility for aid.

It was the philosophy of the business community that public welfare should be constrained. The Speenhamland plan was subsidized by taxes imposed on large employers and property owners; when the plan expanded, the cost became severe for them. Naturally, they favored controls. Thus, wage supports were seen as the lazy man's way of evading work at the expense of entrepreneurs. Adam Smith in *The Wealth of Nations* (1776) declared that man had a natural right to accumulate and possess wealth. He surmised that public assistance interfered with the supply and demand of labor and with the otherwise self-balancing economy because it prevented people from becoming employed. Others subsequently reaffirmed this view.

Between 1803 and 1818, English poor law taxes doubled, and by 1832 they tripled. In 1832, Parliament, concerned with the poor law tax rise, appointed a Poor Law Commission to determine what could be done (see Coll, p. 10). Parishes were solicited for information, but the research instrument was a set of questions that had tenuous validity and reliability. This commission concluded that the poor law was "a bounty on indolence and vice" and a universal system of pauperization. Therefore, a proscription was placed upon all outdoor (home) relief. After the poor laws of 1834, aid was provided only within institutional arrangements. The 1834 legislation was a result of widespread public complaint; both the national authorities and the public were convinced that the local parishes administered the law loosely. Under the new law, welfare administration was centralized, and welfare policies were made uniform across the nation. All local relief units were placed under central control. Emphasis was placed on reform of local welfare administration, on merging welfare parishes, and on separating institutions for various classes of dependents. In spite of the 1834 legislation, there was no increase in the number of persons transferred from public relief to employment. One problem was that there were numerous exceptions in practice of the 1834 law. Local parishes, for example, made numerous grants of home relief. The local authorities explained these exceptions by citing the necessity to keep families unbroken. We do not know whether the parish authorities could have found these clients jobs instead. Many of the parishes also found it cheaper to provide home relief allowances than to establish the workhouses and poorhouses which the law required.

By 1873, one-third of the persons who were receiving outdoor relief were widows in London, and most of the rest were widows in northeast England. We can therefore assume that few complete families were supported by outdoor aid. But despite its inability to limit outdoor relief, the 1834 poor law was praised for two reasons: its firm guidelines for administering relief slowed the spread of abuses in the parish system; and the London (central) administration became more aware of issues related to broader social reforms, including medical care, housing facilities, and sanitation.

The Doctrine of Lesser Eligibility

The lasting effect of the 1834 legislation can be found in the strengthened doctrine of lesser eligibility that prohibited the granting of assistance in an amount greater than the lowest earned wage in the community. This doctrine was originally intended to apply only to able-bodied employables but for the remainder of the century in England and until depression relief measures of the 1930s in the United States the law had a continuing effect on policy for all persons in need.

The principle of lesser eligibility is an important issue in the design of public welfare. If a person can receive more aid by not working this has a deleterious effect on the labor market and general economy. But if a family is so large that it needs more aid for survival, should the law restrict the feeding of hungry children? If the principle is to be applied only to the able-bodied and families with abled-bodied members, will this not encourage abandonment of families by fathers? Thus it can be seen that England focused on a most critical issue in public policy but was not able to satisfactorily resolve it. At best, the English solution was to use the workhouse answer for able-bodied unemployables.

The development of workhouses in England, continued under the 1834 laws, proved an economic failure, and they were closed soon after they opened. At the beginning of the nineteenth century, there were over 4,000 workhouses with approximately 10,000 inmates at a period when England's total population was estimated at 9 million. Within a decade, those workhouses that were not closed were converted to almshouses for special categories of the poor who could not be served in their own homes. The major means of public aid then became home relief, and this pattern has been dominant ever since.

England's 200-year struggle for control during a changing social order was necessary in the face of a disintegrating feudal system, a loosening of church controls over the people, and the development of a dominant economic and industrial commerce. England's empire would have been impossible without the development of a production economy, and that economy would have been impossible without the social controls derived from the Elizabethan Poor Law.

Of the three accomplishments of the 1834 revisions, it is difficult to determine which was the most important, for each supported the economic process. The principle of lesser eligibility prevented the intrusion of welfare into people's motivation to work; the reestablishment of the workhouse test prevented the substitution of welfare for work as a way of life; and the centralization of welfare control and the development of uniform welfare policies presented a united front to prevent welfare abuses by migrants. The Webbs, almost a hundred years later, vehemently criticized the Reforms Law of 1834 as a framework of repression (see Webb). But the Webbs, as well as earlier critics of the law, failed to provide satisfactory alternative solutions for the problems which the 1834 law was designed to control.

The doctrine of lesser eligibility in its basic form is an economic issue. In an industrial and therefore a relatively mobile society, this doctrine proposes an important coordination between economics and management. It is an incentive to provide limits on the welfare family, and it expects self-sufficiency. As most middle-class parents will testify, the decision to have an additional child is often a budget-management issue, and a child is planned only if the family can afford the additional cost. Although the doctrine of lesser eligibility is obviously inhumane when enforced after the fact, it does impose limits on the economy of the welfare family which economic factors constantly impose on the middle class. If poor people are not expected to deal with economic self-sufficiency in the short run, how can we expect them to deal with it in the future?

The workhouse test was important in its time because England was not yet ready or able to retire a major portion of its population from work. When it became possible to retire the disabled, the sick, and the aged, this was done in later legislation, but to exempt the able-bodied from the necessity of employment is something only a utopian society can afford under conditions that rule out most other national expenditures.

Centralized control was necessary to make the policies of the welfare system enforceable. If a different welfare grant were available in each town, and if some towns were more lenient than others, welfare clients would migrate to those with larger grants and more lenient policies. Between 1834 and 1909 in England, numerous changes in welfare occurred. The key changes provided specialized care for certain groups among the disadvantaged, including hospitals, outpatient clinics, specialized institutions for the mentally ill, mentally retarded, blind, and deaf, and foster homes for dependent children who did not have parents to care for them. These amendments did not really change the basic policies in terms of the three principles of 1834. England still suffered the effects of almost 300 years of poor housing, poor health care, and inadequate sanitary conditions for the poor. These conditions became more serious as more and more of the economy was directed toward the accumulation and investment of capital and toward the expansion of industry. By 1909, these conditions were so aggravated that they became a national concern. The Royal Commission on Poor Laws and the Unemployed was established in 1909 to recommend changes (Fink).

The commission's report resulted in policy revisions that stressed curative treatment, rehabilitation, and universal provision instead of repression and the workhouse test. However, the state was expected to continue to exercise compulsion in the care of vagrants, mentally ill patients, children in the hands of unfit parents, and others. Compulsory schooling and vaccination were instituted, and child labor was regulated.

Although the 1909 report of the commission abandoned the workhouse test for most clients, it retained the test in the case of vagrants. This selective application of the principle was based upon the varying, and often unjust, definitions of vagrancy. The majority report advocated the strengthening, humanizing, and widening of the poor law, but the minority went beyond them in ways that were apparent in later years.

The National Insurance Act of 1911 and the Widows, Orphans and Old Age Contributory Pensions acts of 1925 were the forerunners of the American Social Security Act of 1935. The Unemployment Act of 1934 in England provided for unemployment compensation in a plan roughly parallel to the counterpart provisions of the American Social Security Act. In 1941 England undertook still another reform of her entire welfare program. Parliament authorized an inter-departmental committee on social insurance under the chairmanship of Sir William Beveridge. This committee undertook to guarantee a level of income for all citizens. Since that time, England has revised her welfare and social insurance programs again according to the principles of the Beveridge Report which provides for social insurance coverage for all citizens; social insurance protection against the major causes of lost earning power: maternity, old age, widowhood, accident, unemployment, and sickness; a flat contribution paid by all regardless of income; and a flat benefit rate for all who qualify, regardless of income.

Social insurance can be a basic support, enabling families to protect themselves against loss of income. It is another matter, however, when the family has no income, is on welfare, and has been on welfare for decades and generations. This is presently the case for a sizable population in England which is highly dependent upon National Assistance. The poverty problem has not been solved by the English social insurances, and the general income level is constantly bypassed by labor union employees who seek to raise their economic status far above the level of the dole.

The Welfare Scene in Colonial America

In early colonial times in America, the people as a whole faced a life of severity and hardship. Deprivation was common and most communities were close knit, although poverty stricken. The group's survival depended upon communality and mutual aid. Either a community was a true *gemeinschaft* or it did not survive. When any member of the community could not care for himself on his own, others in the community would take him in or help him in other ways. At the outset, there was no official welfare program for settlement members, nor was it necessary.

Strangers had no part in this system. There were no charitable philanthropists to support a welfare program via the churches or local secular authorities. Newcomers to the communities who were not likely to be able to support themselves were "warned away." Those who could support themselves had to do so, and there were usually plenty of opportunities for self-subsistence based on hard work. Newcomers were often encouraged to go to the more rudimentary settlements unless they could work and support themselves in the cities.

Eventually, many communities, especially the port cities, were forced to make some official arrangement for their destitute members and for strangers without means of support. The local poor were provided for by some means or other, sometimes even by passing around the widows and children from one household to another for portions of the year. Strangers, however, were required to register as visitors and to have a resident post bond in their behalf to ensure they would not become dependent upon the community. Only if a visitor stayed three months without being warned out could he claim resident status (Trattner). In time, most established settlements chose overseers of the poor whose functions were similar to the English model. Generally, the communities took responsibility, and decisions regarding the poor were made in town meetings or in the general council or court.

Colonial America adopted the Elizabethan Poor Law of 1601, including the presumed right of the needy to receive aid within the constraints of the law. Actually, this was less a right of the recipients than it was a responsibility imposed on secular state administrators. The American poor law upheld the traditional English legal residence requirement for local aid eligibility. This provision was specifically directed against nontaxpayers, who, it was believed, should neither vote nor be entitled to aid.

(People who owned no property paid no taxes.) The early laws included a process of warning out for newcomers who were believed to have arrived without assets. Town officials would notify newcomers that if they were not able to provide for themselves they would not be permitted to become public charges on the local community. Passing out was a procedure utilized with newcomers who requested aid. This procedure involved taking the indigent persons to the road nearest to their original homes or point of origin and then seeing them over the county line. In the next county, they would often be met by the overseer and escorted to the border of a third county. Considerable costs were involved in suits between counties when disagreements developed over which county was financially responsible for the continued support of the indigents. These suits often took place after the indigents in question had moved away from both counties and were nowhere to be found.

As the American poor law took shape, certain patterns of the English poor law were adopted. First, each county (and later each state) was responsible for local indigents. This principle paralleled the English parish responsibility. Various elements of this position are now expressed in formal law.

A second principle regarding responsibility for dependent relatives was drawn from the Protestant Ethic and was rooted in the English poor law: notably, the economic resources of close relatives were subject to lien in support of dependents. Thus, a grown child, already married and with responsibilities of his own, would be expected to care for his elderly parents. A person who participated in the conception of a child was expected to support him, and this was his primary responsibility regardless of his other obligations. Many elements of natural law can be found in this aspect of poor law.

Third, a firm distinction was made between more deserving and less deserving indigents. Persons who were in need through no fault of their own or who were not able-bodied and employable were given more generous aid and with less stringency. We can recognize elements of natural law in the fact that widows and orphans were considered the community's primary aid responsibilities. In the instance of priority for the handicapped, elements of both natural and cultural-historical law are present. We recognize elements of utilitarian law in the fact that concern for the employment market ruled out large aid grants for the able-bodied. Thus, the categorical relief pattern of England was transposed to the American scene.

Two important principles of the Elizabethan Poor Law were not fully transposed to the United States: centralization of welfare control and uniform welfare standards, and the principle of lesser eligibility. Central administration and uniform welfare standards were obviously impossible in a collection of colonies without adequate transportation and communication facilities. Hence, the local community, and later the county, became the seat of welfare administration. Eventually, the states became centers of service policy and funding. Only recently has aid to the aged, blind, and disabled been nationalized. Because AFDC has not been centralized (the Carter welfare reform proposes to do so), its quality has suffered in the uncoordinated hands of fifty states, a number of territories, and a national government which is a partner with each of the states and territories.

The principle of lesser eligibility was not formally transposed because it would have been unthinkable for any settlement in the New World to give very much help to anyone in the face of the sparse resources. It would have been impossible for any community to provide as welfare more than a man could earn in employment. Although the principle of lesser eligibility continued as a basic point of view, it never became a formal policy. Over the decades, funds were usually so limited as to preclude a violation of the principle. The professional workers of the charity organization movement were also quite alert to mechanisms of client motivation. Hence, in their effort to move a client back to self-sufficiency, they limited private or philanthropic welfare so that it did not compete with the client's interest in finding and keeping employment. This principle did not even become an important issue until federal and state funding of the AFDC program became part of the Social Security Act in 1935. As long as family budgets were limited under the program, the matter was not urgent and had little effect on the nature and pattern of welfare family life. Only in recent years and only in the more urban and populous settings has this principle become so important that it affects the cohesion of families and the nature of welfare children's role-models. Because of the Napoleonic wars, the United States experienced a severe depression in the early nineteenth century which caused relief expenditures to rise critically. Procedures for the granting of aid were relaxed in many states. It was logical for the authorities to expand aid programs and to relax procedures because they were faced with general societal change and structural unemployment. This action reflects elements of sociological jurisprudence. Whereas previously the state was cognizant of only individual unemployment and need, it now was forced to consider events that affected the whole community. In New York State, four major mechanisms were operative in poor law during the nineteenth century: the contract system under which a contractor would undertake, for a lump sum, the care of specific indigents; the "auction of the poor" system under which an auction in reverse was conducted and the poor were farmed out to the lowest bidder; the almshouse or county poor-farm system; and the home relief or outdoor relief system.

Almshouses were often preferred in many American localities. The "idle and dissolute" were required to work in such sites. Authorities assumed that persons who could find jobs elsewhere would avoid the almshouse. In that way it was thought funds would be conserved and morals improved; lazy people would become industrious, intemperate people would become teetotalers, and vicious people would become virtuous. Thus, the administrators who chose to use the almshouse system were utilitarians in direction and approach.

The almshouse format had other advantages for the counties. Because the almshouse was large and centrally located, the county could save money buying supplies wholesale. (It would have cost more to supply individual aid recipients small amounts at retail prices.) Because all inmates could perform some duties, the almshouse could produce many of the goods and services it needed. Many almshouses had their own farms, dairies, furniture shops, and the like. (Some almshouse products were used in other county offices.) Being centralized, the almshouse could make the most of specialized services. For example, a county physician could care for all of the indigents, including those in the county hospital, which was usually located near the almshouse.

The almshouse system had a number of shortcomings. For one thing, almshouses frequently provided opportunities for political favors. All too often, county officials used the almshouse as a means of paying off political debts rather than as a true service to the poor. Another serious criticism of the poorhouse was that it institutionalized its inmates. By separating the clients from the community, poorhouses so inured the clients to the ways of the almshouse that they no longer had the role-skills for interaction outside the institution. That is why most persons who entered the almshouse had little possibility of ever leaving it. Such institutions became expanding storehouses for persons who might have otherwise lived in the community as productive, taxpaying citizens.

The first almshouse in America opened in Boston in 1660. On the eastern seaboard, American almshouses were mostly free hospitals, particularly serving new immigrants. Many immigrants were so ill upon arrival that they urgently required medical care. Of the many immigrants injured while building canals and railroads, most returned to work as soon as they recovered—much to the surprise of almshouse administrators. Almshouses also served what today may be termed urban crisis centers during the epidemics of yellow fever, cholera, and typhoid fever. Many of today's great hospitals, such as Bellevue and Philadelphia General, were once county almshouses.

The function of the almshouses varied (Johnson, 1911, pp. 171–80). The Blockley almshouse in Philadelphia in 1848 (Coll, 1969, p. 25), for example, had the following distribution of clients:

Children without homes	111	
"Lunatic"	718	
Old men and incurables	188	
Men's working wards	79	(presumably unskilled laborers)
Mechanics wards	42	(presumably skilled unemployed workers)
Old women and incurables	256	
Working women's ward	71	
Women in nursery	21	
Children in nursery	23	

Thus, the almshouse had diverse purposes. It sheltered the homeless; provided hospital care; deterred pauperism; provided for the seasonably unemployed; taught hospital functions; and served as a community crisis center.

The almshouse was primarily a product of city life. The small town did not require it for a number of reasons. As a near-*gemeinschaft,* the small town population had tolerance for its idiots, "lunatics," drunkards, and "ne'r-do-wells." Those who foundered were nevertheless accepted, controlled, and provided for, as long as they were members of the community. It was only in the city that lunacy, idiocy, drunkenness, and laziness were identified, and with identification came the need to provide care. Residents of small towns could take each other in during periods of illness and need. The social structure of the city had no such built-in facilities. Because of this need, the almshouse left its mark on American history.

Today, most of our population is urban or suburban in character. It was not always so. During the nineteenth century, most of the American population lived on farms and in farm areas. When cities were still growing and expanding, the American almshouse was only a temporary expedient for the administrators of public welfare.

A discussion of public welfare and poor law in England, Europe, and the United States would be incomplete if it did not also include the humanitarian movement and its effect upon welfare services. During the Middle Ages, it was assumed that need arose as a result of misfortune. Christian charity and justice were considered society's responsibilities. Later, the Calvinist ethic (and other versions of the Protestant Ethic) equated the acquisition of wealth with moral virtue. People believed that the able-bodied destitute were in poverty because of individual faults. They held on to this notion despite the arguments of economists that low wages and lack of jobs were beyond the poor's control. By the early nineteenth century, with the American Revolution, the French Revolution, and the rise of rationalism, public opinion changed. Runes (p. 263) defines rationalism as a theory of philosophy in which the criterion of truth is not sensory but intellectual and deductive. Thus, Plato's rationalist theory of the self-sufficiency of reason became the *leitmotif* of neo-

Platonism and idealism. Rationalism rejected superstition and the supernatural, and postulated that men could achieve a rational society. It therefore rejected the views of Calvinism which blamed the victim for his poverty. These same concepts of rationalism form the basis for much of contemporary social policy and social legislation planning. Under rationalism, determinism is rejected, and man is thought to be perfectible through social reform.

Welfare Reforms in Nineteenth-Century America

There were several approaches to social reform in nineteenth-century America. One was reform by persuasion, exemplified by the Missionary Tract Society and the Sunday School Society movements. Another was reform by legislation—e.g., temperance laws, expanded suffrage, employment legislation, public aid, and the abolition of slavery. Yet another approach involved action programs such as the Society for the Prevention of Pauperism (1819) and the Society for the Improvement of the Condition of the Poor (1840), and the child saving movement. In addition, orphanages, schools for the deaf, schools for the blind, and other institutions were established. The reformers of the time called for moral treatment of deviates in the penitentiaries and reformatories. Probation, parole, and the juvenile court were products of reform. Reformers believed that the problems of society could be resolved and that it was possible to improve both man's behavior and society's ways of controlling man. Unlike the Protestant Ethic, reform entailed an optimistic view of man.

Belief in reason, science, and the empirical method led to emphasis on fact-finding. Dorothy Dix headed a movement which began in 1841 to humanize and reform the treatment of the insane. She began in Massachusetts but by 1853 her influence spread all over the United States and beyond (see Bremner, pp. 67-70, and Trattner, pp. 58-62). This movement led to the use of the medical model for human problem-solving and, ultimately, to the relegation of the insane to mental hospitals. During the reform era, the emphasis was on voluntary (sometimes called private) assistance rather than on government programs. The popular approaches were character reform based upon moral persuasion, patronizing interest, and highly directive intervention in clients' lives.

Reform as a vehicle of rationalism soon gave way to scientific charity in behalf of rationalism. The charity organization movement of England (and later of the United States) evolved and became important between 1880 and 1930. During the same period, the settlement house movement developed. The Charity Organization Society (COS) sought to coordinate and logically plan services for the poor. Members of the settlement house movement sought to live among, and to involve the poor in, self-help programs. In format, the COS was rationalist, while the settlement house movement was more humanitarian. This difference provided separate approaches for each movement.

Both the COS and the settlement house movement had their origins among the upper class. The COS tried to reform people by providing private charity while imposing specific constraints on the use of funds. The COS required intensive investigation of client needs and conditions, and development of and implementation of a supervised plan for the client's redirection toward self-support and responsibility. The COS members believed that public assistance or relief was a means of creating and reinforcing dependency. They viewed uncontrolled charity as a perpetuation of dependency and an unnecessary interference with the sacrosanct principles of the free market. In the COS way of thinking, poverty was usually a forerunner of, or a concomitant to, degeneracy.

The settlement house movement can be traced to the London Workingmen's College (1884) which offered education at convenient hours and locations, so that poor people could improve their economic situations and social status. Around the same time, Toynbee Hall offered a similar program, aimed at developing mutual aid societies. The first settlement house in the United States was begun at the Neighborhood Guild in New York. By 1889, Hull House was set up as a neighborhood settlement in Chicago. This movement combined the efforts of the well-to-do volunteers, who took up residence in the settlement, with the efforts of the poor who lived in the neighborhood. The program of settlement houses included classes for socioeconomic upgrading, classes on political and social involvement in the community, and classes in home care and healthy family development.

The charity organization movement was supported largely through private funds until the Depression of the 1930s when the private charity organizations could no longer cope with the poverty problem. By 1932, more than one of every four American workers was unemployed. Then the Federal Emergency Relief Act (FERA) of 1933 provided for a public welfare program. This program utilized many of the charity organization movement caseworkers as supervisors and administrators.

The Social Security Act was established in the mid-1930s to provide, in part, for compulsory insurance for retirement and survivors benefits. But federally subsidized state programs for old age assistance and aid to dependent children were continued because most clients had built up no benefits or only minimal benefits under Social Security. Most people thought that these two aid programs were only necessary as interim activities and that after a generation, with everyone working and building benefits for himself, the need for aid programs (as contrasted with insurance programs) would diminish (see Witte). The social insurance program was based upon an egalitarian philosophy rather than on an attempt to control the poor.

By 1950, most persons on public welfare in the United States were neither employable nor oriented to preparing for employment. Many were the descendants of relatively small populations which were locked into continued poverty. By 1965, the large cities had become the centers to which the rural poor came, uprooted by changing agricultural methods and federal agriculture policies. Mechanization and regulation made it profitable for landowners to displace sharecroppers in preference to land bank payments or large-scale farming by new equipment. Public attitudes toward the poor were no longer as accepting as they had been immediately after the Depression. The public grew restive at the sight of increasing aid costs and increasing numbers of people receiving assistance. Old Age Assistance (OAA), Aid to the Totally Disabled (ATD), and Aid to the Blind (AB) passed in 1935 remained at a stable level of numbers of recipients and costs. In 1974, these programs were consolidated into the Supplementary Security Income Program. However, the AFDC program has followed a different course.

Poor Law and Social Insurance

Public assistance, in accordance with the Protestant Ethic and the general philosophy of poor law, has five major characteristics.

First, a means test is required of all recipients of public welfare. That is, the client's resources and those of his responsible relatives are examined to determine whether he can possibly use resources of his own rather than become dependent upon public assistance.

Second, categorical assistance is the pattern for establishing public welfare policy. Under this pattern, those categories of persons who are least able to help themselves and least responsible for their indigency are given aid priority, namely, the aged, blind, handicapped, or those otherwise unable to support themselves. Somewhat less priority and access to aid are provided to widows, orphans, and others in similar conditions. Finally, little or no aid is given to those who are able to work and for whom work is available. Recipients of OAA, AB, and ATD receive larger individual grants than recipients of AFDC. The AFDC program was originally established to provide support to widows and orphaned children. Now that the rolls include a heavy proportion of unmarried mothers and illegitimate children, public data show that its function has shifted. The categorical imperative of the Protestant Ethic has been updated to relegate AFDC to a lesser category of deservingness. This matter is discussed more fully later in this chapter.

A third requisite of public assistance is the principle of lesser eligibility. Under this principle, as stated earlier, no public welfare client shall receive more than the lowest paid fully employed worker in the labor market. This principle has not been fully adhered to during the past three

decades. The reasons are probably to be found in the spirit of humanitari-
anism of the 1960s and in the increase in automation and mechanization
which has lessened the need for unskilled, untrained labor. Humanitarian
attitudes and organized minority group pressures have assured the retention of proportionately larger grants to large families, despite the fact that
in a market of potential employment opportunities the unskilled wage-
earners in a large family can probably not earn as much as they are
entitled to on a welfare grant.

A fourth aspect of the public assistance process is the provision of
established item budgets for family needs. Item budgets are crucial to the
construction of family grants. Each item such as food, clothing, electricity, gas, laundry, personal care, and household supplies is listed on a
chart of allowances, with different amounts established for each person
based on age and activity. Persons who must visit clinics regularly or are
involved in part-time work are permitted additional sums for transportation and other related expenses. Rent is authorized on the basis of the
amount set by the particular welfare agency and state. Additional items,
such as telephone, are also authorized when a specific medical or other
need is indicated. These budgets are provided by specialists who have
determined the minimum amount a careful, rational, informed family
needs per person for food, utilities, personal items, household remedies,
and so forth. That the welfare family does not usually plan ahead financially and is not careful, rational, and informed of the best buys is not
considered in the budget construction process, nor can it be taken into
account with a severely limited welfare appropriation. Proportionate calculations are factored into the established budgets in relation to family
size in view of the reality that family group purchases, food preparation,
and household operation can be conducted with less expense than those
for single individuals. Finally, the budgets as established are listed as
ideal, and each state or locality indicates what proportion of the established minimum budget it will seek to support. Thus, the range of support
varies so greatly that grants in some states are five times those of other
states. This explains, in part, why certain localities, particularly New
York City and Los Angeles, have almost unrestrainable welfare costs.
However, in recent months (March 1978-September 1979), a decline in
the welfare case load has been recorded in Los Angeles County,
California.

Public assistance grants are calculated and constructed for families on
the basis of approved need. Hence, a person whose housing is provided
by a well wisher or a relative merely has the rent portion of his budget
omitted. One important concept of public assistance is that of approved,
authorized need as a basis for public relief.

A final aspect of public assistance is that of the way in which other
assets and income are dealt with in public relief. Because the issue of

need must be met in providing public relief to individual applicants, all assets and resources must first be deducted before grants are made. Thus, a public assistance client is theoretically supposed to earn as much as he can on his own, and then the difference between his calculated budget and his earnings is the amount of his grant. It is true that the budget can be amended to provide for bus fare to work, working clothes, and the like. These would be the costs of items occasioned by his employment which are added to his calculated budget. The policy of full deduction of earnings from the budget before a grant is arrived at has a disincentive effect upon client employment. If a person knows he will receive substantially the same amount from welfare alone without working as he can receive from a combination of welfare and earnings, why should he work? In limited and controlled circumstances, some clients are allowed to retain a small proportion of their earnings over and beyond their calculated budget, but this amount has been so small that it has not served as an incentive to work.

The purposes of meaningful work for the public assistance family are more than simply a matter of money. Having a place to go to daily and having worthwhile duties to perform for which people are willing to pay with wages and respect are very important to the welfare client's sense of self-esteem. As is shown in Chapter 8, work provides the individual with a sense of identity vital to self-esteem. An employment opportunity provides continuing life-experiences for the worker which one would not have at home. This type of experience can prevent client deterioration and often provides a sense of hopefulness that would otherwise not be present.

Employment for the adult in a welfare-supported home has benefits for the children as well. A parent who leaves and returns every day, who has a perceived meaningful interaction with other adults, and who reflects these experiences at home in his interactions with his spouse and children makes a better model for a child than an adult whose life is related primarily to children. Even among the middle class, a child-circumscribed world is viewed as less productive in child learning and development than one in which adults who have adult contacts enter into the lives of children. At early ages, it is only through adults (and the less than real television) that children become acquainted with the world beyond their immediate circle. Without contact with an experiencing adult who is continually equipped with the language of other communicating adults, the child's level of conceptual learning falls below that of others. Only in contact with such adults who are respected by others for their work and are so perceived by the children can children build realistic aspirations and expectations for their own future. Finally, only by interactions with such adults can children learn an adequate repertoire of reality-related roles and how to perform them. Without such roles, the child is ill equipped for any career except continued coping with a life based upon the exigencies of welfare.

The welfare mother, in contact only with her children and other welfare mothers, can provide little as a mainstream-oriented role-model for a life outside of welfare. Neither can she compete effectively for continued influence over her children who are easily attracted by the more exciting role-models of the street. This kind of attraction competition is always present as the child grows beyond infancy, but competition with the street by a meaningfully employed parent is less like a "stacked deck." A parental model who is engaged in stigmatizing and demeaning work is not necessarily a more effective role-model than an unemployed parent. Only if the worker is respected by other employees and his employer can work have an important part in child-rearing and the intergenerational resolution of poverty. For that, the work would have to be adequately remunerative, requiring some training and skill, or at least be responded to with respect by the recipient of the work or service.

Because work is important for the parent, the public welfare practice of deducting wages from the budget has a deleterious effect on both client and children. This is so not only in the here and now, but even more so for future welfare generations. As children see, so they do. Children who have never known a continuously employed parent can hardly be expected to look forward to working and to enjoying it. As long as they are not exposed to such experiences, they and their children, whose numbers increase with time and medical advances, can be expected to be outside the mainstream of society and the benefits of affluence. Thus, the deduction of earnings practice in welfare is not only a disincentive for work, but it is also a mechanism for social isolation and exclusion.

The alternative solutions of this problem are discussed in Chapter 5. It should be sufficient at this point to note that not to deduct the welfare clients' earnings from their budget raises problems of fairness for others, primarily the working poor who are not welfare beneficiaries. The problem requires more than budgetary manipulation under public welfare regulations. A revision of the American priorities may be necessary in order to redefine, with adequate wages, the nature of respected work and to provide adequate jobs for all without too greatly disturbing the job market for others.

Another aspect of earnings deductibility relates to retaining the father in the home. If AFDC regulations permitted nonhandicapped fathers as applicants (and this is not so in many states), fathers would still not be permitted to add their earnings to the family income without a commensurate reduction from the AFDC budget. Because the American culture holds that a mother is her own justification in a family but that the father is primarily justified as a family head only to the extent that he provides support for the family, the number of able-bodied fathers willing to stay on in a welfare-supported family is insignificantly small, even in the states where fathers are includable on AFDC. Thus, the deduction of earnings in welfare helps destroy client self-esteem, child role-models, escape mechanisms from welfare for children, and family cohesion.

It is helpful to examine the comparable aspects of social insurance. In public assistance, the threshold admission requirement is the means test; in social insurance, it is one of being included in coverage. Eligibility for social insurance consists of having paid in necessary premiums over an adequate period so that one is included for benefits, or alternatively having had some other party pay premiums in behalf of the beneficiary. Private or commercial insurance is undesirable for broad societal purposes in that those who need coverage the most are (1) least able to pay it; (2) usually the first to be rejected by insurance companies because they present high risks which the insurance fund cannot afford; and (3) least likely to plan ahead and secure insurance.

Social insurance differs from commercial insurance in that broad segments of the population must be covered, and it is not discretionary for individuals to be covered. Anyone who is employed in an occupation covered by Social Security has a percentage of his wage or salary deducted, and a matching percentage is levied on the employer. In the case of unemployment compensation, the employer has a percentage of the total of his employee wages levied upon him by the state authority to cover his employees. In the case of worker's compensation to cover employees injured on the job, employers in many states are required to enter into an approved insurance contract with a private or public carrier. The key to the difference between private and social insurance is that under social insurance almost everyone is covered. The costs are lower inasmuch as those who do not encounter casualties are required to pay benefits to help cover the costs of those who do. Thus, social insurance has an equalizer effect in seeing that everyone is protected against hazards without regard to their foresightedness or lack of it in insuring themselves. Nearly everyone who needs coverage has it.

Social insurance has two major shortcomings. The first occurs in the tooling up or initial phases during which time people who are not yet covered or who have not yet built up an adequate reservoir of benefits encounter casualties. In such instances, the benefits are either absent or inadequate, and public assistance or private charity is expected to take up the slack. The second problem occurs when the population to be served cannot be covered because of social or economic reasons. Where a youngster is brought up in an AFDC family under such conditions that he cannot reasonably expect to have steady work in insured employment over a considerable span of years, it is obvious that he will not be a beneficiary of Social Security retirement, unemployment compensation, disabled worker's insurance, and so forth. Neither will his wife and children be made secure by his death benefits or survivors insurance. Thus, the primary function of social insurance is not to assist those in need but to assure those who are employed that they will be provided for in the event of a casualty. Social insurance serves as a preventative to help people provide for themselves by enforced foresight.

Because of the two faults in social insurance (noncoverage of the noninsured and inadequate coverage or noncoverage of workers taken in by a beginning insurance program), it was obvious at the outset of the United States' experience with social insurance (1935) that some temporary assistance arrangements would be required for those who could not be included in social insurance. Thus, an OAA program was established for the needy aged who reached retirement before they achieved social insurance coverage. This assistance program contains all the elements of public assistance, including a means test, total deductibility of other income from the budget, budgets constructed on the basis of authorized "allowables," and so forth. Over the years since 1935, the program grew until it reached a plateau, and it is now leveling off. As predicted and except for the aged who are derived from the chronic poverty population, the OAA is a shrinking phenomenon eventually to be supplanted by the retired workers and spouses provisions of Social Security.

Under social insurance, disabled and blinded workers who have sufficient coverage are permitted to retire with benefits similar to those of retired workers. Here, too, provision had to be made for disabled and blinded workers and others who were not able to build up adequate coverage before blinding or disablement. As a result, the AB and the ATD assistance programs were developed in 1935. It was believed that when full employment with full insurance coverage was achieved, these programs would shrivel and fade away. For the most part, these programs did just that, although there are residual populations of the blind and disabled who have never had the opportunity to achieve social insurance coverage.

In the case of survivors benefits, the Social Security system designers also believed that under full employment all employable people would find covered work. Thus, their spouses and children would be provided for with death benefits and survivors benefits, and would not have to depend upon private charity or public assistance. Only a temporary program would be needed to cover wives and children of workers who died before achieving adequate coverage. Most of the persons believed to need such care would be those already served in a limited way by the widows pension programs of the various localities, usually under the supervision of a county judge. These persons became the beginning population served by the AFDC. In time, provisions were made to include deserted mothers and divorced wives where the spouse could not be found or could not support his family. Later, arrangements were made to cover unmarried mothers and their children.

Unlike the OAA, AB, and ATD programs, AFDC did not shrink or fade. On the contrary, it has expanded to a point where it has become a financial concern for the participating governments. Its growth can be traced to a number of factors, including the expansion of the AFDC definition to include persons not in the widows and orphans category. Widows, unlike deserted and unmarried mothers, represent a category of persons likely to succeed in placing their children on rising rungs of the socioeconomic ladder. In this way, children in families headed by widows succeed in getting their children out of poverty and into employment and social insurance coverage. One clear advantage of widows is that, unlike deserted and unmarried mothers, they retain contact with both paternal and maternal parents, siblings, and friends. Such contacts provide the child with a variety of role-models, norms for living patterns, life-expectations, experiences, and resources and opportunities.

Another factor is the differential birth rate in families of widows as compared to that of deserted or unmarried mothers. Studies of AFDC families conducted periodically indicate that more births are recorded in the families of deserted and unmarried mothers than in the homes of widows and families headed by a handicapped male parent. Each additional child locks welfare children more firmly into transgenerational poverty. The more children in the family the less opportunity to rise out of the poverty-welfare syndrome. Social insurance is clearly not a solution for poverty when children cannot look forward to extended covered employment in their adult lives. Thus, AFDC as a temporary expedient is effective for the one-generation family. For the transgenerational public assistance family, social insurance is outside its life space, and AFDC has been so extended that it is in no way temporary.

Unlike public assistance, social insurance does not operate differentially in relation to categories of clients. All clients in Old Age, Survivors and Disabled Insurance (OASDI), for example, are required to pay the same percentage of their earnings, and so are their employers up to an established limit. Each beneficiary receives a set amount based upon the number of covered quarter-years and average earnings during a specified period. All benefits are based upon details of coverage, but a floor of benefits is established for those with minimal levels of coverage. We present herewith the mechanisms of social insurance to indicate why it is that social insurance is not plagued by the same problems as public assistance. To indicate this we have to start with a comparison of the two systems and their differential effects on the motivations of recipients.

Unlike public assistance which seeks to relate grants to a level lower than that of the lowest paid full time wage-earner, social insurance operates with fixed benefits that are unrelated to the income levels of others. Social insurance also operates without established family budget allowances, as is the practice with public assistance. Benefits are fixed and are not related to specific needs. Finally, in public assistance, there is usually

TABLE 2.3 **A Comparison of Public Assistance and Social Insurance**

CHARACTERISTIC	PUBLIC ASSISTANCE	SOCIAL INSURANCE
Eligibility threshold	Means test	Broad population coverage; broad access based upon coverage achieved
Categories of clients	Based upon degree of responsibility for being in need	Benefits based upon coverage but with floor
Factors which grants or benefits are related to	Principle of lesser eligibility	Benefits fixed and unrelated to income differentials
Construction of allowances or benefits	Family budgets constructed on basis of specific allowances for authorized needs as recognized	Benefits not related to specific needs
Deduction of outside income	Full deduction of outside income (except in special projects)	Outside income permitted within scope of insured restrictions
Responsibility for care of responsible relatives—parent to child, grown child to parent, and so forth.	Responsible relatives must be interviewed to determine whether they can provide support. If yes, then client is ineligible.	Relatives not involved in regard to eligibility for social insurance
Cultural "stigma," devalued view of others of beneficiaries.	Stigma does exist, both in fact and in the way public assistance is administered.	Social insurance bears no stigma.
Benefits or grants as a right	Until recent legal decisions which indicate that public assistance is a theoretical right, public assistance has been administered as a privilege to be granted by the authority.	One with credits in the system is eligible for benefits. Benefits are a right based on credits paid.

a full deduction of other income. In social insurance, outside income is permitted without deduction within the scope of insurance restrictions. For a comparison of public assistance and social insurance, see Tables 2.3 and 2.4.

TABLE 2.4   **Types of Services under**
            Public Assistance and Social Insurance

SERVICE	PUBLIC ASSISTANCE	SOCIAL INSURANCE
Provision for retired workers	SSI	Old Age Retirement Provisions of OASDI
Provision for disabled workers	SSI	Disabled Workers Insurance of OASDI
Provision for blinded workers	SSI	Blinded Workers Insurance of OASDI
Provision for families of deceased or missing wage support	AFDC	Survivors insurance provisions of OASDI
Provision for families of unemployed parents	AFDC-U (U = unemployed parents—not an operative program in many states)	Unemployment compensation

In Chapter 3 an analysis of each of these programs will be presented, and a discussion of the Beveridge proposal to combine public assistance and social insurance as an income-transfer program will follow (see Friedlander and Apte, pp. 42–44).

References

Beveridge, William H. *Full Employment in a Free Society.* New York: W. W. Norton, 1945.

Booth, Charles. *Life and Labor of the People of London.* 10 vols. London: Longmans, 1900–1911.

Bremner, Robert H. *American Philanthropy.* Chicago: University of Chicago Press, 1960.

Coll, Blanche D. "Perspectives in Public Welfare: The English Heritage," *Welfare in Review,* 4(3):1–12, 1966.

————. *Perspectives in Public Welfare.* Washington, D.C.: U.S. Government Printing Office, 1969.

Fink, Arthur E. *The Field of Social Work.* New York: Holt, 1974.

Friedlander, Walter A., and Robert Z. Apte. *Introduction to Social Welfare.* Englewood Cliffs, N.J.: Prentice-Hall, 1974.

Gould, Julius, and William L. Kolb. *A Dictionary of the Social Sciences.* Glencoe, Ill.: Free Press, 1964.

Hoult, Thomas Ford. *Dictionary of Modern Sociology.* Totowa, N.J.: Littlefield Adams, 1974.

Johnson, Alexander. *The Almshouses.* New York: Charities Publication Committee, 1911.

Kurzman, Paul A. "Poor Relief in Medieval England: The Forgotten Chapter in the History of Social Welfare," *Child Welfare*, 49:495–501, 1970.

Leonard, E. M. *The Early History of the English Poor Relief.* New York: Barnes and Noble, 1965.

Loch, Sir Charles S. *Charity and Social Life: A Short Study of Religious and Social Thought in Relation to Charitable Methods and Literature.* London: Macmillan, 1910.

McClure, Ethel. *More Than Poor—The Development of Minnesota Poor Farms and Homes for the Aged.* St. Paul, Minn.: Minnesota Historical Society, 1968.

Mencher, Samuel. *Poor Law to Poverty Program.* Pittsburgh: University Press, 1967.

Notestein, Wallace. *The English People on the Eve of Colonization, 1603–1630.* New York: Harper, 1954.

Rodgers, Brian. *The Battle Against Poverty.* Vol. 1; *From Pauperism to Human Rights.* London: Routledge, 1968a.

————. *The Battle Against Poverty.* Vol. 2; *Toward a Welfare State.* London: Routledge, 1968b.

Rowntree, B. Seebhom. *Poverty, A Study of Town Life.* New York: Macmillan, 1903.

Runes, Dagobert D. *Dictionary of Philosophy.* Totowa, N.J.: Little Adams, 1962.

Schweintz, Karl de. *England's Road to Social Security, 1349–1947.* 3d rev. ed. University of Philadelphia Press, 1947.

Segalman, Ralph. "The Protestant Ethic and Social Welfare," *Journal of Social Issues*, 24(2):125–41, 1968.

Smith, Adam. *The Wealth of Nations.* Edwin Cannon (ed.). New York: Modern Library, 1937.

Theodorson, George, and Achilles G. Theodorson. *Modern Dictionary of Sociology.* New York: Thomas Crowell, 1969.

Tonnies, Ferdinand. *Community and Society, Gemeinschaft and Gesell-*

schaft. C. P. Loomis (ed.). New York: Harper, 1963.

Trattner, Walter I. *From Poor Law to Welfare State: A History of Social Welfare in America*. New York: Free Press, 1974.

Webb, Beatrice (Potter), and James Sydney Webb Passfield. *English Poor Law Policy*. London: Longmans, 1910.

Webb, Sidney, and Beatrice Webb. "Report of the Royal Commission on Poor Laws and Relief of Distress: Minority Report 1909, Introduction to Part I," in Roy Lubove *Social Welfare in Transition: Selected English Documents 1834–1909*. Pittsburgh: University of Pittsburgh Press, 1966.

Witte, Edwin E. *The Development of the Social Security Act*. Madison: University of Wisconsin Press, 1962.

Woodroofe, Kathleen. *From Charity to Social Work in England and the United States*. Toronto: University Press, 1962.

PROGRAMS OF PUBLIC ASSISTANCE AND SOCIAL INSURANCE IN AMERICA 3

BOTH public assistance and social insurance programs have positive effects as well as serious faults with regard to resolving the problems of poverty. Tables 3.1 and 3.2 list the various social insurance and public assistance programs operated by the federal government and by a combination of federal and state programs. It is helpful to describe each of the programs in an examination of their achievements and faults in the fulfillment of their purpose—prevention and resolution of poverty.

Programs of Public Assistance

SUPPLEMENTARY SECURITY INCOME—AID TO AGED (SSI-AGED)

SSI is operated under the general policies and laws established by the Congress and under regulations of the U.S. Department of Health, Education and Welfare (HEW). These programs were originally operated by the individual states under state and federal matching grants, under the designation Old Age Assistance (OAA). Beginning in 1974, these programs were transferred to the Social Security Administration, and all applications were then referred to the federally operated local Social Security offices. Grants are administered through the same machinery as other clients of the Social Security Administration.

OAA is still restricted to persons over age sixty-five who have limited assets and who are able to pass the means test. Earnings and other income are deducted from the calculated needs budget. The family budget is determined by calculating the authorized need as defined by the program. For a number of years, OAA was criticized for certain of its defects. The multistate administration of the program placed it in a position of differential accessibility and availability, and many states provided less than a minimal existence budget for the aged. (The latter defect has been rectified with federalization.) Many states, probably because they were reluctant to expend funds among massive minority populations, gave their

TABLE 3.1 **Major Programs of Family Support**

| REASON FOR LOSS OF INCOME | FEDERAL | | FEDERAL AND STATE |
	Social Insurance	*Public Assistance*	
Old age.	Social Security retirement annuities (OASDI). Veterans benefits.[1] Medicare-formed needs of OASDI-covered.	Supplementary Security Income (SSI). For persons who have not built up adequate benefits under OASDI and who can prove need.	Medicaid (public assistance) for persons not covered by OASDI.
(Worker) Permanent disability and blind.	Disabled Workers Insurance (OASDI). Blinded workers (OASDI insurance.)	Supplementary Security Income (SSI).	Aid to Families with Dependent Children (where parent cannot support family). (public assistance).
Death of Worker.	Survivors insurance (Social Security).		Aid to Families with Dependent Children (where minor children are among survivors). (public assistance).
Unemployment			Unemployment Compensation (Social Insurance)
Inability to earn adequate funds as a result of less than permanent disability, absence of principal wage-earner; or temporary reverses stemming from medical, legal, or prison problems.	Medicare for medical coverage of certain OASDI-included persons with benefits.	Medicaid for medically needy without other benefits and without other resources.	Aid to Families with Dependent Children (where minor children are present in a family without a wage-earner parent).
Income inadequate to meet basic needs.[2]		Food stamps.	Public housing.

[1]Based on credits earned as a service man, in terms of national service.
[2]Open to all persons in need, whether or not covered by any of the above programs.

TABLE 3.2 **Major State, Local, and Private Programs of Family Support**

REASON FOR LOSS OF INCOME	STATE OR STATE AND LOCAL (PUBLIC ASSISTANCE)	PRIVATE	OTHER
Old age.		Commercial insurance. Private savings.	Company and union retirement programs, Railroad retirement program, Public retirement program (government workers).
(Worker) Permanent disability and blind.		Commercial insurance.	Workers' compensation (when injured on the job).
Death of worker.	General Assistance (where no minor among survivors).	Commercial insurance.	Company and union survivors plans.
Unemployment.	General Assistance.	Private savings.	Company and union —special plans (such as United Auto Workers).
Inability to earn adequate funds as a result of less than permanent disability; absence of principal wage-earner; or temporary reverses stemming from medical, legal, or prison problems.	General Assistance (for families and individuals without minor children).	Commercial insurance (for temporary disability only). Private savings.	Company disability plan (for worker disability). Workers' compensation (for worker injured on job and temporarily disabled).
Income inadequate to meet basic needs.[1]			

[1]Open to all persons in need, whether or not covered by any of the above programs.

OAA programs a low visibility, especially in neighborhoods where the poor lived.

The Social Security Administration, beginning in 1974, enlisted a variety of voluntary organizations including senior citizens' groups, retired persons' associations, disabled persons' groups, and community action programs to promote the enrollment of persons eligible for retirement insurance, survivors annuities, disabled workers' insurance, and SSI in the programs appropriate to each individual. According to a variety of newsletter reports there was a perceptible increase in enrollment over the first few years, especially in SSI, but the increase leveled off over the last five years. This leveling off, it has been suggested, is due to the fact that many persons otherwise eligible for SSI payments are reluctant to apply because of a personal reluctance to become dependent. Persons enrolled in SSI-Aged are also eligible for Medicaid.

The purpose of the SSI-Aged program is to provide assistance to the aged who have not built up, in their preretirement years, sufficient credits under Social Security to receive minimum retirement benefits. The program provides minimum subsistence for the aged who have not been employed in an occupation covered by Social Security. As such, it generally fulfills this purpose.

SUPPLEMENTARY SECURITY INCOME—DISABLED ASSISTANCE (SSI-DISABLED)

Like OAA, this program was previously administered by each state with matching federal funds and operated under federal laws and HEW regulations, as well as under the regulations of the individual states. It was transferred to the Social Security Administration on January 1, 1974, and many of the problems stemming from differential accessibility and levels of grants were resolved after the program was federalized.

The program is limited to persons who have been medically certified as permanently and totally disabled, are unable to support themselves, and are without responsible relatives who can support them. Just as in SSI-Aged, all of the characteristics of public assistance apply including the means test, which evaluates available resources and assets and limitations on the value of personal and real property held by the applicant. Persons on SSI-Disabled are also eligible for Medicaid services.

SSI-Disabled is designed for persons who are not covered by the disabled workers insurance provisions of Social Security (which is described later in this chapter). It provides limited assistance and support for persons who are otherwise unable to maintain themselves and who have not had an opportunity to build up a Social Security work account. Its most critical weakness with regard to coverage is that it does not provide for the partially disabled who are usually the first victims of a weak employment market.

Recently, the Social Security Administration opened up the program to persons who are totally disabled by reason of psychological impairment. This group includes the mentally retarded, the mentally ill, persons addicted to drugs and alcohol, and others whose mental state is such that they are deemed to be unemployable. Much of the SSI-Disabled program serves a necessary purpose in the society. In some situations, enrollment also provides caretaker aid where the disabled person requires aid in daily care. Enrollment in SSI-Disabled also makes the individual eligible for Medicaid services.

Those enrolled in SSI-Disabled must periodically register with the State Vocational Rehabilitation Agency (SVRA) as a means of securing physical or other rehabilitation aid in order to become employable again. This registration requirement is probably little more than that. To our knowledge, there are no empirical data on how many cases these agencies have undertaken for rehabilitation, let alone data on successful rehabilitation by the SVRA.

A major problem of SSI-Disabled has become apparent after five years of experience. Because of the increased availability of SSI, many young handicapped individuals, especially those with less serious handicaps, tend to make less effort to obtain education and employment training.

SUPPLEMENTARY SECURITY INCOME—AID TO BLIND (SSI-BLIND AID)

The SSI-Blind Aid program was also previously operated by the individual states under federal legislation and regulations and on a grant-in-aid basis. After January 1, 1974, this program, too, was transferred to the Social Security Administration. The program aids persons specified as legally blind, as determined by specific tests, if they meet the requirements of the means test and lack other resources. Budgets are established in Aid to the Blind (AB) on the same basis as in other SSI programs. Generally, the program provides limited assistance for persons who are unable to support themselves because of blindness and who have not built up adequate credits for coverage under the blinded workers insurance provisions of the OASDI.

SSI-Blind Aid enrollment enables the individual to receive Medicaid services. In some situations, enrollment also provides caretaker aid where the blinded person requires aid in daily care. Enrollment in the program requires coordinated registration with the State Vocational Rehabilitation Agency. As is the case with SSI-Disabled, this enrollment is probably limited inasmuch as no data are currently available about SVRA-active SSI-Blind cases.

One obvious weakness of the program is that it does not cover those who are only partially blind and unable to find work to support themselves.

✷ AID TO FAMILIES WITH DEPENDENT CHILDREN (AFDC)

Unlike the SSI programs, AFDC was not federalized in 1974. It is operated under federal legislation and under the regulations and supervision of HEW. AFDC is administered by the states and territories of the United States under a matching grant-in-aid basis, with costs borne by the federal and state entities.

Mothers with dependent children (and other guardians of dependent children) who are without financial assets or responsible, financially able relatives are eligible for AFDC if they meet public assistance requirements. AFDC also covers families with disabled fathers and dependent children. Provisions include a means test and an individual budget related to state-calculated need. Outside income and resources are generally deducted from this budget. AFDC primarily serves widowed, divorced, deserted, and unmarried mothers with children. In some states, it also serves families with unemployed fathers.

The AFDC family does not have adequate credits available to it to provide it with survivors benefits under Social Security. Those families that have lost a father who has left behind an adequate Social Security account by reason of a sufficiently steady covered work history are served by survivors benefits of OASDI and do not usually require AFDC assistance.

In its time, AFDC was an improvement over the locally funded mother's or widow's pensions which were limited in funding and by the constraining individualistic attitudes of local boards and administrators. The program does enable a mother to meet part of the needs of her children in most states and almost all of their needs in the more generous states.

AFDC seems to attract criticism from all sides. It varies from state to state in terms of grants, budgets, regulations, procedures, and levels of staff competence. The limited funding, large caseloads, and restrictive state regulations tend to juxtapose the system and its workers to the clients, often to a point of polarization. In this way, circumstances and responsibilities pressure the workers either to control cases or to yield on demand rather than seek rehabilitative mechanisms to help the family find its way out of poverty. AFDC tends to become the "whipping boy" of legislatures which seek to conserve limited state funds. Unlike other programs which have built-in electorate pressure groups (for example, farmers, unions, the aged, the blind, the environmentalists, and businesses), AFDC mothers and children are unlikely to be of much concern at election time. Federal controls are difficult to interpret and use in seeking equal and adequate care for eligible children and mothers.)

Of all the programs established to provide for the supposedly temporary need of persons until social insurance is available, AFDC has shown the greatest resistance to supplantation by social insurance mechanisms. Rather than shrinking in the face of increased employment, AFDC has developed to the point that it has few reportedly employable persons on its rolls. Under Social Security, the lack of employed coverage for an adequate period is equivalent to permanent ineligibility.

Because few legislators or administrators have undertaken responsibility and leadership for AFDC, the program operates blindly, without effective direction and leadership, and is constrained by controls in some ways only to grow uncontrolled in other ways. AFDC and its alternatives are discussed in detail in Chapter 4.

GENERAL ASSISTANCE (GA)

In addition to AFDC and SSI, the local governmental unit in most geographical areas provides assistance to persons who are either ineligible for these programs or are in need of temporary aid until these categorical assistances or other aid or employment become available. In many instances, General Assistance is a necessity until social insurance benefits begin. In addition to such temporary service, General Assistance is important to a large population of others who are ineligible for categorical assistance or social insurance. This group includes those who are not yet of retirement age but have no other resources, childless couples and single persons who are unemployed, and/or unemployable persons who are only partially handicapped or blind, and homeless, unskilled, untrained or transient persons who cannot obtain steady employment. GA programs are operated and regulated primarily by local boards.

On a national basis, the program is spotty with extreme variance in the limits of assistance, policies, personnel, resources to be distributed, and attitudes toward the clientele. Many GA programs refuse service to nonresidents unless reimbursed by the nonresident's own home base, which seldom occurs. Although it is an undependable source of aid, GA does provide minimal relief to some of the families and individuals not immediately eligible for categorical assistance or social insurance. Where it does operate with limited funding, it can be of some help to the client by acting as a referral and information source about other agencies and resources.

Only the GA program is reluctant to accept nonresidents. Unlike AFDC and SSI, which are federally funded in whole or in part, GA is funded locally and is therefore not affected by Supreme Court interpretations. In essence, the Supreme Court has ruled that residency may not be required of public assistance applicants because it would be a restriction of an individual's right to travel in the United States.*

According to Levy, Lewis, and Martin (p. 55), GA programs are financed and administered exclusively by local and/or state government units. In some states, the state authorities have supervisory roles. GA differs substantially from community to community and from state to state. Its only uniformity lies in its much lower grant size than federally aided programs in the same localities and in its perpetuation of Elizabethan Poor Law policies. Many GA programs are limited to short-term help for emergency situations. This aid frequently consists of vouchers which can be exchanged for goods and services rather than cash. Aid is frequently given only to persons who are considered unemployable, and family responsibility provisions of parent to child and adult child to elderly parent are enforced with firmness.

The administrative pattern of General Assistance is extremely uneven in the various states and localities. It serves only those who are considered to be in desperate need, as measured by extremely stringent standards. Comparative newcomers, even though they technically meet legal residence requirements, are frequently refused. GA administrators usually have much greater discretion to refuse aid than the administrators of other programs. For a comparison of GA with other welfare programs in the United States, using the Durkheim topology, see Table 3.3.

MEDICAID

Medicaid (MediCal in California) is a program of medical and hospital service available to all who can prove medical need and who do not have resources with which to pay medical costs. Persons who are eligible for categorical or General Assistance, having undergone the means test and other constraints of public assistance, are eligible for Medicaid. Also eligible are persons who are able to provide their own support except for necessary medical care and can be certified as medically indigent.

The pattern of medical and hospital service to the poor available under Medicaid is similar to that of Medicare under social insurance. (Medicare, which is the social insurance cousin of Medicaid, is discussed later in this chapter.) Both Medicaid and Medicare are victims of a free enterprise growth in demand for service unmatched by a commensurate growth in

---

*"On June 19, 1967 a three judge federal court declared that states relief residency requirements unconstitutional." (Piven and Cloward, p. 307) "In the Spring of 1969, acting on an appeal from Connecticut, the United States Supreme Court held that relief residence laws violated the Constitution." (Piven and Cloward, p. 308)

TABLE 3.3 Comparison of General Assistance with SSI and AFDC, According to the Durkheim Topology

LEVELS OF SOCIAL REALITY ACCORDING TO DURKHEIM	GENERAL ASSISTANCE	SUPPLEMENTARY SECURITY INCOME (FORMERLY *OAA, AB, ATD*)	AID TO FAMILIES WITH DEPENDENT CHILDREN
Geographic and demographic basis.	City, town, county, or borough (urban areas often checkered with a variety of authorities).	Nationwide.	Differs from state to state, with high variances between them in amount of grants and in nature of clientele.
Morphological surface: institutions and collective behaviors.	Successors to the overseer of the poor. City welfare agencies or equivalents.	The Social Security Administration, mechanically effective and uniform.	The state welfare department of each state, usually a civil service-manned entity, with some welfare agencies as delegated.
Symbology: dogmas, procedures, statutes, customs.	Elizabethan Poor Law concepts, as as transmitted by tradition and custom.	A disguised public assistance program carried out under social insurance symbols.	Federal and state regulations, usually formalistically and ritually adhered to.
Collective values and ideals.	Limited aid to the deserving urgent poor under pressure of limited, hard-pressed city budget.	Presumably the aged, blind, and disabled are accepted as deserving poor acceptable for aid.	The emphasis is usually on ritual adherence to regulations for purposes of agency and worker survival. Client (as person) is irrelevant.
Collective state of the mind: collective meanings, memories, responses, "feelings."	Many city authorities view this aspect of welfare as something for which they would rather not be responsible. They see the recipients as outsiders who stay on in "skidrow" as an embarrassment to them.	The aged, blind, and disabled are accepted as they are and are not usually resented.	AFDC is a program which no one knows what to do with. Clients are perceived in their present state to have no hope of changing themselves or of being changed by the welfare programs. Both workers and clients are generally resented by the public.

available practitioners and facilities. Costs and charges have grown, although the volume of delivery of services to the beneficiaries has not developed commensurately. The expansion of charges by medical vendors has brought with it administrative reactions in the form of state and federal regulations limiting the number and frequency of services. These constraints and a growing volume of complex restrictions have created the need for specialists in the management of reporting and billing. The complex of regulations has even further limited the availability of medical care for the poor in that individual practitioners have less interest in becoming involved in the program and fewer clients can find their way through the Medicaid maze. Medicaid customers usually become less favored clients. Increased restrictions on Medicaid and other factors discussed in Chapter 6 limit the use of Medicaid as an instrument of preventative medicine among the poor. To the extent that chronic ill health is a factor in unemployment and unemployability, Medicaid is criticized for inadequate funding for preventative medicine.

Spotty as Medicaid is, it is a vast improvement over no medical program or policy for the poor, which was the case before its establishment. In its present format, it provides limited medical care to the poor if they are also informed of Medicaid's existence and procedures, and if they are able to process themselves through the available eligibility mechanisms. This problem has diminished in recent years.

FOOD STAMPS

The Food Stamp program developed as a successor to the Surplus Agricultural Products program of the U.S. Department of Agriculture and was adopted nationally in 1964. It was originally established to aid farmers who were in jeopardy of financial losses by falling prices when a surplus of commodities were produced beyond the normative market demand by those who could afford them. The basic method of aiding the farmers was to have the federal government buy all surplus food products from the market at profitable rates for the farmers and then to distribute these products to the poor through local governmental welfare programs. This method of distribution had disadvantages for the federal government, the local welfare administrations, and the welfare clients. The federal government found that the preservation, packing, wholesaling, and distribution of such foods was an unwieldy and expensive process; the local welfare administrators found that preservation, repackaging for retail, and distribution of commodities were costly and difficult; and the local clients found that pickup of stocks of huge monthly or semimonthly supplies, often by persons without personal transportation, was difficult and the commodities available were not too easily fitted into the needs of individual families. Over a period of decades, the surplus commodities program was phased out and a food stamp plan was substituted.

Under the food stamp plan, every needy family, whether or not on welfare, can be certified by the local governmental welfare authority or by its officially delegated agencies. A family with a financial gap between the official calculated need and its income is given, or sold at a discount, whatever food stamps it requires to bring it up to the designated and budgeted level. Thus, a limited income family is permitted to purchase food stamps yielding up to five or more times the value of the money used in purchasing the stamps. Because food stamps can be used only to purchase food (and related home-use products), the farmers are aided in that more of their products are purchased by consumers at the prevailing prices. (The purchase of food stamps is no longer required for families eligible to have them.)

From the clients' viewpoint, food stamps have many advantages over surplus commodites, the primary advantage being that they can purchase what they choose for their families rather than what is needed to satisfy the needs of the farming economy. Food stamps have become a major item in the federal budget. Expenditures by the Department of Agriculture for food stamps far outweigh all of its other expenditures. The department now advocates that the Food Stamp program be administered as part of the welfare administration of HHS, but HHS is reluctant to accept the program because of its size and unwieldiness. The agency also fears that transfer of the program will be a precursor to a merger of the Food Stamp program into the other established public assistance programs, with a lessening of the total assistance provided to clients and a cutting back of staff.

Thus, food stamps are provided by a department which is oriented more toward aiding farmers than toward serving the clients who use them. Food stamps are administered in a manner which is separate and apart from other welfare programs and through policies that are not necessarily integrated or consonant with other welfare programs. Because of the heavy financial contribution of food stamps to the crazy-quilt of various welfare and related programs, many clients are underserved, overserved, or served less than effectively. (This subject is dealt with in Chapter 4 under the subject of multiple benefits.)

BASIC EDUCATIONAL OPPORTUNITY GRANT (BEOG)

The Basic Educational Opportunity Grant program is administered by the Office of Education of HEW. Grants are provided to individuals who establish eligibility under a relaxed means test based upon a normative rather than a subsistence- or poverty-level budget. The grants are awarded to college students who do not have adequate funds to secure their education, whose parents are unable to help, or who are no longer dependent on and responsible to their parents. The individual universities distribute the grants under contract with the Office of Education. The amount of each grant is limited and generally represents about one-fourth of the student's annual financial needs. It is assumed that the student will use his own savings and earnings and will secure bank loans for the balance of his educational costs.

The BEOG program is also generally devoid of the stigma involved in many other public assistance programs. The reasons may be that it is administered by college counselors rather than by public welfare workers; that its inherent sense is of goal orientation rather than of mere subsistence; and that it is tied to self-secured earnings and loans that provide the grants as supplementation rather than primary support.

BEOG grants, like student educational loans, have come under fire from a variety of sources. Because they are administered by financial assistance officers of colleges and universities who have little or no interest in policing them, there have been frequent instances of students accepting them without attending the college. An improved administrative pattern may have to be devised to ensure a better followup of student grantees.

EMERGENCY EMPLOYMENT PROGRAMS (EEP)

States and cities that experience high rates of unemployment receive annual assistance from the federal government in creating public service employment openings. In some localities, the local government is permitted to enter into contracts with agencies, hospitals, and similar institutions for temporary public service employment. Public service employment is also offered to unemployed youth under similar sponsorship. From the definitional standpoint, such employment may be viewed as a modified form of public assistance in that it is not available to persons who already have employment or a steady income. (These matters are discussed in detail under the employment section of Chapter 7.)

Federally funded public-service emergency programs are severely limited in breadth, scope, and time. Because of limited funds, these programs provide opportunities for perhaps one out of every hundred persons seeking employment. These jobs may not be a substitute for regular work done in governmental service, for to permit that to occur would open a door to local government budget cuts at federal expense. As a consequence, these jobs provide little in the way of employment, skills training, and experience. Similarly, because of the tenuous funding pattern, they provide no hope for future or continued employment. These jobs may therefore be viewed as a limited stopgap which provides little for the unemployed and even less for the usually unemployable. An alternative to the stopgap approach is probably necessary, particularly during periods of high unemployment. A more comprehensive alternative program might include a tier system of public service employment funding. Such a system would provide opportunities for states and localities to undertake long-range projects of public service and construction, with job opportunity ladders provided to enable the less skilled and experienced to build a background of employability for themselves. As an alternative for public welfare, it is highly desirable in terms of prevention and resolution of transgenerational poverty. This topic is dealt with later in Chapter 8.

The EEP is too limited in scope, funding, concept, and duration to be anything more than a political tool used for cooling off urban communities during recurrent crises. As a mechanism for public service jobs, it is illusory and tenuous, and as a mechanism for poverty prevention and resolution, it is too feeble a reed for social policy planning.

Programs of Social Insurance

OLD AGE, SURVIVORS AND DISABILITY INSURANCE (OASDI)

All OASDI benefits are controlled by certain basic principles:

Work related: Security for the worker is based upon his entitlement to benefits which grow out of his employment in employment settings where he has been covered for Social Security. In general, the more a worker earns up to a specified ceiling, and the more consistently he has been employed and over a longer time span, the greater the protection to him and his dependents.

No means test: Benefits are an earned right to be paid regardless of income from savings, pensions, investments, or the like. Absence of a means test tends to encourage the foresighted worker to provide additional protection for himself and his family through other private insurance programs, savings, investments, home ownership, and so forth.

Contributory provision: The concept of an earned right is reinforced by the fact that workers make contributions to help finance the benefits. The requirement of an earned right encourages a responsible attitude toward the programs.

Compulsory provision: Most of those who are covered in social insurance programs are in them because they are compulsory. The compulsory nature of the program strengthens the soundness of its funding in that poorer risks are offset by others who present better risks at any particular time. This sharing of risks tends to keep the costs of the program from rising beyond the point of feasible operation.

Rights of beneficiaries clearly defined by the law: A person's rights to benefits and the amount of his benefits are clearly and legally defined. The benefits are related to specific facts rather than to unclear variables connected with administrative decisions. Thus, the program is open to all who have become eligible, and no one can be arbitrarily denied his benefits because of personnel attitudes.

Social Security funding: Social Security funding is currently funded under the Compact Between Generations Plan. An alternative plan for Social Security insurance is the traditional funding plan. Both plans are presented in Table 3.4.

TABLE 3.4   **The Compact Between Generations Plan and the Prepaid Plan**

THE COMPACT BETWEEN GENERATIONS	
For people who are currently employed in covered employment.	Payments are made during the years of employment and *these pay for concurrent benefits* below.
For people who are currently retired, or survivors of covered deceased employees, and so forth.	Benefits are received by retirees and survivors from funds collected concurrently from workers.
THE PREPAID PLAN	
For people who are employed in covered employment.	Payments are made during years of employment, and are recorded just as in any commercial insurance program.
Future benefits are paid after retirement or to survivors after death.	These funds are set aside and invested in order to provide benefits to the same people who have made these payments.

Compact Between Generations Plan provides funds at the same inflationary (or deflationary) rate as are needed in providing the benefits. Its disadvantage is that changes in the birth rates of workers and in the health survival rates of beneficiaries create a heavy payment rate on workers when the birth rate of their generation is low and when advances in health care provide a larger population of beneficiaries. The Prepaid Plan offers the advantage of a direct relationship between the persons to be paid and the benefits received. In this respect, the plan is similar to the funding plan of commercial insurance and is more easily understood by the public. In addition, the proportion of the number of beneficiaries receiving benefits is in direct relation to the number of workers who made payments for this purpose. The plan has two disadvantages: Benefits for the population cannot be provided until an adequate fund has been built up, which may take as long as a generation; and inflation can make the benefits very inadequate in a period of inflation without any possible adjustment.

The OASDI program commonly known as Social Security has a number of beneficiary functions. These functions are related to retirement, survivors' benefits, blinded and disabled workers' insurance, unemployment compensation, workers' compensation, programs of special employers, Medicare, and vocational rehabilitation.

Retirement

Persons over age sixty-five who are otherwise eligible for benefits or others who elect to accept less benefits at the lower age of sixty-two receive a retirement benefit during their remaining lifetime. In the case of a retired worker and aged spouse, a larger benefit is provided than for unmarried retired workers. Unlike public welfare, Congress has periodically upgraded the program in order to keep abreast of inflation of the economy. Even so, the level of retirement benefits is such that it is only slightly above established poverty norms. Retirement benefits do provide a base for aged workers. In an age of disintegrating nuclear families, this program provides service that was once the province of grown children and the extended family. Law and regulation clearly define the nature of retirement. Benefits are to be paid only when the beneficiary has actually retired within specified financial earnings limits.

The program is designed to replace some of the earnings from work lost following retirement. It encourages retirement and thus provides labor openings for others, particularly the young. The program is criticized in that too many marginal and sporadic workers are either not covered or avoid coverage. This is especially the case with female home maintenance workers (Lawrence). Many of these persons work in middle-class homes for one or two days a week for housewives who are either uninformed or reluctant to bother with completing forms for withholding taxes and Social Security. While the forms are simplified and not time consuming, they do require that a portion of the employee's wages and Social Security taxes which are to be withheld from wages be submitted. They also require matching Social Security taxes from the employer. It is difficult for a housewife who uses household help only once or twice a week to understand the relationship between filing these forms and security for her employee's old age and family. Many of the newer house maintenance service companies hire both men and women and do carry out the social security and withholding payments obligations but this is much less so among the many female day workers who view social security as a "rip-off" from their pay.

Female household employees are also reluctant. Many women with children to support work five or six days a week, each day at a different home. It is difficult for such a worker earning marginal wages to agree to turn back a sizable percentage of her wages which she believes she will never see again. People in limited income families have to live from day to day and have difficulty planning for their old age and for insurance for their families even when it is a violation of the law not to do so. An additional problem in securing adherence to withholding and Social Security law is related to the marginal employee's perception of government and society. Lower class workers, especially minority workers, tend to view the law with suspicion and with a pattern of avoidance. Such employees may also be receiving public welfare. In such instances, employees are reluctant to have their outside income reported because such earnings would be deducted from their budget or might even make them ineligible for welfare. To submit to such withholding processes, an employee must submit to having a Social Security account which can easily be traced to her public welfare account. Thus, because of inadequate provision for the incentives and disincentives presented to marginal workers and their employers, the purposes of Social Security are contravened for a priority population group in need of Social Security protection. Such persons could be served by social insurance at a sizable possible saving to SSI expenditures in future years if the obstacles of compliance by employers and employees were overcome.

Benefits for retired workers and their families can be supplemented by SSI and other categorical assistances when such benefits are lower than a public assistance budget calculated for them if they are otherwise eligible for public assistance. Hundreds of thousands of OASDI beneficiaries are also public assistance recipients, particularly under SSI.

Survivors Benefits

Upon the death of a worker who has had an adequate period of coverage, benefits are paid to the widow and children until the children have completed their schooling (up to a specified age when adulthood is assumed to begin). This program provides a basic income for such families and often makes it possible for the household to remain intact. It is usually a preventative factor in keeping the family independent of public welfare. By helping to keep the children in school, it prevents the flooding of the employment market with marginal, untrained workers who are inadequately prepared for competition in the employment market place. Adolescent employment candidates, especially from marginal-income and public-assisted families, are believed to drive wage rates down, thus interfering with employment and family stability generally. Although benefits have been regularly upgraded to maintain a rational relationship with the costs of family maintainance, it is doubtful that families can make ends meet with only survivors benefits as support. Still other problems are occasioned by the discontinuance of benefits of young adults who need much more preparation for employment than is allowed in the age period covered.

Blinded Workers Insurance and Disabled Workers Insurance

When a worker's sight has become so poor that he is judged to be blind, if he has an adequate OASDI earnings account he becomes eligible for Social Security purposes. In such a case, he would be provided with benefits for the remainder of his life as if he were retired. Similar determinations and benefits are available to disabled workers. The disablement test of Social Security is clearly defined by law and is not subject to the arbitrary views of administrators. This test generally provides assurance that benefits will be paid only when the beneficiary has actually discontinued employment (within the financial limits specified). Blinded and disabled workers insurance provide some replacement of the earnings from work lost because of blinding or disablement. These programs have the same features as other Social Security programs in providing assets to keep the family together and in withholding children of workers from the labor market. The programs have inadequacies similar to other Social Security programs.

Unemployment Compensation

Unemployment compensation programs are individually administered by state offices of employment security with federal and state funding of administrative costs. The income of unemployment compensation funds is derived from premiums or levies provided by employers. Each employer's payments are related to a preestablished formula based upon numbers of employees, payroll, and stability of the work force retained. Employers who have periodic layoffs, who hire masses of new workers and then replace them with other new workers, or who maintain erratic employment hiring and retention patterns are rated as higher risks. This rating is reflected in the higher premiums they have to pay. Only when employees are laid off are they eligible for unemployment compensation. Employees who are fired for cause are not eligible, and they are not charged as a risk against the employer's premium. For this reason, employees are provided with access to appeal hearings before examiners if they have been reported by their employer as fired for cause. It is in the employer's interest to have affirmation of the justification of such action. It is similarly in the employee's interest to appeal such employer action if he is to be provided with unemployment compensation. An employee who leaves voluntarily is ineligible for unemployment compensation. Employees are considered covered only if they have worked for an included employer for an adequate number of quarters prior to being laid off.

In addition to the requirement of having been laid off rather than fired for cause or left voluntarily, an employee must make himself available for suitable employment when offered such employment by the state employment service. Unavailability or unwillingness for such potential employment will make an employee ineligible for unemployment insurance. The length of time of coverage is limited both by legal restrictions and number of previous covered quarters of employment.

Unemployment compensation provides a reasonably adequate financial base for temporary unemployment. Thus, seasonal unemployment, or temporary unemployment occasioned by technological or model changes or by a disturbed supply or transport system is served well by unemployment compensation. The problem of chronic unemployment is, however, a more serious problem on which unemployment compensation has little effect.

Unemployment compensation can be faulted for a number of reasons. First, it is available for only a certain number of quarters and thus is of limited value in cases of a lengthy period of unemployment. Second, it does not cover many types of employees and employers. It is these employees who probably most need unemployment compensation. Third, it does not serve those with an inadequate work history. Youths, especially public assistance family youths, have never had employment with coverage, and such youths are reported to have the highest rates of unemployment.

An additional problem of unemployment compensation is related to its structural tie to the state employment placement services. The tie is necessary in order to ensure that those who draw unemployment benefits are exposed to available employment. If this were not done, the fund would soon be completely exhausted and no further payments could be made to the unemployed. The connection between unemployment compensation and employment placement presents problems in terms of employment candidates who are either ineligible for unemployment compensation or have exhausted their unemployment benefits. It is in a state program's interest to conserve its unemployment compensation fund as much as possible. If a job is available, in the interest of conserving that fund the job should be offered to a person who is drawing compensation. Thus, we arrive at a de facto pattern of employee preferment classification in employment referrals.

Still another weakness in the unemployment compensation program relates to its use as a mechanism for worker "sabbaticals." Many unemployment compensation offices merely require registrees to certify that they are actively looking for work without requesting details of how the registree is going about the task. Names of employers interviewed by the applicant are not taken, nor are any employers contacted to check whether the applicant actually attended an interview. This pattern of not monitoring availability for employment is particularly evident during periods of high local unemployment when the unemployment compensation funds are supplemented from federal sources and when the period of coverage is extended for applicants. During such periods, applicants are often not required to check at the jobs available desk for possible referrals. In many unemployment offices, the negligence in not monitoring availability for employment extends beyond the periods of heavy unemployment to the detriment of fund stability and to a point where unemployment compensation becomes converted from social insurance to public assistance for many.

When applicants for unemployment are required to report at the jobs available desk at the state employment service, they have an incentive to report, if only to ensure the collection of a check. The person who is ineligible for unemployment compensation or who has exhausted the benefits, on the other hand, often tends to view a visit to the state employment service as an exercise in futility, if not as an added traumatic experience. Thus, unemployment compensation helps the recently unemployed, but some other mechanism is needed for others.

By and large, unemployment compensation insurance is conceived as temporary insurance. It cannot operate effectively without a program of full employment and without making special provision for the never-employed, the inadequately trained, and the marginal workers as described in Chapter 8.

Workers' Compensation

Most states and territories of the United States have unemployment compensation laws. These laws usually require employers to pay premiums into either a state-operated fund or to be covered by programs of private commercial insurance firms. Benefits are usually paid to workers (or their survivors) in connection with disablement brought about by injury on the job. Workers' compensation provides medical expenses for covered injuries whether the injury results in disability or not and provides partial restoration of wages lost; and also provides partial restoration, often for life, of wages due to partial permanent disability (see Levy, Lewis, and Martin, pp. 456-57). In some localities, lump sum payments are also authorized. Where workers' compensation is available and adequate provisions are made, it provides a carryover income base for covered families whose resources are limited. The programs are spotty in coverage, adequacy of benefits, availability, program accessibility, and transferability of benefits where the employee moves out of the locality. In many states, the securing of workers' compensation in important cases involves an advocacy proceeding with confrontations between the attorneys of insuring companies and representatives of claimants. This proceeding causes a servere drain on funds which should logically be available for claimant payments.

The involvement of commercial concerns in workers' compensation (formerly workmen's compensation) has some advantages in the interest of program efficacy. Many companies seek to prevent payment of compensation by accident prevention programs. In such instances, employers are provided with premium deductions if they comply with recommended installation of safety devices and with suggested safety education programs.

In the more advanced programs, workers' compensation provides a useful protective and supportive function for workers. Its shortcomings are in terms of coordination between localities and of floors for standards of the various programs.

Programs of Special Employers

The Railroad Retirement Act provides retirement, survivors insurance, and unemployment compensation for covered railroad workers similar to programs of the Social Security Administration. The Public Employee Benefit program of the U.S. government provides retirement and survivors benefits similar to the benefits of the Social Security Administration. Various states and localities furnish limited protection for the retirement and survivors of their employees which are constrained by problems of nontransferability. Many of these programs have some of the same shortcomings as other retirement and survivors programs.

A recurrent issue is the problem of double dippers into the social insurance programs. Although the Social Security and railroad retirement programs are integrated, there is no integration between the Social Security system and the federal employees and military pension programs. Thus, many federal workers after twenty to thirty years of civil or military service are retired at sizable pensions only to find employment in Social Security-covered jobs in private industry or at the local or state government level. When such an employee reaches age sixty-five, the retirement benefits are quite large. Attempts to integrate federal employees benefits with the Social Security system have met strong opposition from federal employees lobbies. It can also be argued that employees who have already invested years of service and money in the federal programs cannot legally be forced to release a part of their retirement investment in order to provide better articulation between the two major governmental retirement programs.

Health Insurance for Aged and Others (Medicare)

The Social Security Administration provides a basic compulsory program of health insurance for persons retired under Social Security and others under similar coverage. It also provides an associated program of voluntary supplementary medical insurance for the same clientele. Basic medical and hospital protection is financed through health insurance taxes paid during employment years through OASDI deductions. The volume of care given is based upon the number of quarters built up in the account. Additional medical and hospital care is funded by monthly premiums provided by those who elect such coverage.

Medicare supplies necessary medical care for covered persons usually at a time in life when they are unlikely to be able to meet the high costs involved and when their relatives may not be available to provide such care. The program spreads the risk of major medical costs for those who are covered. Medicare has a number of drawbacks. The demand for medical and hospital care has always exceeded the available facilities and personnel. Passage of the Medicare bill made it possible for many who had medical need to compete for it, as a result of which medical facilities have been swamped with demands for care and have imposed a commensurate rise in charges. Management of the program has entailed considerable administrative difficulty and has usually been farmed out to various medical insurance administration programs and carriers.

Medicare, unlike Medicaid, does not cover a wide age range of clients; it primarily serves the aged. Its major inadequacy is its lack of scope in population served. Other populations who need medical and hospital coverage and who might conceivably be included are (1) spouses of aged retirement annuitants who have not yet reached age 65; (2) children of disabled parents who are covered by Social Security disability annuities; and (3) children and spouses of deceased workers who are dependent upon survivors annuities of Social Security. In each instance these are population categories for whom Social Security deductions could be easily provided. The reasons for a medical social insurance such as Medicare apply equally, in principle, to the above population groups.

Other programs of public assistance and social insurance serve special population groups. For example, veterans benefits provide educational, housing, and employment-training benefits for honorably discharged veterans. If the veteran's national service is viewed as his contribution, then such benefits can be considered as social insurance. Other veterans services, especially those that require proof of need, can be considered as forms of public assistance.

Vocational Rehabilitation

Vocational rehabilitation programs provide education and training for handicapped persons to aid them in preparing for employment. These programs are operated by the states with heavy matching federal grants. If the programs are sufficiently funded by state and federal sources and the retraining is intelligently and skillfully administered in terms of client and agency goal choices, they can reclaim in taxes up to $70 for each dollar spent in the rehabilitation effort. The original vocational rehabilitation act was passed in 1920 and has since been amended a number of times, each time with an expansion of provisions and of the clientele to be served.

Vocational rehabilitation has been particularly useful in retraining uninsured, injured workers who, along with their families, would otherwise have had to become dependent on public welfare. The program provides such persons with necessary prosthetic devices, training in the use of these devices, and training in a new occupation where the physical handicap would not be a problem. The program also provides for the education and occupational or career training of handicapped adults, regardless of whether the disability is the result of a birth defect or injury during childhood or adulthood. The vocational rehabilitation program may cover costs of tuition, room and board, medical care, and any other related costs. The definition of disablement has been broadened to cover mental retardation and mental illness, and many thousands of such clients have been trained for useful occupations.

A major strength in the program is the flexibility with which it is permitted to operate under federal regulation. State programs are encouraged to cooperate with voluntary agencies and schools in training the handicapped. Contracts between such agencies and state programs allow the development and improvement of retraining services. A major weakness in many state vocational rehabilitation programs is the lack of leadership needed to foster the development and growth of innovative and effective rehabilitation projects.

Vocational rehabilitation lacks the implied stigma of many other public assistance programs. The reason presumably derives from the higher level of financial standards set in the test for eligibility and the pervasive difference in program emphasis between vocational rehabilitation and other public assistance programs. The vocational rehabilitation program consistently emphasizes a rehabilitative goal rather than maintenance and subsistence. That is, the ideal vocational rehabilitation model focuses on hope and on movement toward a specified goal. Reaching such goals gives both counselors and clients a sense of achievement. The social-psychological effect of such goal achievement is to build and validate the sense of self-esteem held by the client, upon which further self-sufficiency can be structured. In a sense, where the welfare worker or eligibility worker must necessarily serve primarily as a conservator of public funds, the vocational counselor must necessarily serve primarily as a coach and advisor in goal achievement.

One weakness of the vocational rehabilitation program is its pervasive emphasis on vocational success for clients. In many states, too many counselors tend to select for training those clients who have the greatest probability of succeeding. This policy of creaming tends to leave unserved too many potential clients who could be made self-sufficient if provided with the services. Many counselors also tend to emphasize quick, low-cost programs that provide only transitory and marginal occupations for clients rather than the more expensive and lengthy career plans that are more likely to assure long-term self-sufficiency and long-term returns of client maintenance savings and tax earnings.

In 1967, the vocational rehabilitation program was expanded to permit a redefinition of disability to include the culturally and educationally deprived. This aspect of the program, however, has never been supported with matching appropriations. To expand the program to include the culturally deprived and transgenerational poverty population is logical only if the job market is expanded to provide employment for such graduates of the program.

Under Social Security regulations, clients who are assisted under the disabled provisions of the SSI program or who receive benefits from the disabled workers insurance program must be registered with their state vocational rehabilitation program. This provision seeks to bring the disabled client into contact with opportunities for rehabilitation, wherever possible. However, while the handicapped person can be made to register with the vocational rehabilitation office, he cannot be made to choose and undertake a retraining program unless he already has the motivation.

The vocational rehabilitation program is a very useful program for the disabled who are retrainable. Its usefulness can be extended even further through an expanded employment market, expanded program resources, and improved outreach services.

Because of the proof of need requirement, vocational rehabilitation can be considered a form of public assistance, despite the fact that the public assistance constraints are quite flexible. The line between public assistance and social insurance has been somewhat blurred by court decisions rendered in behalf of public assistance clients. Many such clients have had the aid of legal services attorneys who have sought to prove the clients' right to assistance. The major differences between public assistance and social insurance are still the means test and differential categorical assistance, these remain intact as features of public assistance (see Table 3.5).

The Current Debate

A variety of social policy suggestions have been made to eliminate the distinctions between public assistance and social insurance. For example, Irwin Garfinkel urges the establishment of a universal program to sub-

TABLE 3.5 **Differences Between Public Assistance and Social Insurance**

PUBLIC ASSISTANCE	SOCIAL INSURANCE
Admission by means test; no prior payment required.	Admission by prior inclusion on broadbased nonvoluntary coverage where person has paid premiums (or had them withheld or paid for him).
Categorical assistance (based on presumed degree of need).	Benefits based on coverage amount and period of prepayment, but with floor for greater risk groups.
Principle of lesser eligibility (recently eroded in past two decades).	Benefits are fixed and unrelated to income differentials or outside income (except for retirement test).
Budgets constructed on basis of specific allowances for authorized needs, as recognized.	Benefits are not related to specific needs.
Full deduction of outside income (with some special exceptions).	Outside income irrelevant within scope of insured restrictions.
Unshared risk (some prepay not at all, but benefit).	Shared risk, involuntary inclusion.
Stigma (as carried over from Protestant Ethic tradition).	Because it is a right, no stigma.
Close relatives (such as parent for minor child or husband for wife) responsible.	Relatives not involved.
Funded by taxes.	Funded by client (and employer) prepayment, and so forth.
May be reevaluated for eligibility at any time, at discretion of staff administration.	No (or very little) discretion left to administration.

sume Social Security, unemployment insurance, income tax credits, and the means-tested programs of AFDC and SSI. Under his proposal, all income tests would be eliminated and all persons would be permitted to draw on benefits regardless of whether they had built up credits in the programs by previous employment or by other previous participation.

According to Garfinkel, such a universal program would have the following advantages. "(1) It would increase the self-respect of the poor; (2) it would decrease the chances that the poor will be treated like second-class citizens"; (3) it would increase "social cohesion by eliminating sharp distinctions between beneficiaries and non-beneficiaries"; (4) it would "provide more aid to the poor"; and (5) it would "increase the chances of the poor to improve their lot through work and saving" (p. 1).

It is helpful to examine these claims. Garfinkel's assumptions are based largely on the degree to which perceived stigma is attached to the SSI and AFDC programs. For those on SSI, the only differences between social insurance and the SSI programs are that (1) the SSI applicants must account for lack of income or assets which make them eligible for coverage, just as social insurance applicants must make their claims on the basis of earned coverage; (2) the SSI applicants receive a gold-colored check, while social insurance applicants receive a green check; and (3) the SSI payments are usually set at a lower level based on a needs floor, while social insurances are based on calculated accumulated prepayments.

Most aged, blind, and disabled people tend to view their checks as benefits, but few make the distinction between aid or pension. Applications and complaints are made at the same office, and no one but the applicant and the clerk really knows whether the matter under discussion is an aid or pension. To eliminate the differences between SSI and Social Security annuities would merely cost the government much more (if all were paid at the higher level), or it would result in serious disruption among those who have paid into the system (if all were paid at the lower level).

The issue of stigma is important only in regard to the differences between AFDC and survivors benefits. By and large, survivors benefits are paid to widows and their children, while AFDC is paid primarily to women (and children) who have been deserted, separated, or divorced, or are unmarried mothers. The families in the survivors benefit programs are usually intact, except for the loss of the principal wage-earner. For those who are temporarily on AFDC, AFDC stigma serves to help shorten the family's period of public dependency. Those who are chronically on AFDC apparently feel little stigma, either on the families or on their choice of life-style. Studies of public aid versus income maintenance (which are presented in the next chapter) indicate that the provision of a regular, stable public grant does not alter the poor's sense of self-worth in relation to others in the society.

Garfinkel's claim that universalization would increase the poor's chances to improve their lot through work and saving is questionable, unless the grants are so sizable as to leave the poor with excess funds for savings. Similarly, the provision of sizable grants might remove the little incentive for work which currently exists.

…man recently made a proposal similar to Garfinkel's. He suggests
…ination of means-tested welfare, and even the negative income
tax, because the more the poor person works, the more he is taxed (by
deductions from the welfare grant) and thus is discouraged from employment. Instead, Stockman suggests a universal child payment system
"since no change in income status would affect eligibility." He views this
mechanism as an alternative to AFDC and the personal income tax exemption. He also suggests a tax credit of 20 percent of gross wages earned
for low wage-earners in place of the AFDC and the personal income tax
exemption. He describes this credit as a negative withholding system to
encourage work in poor families (p. 41).

Stockman's plan for a child payment system would entail a sizable cost,
for it would require reclamation of child payments made to other than
poor families. It is doubtful that the income tax system can be sufficiently
revised and other deductions so reduced or eliminated as to make such
reclamation possible at the middle- and upper-income brackets. The prob-
abilities are high that most of these payments would be lost to the general
treasury and thus be highly inflationary.

An even more serious fault lies in Stockman's view of welfare grant
deductions as a tax. A tax is a levy on income earned by a person. A
welfare grant is not *earned* income, and a deduction from a welfare grant
is clearly not a tax but a lessening of support *from* tax sources. To equate
the two is to deny any difference between self-support and welfare dependency. To eliminate this difference and to assume one has eliminated
welfare dependency is the equivalent of solving the problem of crime by
removing criminal law from the statute books. Not to clarify the welfare
client's understanding of the difference between tax and grant is to ignore
the nature of welfare dependency problems.

Such reductionist analyses appear in many contemporary discussions
of welfare policy. The literature commonly refers to both welfare and
social insurance benefits as income transfers, based on the presumption
that the persons under social insurance protection make no connection
between Social Security wage deductions (paid by the individuals and
employers) and the expected size and arrangements of their retirement
annuities. The equating of Social Security deductions with taxes unrelated to personal interests is a similar pattern found in social policy writings. Both patterns are incorrect in that workers and employers do not
view withholding income tax and social security in the same light. Most
workers see income tax as a tax on their earnings but they view social
security as an investment for their future and as a protection against being
penniless in old age or when disabled.

In support of such labeling, it is argued that Social Security deductions
are not fully tied to benefits on a strict actuarial basis, since benefits at a

lower income level are greater than are actually accumulated by the worker and benefits at a higher income level are much smaller than are actually accumulated. But this argument merely indicates that the Social Security program is a social insurance because it reflects the shared risk pattern between rich and poor. A second argument used in support of this position is that the Social Security system is not a funded system, and thus a worker's investment in the system is untraceable. This argument is questionable in that the amount the worker and employer pay in can easily be traced. The only issue is that the money to pay the benefits has not been accumulated and segregated on behalf of the worker. But this is no problem when the same government which controls the treasury and monetary system owes the worker the money.

The two systems are also commonly blurred in many statistical government reports which list the expenditures for total welfare or income maintenance in such a way as to include public assistance and social insurance benefits as paid. But social insurance benefits are not really governmental income maintenance expenditures; they are merely repayments of money loaned by workers to the social insurance system. To give the social insurance beneficiaries the view that they are dependents upon government-income maintenance carries an undercurrent of "fuzzing" in a relationship based on a lifetime of forced premium payments.

According to Williamson, "Social Security has made it possible for an increasing proportion of the elderly to maintain independent households" rather than to have to be taken care of in the homes of their adult children as dependents (p. 12). Obviously, this independence is not only financial but also psychic in nature, in the sense that the aged have viewed their benefits as self-achieved rather than government-conferred.

Those who have administrative responsibility for both a problem and successful program are easily tempted to hide the problem one within the successful one. The rate per 1,000 covered aged population for the social insurance program grew from 0 in 1940 to over 900 in 1978, but SSI-Aged currently (1978) rests at about 100. Similarly, 95 out of every 100 young children are protected by social insurance (a benefit not earned by AFDC recipients). Four out of five persons of working age are insured with disability protection. One out of every seven people receives social insurance benefits each month. For every 1,000 orphans (a child who has lost a parent by whatever means), about 800 are served by survivors benefits and about 125 by AFDC. For every 4,000 disabled persons, about 3,650 are served by disabled workers benefits (social insurance) and 2,200 by SSI. Those receiving both minimum benefits under disabled workers social insurance program and SSI-Disabled assistance programs represent 1,850 out of every 4,000 disabled persons.

When the total number of persons served by public assistance and social insurance, and the costs of both, are presented as if they were homogenized welfare (income maintenance), the public relations problems of AFDC are easily resolved for administrators and the growing problems of AFDC easily hidden. The seemingly magical removal of the problems of AFDC under such a program can only be accomplished, however, by a twisting of definitions and meaning not intended in the original legislation and not so understood in the unwritten contractual understanding of the worker, employer, and government.

There are many reasons why the distinctions between public assistance and social insurance should *not* be blurred. If there were no longer a difference between the two, and if the basic grants for all were sizable, public aid could easily become a life pension for nonworkers. If this occurred, the society's productivity would probably fall drastically, and inflation would become even more of a problem than it is currently. With no difference between the two, those persons required to submit to Social Security deductions from their pay would exhibit increased resistance to such deductions. If there were no difference and if the payments were sizable, resistance to employment would be encountered among the skilled, the semiskilled, and the working poor for whom employment would offer less advantages than the grant. Similarly, if there were no difference in the payment level between public assistance and social insurance, then the never employed and the seldom employed would have little incentive to achieve employment training and to prepare for reentry into the employment market. Those currently on public assistance (AFDC) would probably view themselves (even more so than now) as justifiable beneficiaries of the government for life. In the process, the dole or "nonparticipatory dependency" would become even more of a problem with their children and grandchildren, because children not motivated to employment (and school as a vehicle for employment) become available candidates for delinquency, crime, and other antisocial activity. If no difference existed between public assistance and social insurance, and if the grant was sizable, then people in the society who tend to save for emergencies and old age and who secure private insurance would be less motivated to do so. The cessation of savings and insurance practices might have a noticeable effect on the capital available for investment and thus a negative effect on the economy. The provision of an unearned pension for all has been known to have a deleterious effect on family cohesion in a number of guaranteed income tests (see Chapter 4). The removal of all differences between public assistance and social insurance would no longer make it possible to identify the residual poor whose problems amount to much more than a lack of income and who require considerable help in resolving their nonmonetary problems.

In brief, universalization would amount to an unwarranted expansion of the Social Security program whose social hidden costs would be multifarious. Perhaps the dual goal of the two programs could be combined in two ways. First, a keen separation could be made between the wage-related provisioneering and nonwage related transfers. Second, separate financing methods might be used to delineate the two (wage- and non-wage-related benefits). A flat payroll tax on income could be levied and a personal income tax based on the earning structure could be used to finance government programs (Munnell, 1977 and 1978). After all, why should a working person be taxed via payroll to finance a nonwage transfer program?

Protective Laws

Still another form of social legislation—categorical protection laws—falls in neither the public assistance nor social insurance category. Each of these laws focuses on the protection of a target population or category of persons in order to prevent their suffering at the hands of some powerful group, social institution, or even a popular majority. Many of these laws seek to protect the financial and other interests of the target group, and in that sense they often serve as antipoverty legislation.

One example of this type of legislation is categorized as child labor law. At the turn of the century, according to Axinn and Levin (p. 126), children ten to fifteen years of age constituted 2 million of a total labor force of 29 million. A coalition of the National Child Labor Committee, consumers' groups, women's groups, and labor unions sought to secure laws controlling the conditions and hours of child labor in factories, mills, and workshops, By 1914, almost all states had passed such laws, setting minimum ages for child employment. Because these laws were relatively weak and inadequate, attempts were launched to establish federal child labor laws relating to industries dealing in interstate commerce. In 1912, the Children's Bureau was established to report on such matters as dangerous occupations involving children, children's accidents and diseases, and recommendations on employment legislation for children. By 1930, after several attempts to secure constitutionally valid federal child labor laws, improvements on the state level were achieved which secured relatively effective legislation for this purpose. Since that time, child labor declined steadily throughout the United States, except in certain industries and localities where exemptions were retained or where enforcement was particularly difficult. The problems of coverage and enforcement are brought about by unequally effective laws in the various states, by staffs limited in number, equipment, and authority and by exemptions relating to agriculture and other settings. (See Friedlander and Apte, pp. 379-380.)

The relative success of child labor law stands as an exemplary study for social legislation. Its success can be analyzed from the point of view of initial support groups, subsequent institutional support, and the cultural, economic, and technological trends of the times.

The National Child Labor Committee provided leadership to the child labor legislation movement, supplying professional and technical knowledge on a consistent and constant basis. Another not inconsiderable support group was the women's clubs of America. As middle-class mothers, they were in general sympathy with the mothers of poor children who had to support their families under dangerous, unhealthy conditions, at very low pay, and for long hours without rest periods. But support by women's groups was not enough, especially since their support could be expected to rise and fall with their degree of emotional involvement in a subject that competed for their interest and attention with many other concerns. One consistent and stable supporter of the movement was the leadership of organized labor which was concerned more with the effect of child labor on the wages and employment levels of union members than with the effect on the children of the poor. When factories lured children at low wages and under hazardous conditions, the wages of men in factories were accordingly undercut. Thus, the labor movement consistently pressed the legislatures for child labor laws, especially where large employers were concerned and in those unions where labor organization was most feasible. This is why child labor laws for migrant argricultural work and many retail trades were secured at a much later period.

A hidden supporter of the movement was institutional American education. To the supporters of the American schools, anything which kept children out of school was somehow un-American and antidemocratic. The history of the early enforcement of child labor law is replete with tales of factories with secret bells and buzzers to warn of the entrance of a child labor investigator and of factory drills, similar to fire drills, to quickly direct the children to the restroom for the sex other than that of the investigator. This kind of evasion was soon eliminated because the American labor union movement viewed child labor as scab labor, which was seen as an enemy of the worker in his search for his daily bread.

Still another support of child labor legislation could be found in the degree of technological development in America at that time. The employer or entrepreneur was faced with the narrow alternative of hiring children cheaply or adults at a more expensive rate. His spectrum of choices also included arrangements involving mechanization and, later, automation and computerization arrangements. If an employer could hire a small number of skilled men using a sizable collection of machines for less money than a horde of difficult-to-manage, unskilled children and a less expensive collection of machines, the critical factor was bottom-line cost. If he could make a profit, have less personnel difficulty, and at the same time avoid the notoriety and negative public relations of being designated the operator of a children's sweat shop, why not be a "hero?" As more employers saw their way to this type of factory conversion, they, too, took advantage of the public relations benefits of the move, and they frequently became supporters of the child labor legislation movement.

In a study of social legislation generally and in an issue such as the restriction of child labor, it is important to examine both the immediate and long-range societal tradeoffs that occur. When such laws are instituted, who benefits and who loses in the long run? What long-range societal trends does such legislation set in motion?

In the short run, the family which is partially or, in some instances, wholly dependent upon children's employment is, of course, negatively affected by the loss of income. To a certain extent, the growth in the AFDC program can at least partly be traced to the effect of the child labor laws. Similarly, the loss of beginning employment opportunities and work conditioning for children resulting from the child labor laws has left many children with the considerable problem of finding their first job after years of schooling without experience.

In the short run, these laws have ensured the effectiveness of school attendance laws. No parent could justify nonattendance if the child were not otherwise meaningfully involved in some activity necessary for the family or for his own development. In part, child labor laws have assured children the education needed to gain socioeconomic mobility. Child labor laws have also had a counterproductive effect in keeping some children in school beyond the point where they have been able to make continued progress. The result has been the introduction of social promotions for youngsters too old for one grade who are not academically ready for the next one. To some extent, in many locations, child labor laws have been an important factor in the problems of educational dropouts and pushouts,* and in the deterioration of American education in many locations.

In the long run, child labor laws have had the positive effect of supporting public sponsorship of high school and even college education. The laws have also helped maintain the wage levels of adults and the increased

---

*A pushout is a child who is supposedly perceived by the teacher and principal to be making no progress in school and who may be difficult to manage in class. The child is therefore encouraged to drop out by either cooling him out (counseling the child elsewhere) or by increasing pressure so that he/she will quietly drop out. This is a term used by many community action workers who have been disturbed by school personnel who do not try hard enough with minority children.

specialization brought on by a higher adult wage level and a higher level of mechanization. Another long-run effect of child labor legislation has been the increased separation of school and work, to the point that the creation of a work-preparation-oriented school program is not easily achieved in the United States. School-connected work apprenticeship on the American scene is usually not available for the mass of youths seeking to prepare themselves for a lifetime of employment. Thus, child labor laws have helped minimize the readiness of youth for employment and have helped create the massive portion of the population which either has never been in the work force or has been only sporadically involved in work activity.

An analysis of child labor laws shows that no law ever has a clear and unidirectional influence. To some extent child labor laws have kept many children in school and on the path toward securing a necessary education. But in the process of trying to eliminate children from the labor market in order to provide employment for adults, the child labor laws have removed thousands of unskilled jobs from the market place and many of these children have been replaced by labor-saving machines and fewer adults. The adults who have succeeded the children have had to bring more skills and education into the factory. Child labor laws have consequently helped escalate the process which has left the unskilled adults behind as superfluous and welfare-ready. Yet, few people would object to child labor legislation. It is important, even in the case of what is now a relatively noncontroversial law, to examine the short- and long-term productive and counterproductive effects.

Another set of protective laws is related to work conditions for women in the various states. At the beginning of the twentieth century, women's employment laws in many states followed the development of sweat shops in many of the population centers where new immigrants settled. Textile factories, garment factories, and production plants for a variety of products found that women could be as quickly trained as men for the simple but careful tasks needed. Women seemed to have more patience in some jobs, and were satisfied with less wages than men. Women would accept lower wages than men partly because they were supplementary rather than primary wage-earners, and they seldom viewed their income as the basis for supporting the entire family. When a wage basis was used for worker payment, many of the sweat shop employers rode their workers hard, seeking to get maximum production out of each day's wage. Many factories had limited and often rudimentary restroom facilities, and did not even have separate facilities for women. Many were unsafe fire-traps and were badly ventilated and seldom cleaned, since cleaning of the plant was not a profitable activity. Many of the sweat shop operators were themselves former factory workers who had opened their own shop on a shoestring of borrowed money and attenuated credit.

When various states passed laws specifying mandatory rest periods for women workers, many factories shifted to the piece-work plan whereby a standard price was set for each multiple of products which the workers serviced with a particular process. Workers could either work intensively or rest, as long as they did not occupy the factory machine unproductively. Thus, many women who used to rest each hour under the wage plan were tempted not to rest at all or to rest less.

The employment regulations for women also specified conditions for women's restroom facilities in factories, standards of cleanliness in the plant, and other necessary changes. Where these changes could be effected without too much of an expenditure, they were carried out. If they brought costs up beyond the range available in the profit margin, however, some employers were no longer able to compete, and these shops closed and were usually not reopened. Many little firms gave way to larger firms which were better able to provide the facilities. In time, the women's employment laws became a spur to improving men's facilities and to providing rest periods for men as well, particularly when equal provisions under the Constitution became a concern for court interpretation.

Another area of protective law which relates to potential threats to workers can be described as occupational health and safety laws. Many occupations in the United States, especially during the early growth of American industry, required that workers expose themselves to a variety of hazards, including fumes, dust, activity in proximity to dangerous machinery and to overhead weights, and life and limb-threatening situations. The President's Conference on Industrial Safety in 1949 set up a typology of hazards: (1) Uncontrolled and therefore hazardous movement of men, materials, and equipment deriving from plant layout, material-handling methods and transport, congestion resulting from inadequate storage planning and facilities, and waste-reject disposal arrangements. (2) Lack of hazard-proof installations arising out of process equipment operation, pressure and temperature control, flammable, explosive, and toxic dusts, gases, liquids, and solids. (3) Structural failures of cranes, hoists, elevators, and permanent structures. (4) Practices of workers arising out of lack of knowledge of the necessary control of machine and equipment operation or of safe handling of materials.

Research into industrial safety shows that only a small proportion of injuries stem from mechanical or process failures. The vast majority of accidents result from human failure to act carefully, protectively, or logically. Accordingly, the President's Commission on Health Needs in 1952 recommended greater emphasis on employee training in addition to accident prevention planning.

In prior years, worker loss or injury was viewed as a necessary, although regrettable, byproduct of factory, mine, and plant operations. By

1877 (Hogan and Ianni, p. 429), the first state law was passed requiring factory safeguards. Prior to 1885, employers were protected from liability for accidents and diseases suffered by their employees under general interpretations of the law. Some employers even deducted some of the costs of accidents. By 1910, some of the states began to enact workmen's compensation laws. The plans set standards for plant safety conditions utilizing such definitions as maximum allowable concentrations, permissible limits, and safe limits for ventilation and other factors in worker conditions. Protective clothing was specified where appropriate, and machinery guards were specified. Mechanical hazards were defined and safeguards were noted. Job specifications were required, and accident-prone employees were defined and specified for transfer away from hazardous plant sectors.

As a result of the emphasis on plant safety, many states now require plant accident and hazard insurance. Each plant operator must necessarily pay premiums that reflect the accident potential and hazard present in his plant. A manager of a dangerous plant must either pay a high premium, improve the conditions in the plant so as to secure a lower premium, or go out of business. He will usually do what is most profitable for his company, but at least the law prevents him from operating a plant that is dangerous to his workers. Commercial insurance is usually available to nonhazardous plant owners. States usually provide for intercompany- or state-sponsored, high premium insurance for the less insurable plants.

Insurance companies, of course, desire fewer and less serious accident and hazard claims (and thus greater profits). In this regard, they devote considerable time, energy, and expert consultation in seeking to make the plants of their customers as accident- and hazard-free as possible. If an insurance company finds a plant to be too much of a hazard, it may decide not to renew the insurance on the plant, and, if state law requires such insurance, the plant may have to be closed. This situation has occurred many times, with little publicity or public notice. For example, in one Texas town, an asbestos insulation manufacturing plant was closed down when it was found that ventilation in the plant could not be improved without entirely rebuilding it, and when a direct tie between inadequate ventilation in the plant and lung cancer and emphysema was clearly proven. The plant was closed down over the objections of many of the town leaders, businessmen, and plant workers.

When state law requires workers' compensation, (although the compensation may be a form of social insurance since protection is an earned employee benefit), the requirement for such insurance can be considered in the protective legislative category. The requirement that an employer improve the conditions under which the employees work can also be considered protective law.

Most states have enacted occupational health and safety laws. These laws are usually operated by the state health agency, or the state employment or labor agency. The federal government has become involved in occupational health and safety in jurisdictions under its purview and over plants that can be controlled by federal legislation or regulations. The U.S. Department of Labor, through a number of its bureaus, seeks to provide leadership and coordination to the various governmentally concerned entities.

Where plants have been required to insure themselves against losses by workers from accidents and hazards, and where these plants could not bypass the requirements by moving away or by automation, the occupational health and safety of the workers has been enhanced by the resultant plant planning and activity. Thus, the occupational health and safety laws tied to required workers' compensation insurance plans have often served as an exemplary demonstration of utilitarian jurisprudence.

Another instance of protective law can be found in the various forms of federal and state fair employment practice laws, fair housing laws, equal educational opportunity laws, equal access to public facilities laws, and affirmative action laws. Here the rights at conflict are not only between the employer and potential employee, the landlord and tenant, and so forth, but also other potential applicants and aspirants for employment, housing, education, upgrading, and the like. These laws juxtapose the rights of minority members to the rights of those who are already established in jobs, for example, and who would be necessarily displaced if the rights of the present applicants were upheld. These laws, especially the affirmative action mechanism, introduce a conceptualization of rights that are no longer tied to individuals but to ethnic and racial categories. Previously, this approach was neither practiced nor considered valid under American law. The fact that a person was a member of a particular ethnic or racial group was considered irrelevant, under the law, in any attempt to substantiate the rights of any individual. Any attempt to show favoritism to certain ethnic group members was considered a gross violation of the principles of equity and justice.

Under the Napoleonic Code each minority was permitted a quota of openings in French medical schools, engineering schools, and other upward socioeconomic institutions based upon the percentage of that minority in the general population. For a few years, this system was gratifying to the minorities of France, but the quotas were soon filled and further opportunities for minorities were then closed. After many decades of struggle against the quota system, opportunities to enter such programs were restricted to competence only, on a competitive basis, using whatever tools were available to determine relative competence.

In the United States, the quota system for entry into higher education programs and professional schools was tested in 1978 (*University of California* versus *Bakke*). In earlier decades, American law focused on the rights of the individual rather than on the rights of the ethnic or racial groups. The reasons given for this view were that each person had the equal right to seek and achieve opportunities. When equality was restricted, such as when the vote was limited to property owners or when blacks were calculated as three-fifths of a white citizen in terms of representation, these discriminatory laws were overturned because they were inherently antidemocratic. The immigration quota established under labor union pressure to keep non-Nordic immigrants out of competition for jobs on the American scene was constantly under attack. The law was finally revised so that each applicant for immigration could be viewed as an individual rather than as a member of a group.

Thus, the establishment of quotas, or goals as they are now euphemistically designated, in the hiring of employees and in the selection of candidates for professional programs is retrogressive in the direction of an equal opportunity society. To close out any person's chances because of an irrelevant factor like his ethnic or racial background is to deny him his opportunity to compete. Once the quota is filled, the system can be used to deny entry for otherwise qualified people who, by chance, may be black instead of Chicano or vice versa. This has already occurred with Orientals, who in many cases are no longer given priority for affirmative action.

It is important to compare the basic democratic pattern of equal individual rights to opportunity with the ethnic quota pattern (Glazer). Under the basic pattern, the individual is judged only for competence, and under the ethnic pattern, the group becomes the key criterion and the individual's competence or effort to succeed is less important than his ethnic designation. Under the basic pattern, the individual is autonomous, while under the ethnic pattern, he must rely for his focus of concern on group patterns. Under the basic pattern, an individual can move ahead regardless of his ethnic membership, and under the ethnic, he can move only if his ethnic group has a favorable quota position and if his ethnic group provides him support. Under the basic pattern, the individual could seek a career in the larger society, but in the ethnic, the scope of his career would be linked to his contribution to his ethnic group. Under the basic pattern, an individual's failure can be judged to be his own fault, and under the ethnic, failure can be traced to an unjust system or an unfortunate ethnic membership factor. Under the basic pattern, a constant effort is necessary to enforce equal treatment in evaluation and grading of competency, while under the ethnic, there is greater reliance on ethnic membership with lesser regard for performance and competency. Under the basic pattern, individuals have constant opportunities to interact regardless of ethnicity, but under the ethnic, since upgrading will occur only through one's ethnic group membership, motivation of interaction beyond one's ethnic group will probably be lessened. Under the basic pattern, due process can always be questioned and the data examined. Under the ethnic pattern, ethnic factors become necessary for decision-making, and the unknown degree of relevancy of these in relation to competency factors make examination of such decisions difficult, if not impossible.

Affirmative action quotas have come into use because of a series of inefficiencies and "short-circuits" in the competitive hiring and appointment process. First, people hire and appoint those people whom they know. In order for people to be known, social interaction and association must take place. If a person is not known to the hirer, the personnel manager, the admissions officer, or whoever is in charge of opportunity, then that applicant is a mere number. The process of choosing people involves not only selection for competency, where individuals are considered, but also idiosyncratization. If the candidate is not perceived as special, then there is little chance of being selected. To this calculation should be added the fact that examiners and hirers tend to consider as special those people they can best understand. Those who are strange or incongruous are not usually idiosyncratized.

Not enough effort was put into the process of equality of opportunity to be idiosyncratized, especially for minority group members. That is one reason why nonminority ethnics predominated in the sought-for positions. Some minorities, such as Jews and Orientals, pierced the communication barriers through increased competency and stronger preparation. In the process, they became increasingly able to be idiosyncratized or recognized as special and of being perceived as such. Thus, the ability to be perceived as a uniquely prepared and skilled individual is also a critical quality of competency.

Second, many of the valued posts in universities, industry, and government were never adequately made known to the public. Because only those people who knew of such openings applied, many such valued positions were filled on an "old boy" basis—by colleagues who had attended the same universities and who had lived in the same elite conclaves. This pattern existed throughout the history of the country. Only when no friends or acquaintances were able or willing to take the position was the job advertised. In recent years, partly because of the influence of affirmative action programs, this is no longer the case. All positions must be publicly announced in periodicals with broad and appropriate circulation. As a result, more people know of the opportunities and are free to compete for consideration. This pattern has been used in English universities and public institutions for many years. Its earlier adoption in the United States might have prevented the pattern of upper level elitism which prevented open competition and maximized competency as a basis of appointment.

Third, many of the tests which appointive authorities used for selection were irrelevant to competency on the job. Some have viewed these tests as traps to screen out minority or ethnic candidates. It is more likely, however, that such tests were adopted more out of laziness than connivance. A test for ability in the use of concepts and English writing on a civil service exam might be very appropriate for the choice of an editorial assistant, but irrelevant for the choice of a computer trainee. Similarly, a test in algebraic ability might be very necessary in a search for a research and analysis trainee, but irrelevant and counterproductive in a search for an editorial assistant. Yet, both tests have been used for both types of positions on civil service exams, and eligibility has been based upon the total score. Such a combination of tests may well have been counterproductive in the attempt to select the best candidates for each position. In the process, it may also have unnecessarily and purposelessly screened out minorities and others. Where this test is irrelevant to the job function, it is not only counterproductive but also a violation of the equal opportunity principle.

In recent years, there has been increased pressure, by legal suits and political endeavors, to resolve this problem. The anomaly still exists. Either it will be corrected, or the pressures will mount to eliminate civil service testing generally. If it is eliminated, the result could be a pattern of ethnic politicization as destructive to justice and productivity as the spoils system was prior to the enactment of civil service.

It is possible that the affirmative action quota system can grow into a permanent negation of equal opportunity. Who is to designate which ethnic and racial groups shall be given priorities? Who is to judge priorities after all opportunities are narrowed and ethnic and racial groups begin to compete for juxtaposed openings? What is to happen to those who, through no fault of their own, are born with unfortunate ethnic quota allocations? What will happen to motivation for individual enterprise when ethnic and racial quotas, rather than competency, become the basis for social mobility? What will happen to productivity when position is assured not by individual effort but by favorable location and involvement in ethnic politics? Is the matter of ethnic quotas as a determinant in life any less inimicable to American concepts of justice than prior patterns of life positioning on the basis of noble or non-noble birth? Will the mass of society, finding that social mobility is closed to them on the basis of individual efforts at self-improvement, then move to collective efforts which may be uncontrolled and repressive of the preferred ethnic and racial groups?

Neither affirmative action nor the past imperfect practices of selection for mobility can solve the problems of delivered equality. Reverse racial and ethnic preferment can be as unjust as primary discrimination. The answer to the question probably rests with creating increased equality of opportunity by providing safeguards to ensure honest competition and by providing increased services to give children at an early age the competency necessary to compete in their adult lives.

Any country that relies on caste rather than on competency can expect declining productivity and lessened social mobility for all. Affirmative action will not compensate for the inadequate preparation given poor children to compete when they reach adulthood.

Other laws designed to protect minorities include guarantees against garnisheement of workers' wages by creditors in some states. Homesteading of a family home, car, and furniture of a person is another example of some state provisions to protect families from being pressed into extreme poverty by creditors. Many states have tenant protection laws which provide for eviction only after careful due process. In the interim, tenants in danger of losing housing have the opportunity to retain their housing or to seek other housing. Consumer protection law requires manufacturers and retailers to make good on their products, and in this way families are protected against these financial hazards. Recent laws requiring truth in lending also protect borrowers by clearly setting out the costs of loans and credit.

Another type of legislation in the protection category relates to protecting the individual's right to equally effective public education. This law can mean a great deal in preparing the individual to compete on an equal basis. (This legislative effort is presented in Chapter 8.)

All of the laws in the protective category safeguard individuals and families from hazards that would interfere with their equal opportunities and that might otherwise be beyond their control. As such, they are designed to protect individuals and families from a certain degree of poverty deriving from their less secure position in the society.

In 1980 the Department of Health, Education and Welfare was divided into a Department of Health and Human Services and a Department of Education. Presumably, the programs listed in this chapter (other than Basic Educational Opportunity Grants) will be delegated to the Department of Health and Human Services.

References

Axinn, June and Herman Levin. *Social Welfare—A History of the American Response to Need.* New York: Dodd, Mead, 1975.

Durkheim, Emile. *Division of Labor in Society.* Glencoe, Ill.: Free Press, 1933.

Friedlander, Walter A., and Robert Z. Apte. *Introduction to Social Welfare.* Englewood Cliffs, N.J.: Prentice-Hall, 1975.

Garfinkel, Irwin. "Universal vs. Income Tested Debate Focuses on Income Maintenance Programs," *Socio-Economic Newsletter,* 3(9):1–2, 1978.

Glazer, Nathan. *Affirmative Discrimination—Ethnic Inequality and Public Policy.* New York: Basic Books, 1976.

Hogan, John D., and Francis A.J. Ianni. *American Social Legislation.* New York: Harper, 1956.

Lawrence, John F. "Household Help Laws Discourage Hiring, Encourage Cheating," *Los Angeles Times,* September 17, 1978, Part V, p. 3.

Levy, Robert, Thomas P. Lewis, and Peter M. Martin. *Social Welfare and the Individual: Cases and Materials.* Mineola: Foundation Press, 1971.

Munnel, Alicia H. *The Future of Social Security.* Washington, D.C.: Brookings, 1977.

———. "Social Security: Public Financing for Human Needs," *The Pioneer,* October 19, 1978, pp. 6–7.

Piven, Francis Fox, and Richard Cloward. *Regulating the Poor, The Functions of Public Welfare.* New York: Vintage, 1971.

Social Security Administration. *Social Security Program Charts.* Chart presentation for 1979 Advisory Council on Social Security. Washington, D.C.: U.S. Department of Health, Education and Welfare, 1978.

Stockman, David A. "Welfare Is the Problem," *Journal of the Institute for Socio-Economic Studies,* 3(3):39–50, 1978.

Williamson, John B. "Social Security: Insurance or Welfare?" Paper presented at the Annual Meeting of the Society for the Study of Social Problems, 1978.

SOCIAL INTERVENTIONS AGAINST POVERTY

4

AS NOTED EARLIER, the Aid to the Blind (AB), Aid to the Totally Disabled (ATD), and Old Age Assistance (OAA) programs were federalized and transferred to the Social Security Administration in 1974. A basic minimum for all grants has been established, and where states desire to supplement these grants, they make their payments via the Social Security disbursement system. Potential aid recipients apply to the local offices of the Social Security Administration, which processes them in the same manner as OASDI applicants. The only difference in procedure is that grants are based upon nationally established standards rather than on earned benefits. The amounts also differ in that the grant levels are smaller than Social Security annuities. Where a client is eligible for a small OASDI benefit or has other outside income, the Supplementary Security Income (SSI) program provides him or her with a supplementary monthly grant to bring the income up to SSI established levels.

The SSI program is public assistance in that a means test is used and the grant is subject to deduction of outside income. The administrative procedures introduced by the Social Security Administration, however, have eliminated much of the stigma of public assistance as well as many of the discretionary controls previously used by the local welfare systems. To all intents and purposes, the revised program has established a floor under the incomes for the aged, the blind, and the disabled. Although it is a public assistance program, it is operated as if it were social insurance. Much of the adverse publicity previously focused on all public assistance has been removed from these programs. The removal of these aid categories from the local welfare administrative scene and from the debate about welfare leaves only one category, Aid to Families with Dependent Children (AFDC), in the center of public concern.

During fiscal 1977, the SSI program provided $5.3 billion to the aged, blind, or disabled clientele (Budget, p. 199). This total was over and above supplementation to the program provided by most of the states, which amounted to $1.6 billion (Rush, Table A). A total of 2 million aged, 77,000 blind, and over 2.1 million disabled were served as of December 1977. Of this client group, 175,000 were blind or disabled children. The average monthly grant for the aged was $102 for an individual and $141 for a couple. Blind individuals received an average grant of $163, and couples $241. Disabled or blind children received an average of $170 (Rush, Table B). The aided clientele, as of June 1977 (Thomas), included a total of 10,000 persons disabled by reason of alcoholism or drug addiction. Of these, almost 8,700 were New York clients. As of August 1977 (Rush, Table 1), after this subcategory had been subjected to reexamination and eligibility review, the number declined to 6,233, of which New York accounted for approximately 4,700. Of a total of 357,000 disabled and blind served in 1975 (Rush, Table 2), 18 percent were disabled because of mental disorders and 13 percent because of mental retardation.

The proportion of clientele covered by SSI shifted from 1974 to 1978. Although the number of blind persons remained relatively steady, the number of aided disabled grew from about 1.2 million to 2.1 million people. The number of aged during this period has increased from 1.8 million to approximately 2 million.

The data on SSI beneficiaries during 1967–1974, as reported by Treitel, showed that about 36,000 of the 2.4 million blind and disabled referred to vocational rehabilitation were reported recovered, but only about 3.1 percent, or about 1,100 persons, continued in what was designated an active recovery. Thus, efforts at rehabilitation, as provided for by Congress and the state vocational rehabilitation programs, account for a rehabilitation rate of less than 5 percent.

Not all persons eligible for SSI apply for such aid. For example, Bishop (p. 171) reports that half of the aged poor whom the Social Security Administration expected to apply in 1974 did not do so. Based on the reported data, there is no reason to believe that this situation has changed since 1974. Presumably, a sizable proportion of the needy aged now know about SSI but prefer to be self-sufficient.

Doolittle, Levy, and Wiseman (p. 87) report that the SSI has not been an unmitigated success: "Since its inception . . . the program has been charged with delays in disbursing checks and other administrative inefficiencies." "Significant numbers of recipients [were found to have] unreported income, including incomes from other federal programs," which would probably have made them ineligible for SSI had the facts been revealed at application or on rechecking. Numerous calculation errors were believed to account for almost $56 million in the annual SSI budget. A computer-managed distribution program presumably lacks the evaluative judgment and the continued contact that only a system dependent upon frequent worker and home contacts can provide.

The social insurance programs of the Social Security Administration are much larger than SSI in both funds distributed and in numbers of beneficiaries. In 1977 (Budget, p. 192), more than $82 billion were distributed to 33.2 million individuals. The programs were expected to grow to 93 billion in 1978 and 103 billion in 1979. These programs are estimated to be almost universal for all workers except for federal civilian employees and the employees of some state and local governments, nonprofit organizations, and irregular workers. "The system is financed almost entirely from payroll taxes paid by covered workers and their employers" (Budget, p. 192). The Social Security Administration experienced some funding problems in that "a long-range decline in birth rates was not foreseen in earlier projections of program costs." Consequently, "there will be fewer workers in future years to pay for the costs of benefits." Congressional action was secured to balance the expected cost overrun with increased employee and employer taxes (Snee and Ross). This action occasioned the trustees of the fund to declare it financially sound as of mid-1978 (Social Security Items No. 21). According to Munnell, if Social Security continues as a self-supporting system, financed exclusively by payroll deductions,

expenditures for OASDI will rise by 18 percent of taxable payrolls by 2025, with Medicare requiring another 8 percent, if the current ratio of benefits to preretirement earnings is maintained. If, however, the retirement age is shifted to 68, which is probably reasonable to consider in the light of contemporary health advances, that would substantially reduce costs (p. 6).

The railroad retirement system also amounts to a social insurance of sizable proportions. In 1977, payments were made to over 1 million persons in the amount of approximately $3.8 billion. The total was expected to grow to 4.3 billion by 1979 (Budget, p. 194). Benefits under this system cover all of the same categories as under the social insurances of the Social Security system.

Aid to Families With Dependent Children

(AFDC is a small program compared with the social insurances, but its size is nevertheless of fiscal concern inasmuch as the social insurances are entirely self-sustaining while AFDC is fully dependent on public funding. In 1977, an estimated 11 million persons, or 3.6 million families, received approximately $6.8 billion in federal funds, supplemented by matched funding from state governments (Budget, p. 199). The average grant varied with each state, but the national average per family under AFDC was $250 in 1978 and was expected to go to $261 in 1979.

years previously (1969), AFDC represented 53 percent of the total e financial outlays (OAA, ATD, AB, and AFDC). In 1977, it was responsible for $10 billion (Research and Statistics Note No. 10) of welfare disbursements, which now places it as approximately 60 percent of the total welfare outlay. The expenditure for the same number of clients served (11 million) was approximately $9 billion in 1975, an increase of 10.7 percent (Research and Statistics Note No. 10). Although AFDC grew phenomenally from 1969 to 1975, the number of persons it has served since that time has remained steady. Thus, a program of 2.2 million persons in 1950 became one of 3 million in 1960, 4 million in 1965, 6.7 million in 1969, 10.8 million in 1974, and 11 million in 1977. Expressed in percentages, the total number of beneficiaries has grown 500 percent since 1950, and its costs have grown from $550 million in 1950 to $10 billion in 1977. In other words, it has doubled itself every four to five years, reaching a growth of 2,000 percent since 1950. An examination of all other aid categories of the United States indicates that AFDC has no parallel in terms of expenditure growth. For a temporary program scheduled to wither away and disappear between 1936 and 1945 (Hefferman, p. 110), it has shown considerable robustness and longevity.

Piven and Cloward claim that the dramatic growth of AFDC in the 1960s occurred as a result of the government's response to urban unrest. According to these authors, by providing welfare the government was able to continue to "regulate the poor" and to keep them under restraint. Eugene Durham is highly critical of the regulation of the poor thesis. He agrees that "official response to agitation by disadvantaged blacks" was an important factor in the growth, but he contends that the growth of AFDC was even more an unintended consequence of welfare and employment policy enactments, migration within the United States, changing aspirations of the Spanish-speaking people, changing social mores, and, most importantly, social stress which created a large number of female-headed families among whites and nonwhites.

The *New Republic* editorial on the Planned Parenthood study for 1974 reported a drop in the birth rate among poverty families. Their annual birth rate declined from 152.5 births in 1970 to 108.5 births per 1,000 families in 1974. Unfortunately, the report did not list separate statistics for the working poor and welfare-dependent populations. Other studies have indicated that as the working poor move toward middle-class status their birth rate falls even lower than that of the middle-class family, which was about 71 births per 1,000 in 1974. (The middle-class rate has dropped from 98.1 births per 1,000 in the 1960s.) Thus, a conservative estimate of 110 births per year per 1,000 for the welfare-dependent population could present us with an annual increase of 11 percent with welfare-dependent population (with few losses from deaths in that the AFDC is a young population). This is double-digit population inflation. By 1980, we could expect an AFDC welfare population of 16 million instead of 11 million. With expenditures doubling every five years, the cost would increase to $15 billion by 1980. Because of its size and its cost (not only in terms of money but also human resources), AFDC is a matter for careful concern. The program is particularly important as a case study in the problems of public assistance.

More recent figures reported by McCormack show a steep growth in teenage pregnancy, estimated at 1.1 million girls annually, of whom more than a majority elect to bear and keep their children. According to the study reported by McCormack, these mothers choose to be supported by AFDC. In fact, half of the AFDC expenditures currently goes to mothers who gave birth in their teens. By 1984, the indications are that 21 percent of all the present fourteen year olds can expect to give birth, and 35 to 39 percent will have one or more pregnancies during the teen years. In May 1979, the House Select Committee on Population reported that there were more than 3 million fertile women in the United States with no access to contraception, of whom more than 2 million were sexually active teenage girls. One-third of all girls fifteen to twenty years of age have had at least one unwanted pregnancy. The committee also reported that half of all AFDC money was going to women who had had their first child during the teen years. Very few girls were reported as giving their children up for adoption, probably because of the diminished stigma and taboo against out-of-wedlock pregnancies (Holden). Among many ghetto young people the process of becoming an adult requires a pregnancy for the teen-aged girl and a series of successful seductions for the young male. The process may seem initially exciting, but for many of the young girls motherhood soon becomes boring and a hinderance.

According to McCormack, the teenage mother, and the usually unreported father of her child, have completed fewer years of schooling than their classmates. These who become mothers, even if they finally escape a life on AFDC, end up with less prestigious jobs, have much lower incomes, and report much less satisfaction in their work. Most such mothers, however, never become entries in the employment market. McCormack finds that such adolescent parents experience greater separation, divorce, and desertion rates and are more likely to marry persons of limited educations and occupations. After eleven years out of high school, less than 10 percent of the spouses of such mothers had college degrees, as compared with 40 percent among their classmates' husbands, but those who do marry at all and have viable marriages are a small minority of that population after eleven years. Teenage parents also suffer from a variety of social and psychological ills, according to the report, but whether these disturbances predated the pregnancies or were sequelae of the birth is not known (p. 6).

The Planned Parenthood Association has declared this trend of children bearing children an epidemic. Obviously, this epidemic can be expected to have serious consequences in terms of further increase in the rate of growth of the AFDC population and their costs. The older the applicant to AFDC and the more socialized to the mainstream, the more likely it is that the AFDC applicant and her family will experience a dependency of shorter duration. Conversely, teenage applicants can be expected to remain dependent for longer periods, to present multiple problems, to be much more expensive to the society in terms of AFDC and Medicaid costs, to be less employable, and to rear children who are more likely to continue to be dependent on the society. Thus, the current growth of the AFDC, plus the contemporary teenage childbirth epidemic, represents a potential explosive threat to American social and economic stability and development. Nash, a former organizer of the Student Nonviolent Committee of the 1960s, has cited the spread of such dependency to former middle-class children.

Welfarization and AFDC

Before further examining the social basis of the AFDC mechanism, it is necessary to understand the fundamental process of welfarization. Freeman's analysis of the metamorphosis of AFDC has shown how the original program of aid for orphaned children not protected by Social Security annuities has been converted, over the years, into a program to provide care for any child and his mother without regard for the makeup of his family, the past history of his parents, or their readiness and capability to care for him. Most humane social policy planners, and indeed most people, would tend to support such an expansion of orphans' aid to include aid for other fatherless or deserted children. The problem with such a policy is that it does not take into account the effect of the availability of such aid on others. In his 1935 State of the Union message, President Franklin D. Roosevelt described continued aid as a "narcotic, a subtle destroyer of the human spirit," and believed it to be "fundamentally destructive to the national fibre." Moynihan presents an overview of the transformation of the AFDC. Originally, it was highly rehabilitative for relatively stable families with generations of work experience and self-sufficiency, which had lost a breadwinner (Moynihan, 1968, p. 15). It has now become a highly antirehabilitative mechanism for unmarried younger women who are unprepared for self-care and self-sufficiency, much less for responsible parenthood.

Thus, AFDC, a program originally established to aid helpless victims of uncontrollable circumstances, such as death by disease or accident of the principal wage-earner, has somehow been converted into a program to

serve women (and their children) who have experienced a loss
principal breadwinner by reason of divorce, desertion, or sep:
Divorce, desertion, or separation cannot be equated with widowhood in
that none of the three conditions is an "act of God" over which the
principal applicant has no control. Hefferman (p. 110) states that the
legislative planners of the program did not intend it to deal with poverty
resulting from divorce, desertion, and illegitimacy. These states were not
considered to be the responsibility of society. Steiner (1971, Chapter 5)
also supports this reading of the legislative history.

When AFDC was expanded to serve teenage and young adult unmarried mothers, it was further broadened to include not victims but those
persons who were not sufficiently responsible or mature to make life-
defining decisions. A program can probably be designed to serve the
victims of uncontrollable factors and still be expected to be efficiently
limited in terms of numbers included and costs. No program, however,
can be expected to remain reasonable in numbers and costs if it provides a
form of unearned insurance against the results of one's own failures of
interpersonal relationships and/or of activities. The insurance industry
long ago learned that protecting a person against the hazards of his own
foibles was a policy of bankruptcy. The expansion of AFDC to protect
clients from the consequences of certain hazards when they make no
effort to avoid such hazards in the first place has resulted in a program of
infinite size and costs. Moreover, it has probably helped dilute individual
inner restraints by letting it be known that regardless of any consequences
third-party funding (AFDC and other public welfare support) will be
provided.

Over and beyond the voluntary factor in the creation of AFDC applicants, a number of other changes have affected AFDC. One such change
involves the effects of technical, medical, and other developments in the
target population. Rein (1966) indicates that as the society develops a
number of processes related to the target group occur. "Selection for
excellence" is the first of the processes. As industrial man (and woman) is
tested for rational productivity by the society and its selectivity mechanisms, some individuals are given opportunities to get ahead in the society. Others, because of their inactivity or failure to get past the selectivity thresholds (tests, class grades, employment interviews, and the like)
or because of their own actions (for example, unmarried motherhood,
juvenile delinquency, and inadequate self-preparation or training), just do
not make progress within the mainstream society. Such persons are excluded from the mainstream or relegated to a realm of marginality, which
minimizes their interaction with the mainstream. For the purposes of this
discussion, it is irrelevant to question the objectivity of the selectivity
thresholds or the standards used for excellence. The effect is the same no

matter what type of selectivity thresholds are used: that is, sizable numbers of individuals are "washed out" of daily interaction without which a person cannot equip himself for advancement in the mainstream of society.

Another factor which Rein (1966) considers important in the process of "making industrial man into the object of rationalized production" is technical progress. As automation proceeds, production increases and the number of factory workers decreases. Efficiency makes the less skillful and the less prepared people superfluous. As the requirements for continued employment are raised to match the needs of an automated society, the chronically unemployed and unemployable become categorized as incompetent in relation to industrial requirements. They are too young, too old, too uneducated, too impatient with social systems, or too inflexible to change with the changing job market. Their primary fault is that they had been inadequately prepared by parents who were themselves dropouts or pushouts from society.

Still another factor that makes people superfluous in the society is medical progress. In earlier times, the poor and the unfortunate who became ill would die. The children of the poor had smaller chances of survival than those of other classes. Our present medical technology and medical service delivery and public health programs keep more people alive. Many of these never make it to the employment marketplace. Millions are kept alive in order to exist in sheltered environments in which the deprived, rejected, handicapped, weak, sick, and drug addicted or disturbed survive longer. If anything, these groups of people have become more dependent than ever. Their chronic condition usually precludes interaction with others in the social mainstream and prevents opportunities for them to improve their lot.

Rein (1966) also lists the labeling process as a cause of increased dependency. He describes "social disservices" which anticipate and prevent trouble by early diagnosis and intensive treatment. These services inform the individual that he has been singled out as a potential dependent, delinquent, or other kind of loser. Potential failures are saddled with the images of actual failures and the program boomerangs. In Rein's words, "labelling increases dependency." Such a process did not occur in earlier public welfare populations because the clients were of a far different mettle. Unlike the transgenerational public assistance client, the person in temporary need came from a long line of work-conditioned, socially involved, self-sufficient people. Public welfare carried a stigma, and the client therefore used it for as short a time as possible. Such a client would more readily reject public welfare than become dependent on it. Several labeling theory researchers, including Steele (1973, 1974, and 1975), indicate that, in the last analysis, labeling is dependent upon the process of self-labeling (also Goffman, pp. 20–21). If the individual is reluctant to accept the label because he has already been immunized against it by preparatory socialization, self-recognition and achievement in other settings (such as in the family), and from past experiences, the client will not be labeled.

Garmzey (1971, 1976) and others have written about "the invulnerables" who do not accept labels of failure despite overwhelming factors. We hypothesize that the success of such people can be attributed to the influence of an effective significant other in their lives who is not necessarily always the parent. Nonetheless, it must be conceded that for persons who are chronically on AFDC and their children, and whose internal defenses have not yet developed because they lack realistic self-worth validation, the problem of labeling must be considered to be unavoidable.

Rein (1966) describes yet another counterproductive process: the usual retraining and remedial program which is ostensibly designed to move people out of unemployability into mainstream employment and involvement. This service has two built-in flaws. When the service is effective in fulfilling its purposes, successes are usually based upon a creaming activity which selects those candidates most likely to benefit from the program. Those with less capability and/or motivation for success are overlooked. The very success of the program and of its graduates ensures that a sizable population will be left behind, and these become the permanent underclass. Where retraining is less effective, the program processes failures who cannot move out and up from dependency. The less successful retraining program reinforces the labeling process for the trainees who conclude that they, or the retraining program, have failed again.

Aside from Rein's indications, we need to consider the very nature of the process of public helping. The young man or woman away from home at college knows full well that every act of support provided by parents also serves as a constraint. People who get help and who have little hope of changing their situation tend to behave in ways that will ensure continued help from the same sources. If evidence of self-sufficiency will reduce the chances of continued assistance, they will avoid the appearance of self-sufficiency. In time, most of their behavior and life-style is shaped by a desire to live as comfortably as possible within the constraints set by the helpers. Thus, for the less competent or for those who perceive themselves to be less competent or excluded, every support becomes a constraint. Such help provides one of the few guidelines which the dependent person perceives clearly. Conversely, the constraints set by the helper become a basis of support for the dependent person. From these constraints, he finally knows what is expected of him and he depends on these guidelines for emotional support in an otherwise bewildering and complex world. Just as the young child both hates the prison of his crib

...ioves it for the protection and security it provides, so the public welfare dependent views public assistance as the most important feature of his life. It provides him with the concurrent support and constraints necessary for his physical, social, and emotional survival (Wishnov, pp. 32–34; Klausner; Rein and Rainwater, p. 23).

According to Henry Aaron (President Carter's key advisor on welfare reform in 1978), the welfare system provides for the clientele "more total income, cash and . . . non-cash (resources and services) than many . . . could earn from regular private or public employment . . . so it is entirely to their advantage . . . that they remain on welfare" (oral response at a welfare symposium). It is therefore quite understandable that the dependent views welfare as a protection against all hazards, both external and self-created. This protection is a form of nonliberating parenting which has a destructive effect on the client and the society: it provides a haven for all who fear failure, competition, personal incompetency, and particularly the discomforts that accompany the constraints of personal development.

The analogy between a baby's crib and emotional security necessarily dissolves at some point in most people's lives. The child almost always outgrows his crib. As his competency grows and as he begins to be more self-sufficient, he learns to climb out of his crib and progresses to the next level of familial support and constraint. Eventually, if his development is successful, he grows beyond the supports and constraints of his family and peer group and becomes relatively independent. This is not the case with the chronic AFDC clientele.

The parent of the young man or woman at college previously referred to usually has some realistic limits on the amount of money he can afford to give. If he maintains his son or daughter at college in a style of living that the child cannot expect to earn after graduation, and if he gives his offspring, consciously or otherwise, reason to believe that this type of help will be eternal, then the son or daughter can be expected to make little or no progress toward graduation and independence. If the student does free himself or herself from dependence on the parent, it will be only because of other influences, such as the examples set by peers and professors at college. Thus, the percentage of college students who remain dependent is relatively small. This same analysis can be applied to welfare clientele. The style of living of the welfare family based on AFDC and other programs is much higher than what they could possibly afford on entry into the unskilled and beginner's labor market, especially after deductions. There is no time limit beyond which welfare will no longer be available. The residual welfare population is surrounded by a subculture that does not expect to achieve self-sufficiency for its members, for their children, or for their grandchildren. It accepts the inevitability of welfare as a way of life.

Still another factor in the problem relates to the parents' and youth's understanding of the social structure and the mechanisms by which a person may advance himself upward by legitimate socioeconomic efforts. Oblata refers to this problem in his discussion of successful middle-class blacks who are ignored by ghetto youth. He states that the black youth no longer dreams, that many young people in the ghetto have been led to believe that easy success and quick money are always near. "All anyone needs is a good 'con' game and a little tough talk." Sooner or later, most ghetto youths find this stance to be not only ineffective but traumatic as well, in terms of advancement in both legitimate and illegitimate activities. Hence, after numerous, ill-fated attempts at a quick grasp at success, many ghetto youth fall into the apathy of living each day as it occurs, aspiring to nothing, making no plans for the future, and making no efforts on their own.

This psychological state is epitomized in a statement by an Urban League representative, Maudine Cooper, about a proposed extra grant of $80 to be given as a tax rebate to taxpayers and as a gift to others. She said that "Eighty dollars . . . won't pay the rent for a person's flophouse. It won't buy some wino his wine. And it won't even pay the busfare for a person to pick up his unemployment compensation, if he qualifies." This kind of subjectivity, which middle-class sympathizers maintain as an eternal truth and as a fatalistic self-fulfilling prophecy, is mirrored in many welfare clients who view themselves and their children as permanent dependents of the state. That the Cooper statement is factually erroneous is obvious. Eighty dollars may pay a major portion of a poor person's rent. It would provide at least 20 gallons of a cheap wine or 5 gallons of an expensive one. It would pay not only busfare to the employment office, but also taxi fare. It might do much more than that. It could provide tools for a semiskilled worker seeking to start his own repair service, or it could provide some other kind of basic opportunity fund for someone seeking to break out of welfare. Oblata expresses his concern for the future of poor black adults and their children who have lost their respect for work and their will to succeed outside of the welfare system or illegitimate enterprises.

Aside from subjectivity and apathy, many residual poor use other mechanisms which are self-defeating and destructive to life opportunities. Liebow, in his article "Fathers Without Children," describes the shallow and unsatisfying life of the unmarried, absent black father. The implications of this pattern for the black population is clearly set out in Jackson's article in *Ebony*, "Where are the Black Men?: Scarcity of Males Upsets the Life Style of [Black] Women." Thus, the alternative stances of apathetic dependence, illegitimate street activity, or escape on the part of black welfare youth are self-defeating and destructive for the future of family life for a major sector of the black population in America.

Similar patterns are beginning to develop among other sectors of the population (Nash).

The residual public welfare client, unlike others, never gains enough self-sufficiency, competency and self-assurance, and realistic aspirations and expectations to challenge the constraints of the system that supports him. Through his own inadequacies, or through the structural nature of public welfare (which provides disincentives for emancipation) or, more likely, through his own inadequacy in interaction with structural public welfare disincentives, he never succeeds in leaving the sanctuary.

Sean O'Casey, in one of his plays about the IRA movement in the Irish liberation movement, discusses why some individuals fail to gain their objectives in the society. He says, "All the world's a stage but some of us are bloody under-rehearsed." In the mainstream society, the public welfare dependents constantly remain on the "don't call us, we'll call you" list because they are under-rehearsed for life in the mainstream. Whether their under-rehearsed condition derives from their own activity or lack of it, or from a lack of opportunity, or more likely both, is not the point. What is important is that in a competitive society, many are not chosen, many are relegated to dependence on public welfare, or many relegate themselves to public welfare. In time, they produce progeny who are even more relegated to public welfare and nonsocial or antisocial activity.

A complex of factors relating to the AFDC population makes it clear that the process of becoming a public dependent is hardly a linear one as it moves through the generations. Goodwin (August 1972) indicates that

welfare mothers [transmit] to their sons a greater tolerance of government support than is found among white middle-class families. To the extent that acceptability discourages work activity, one could argue that mothers are transmitting a negative attitude toward work. . . . [a] lack of confidence orientation [applies] to both welfare mothers and their sons. Mothers . . . hinder their son's entrance into the work force by transmitting their own uncertainty to them (p. 36).

Work is the only possible vehicle for bringing the AFDC boy into contact with a world where he can learn about family stability, self-support, self-assurance, and life as an actor rather than as a welfare object or operator in a ghetto crime jungle. Many factors discourage the welfare child from seeking employment: his mother, the welfare structure, the minimum wage, child labor laws, and school attendance laws. A boy would have to be a moral hero to stand up against such forces and seek more than a marginal entry into the legitimate employer marketplace. Yet, there are hundreds of thousands of boys who do it every year. Hartung (pp. 84–88) describes the "good boy" of the ghetto who makes it when others fail. He finds that such boys are deeply influenced by relatively competent parents or other adults in their life space and by solid nuclear and extended family structures where failure would not be countenanced. Even against the enticements of being dependent on some young public welfare mother, and against the strictures of discrimination and antiwork laws, such a youngster finds his way into the world of work. The saving difference is in the nature of his own self-confidence and competency as a person, which he derives from competent parents and other adults in his life space.

Hamilton provides a clue to the difference between the "good boy" and the boy who doesn't make it. He says that "the welfare problem is the poverty problem but the poverty problem in its most intractable form is not the employment problem; it is the fatherless family problem." Hamilton could be refuted by the data related to residual public dependency found in numbers of ostensibly complete families, but careful study of such families will probably reveal that these fathers might as well be absent for all their effectiveness as fathers in the families. The point is that it takes at least two adults who are equipped with the necessary qualifications or potentialities to rear a competent child; at least one of the two parents must be in constant interaction with the real world of the mainstream and marketplace. If either parent is employed and involved in the society, then the child can be expected to have some knowledge about the outside world, its potential opportunities for him, and the requirements to be made of him. Without this knowledge of the outside, the child's life is circumscribed by the parochial and subjective interests of his mother and neighborhood.

Because of the limitations of the one-parent welfare family as a training ground for life in the real world, Williamson (1974) questions whether it will be possible to provide sufficient welfare and resources "to assure that children of the poor will escape the poverty of their parents to have large families." Census Bureau reports (1974) show that, while the overall number of poor families dropped 4 percent from 1971 to 1972, the number of poor families headed by women rose by 9.1 percent. In the thirteen-year period 1960–1972, the proportion of poor families headed by women rose from 23 to 43 percent. Black families headed by women rose from 33 percent of all poor black families in 1959 to 66 percent in 1972. The Census Bureau stated that "the presence of children appears to be an important factor in . . . the poverty status of families headed by women while it hardly affects the poverty status of those headed by a man" (p. 3).

According to Johnson, nearly one out of every seven families was headed by a woman in 1976. Of this group, one out of every three such families was living below the officially defined poverty level, compared to one out of eighteen husband-wife families in that economic category. There were 7.7 million families headed by women in 1977, or 13.6 percent of all families in the United States. This proportion of female-headed families has grown steadily each year since 1970 when it stood at 10.9 percent of the total. Since 1970, about 60 percent of the increase has been among divorcees.

The number of female-headed families in 1977 was more than five times as large as male-headed, single-parent families in the United States. Female-headed families under the poverty line represented over 4.5 percent of all families in the country. Thus, approximately 3 million female-headed families were believed to be living under the poverty line in 1977 (Johnson, p. 32).

In 1970, there were 6.7 million women with children under eighteen, but by 1977 this number had grown to 9.5 million. Only 3.5 million women were in the labor force in 1970, but this total grew to 5.5 million by 1977 (Johnson, p. 35). By 1978, over half the women with children in the United States were in the labor force (Bell, p. 11).

Hence, two trends are visible. One is an increase in working mothers, and the other is a continued increase in the number of female-headed families, with a sizable increase in those families below the poverty line. Johnson also reports that

there are a disproportionate number of children in the families where the mother neither earned an adequate income nor obtained it from other sources. More than half of the 10 million children living in families with income below the poverty level were in these single-parent homes.

In both 1970 and 1977, 52 percent of children under age eighteen in families headed by women were living below the poverty level. In contrast, only 8.3 percent of the children in intact families were living below the poverty level (p. 37). It is therefore clear that family breakup, which usually leads to female-headed families, also leads to a high probability of poverty-level living and welfare dependency.

Hess points out that the growth of the permanent welfare class is not an accidental phenomenon. Rather, it has derived from a number of factors: (1) All families in the category of AFDC support are kept at a level of marginal subsistence. (2) AFDC families are disrupted by restrictions on fathers in the home. (3) Self-help and economic improvement result in punitive action in the form of deductions from the aid budget (with a few exceptions). (4) The natural and normal sexual drives of the mother for male companionship are frustrated by the constraints of AFDC rules (at least in orientation, if not in fact). (5) All families, by reason of their status, are suspect in relation to their eligibility for AFDC (in terms of possible unreported income or assets). This condition has changed considerably since the self-declaration eligibility process was adopted. (6) All families and their members are deprived of their self-direction and autonomy because they are directed as objects rather than as actors. (7) All families are subject to a stigmatizing public image. They are viewed as dishonest, lazy, immoral, and illiterate. (Here, Hess's unilateral effect view is probably questionable.) All of these conditions, Hess concludes, build up a complex which is antimental health. Hess, of course, arrived at his conclusion in 1964, when a variety of AFDC rules were still enforced.)

Since the late 1960s few research programs on patterns of welfare mother child care have been funded by HEW, and for good reason: too many people were drowned in criticism after the Moynihan report. Ideologues in great number openly charged scholars who focused on the subjects as "racists." There is nothing to indicate that it is not still valid.

Hess compares the communications methods welfare mothers use with their children to those used by other mothers. After careful study, Hess and his colleagues found that mothers who were more optimistic about their chances to improve their own lives and the lives of their children (as compared to welfare mothers) tended to put greater pressure on their children to achieve in school, to have a higher personal-subjective orientation, to monitor their children's communication responses more or to anticipate their needs, and to build up the children's self-assurance and competency. Welfare mothers tended to concentrate on their children's performance of the nonverbal aspects of tasks assigned them, nearly excluding verbalization of their impulses. Whether intentionally or not, their method of child control focused more on coercion than on other means of motivation. As a consequence, they usually succeeded only in repressing their children's overt resistance without changing their lack of cooperation and interest. Because of this lack of verbal communication, even when the mother was interested in her child's getting the most out of school, she was unable to build the child's interest in scholastic success as a means of escaping poverty.

Many mothers unintentionally used socialization methods that had deleterious effects on the child and his expectations for himself. Hess et al. found that a mother's ability to convey positive attitudes toward school and realistic expectations of the child's behavior were more important than other factors in enabling the child to profit from the school experience. Some evidence was found of a correlation between the absence of the father and aimless behavior in children. Hess and his colleagues found that maladaptive attitudes and behavior in welfare children can be seen as learned responses to the environment, deriving primarily from mother-child relationships. These responses become functionally fixed. The problem of eliminating them (so that the child can have a chance for a future) can be viewed as a resocialization rather than socialization problem.

Minuchin et al., in their research on the disorganized and disadvantaged family (pp. 192–243), found many of the same family child rearing patterns which were dealt with by Hess et al. Minuchin and his colleagues found that such families are generally one parent, with the mother in a succession of liasons with unstable father figures. The researchers found that the parents including the "temporary" father form a sub-system often in competition with the sibling sub-system and the peer sub-system. It was revealed that in such families the parent (usually the mother) relinquishes executive functions by either delegation of instrumental roles to a "parental" child or by totally abandoning the family either psychologically or physically. It is the sibling sub-system that takes over as the socialization agent. Communication between the parent and the children finally breaks down and the sibling sub-system undertakes the promotion of opposition expression to parental control (p. 219). The Minuchin researchers studied both black and Puerto Rican families in the category of the disorganized and the disadvantaged. They found a significant feature of the black families in that the grandmother figure so often believed to be the substitute for the missing adult parental figures was often nonexistent. Although the grandmother might be present soon after the birth of a child to a teenage girl the researchers found that she was not a lasting figure in the family constellation. The peripheral male, however, was found to be a constant disturbance to the children's socialization process. In any event the so-called "cooperative collective" of the black extended family and the mother's ghetto friendships were found to be tenuous as a stabilization agent for the children. Much of the time such collectives were found to fail to evolve satisfactory regulating principles for sustaining and revising the interpersonal transactions required by children for productive development. Thus it becomes clear that there are special transgenerational socialization problems to be found in the residual AFDC family for which welfare grants alone would not suffice.

The problems posed by AFDC are unlike those of other assistance programs such as the SSI. The non-AFDC populations do not tend toward geometric growth in number of recipients. They contain few elements that have strong possibilities of hope for behavior change. They usually have had considerable life-experience as participants in the societal mainstream and therefore are not as socially and culturally isolated. They represent neither potential sources of disruptive unrest for the society nor huge manpower reservoirs for manning criminal or other antisocial activity, both organized and independent. Finally, they seem to have a more organized and purposeful life-style than does the AFDC. Unlike the AFDC residual population, they seem to have fewer crises in daily life and are less beset by multiproblems.

While the SSI may have relegated the aged, disabled, and blind to financially unproductive lines, by and large, their children are not affected by their current nonwork status. This is hardly the case with AFDC families.

It would be useful to examine some of the built-in concomitants of AFDC regulations in order to determine their effects upon the clientele. Among these concomitants are stigma, lesser eligibility of able-bodied males, restricted family budgets, the means test, and work disincentives.

Stigma has been an integral part of poor law since the 1800s. The Elizabethan Poor Law and the local overseeing of the indolent carried with them a consistent adherence to the Protestant Ethic view of welfare man (Segalman). Public welfare stigma had a number of societally desired effects. It made welfare so uncomfortable that clients sought relief from its onus as soon as they could find other resources. Many of those who were eligible often avoided welfare because of the discomfort of stigma. Stigma made possible a continually available supply of unskilled labor which was necessary during the early years of industrial growth in the United States.

Conditions have changed but stigma remains. For the family that is temporarily in need, stigma tends to keep them away from the welfare office if they can possibly survive without it, or to drop out of the welfare system as soon as it can be managed. For the family that cannot avoid the welfare office and the welfare trap, stigma apparently has a reverse effect —locking into the welfare system a family that would otherwise want out. To a considerable extent, the curvilinear effects of stigma and other welfare mechanisms are probably reflected in the growth in numbers of those who have become residual welfare dependents.

Over the years, most of the states have limited AFDC to families without able-bodied males. The reluctance of males to see their families starve while they remain at home has probably speeded their departure by the mechanism of what has been described as the poor man's divorce (desertion). Still another frequent condition is what Banfield describes as fiscal abandonment, a process whereby the husband (father) plays absent while still remaining at home, and thus the family enjoys part of his wage plus the AFDC grant. Still another pattern, one that cannot even be described as desertion, occurs when a man leaves a family he has only informally joined without enduring commitments. The problem is complicated further by the reluctance of many poor women to submit to legal marriages that are difficult and expensive to dissolve after a man has deserted. The conventional culturally defined masculine role in the family is hardly congruent with house and child care while the woman of the family works for wages that are too low to be offered to male heads of families. Thus, the tired wife need return home to find a neglected mess only a few times before she expresses her rejection of the man as useless and as a barrier to the family's welfare eligibility. Under such circumstances, men can be expected to leave, only to join other families and to propagate additional children for families that have lost their own family heads. An example of the effect of this pattern is seen in reports of the National Center for

Social Statistics, Office of Research and Statistics, HEW. In long-term poverty families, the cultural devaluation of the position of an unemployed male head of family has made the father somewhat less than fully welcome at home. Information on the constituency of families on AFDC also supports the view that the AFDC mechanism hastens the breakup of families and serves as a locus for broken or never-completed families.

The HEW reports indicate a 550-percent growth in the number of children in the father absent category from 1950 to 1969. By 1977, this category accounted for 83.3 percent of all AFDC cases (Social Security Administration, *Chartbook*, p. 7). This population grouping may be viewed as the locus of the concern of welfare revision. It provides two aspects for concern: an index of expansion of the population locked into the welfare nexus, and an indication of what may occur with other families unable to prevent the slide into the welfare nexus.

One might hypothesize that the combination of public assistance regulations, administration, and the patterns of child conception and socialization among families in poverty results in a continued distillation out of poverty of families that retain their male heads. One might also hypothesize that the combination of contemporary employment hiring and retention patterns, external racial barriers, internal withdrawal barriers, and the like produce a growing pool of nonwhite female-headed families which permit a few individuals to escape but "distill" the remainder in an expanding, self-perpetuating subculture of deviance.

Restrictions on the welfare budgets allowed to AFDC families also have a counterproductive effect on long-term clients. For the family temporarily aided by AFDC or General Assistance, the possibility still remains that some family resources, either material or social-psychological in nature, may be drawn upon to help the family survive and perhaps scratch their way out of poverty. For such a family, members of the extended family, friends, and even past employers and creditors can be approached for special help. This kind of aid, as well as the momentum and experience of past achievements in dealing with life's problems, makes it possible for family members to complete their education, seek out retraining and new employment, maintain their children's immunizations, avoid late payment penalties, prevent falling further into financial difficulty, and maintain the nutritional levels and health conditions necessary to avoid illness and deterioration. Thus, a limited family grant may not do much harm to a family's cohesiveness, stability, and health during a limited period on AFDC. Through restricted budgets, the welfare authorities assure the dropping of welfare as soon as employment takes place if such employment pays more than a budget designed on the principle of lesser eligibility. The limited budget also assures the lowest possible costs to society.

For the family with many children, however, and for the family that has been on AFDC for more than a few years, this minimum budget becomes a problem budget. According to Stone and Schlamp (1967):

In the case of short-time aid families, economic, social-psychological and health handicaps combine in a feedback cycle to reduce the family's capacity to cope with crisis. The result is a resort to welfare dependency. The husbands . . . show a strong capacity to respond to employment opportunities, though they may well return to welfare status again if overwhelmed by crisis. . . . The longtime welfare cases are subject to a second feedback cycle that erodes away the husband's self-conception as a breadwinner . . . [and his] capacity to respond to employment opportunities (p. 2 of Abstract).

The limited budget is, of course, not so limited in the case of families with large numbers of children. In many such instances, a man who is employed even at skilled wages cannot earn as much as he would receive in a welfare budget. Many welfare clients have been unable to accept employment without having to accept a concomitant cut in income and a rather disastrous cut in available family support. Families with low budgets and little financial management capabilities spend a disproportionate amount on food and other household items. The food that is purchased is usually bought on the basis of impulse rather than planning. Thus the family usually buys a disproportionate amount of frozen dinners and "junk foods," high in carbohydrates and low in proteins and other necessary nutrients. For such families this can become a nutritutional problem, particularly for pregnant women. Children who have inadequate protein intake during the fetal and infant stages constitute a population-at-risk for somatically induced mental retardation.

Stone and Schlamp (1967) found that long-time welfare cases showed less stability on the job and lower skill levels: "A persistent pattern of withdrawal from relatives and friends was manifested, . . . a higher percent having illnesses which interfered with working and a higher degree of alienation and psychological dependency. . . " (p. 2, Abstract).

When a wage-earner does secure a job, the wages are usually deducted from the welfare grant (except where employment is thirty hours or more per week, in which case the family is usually no longer eligible for welfare). This disincentive for employment also has its roots in Elizabethan Poor Law policy. In the short run, this policy minimizes government expenditures for the poor. In the long run, however, lack of recent work experience provides a further handicap for reemployment and deprives the children in the family of an employment role-model. The employment disincentive therefore ensures that welfare as a way of life will be the only role-model available to the upcoming generations. The combined factors of race, matriarchal familial history, stigma, work disincentives, lack of suitable alternative child-care facilities, less welfare eligibility for males, and time are producing a fast-multiplying population that is deeply deprived culturally. This population is excluded from operative realities and from mechanisms for utilization of opportunities provided by education and employment available to other populations in terms of treatment and prevention of physical, social, and emotional difficulties.

Work Incentive Program (WIN)

Related to the AFDC program and serving as an adjunct to it is the Work Incentive program (WIN) which was established in 1967 to provide job training and jobs for adult recipients, including mothers (Feagin, p. 64). Allen states that the WIN program was established "to remove large numbers from the welfare rolls [because there was] no built-in guarantee of permanent, well-paid work at the end of the training period, it was necessary to establish some coercive aspects . . . such as categorizing some recipients as 'mandatory registrants'" (p. 37).

Out of 3 million people eligible in 1971, only 300,000 were trained, and of these 300,000, 20 percent secured employment (Allen, pp. 37–38). By 1977, out of approximately 3.6 million adults in the program, about 270,000 persons were placed in unsubsidized jobs after training and intensive employment services, but no data were reported on the number of trainees who remained on the job after placement (Budget, p. 123). Along with training, child care and other services necessary for training and employment are provided for those in the WIN program. Feagin indicates that the problem in finding dependable employment for welfare mothers can be traced to the nature of current labor demand in the local economy. He also indicates that the extent of unemployment generally and the attitudes of employers to accept trainees for better paying jobs all affect the level of success in employment of welfare mothers. Allen (p. 65) and Harrison (p. 143) also underline the fact that employers who need skilled persons will not hire the poor regardless of their training and that marginal employers who have no pressing need for skilled labor will hire the poor regardless of whether they have had training or not. This conclusion is unconvincing when we examine the number of AFDC mothers reported to be employed in such secondary employment. The reasons for limited employment of WIN trainees can probably be found elsewhere: (1) in the quality of training and job readiness; and (2) in the motivation to accept the demands of full-time regular employment at the cost of other, greater benefits (loss of AFDC, food stamps, and Medicaid).

Maynard, Garfinkel, and Leach assert that the failure of the WIN program to substantially reduce caseloads is due largely to the program's failure to provide jobs to large portions of the eligible population. They also indicate, however, that the incentives aspects of the program, including the earnings, disregards the tax rate, and even if the clients were to find employment, would result in a large number of individuals eligible for assistance while still employed.

Still another group of researchers, Mildred Rein and Barbara Wishnov (p. 11) reported in 1971 that they found a small group of AFDC families that use welfare assistance continually. They found a larger group that rotates on and off the program. In their view there are certain incentive benefits, such as food stamps, Medicaid, and welfare which make welfare competitive with work. Because of this they found that the incentive system has made it even more difficult for recipients to move from welfare to work. During their period of study (1967–1971), case closings did not increase, despite the efforts of the WIN program and other mechanisms.

Any effort to obtain employment for public welfare mothers, Rein and Wishnov report, will have to assure wages that compete with welfare. If it is to succeed with this clientele, the work must be sufficiently regular, steady, and remunerative to override the secondary benefits of welfare. Rein and Wishnov do not, however, suggest how this could be made possible without disturbing the rest of the job marketplace.

The problem of welfare benefits versus work is borne out by Abrahamse, et al. (p. 131), who indicate that for the family group caseload on AFDC, "our findings imply that employment fluctuations account for a much smaller portion of caseload movement than the combined effects of population and family status variables." In a study of the lives of AFDC women, Klausner also found that motherhood was more attractive as a full-time occupation and fulfillment than potential employment in the decision-making process about work or welfare, even after training. The focus of the lives of such women is neither employment, nor self-sufficiency, nor husbands current or potential.

With welfare women receiving about three-fourths of their income from welfare and with welfare grants, food stamps, medical care, and other benefits available on a rather dependable and steady basis, and with no income tax deduction on the total of such benefits, it becomes obvious that an AFDC mother would have to act against her own and her children's best interests to undertake the extra costs of regular employment (day care costs, transportation costs, work clothing costs, and so forth) in order to earn less take-home pay. The psychic reward of self-sufficiency is offset by the fear of not being able to compete on the job and of not being able to get back on welfare again. This condition has also been reported by Hausman and Durbon.

Klausner's longitudinal study arrived at a number of useful conclusions. He found that husbandless mothers can be divided into two groups on the basis of their commitment to a traditionalist or modernizing life-style. The modernists use their own resources (and also WIN to some extent) to become self-sufficient, even if their beginning wage is less than what their total welfare benefits would provide. The traditionalists tend to use AFDC as a husband-surrogate and not to elect to undergo WIN training and placement.

His study also concluded that the absence of the father depresses the children's level of achievement. As for women, higher levels of education do not translate directly into higher levels of earning. The higher earnings of the better educated result from working more. A high school or vocational training diploma does not influence later job success unless it is followed by labor force participation. Involvement in work for AFDC women has an antinatal effect, and the anticipation of a larger family (or extended motherhood) is associated with a decline in (or barrier to) efforts for economic independence.

According to Klausner, the greater their father's authority in the household, the more likely the sons are to advance socioeconomically. The major factor for generating success, employment, and income among whites is the father's occupation and for blacks amount of education. For men, a delay in marriage and fatherhood is conducive to socioeconomic success. Women who marry early report more marital conflict, more fighting over adultery, more sexual problems, and more alcoholism and drug problems.

AFDC women, Klausner states, do not constitute a community but rather an aggregate of several social types. These include social outcasts —those banished from the regular social stratification system; unemployed proletarians—those who are impoverished [usually temporarily] because of a fault in the social system of production, and the abandoned dependents—persons who are affected by desertion, divorce, and the like, and who do not have the equipment (social, psychological, physical, or otherwise) to become self-sufficient.

Poverty is often only one of the facets of the failure of families. In Klausner's opinion, poverty is less a scientific than an ideological term (pp. VIII–IX). He believes that it is not sufficient to increase the skill level of the clientele in order to increase the attractiveness of such workers to employers. Wider socialization policies and measures to increase the motivation of the clientele for work are necessary if employment efforts are to become effective.

Wishnov supports Klausner's conclusions on the AFDC work-welfare choice dynamics. She found that many of the AFDC mothers view welfare as "more than just a source of income"; rather, they regard it as a "substitute husband." For those women (see Klausner's traditionally oriented group), "self-respect was more closely linked to home and family" than to a job, especially for women who had never been productively employed in the past. She concluded that a "considerable number of the women had no intent to get off welfare . . . [and] were quite satisfied with their status" (p. 32). Wishnov believes that AFDC "provides the security of a stable income [and] may provide greater financial and emotional security than does an employed husband." When the man leaves, the woman's identity continues and she becomes more secure as a home-maker, home manager, and mother. Welfare is presumably a rival to the husband in that it is a nonjealous, nondemanding, consistently providing spouse who requires few interactive relationships and few or no compro-mises on the part of the wife. The AFDC mother may therefore "perceive her options with regard to child care as if she were married. . . . She does not feel compelled to go to work . . . [if such work] would interfere with [her desired maternal activities]." The AFDC welfare-oriented mother attaches little stigma to welfare since it provides her with the wherewithal to define her role more freely than if she were accountable to a spouse. For her relatives and friends as well, welfare is not seen as stigmatizing, and her desire not to go to work is applauded as good for the children (pp. 33–35).

Rein and Rainwater found that "short term users [of welfare] are a smaller proportion of the ever-welfare population" (p. 16). Goodwin (1972) verifies that "women who find welfare most acceptable tend to show the lowest work activity." "The picture [which] emerges is one of black welfare women who want to work but who, because of continuing failure in the work world, tend to become more accepting of welfare and less inclined to try again" (p. 113). Thus, one gets a picture of women who would rather fall back on what they can do more easily (motherhood and homemaking) than try that which the mainstream society expects of its self-supporting participants. It would probably be futile to explain to such a mother that by electing for continued welfare dependency she is depriving her children of improved life-chances. The effect of welfare on such families has apparently been similar to that of hard narcotics in that the person affected has almost no interest or incentive to become inde-pendent because dependency is less threatening and much more gratifying.

Lyon, et al. in August 1976 and in December 1975 found similar welfare dependency conditions. Patterns of welfare dependency also similar to those of Klausner, Wishnov, and Rein and Rainwater are reported by Rydell, Palmerio, Blais, and Brown in that "cases tend to become in-creasingly dependent on welfare the longer they stay on it" (p. xi). Lyon, Rydell, and Menchick arrived at similar conclusions during research in 1967–1972 on cases continuously on welfare three or more years. Lyons et al. (1975) also indicate that "welfare cases become increasingly dependent on welfare the longer they stay on" (p. xi). Smith found support for the Klausner and Wishnov studies of AFDC work-welfare choice in his finding that children under seven seem to decrease the family's chances for savings and upward mobility by decreasing the mother's opportunities in the job market.

For the residual AFDC mother, it is therefore irrelevant to discuss Levinson's findings that, nationally, the employment potential of recipients, as measured by educational and occupational attainment, increased from 1961 to 1968. What is relevant for this group is that social and emotional factors are much more powerful in the work-welfare choice and that the problem requires careful scientific analysis and treatment if it is not to become a deep and ubiquitous pattern in society. It is relevant, and perhaps even urgent, that studies be conducted to determine if the United States wants such a residual welfare population and, if not, how the social and emotional pulls of the mother long dependent on AFDC can be reconciled with the needs of the society for more skilled participants and self-sufficient workers. This issue cannot be viewed in a vacuum; rather, it must be seen in the context of such problems as a rising inflation rate and the related economic problems of the society.

AFDC and Grant Size

Still another problem in AFDC relates to the variance in grant size among the states. In 1977, for example, the states (or commonwealths) of Alabama, Georgia, Louisiana, Puerto Rico, Tennessee, and Texas gave the following average grants for each individual: $37.01, $35.42, $36.23, $11.17, $36.18, and $32.54, respectively. In that same year, the states of Alaska, California, Hawaii, and New York gave grants that averaged per individual as follows: $111.62, $100.27, $113.08, and $114.41, respectively (Office of Research and Statistics, Note No. 10). Although one might make an allowance for differences in living costs between Alaska and Hawaii and the mainland (25 percent higher), it still does not explain the discrepancy in size of grants between New York or California and the low-grant states. New York's and California's grants averaged about 350 percent larger than those of the first group of states listed here. (Because of this large size as well as the large number of AFDC recipients who have settled in these two states, New York and California in October 1978 accounted for 31 percent of AFDC payments to recipients [public assistance statistics].)

In 1977, then HEW Secretary Joseph Califano reported that in twenty-four states the combined benefits received from the AFDC and Food Stamp programs that year provided a family with a total income 25 percent below the official poverty line. But the General Accounting Office

(GAO) study quoted by former Congressman Martha Griffith indicated that in six areas of the country "a woman with three children who could connect herself with five benefit programs (AFDC, food stamps, limited medicaid, etc.) was in fact getting more in benefits than the average woman could earn in the cities of the survey area." Griffith reported that about 20 percent of the women were drawing all five benefits (p. 49). Califano, in his special HEW report on welfare reform, also indicated that 28 percent used four benefits and 43 percent three benefits.

Former Congresswoman Griffith rejected the notion that payments made by California (and presumably New York) are larger because it is more expensive to live in California than elsewhere. She said, "Let me dispel that right now! There is a greater difference in the cost of living within a state than there is between states. There is no excuse for changing the amount paid because you live in New York as opposed to Podunk!" (p. 48).

According to Griffith, the number of recipients in these states is probably indicative more of the size of grants than of the state population size. In New York in 1977, there were 374,000 AFDC grantees and in California, 477,000. The low-grant states previously listed showed grantee populations of 56,000, 85,079, 65,000, 43,000, 63,000, and 97,000, respectively. The total AFDC expenditures for California and New York were $1.7 billion each, and these two states made up more than one-third of the total national expenditure for AFDC (Office of Research and Statistics, Note No. 10).

The disparity in rates between states is a severe problem in terms of both policy and administration. A nationalization of AFDC with more uniform grant sizes might stem movement to the preferred states and might encourage AFDC families to find, return to, and/or remain in localities where living costs are lower, especially if such areas offer familial, community, and other supports and opportunities for the AFDC families. For example, the fact that many of the AFDC recipients are racial minorities and that many of the small southern communities are now less segregated, especially in regard to schooling, might provide the children in such families with increased opportunities to learn about the mainstream and eventually to join it.

Aside from the internal aspects of life in the AFDC family, there are other flaws in the program. Among the most difficult is the problem of coordinating its administration. In the special HEW report, Califano lists 9 executive agencies, 21 congressional committees, 54 state and territories involving 54 legislatures and 54 state or territorial departments, and over 3,000 local welfare agencies.

Unlike the administration of the new SSI program, that of AFDC differs from state to state. In some states, the cities or counties are responsible for clarifying the eligibility of welfare applicants, calculating the payments to be made, processing the payments, overseeing the client group, administrating the operations, and processing federal and state payments. In other states, the entire operation is administered by the state, and neither municipality nor county is involved. All states establish standards for operation that are proportedly in line with federal statutes and administrative regulations of the Welfare Administration of HEW. Generally, it is HEW's responsibility to ensure that the states operate the program as honestly, competently, and nonpolitically as possible within the built-in structural constraints of the system. For its part, HEW must ensure that the program operates throughout the state and that state (and, where applicable, local) contributions are actually made in the construction of matching grants. It is also up to HEW to enforce other constraints on the states. These constraints include a merit system for all welfare employees, supervision or administration by a single state agency, and availability of grants to all state residents. No unduly restrictive residence requirements may be imposed. HEW also has responsibility for policing the grants to ensure that aid is given only to those in need (enforcement of the means test) and that all applicants are given fair hearings, opportunities for appeal, and prompt service.

According to Weinberger, the administration of welfare, particularly AFDC, to the degree that such administration is directed from HEW, is dichotomous. That is, its original intent, as "aid for the needy while they are in need," has been redesigned and redirected in recent years as if it were "a permanent government-ordered attempt to redistribute income from those who have earned it, or inherited it, or both, to those who have not" (p. 2). Weinberger states that the federal government never made an official decision to drop the original aid purpose of welfare and to adopt a policy of income transfer of money from rich to poor and thus move toward income equalization for all. There was no debate on the subject, no vote, but "by steady and rapid additions to existing programs," by policy decisions, and by a variety of formulated regulations or interpretations of regulations, the income transfer purpose has been formed out of what was a more limited original purpose for welfare. With such a dichotomous administrative orientation, the direction and leadership from Washington have been less than effective, especially in states other than California and New York where the aid purpose generally prevails.

Welfare and Grant Structure

Weinberger also indicates that the structural separation of welfare and employment services hampers the administration of welfare. This occurs because the AFDC programs in each state's welfare department relate directly to a division of HEW, and the employment placement programs that are proportedly needed to serve the welfare clientele are related to the labor departments in most states and these state labor departments are related to a division of the U.S. Department of Labor. Thus, the coordination of employment referral and placement of welfare clients at best becomes a paper transfer between state or local agencies, neither of which is responsible for ensuring that the purposes of employment referral are carried out. Similarly, the direction and leadership of state agencies by the appropriate division of HEW and the U.S. Department of Labor are usually less than effective for welfare client placement purposes.

Needs standards are variously defined in the states; the result is a variety of different-sized grants. The definition of resource and income limits and how these are calculated also differs, often incidentally, from state to state. In most states, the procedures and regulations are complex. Issues such as the work requirement and school attendance for welfare children are differentially interpreted in each state and contained within its body of implementing regulations and procedures (Weinberger, pp. 7–10).

Administration is also made more complex by legal constraints which have, for the most part, been spelled out by a variety of state and federal court decisions (Brieland and Lemmon, pp. 67–88). Among the issues resolved by the courts are those relating to the discouragement of immorality and illegitimacy by disqualification of applicant children, the disqualification of substitute fathers, the authority of county or state authorities to inspect client homes without notice or consent, the requirement of a residency or waiting period for AFDC, the authority of public welfare to establish or enforce a work requirement if these conflict with state law, the eligibility of unborn children, and the responsibility of a state or local program to operate uniformly (regardless of therapeutic purposes intended in dealing with one recipient differently than another) (pp. 554–97). In each of these instances, the courts decided in behalf of the beneficiary. The result has been a veritable explosion of the right to welfare without any reference to the client's responsibility to carry out the duties that all parents should perform in preparing their children to be mainstream participants. Thus, from a legal or authority viewpoint, a welfare administration, local, state, and national, is quite unable to focus on or enforce any rehabilitative requirements. By and large, if rehabilitation is to occur, it can come about only if the client so directs himself, or only if the public agency is able to counsel the client into setting the necessary constraints upon himself.

We have discussed the myriad patterns of state and national regulations as amended by court decisions, as well as differential national and state directions. Over and beyond these are the regulations and established procedures of the various local or county administrative boards governed by the local board of supervisors or an equivalent body. Thus, the management of a public welfare agency, which is ostensibly mandated to rehabilitate dependent clients, is instead bound by a complexity of constraints that make the more limited goal of mere operation a very difficult matter.

(ELIGIBILITY

A key issue in administration relates to the process for determining eligibility. Prior to 1969, AFDC clients were cleared for eligibility by public welfare workers, who also worked out the client's budget entitlement and provided social services for clients with problems and special requests. Under pressure from the social service professionals to reorganize AFDC administration (MacLatchie), the plan was revised. Social services are now provided by the public welfare workers, as distinguished from eligibility workers.

(Applications are based upon the client's self-declaration, aided and checked by an eligibility worker, who is often an indigenous worker or former welfare client. Under the revised plan, a number of employment opportunities opened up for AFDC clients and for unemployed persons with limited education. The eligibility workers, with backgrounds similar to those of the clientele, are presumably better able to understand the problems and life-style of AFDC clients and to communicate with them. One assumption underlying this plan was that the eligibility worker whose social distance from the clients would be less than that of the public welfare worker might seem less like a policeman and more like a helper to the clients. Another assumption was that the public welfare worker, when relieved of responsibility for administering a caseload, might be able to spend more time helping clients with social services. The eligibility worker is supposed to review his caseload periodically and to refer clients with problems to public welfare workers. In the past, when public welfare workers handled eligibility, caseload administration, and social services, eligibility and caseload administration took up so much time that there was little time left for social services and rehabilitation. In January 1969, HEW permitted the states to reorganize under the new plan. States now had the option to use either method. By the early 1970s, almost all of the states had adopted the new plan.

(The simplified method for determining eligibility for AFDC involves decision-making based upon unverified information derived from a form completed by the client. A spot check of cases is conducted regularly, but the clients' applications are not delayed for prior verification. A study by the comptroller general in 1971 indicated that "there was not a great deal of difference between the verifications made under the simplified methods and the traditional methods," except that a check of eligibility at the time showed that under the simplified method the rate of incorrect approvals for ineligible clients was found to be high.

The self-declaration or simplified method of establishing eligibility for welfare was based on the theory that what works for most taxpayers in their use of income tax forms should work equally as well for welfare applicants. Banfield challenges this position, maintaining that the two populations differ considerably. Some taxpayers may report the facts in a manner that is more economically advantageous to themselves, but most, realizing the high probability of being checked on and verified, are careful not to lie. Welfare applicants, on the other hand, know that the probability of a careful check is very small and that, even if it does occur, the probability of being held responsible in a court is very remote. At any rate, they feel that whatever might happen is too far off in the future to cause any concern in the present. In addition, most welfare applicants have informal help in completing such self-declarations, usually some community worker who is neither identified on the forms nor responsible for his actions. No judge can be expected to assign blame to a welfare applicant who pleads ignorance when the form was completed by someone else. The welfare client, unlike the taxpayer, is almost never held to have committed eligibility errors if he presents himself as ignorant and helpless. Only in the case of the informed and competent-appearing welfare fraud are penalties actually enforced.

An example of how this change in procedures has affected the integrity of the means test (which in turn exists to conserve government finances) was reported in the *New York Times* in 1977. An audit of the New York City welfare mechanism indicated that 90 percent of the welfare recipients who got married failed to report the marriages. Because these marriages made them no longer dependent, they "were fraudulently collecting relief payments totaling 24 million dollars a year." This represented about 6,600 AFDC women per year. Thus, about 21,000 women and children "were illegally on public assistance rolls" (*New York Times*, p. 37).

Similar problems relating to employment in non-Social Security-covered jobs, income from other sources, and gifts are not usually traced because these items are not generally recorded and audited. This type of fraud is perpetrated not by the few, but by a sizable proportion of the beneficiary population. The fiscal 1976 report of the National Center for Social Statistics on Fraud dispositions of HEW indicates that there were over 166,000 reported cases of possible fraud compared to about 144,000 such cases in 1975 and about 111,000 in 1974. About 41,000, or 47 percent, were referred to law enforcement officials, and some 29,000 were disposed of by reimbursement or other action. An increasing number of states have introduced quality control methods to detect and reduce both fraud and errors. According to the report on welfare fraud cases, the courts tend to give welfare recipients the benefit of a doubt when recipients use such excuses that they were not aware they were supposed to report income.

California, Pennsylvania, and New York had the greatest number of AFDC fraud dispositions in 1976, as in past years, accounting for 60 percent of the national total. Six other states—Arkansas, Colorado, Connecticut, Maine, New Hampshire, and Wisconsin—regularly refer for prosecution 100 percent of all fraud cases found in their programs.

Other studies, including a staff study prepared for the Subcommittee on Fiscal Policy of the Joint Economic Committee of the U.S. Congress on December 31, 1972, on the subject of welfare administration, found that many of the purposes of the plan to separate eligibility from services were not fulfilled. Confusion, chronic understaffing, errors, and uncontrolled fraud were found to be pervasive in public welfare administration. It was also found that AFDC clients had no more liking for the new eligibility workers than they had for the earlier public welfare workers. Clients made less use of social services under the new plan, either because eligibility workers were not interested enough to make referrals or because AFDC clients no longer needed to put their requests for extra financial assistance in a social service context in order to deal with eligibility workers. As a result, AFDC's reputation as a rehabilitation agency has suffered, and any opportunity for rehabilitation to be aggressively offered to welfare clients has been eliminated. For a passive population, passively offered behavioral change services have little effectiveness.

The AFDC administration has had persistent problems with errors in eligibility and budget fraud calculations (Staff Report No. 15, p. 8). For a time, the AFDC administration sought to penalize state administrations by limiting funds for those states that had exceeded announced error norms. When the courts ruled out these mechanisms, the AFDC administration attempted to improve eligibility and caseload administration by educational efforts directed toward eligibility workers. Aaron H. Goldstein's booklet, *Interviewing for Eligibility Determination*, and Benjamin Winslow's book, *Wage Record Clearance Systems*, are examples of this effort. The federal government pays approximately half of the states' administrative costs and a larger proportion for special services provided by the state welfare programs, as authorized by law.

The AFDC program does not cover people in poverty unless there are minor children in the home. It does not cover families in which both parents are present unless the father is physically handicapped or otherwise unable to work. An exception is made in some of the states that operate a very limited program of AFDC-U (unemployed fathers). Thus,

AFDC does not cover all who are in need; in many states, it also fails to cover the full needs of those it accepts for grants. Generally, the amount of assistance to be given is supposed to equal the difference between the income of the applicant and the amount required to meet an authorized budget which would keep the family at subsistence levels and which would meet only the most urgent needs. In some states, even the authorized budget is subject to a percentage deduction because the allocated state matching funds available are limited.

We have already discussed the matter of multiple benefits in relation to the welfare-work choice made by AFDC women. In 1973, a staff study on the incidence of multiple benefits and the issues raised by their receipt was released. This report indicated (p. 2) that the great number of overlapping assistance programs appreciably aggravated other faults in the AFDC system. Work incentive legislation was made ineffective by multiple benefits. The report states that "any disincentives for recipients to work which are caused by the design of one program are almost always worsened when additional benefits are available to those same recipients under other programs."

Another area of legislative concern, family stability, has been disturbed by multiple benefits. The report states that "other financial incentives, which may prompt such behavior as family splitting and which grew out of program design are . . . magnified by benefit combinations." Still another legislative intent relates to levels of income adequacy. As the report indicates:

Overlaps among programs may result in income levels . . . in some areas that [are] overly generous but the same combination of programs still leaves recipients poverty-stricken in other areas. Multiple benefits also multiply administrative errors. . . . the costs of inefficiency and error in one program [are] multiplied through [a] link in eligibility rules and other administrative procedures among different programs.

Still another effect of multiple benefits is the variety of treatment given clients based on personal characteristics. In this regard, the report states that "the differential provisions of individual programs with respect to such eligibility factors of age, sex of [the] family head, place and type of employment and family size [can] be intensified by other programs with similar provisions." Multiple benefits also exacerbate program inefficiency. The report states that "program interrelationships often serve to undo the intent of Congress in passing legislation for a single program." As an example, the report cites the increased benefits to one program which only result in a dollar-for-dollar substitution for other benefits, thereby producing no net gain to some of the intended beneficiaries.

Finally, multiple benefits aggravate administrative problems. The maintenance of eligibility for a series of benefits for the same beneficiaries increases the workload involved in assistance distribution and in agency audit procedures. It requires applicants and recipients to deal with many physically separate bureaucracies, whose offices may be many miles from each other.

Another more recent staff study on welfare benefits (Paper No. 15, pp. 6, 7, 8) has determined that multiple benefits result in large disincentives for work, considerable encouragement for motherhood, and family breakups. Lawrence and Leeds have completed *An Inventory of Federal Income Transfer Programs* for fiscal year 1977 which lists 182 programs accounting for an annual expenditure of $250 billion in fiscal 1977. This total, of course, includes the social insurance programs which are entirely offset by payroll payments; even so, sizable multiple benefits remain open to the welfare client. Of these, seventeen are cash and in-kind programs, seven are cash and other programs, and three are credit and in-kind programs. Of the forty-one programs conditioned on need representing $41 billion, 42 percent are paid in cash, 55 percent are paid in-kind, and 3 percent are granted in the form of tax relief.

Advocates for the poor often raise the question of why one should resist multiple benefits for the poor when so many multiple benefits already exist in the tax structure for the middle class and the rich. One answer is that such special arrangements should not be available to anyone, and because they promote dependency, they should particularly not be available to the poor. Yet another argument that could be made against multiple benefits for the poor is that such benefits are unearned by the poor, while benefits for the middle class are merely deductions on taxes on the money that have already earned, and it is merely a matter of letting them keep more of their own earnings. Other arguments can be made that most tax deductions exist because they provide an incentive for some action made in behalf of the common community good.

Social Costs of Welfare

Banfield (pp. 93–94) considers such benefits from the viewpoint of their social cost to the society and the welfare recipient. In his opinion, the undesirable side-effects of welfare are reason enough to be wary of it in its present form. One of these side-effects is that the welfare system causes the breakup of families since the funds are available only to fatherless families. Thus, fathers leave willingly for the sake of the family, or are eased or kicked out. The welfare system also removes any material incentive for a pregnant girl to seek marriage with the father of her unborn child. Another side-effect is that the available benefits enable many people who should work to escape it. Banfield is not, in this sense, thinking of mothers with young children. He is instead referring to the men who, without welfare, would be supporting the women and children but who are relieved by welfare of the necessity of work. Those who do work probably work only enough to support themselves according to the standards of a street-corner society. The welfare system deters people from moving to places where their opportunities would be better and where the costs of supporting them would be less. In addition it offers a sizable incentive for wholesale lying and cheating. Finally, welfare benefits promote a view of the society at all social stratification levels which is unjust and chaotic. As such, it promotes a short-sighted disorganized orientation to living for all who come in contact with it.

Banfield maintains that no one knows how many fiscal abandonments of families are actually being carried out in welfare families, where the husband (or common-law husband and father) is still in the home but is merely reported as absent. The lower class black family exhibits a certain pattern relating to income, as reported by Rainwater and quoted by Banfield (p. 97). If the wife works, she and her spouse treat her earnings not as family income but as "yours" or "mine." When a family is on welfare, the probability is that the welfare check is treated as "her" money and the husband's earnings are "his." There is little likelihood that much of his earnings will enter into supporting the family, and there is no material incentive for him to be retained in the home or for his authority as husband and father to have any effect. From this explanation by Banfield, one may conclude that welfare benefits have a strong side-effect, probably unintended, in creating a large matriarchal underclass.

Moynihan (1968) also expresses concern for the social costs of welfare. "[T]he present welfare system," he states, "is serving to maintain the poorest groups in society in a position of impotent fury—impotent because the system destroys the potential of individuals and families to improve themselves—fury because it claims to do otherwise" (p. 22). Multiple benefits, when they include AFDC, Medicaid, food stamps, and public housing, can provide an attractive aid package for an otherwise resourceless woman and her children.

On the matter of multiple benefits and family breakup, Staff Study No. 15 indicates that AFDC assistance alone is sufficient to "establish large incentives for low income families to break up or to never form in the first place. If a woman with children on AFDC does marry, the incentive is for the stepfather to refuse any obligation to support her children, thereby keeping them on AFDC" (pp. 6, 7). This effect is even more apparent when food stamps, public housing, and other public assistance benefits are calculated into the analysis.

The report also suggests that AFDC provides "a sizable financial incentive for a woman to have her first child in order to receive AFDC and Medicaid benefits." This financial gain from increased AFDC grants for married couples follows a similar pattern, but the gains for couples are lower than for single-parent households, especially in states with no AFDC-U program. The offset of benefits serving as a financial incentive, or at least as a nondeterrent for additional children, is even more apparent when food stamps, public housing, and other assistance programs are totaled.

On the matter of work incentives, the report makes the following observation:

[T]he return from working is measured by subtracting from the wages the taxes paid, the expenses incurred because of work and welfare benefits lost. Due to the way income is counted (in the calculation of AFDC grants) AFDC and food stamp benefits do not decline very rapidly as earnings rise, but net income left after work expenses for working mothers on AFDC and foods stamps averages as little as twenty cents per dollar earned: for such women who live in public housing, the average gain drops to as low as eleven cents.

The report also indicates that "low wage workers now excluded from AFDC may face high disincentives to work due to the combination of taxes, work expenses, and benefits lost from general assistance, food and housing problems" (pp. 39, 41, 42). Tropman concludes that a study of any one program does not present a fair picture of the condition. All benefit programs must be included in a study of the effect of welfare on clients. Similarly, Chapman reports that "it is simply not to the advantage of many recipients to give up welfare and go to work." One irony of the situation is that conditions in the welfare system and its clients "perpetuate a system [which] everyone says is supposed to 'wither away'" (p. 17).

Welfare administration poses constant problems. In order to assure that only persons who are supposed to receive grants for the established purposes receive them, and that the grants are in the appropriate amounts established for these purposes, myriad administrative processes have been established. The incessant criticism of AFDC in various state legislatures, in Congress, and in the various executive administrations has created a kind of defensive administration in the program. This kind of pressure has heightened the call for financial accountability, a call that has been met by an almost automatic introduction of additional forms and procedures. Such a response has added to the operational burden without in any sense increasing the services to the clients or significantly increasing the manageability of the program.

The relationship between grantee and the welfare administration has varied from active to repressed hostility. In large cities such as New York, the relationship between public welfare or eligibility worker and clients has been made closer by a mutual repugnance and disdain for the welfare system, by the administrative maze, and by the high turnover in welfare workers. In the process, workers have often been laid off to give clients as much as possible in the way of benefits, and little concern has been exhibited for designing regulations to prevent assistance from becoming a disincentive to work (Moynihan, 1968, p. 22). Where little concern has been exhibited to prevent assistance from becoming a work disincentive, clients who can make demands have been aided when the less aggressive have been given only minimum grants. This condition has led to a sense of injustice which pervades the system. Jacobs discusses the attempts of workers and clients "to manipulate the other in the hope of gaining either personal or material rewards." The massive paper workload, matched by the overload of growing welfare but unmatched by a trained, stable staff, has led to generally low morale among welfare recipients and workers. The result has been a further distortion of the legislative purposes of AFDC. In the process, welfare workers and clients have operated in a system that in no way relates to mainstream reality. Ernest van den Haag (p. 74) states that although welfare workers have been hired to check eligibility they have not been very successful. Any attempt to remove someone from the welfare rolls, he says, leads to contention and endangers the welfare worker's job. So the welfare worker has every motivation not to take a hard look at a client's eligibility.

The issue that welfare dehumanizes both the welfare client and the worker may be valid when examined in light of both the unreal requirements of complex regulations and the need to help the client become independent and self-supporting. However, the requirement that a client show good faith, by revealing all assets and income and by openly discussing why he now finds himself in need and what can be done, over time, to resolve the problem is probably not dehumanizing. Rather, it is a necessary first step in planning rehabilitation. Far more dehumanizing are the failure to proceed to such a discussion or to plan the client's return to self-sufficiency; assistance that leads to a habit-forming, permanent dependency; the granting of funds via mechanical procedures; and enforcing rules without understanding or knowing their purpose. Thus, both the client and the worker will likely continue to be degraded by the welfare process until the rehabilitative process in welfare is reinstated, particularly with the residual AFDC poor.

Prior to the installation of the self-eligibility declaration process, in order to make a grant to an applicant it was necessary to officially determine his eligibility. Whether the father was dead, physically handicapped, absent from the family, or unable to support the family had to be verified by documentation. The program required the presence of minor children in the home whose existence and ages could be verified. It was also necessary to verify lack of an income, the amount of income if an income existed but was insufficient to meet budgeted needs, and, in the construction of the approved family budget, the need for specific budgetary items. The earnings of family members had to be deducted from the established budget in order to arrive at an amount for the monthly grant. If the income changed from month to month, or if the budgetary needs changed, appropriate changes in the grant had to be regularly calculated and administered through a cumbersome payment machinery. If the applicant had property of other than minimal value, this fact had to be verified, and it had to be determined whether valuable property had been given away (or sequestered with relatives) in order to make the family eligible for aid. This process included consideration of other resources as well, such as insurance policies, bank accounts, and automobiles other than one needed to maintain necessary family services. If the applicant owned a substantial home, it was necessary to examine its equity, which might be usable as collateral for a family loan.

The present eligibility rules view the earnings of family members as income, which reduces the welfare budget or grant. In some instances, adolescent children are permitted to retain a portion of their earnings for their own needs. In other cases, family members can retain enough earnings, work-related costs, and child-care costs, without deduction from the welfare grant. In general, earnings reduce or preclude aid. In some states, a family member employed thirty or more hours on a job makes his family ineligible for AFDC, even though his earnings represent only a portion of the eligible grant he would receive if he remained on welfare.

Income from absentee fathers (or ex-husbands) must be treated as a deduction from the family budget. This rule is particularly difficult to administer when payments are erratic and undependable. If they are calculated into the initial family budget as income and do not continue, a hardship on the family is the result. If they occur after the budget is calculated, the outcome is an unauthorized additional grant to the family. Locating and verifying absent fathers present an administrative nightmare. If they are apprehended and incarcerated, such fathers earn nothing while in custody. The cost of enforcing the liability of such relatives is usually much larger than the amount that could be secured from them. Table 4.1 presents the previous and present system of eligibility processing.

HEW has made a continuing effort to secure income from spouses absent from the home and who are not supporting their families. In 1975, a new program, designated as Project Responsibility, was established to help state and local government agencies reclaim $1 billion per year from spouses by the end of fiscal 1979 (Social Security Information Items, No. 23, September 1978). This program was created to deal with the growing costs of AFDC caused by noncontributing absent parents. An Office of Child Support Enforcement was established, and branches partially

TABLE 4.1 **Systems of Eligibility Processing**

	PREVIOUS SYSTEM OF ELIGIBILITY	PRESENT SYSTEM OF ELIGIBILITY
Application	made out by the worker in an interview with client usually followed by an investigative home visit to verify home, children, etc.	made out by client with or without help from friends. Application accompanied by children's birth certificate, etc. Grant approved without delays but subject to periodic reevaluation (3-6 mos.) by an eligibility worker.
Follow-up	only temporary assistance was given, during which time worker documented the application, checked bank assets, mortgage, rent, presence of other earners in home, etc.	no follow-up unless the client asks for social services which are then rendered by a social worker who is not involved in eligibility.
Grant	was made after above but worker periodically visited the client to check on rehabilitation (social service) needs and procedures as carried out by the client, and eligibility.	proceeds regularly unless some problem in eligibility becomes apparent or unless the case is selected (often at random) for audit (very few are audited).

funded by HEW were authorized in each of the states. (The states pay 25 percent and HEW 75 percent.) From August 1975 through March 1978, these state and local agencies collected $1.1 billion. A National Institute for Child Support Enforcement to train personnel at all levels is planned, and the project has begun to utilize computer-exchanged information in tracing absent spouses and in checking the income of absent spouses. Some of the restrictions that formerly prohibited exchange of information necessary for enforcing child support have recently been lifted. Similarly, *Program Instruction* on "good cause for refusing to cooperate" provides detailed procedures for determining whether a client may be refused aid if that person does not provide information relating to paternity and to securing child support.

High costs and long delays discouraged enforcement of child-support in regulations in the past. "Even when paid the average court-ordered amount per child was less than half the amount" required to support the child (Winston and Forsher). Winston and Forsher have noted that fathers' willful nonsupport is on the rise and was the cause of the 36-percent increase in poverty among female family heads in 1974. The same resistance to paying support for children persists among absent fathers, who presumably resent the intrusion of welfare into the lives of their families as much as they would resent another man taking over their family role. A concomitant problem in enforcing child support is that of cost. Although an itemized program budget has not been made available, it is probable that the $40 million currently collected per month is in great part offset by the national, state, and local costs of the program. Even if the $1 billion in collections per year were achieved, and even if it were not made at a sizable cost, it would still amount to less than 10 percent of AFDC disbursements, let alone other payments made for food stamps and Medicaid.

State and federal government regulations relating to AFDC were originally designed to encourage a particular type of client behavior, based on the original intent of the program. This behavior includes a mother who will stay home with her children and who will see to it that they are clean and under control, and attend school regularly. She presumably will have no male visitors who are not relatives, and she will report all income and gifts so that they can be deducted from the family budget. It is also presumed that she will be a careful home manager and budgeteer, so that she and the children will survive without going into debt; that she will seek opportunities for employment for herself and the children to relieve the government either entirely or partially for the family's care; that she will encourage the children to work toward self-responsibility and financial independence; and that she will keep her children away from unsocial and antisocial elements, thereby helping them become productive, lawful citizens (Williamson, 1973).

In previous decades, AFDC was administered by welfare workers who were encouraged to promote this model of the welfare client. In many instances, grants were overtly denied when welfare workers became aware of extramarital relationships. The logic of denying AFDC to a woman maintaining a household with a built-in surrogate husband can be explained in terms of the definition of AFDC. If a man is employed regularly, lives in an AFDC home as if he were the father and husband or surrogate father and husband, in what way is this family not self-sufficient and nondependent? For this purpose, the test of nonmarriage is invalid because such a relationship in many states can be considered a marriage under common law. The test of financial contributions to the family or lack of financial contributions is also weak because local domestic relations courts are responsible for enforcing financial support by husbands (and common-law husbands). If a husband and father does not contribute to the family with which he lives, is this not a problem for the domestic relations courts rather than a problem of federal-state welfare support? If welfare does support such a family, does this fact not convey to the father and husband that he and his financial support are not needed? Does it not encourage such fathers/husbands to leave? Similarly, does the provision of welfare grants as a mechanism to permit husbands to remain home but without responsibility not constitute an injustice to other husbands who are responsible and to the people whose taxes provide the AFDC funds? On the other hand, disallowing grants for families where "boyfriends" are regular visitors, and even members, does not induce the kind of behavior in mothers described in the model presented earlier.

A 1971 study conducted by the comptroller-general of the United States of the eligibility processes in three major cities revealed that the simplified method of determining eligibility through the client's own statement was no more accurate than the traditional cursory method utilized previously. A 1974 staff study of the Welfare Administration, conducted by the Joint Economic Committee of the Congress, found that chronic understaffing, complex regulations, inadequate training, and inadequate supervision, as well as client ignorance of procedures, lead not only to fraud but more seriously to a Kafkaesque operation that cheats the entire nation.

The eligibility determination process, when originally conceived of in the early AFDC, OAA, ATD, and AB years, was viewed as a method not only of evaluating eligibility but also of educating the client to the notion that the society values self-support and independence. Such a process was expected to help the client design and work out a plan for regaining independence and self-sufficiency. Only in recent decades has the process become a bureaucratic investigation, at worst, or a meaningless set of irrelevant questions, at best.

A particularly difficult aspect of AFDC administration relates to the problem of lost checks, especially in large urban cities where mail deliveries are made to large apartment houses and tenements. In the absence of provable fraud, federal regulations forbid welfare agencies to reduce a recipient's grant because of prior overpayments. Lost checks are reported by clients, and emergency substitute payments are made. Few of the welfare administrations pursue investigations of fraud in instances where both the regular and substitute checks are cashed. The reasons are that intent to defraud is hard to prove and that criminal charges against husbandless families are highly unpopular.

The AFDC system has a myriad complex of built-in disincentives which are counterproductive to the purposes of AFDC. Central to the complex of disincentives is the problem of AFDC's effect upon family life. The percentage of fathers absent in 1978 was 84.7 (*Chartbook:AFDC*, 1979), up from 76 percent in 1971. This proportion of families with absent fathers has increased approximately 1.2 percent per year since 1971. In 1971, HEW reported that 13 percent of the absent fathers contributed to the children's support. It should be noted that a noncontributing father is usually a never-visiting father. As a result of the AFDC regulations which seek to obtain the fathers' financial participation, the family's situation changes from divorce or separation to the extreme one of "never heard from again." This structural constraint on AFDC makes the children in broken families half-orphans. The converse of this situation is also evident. According to the staff report of 1971, "as long as a family remains on welfare, it generally receives no financial [or other] benefit [from the absent father]" (p. 22). In addition, "A mother's cooperation in support proceedings [against her husband] may be discouraged by her fear that such cooperation would subject the family to abuse from the father or lead to a loss of unreported payments already being received" (p. 23).

The report also indicates that "by enabling married persons to maximize their incomes by separating (or reporting a separation) and unmarried persons to maximize their incomes by not marrying," federal welfare law tends to encourage welfare dependency. Conversely, "since the income of a man who has no legal obligation to support a family cannot be deducted from the family's welfare grant . . . a mother can live with a man who is not—or claims not to be—the father of her children" and still collect welfare, but not if she lives with a husband or the father of her children (p. 23). Thus, if a woman has illegitimate children she receives welfare, but if she marries their father, welfare ceases. If a man lives with his family and he has no money, they go hungry; if he deserts them (or makes believe that he has left), then they can survive. This regulation breaks up families, or at least inserts an emotional wedge between the unemployed father and his family in the knowledge that his presence keeps them financially insecure.

The dollar for dollar deduction of family income from welfare grants is a work disincentive. Whether AFDC mothers are concurrently employed while on assistance is usually uncertain. Unskilled labor is generally day labor. It takes time to be approved for AFDC, but it takes only one day to be discontinued. If a not-too-secure job is accepted, the implication is that the family is putting its hopes on an uncertain job in place of a certain monthly welfare check. It would be difficult to conceive of an arrangement more discouraging for employment, self-sufficiency, and independence.

AFDC was designed not as a permanent substitute for irresponsible or negligent parents, but as a residual program to care for those who, because of uncontrollable circumstances, could not provide for their family. It was intended to provide a minimum of subsistence for the broken family (Wilensky and Lebeaux, pp. 283–334). It was regarded as a temporary palliative rather than a restorative cure for chronic transgenerational poverty, providing a way station on the road back to self-sufficiency. The poor it was to serve were "pioneers," immigrant poor, or the children of self-sufficient Americans whose problems derived primarily from acts of God rather than from family problems, personal deterioration, or interpersonal conflict or difficulty.

Most of the nonpoverty population still views welfare as a temporary assistance program, as seen in Williamson's research on the subject (1973, 1974). The public at large believes that those who remain indefinitely on public welfare are failures because of their individual shortcomings.

The Changing of AFDC

Social services were provided to AFDC families on a limited scale until 1962, at which time the policy was changed to provide services in depth. These services included health care, vocational services, educational programs, job conditioning, counseling, and placement, day care for infants, family planning, child protection against abuse or abandonment, and special needs grants (Moynihan, 1970; Morris). Steiner (1974) presents a review of the social service welfare strategy and its failures.

The image of the client under the original AFDC program model was one of a competent victim for whom circumstances had been unfortunate. This family did not need guidance as much as it needed temporary financial help. It knew where it was going and what had to be done to rehabilitate itself economically. Thus, a grant program was justified, and this policy was validated by the hundreds of thousands of families which moved from AFDC status to independence. Since the 1960s, it became clear that another family model has appeared on the AFDC rolls. The parent in this family is less emotionally mature, less competent in life activity, and has a weaker sense of responsibility, less ability to plan and to manage, and almost no organization or impulse control. This kind of client has needed much more guidance and emotional support and constraints in finding a way out of dependency. The first model is a financial-need problem, but the second is one not only of financial need but, more importantly, also of emotional dependency, inadequate socialization, lack of control over the factors in life, and ignorance of survival and improvement routes within the mainstream of society. The problem that arose in the 1960s was how to use a program designed for one model to serve another.

With the first model, the appropriate service approach is to provide the resources and tools to the family and let them make their own way. To restrain such a family, to hold tight reins on their activity would create dependency or unnecessary resentment in an otherwise competent family. On the other hand, to provide a no-restraint welfare grant to a highly dependent client would probably be as destructive as to hand $1,000 in single dollar bills to a sixth grade child, especially if you promise to keep giving him such sums regularly. What has happened in the AFDC program is that the self-restraint and independent clients have graduated from the welfare system, while the chronically dependent families, hidden among the others, stay on indefinitely and propagate new applicants.

A number of policy scholars, of whom Waxman is a good example, tend to view welfare stigma as if it were a continuing destructive element in relation to welfare policy. Waxman (pp. 68–69) insists that stigma must be viewed as a "definition of the situation," or a social perception of self which he ties to Goffman's language of relationships, such as was presented in Goffman's work on stigma in institutions and elsewhere. Waxman states that the welfare client has been relegated to a stigma of "blemishes of individual character perceived as weak will." He sees the process of stigmatization as "interfering with what otherwise might have been a normal social relationship," and the stigma of poverty, he suggests, confers a less than human or at least disreputable status on the poor.

Waxman is probably correct in his belief that stigma tends to reinforce the residual poor's sense of unworthiness and incompetency. As such, it increases the social distance between them and people in the mainstream, and keeps them uninformed of opportunities that might otherwise be available to them if they became involved in the related preparatory processes (schooling, training, and the like). However, Waxman is quite wrong in his overwhelming condemnation of stigma. He does not acknowledge that stigma also keeps people off welfare who might otherwise become dependent and helps motivate others (the majority on welfare) to get off welfare as soon as possible. If welfare carried no stigma, many more would apply for it and would convert their temporary dependency into permanent dependency.

A simplistic act, such as hiding welfare within a social insurance program (which is Waxman's primary suggestion), would probably make dependency much more palatable, and it would make work as a way of life synonymous with playing the sucker role. A better social policy would be to accept stigma as a logical concomitant of social stratification and to help those of chronic low status learn how to retool themselves and escape poverty.

The complex of stigma and the multiple problems of the residual welfare family apparently provided the rationale in the late 1950s and early 1960s for HEW and the social work community to focus on the increased provision of social services, particularly to such families. The 1956 amendments, for example (Heffernan, p. 111), strengthened the service strategy policy by requiring that "specific plans for rehabilitation be developed for each case before the federal share of the assistance costs would be validated." These amendments also specified that services should supplement public assistance in order to achieve rehabilitation.

In 1962, Abraham Ribicoff, then secretary of HEW (Ways and Means Committee, "Hearings," p. 113), proposed six basic objectives for social services for the welfare population: services to help families become self-supporting; prevention of dependency by dealing with problems causing dependency; incentives to recipients to improve their condition so as to make public assistance unnecessary and incentives to the states to improve their welfare programs; rehabilitation of recipients or those likely to become applicants; independence—useful community work and training programs, and the like to assist recipients to become self-supporting; and training—assistance in the provision of training in order to increase the supply of adequately trained welfare personnel.

In 1962, HEW adopted an in-depth approach to social services. The purpose of this strategy was to inundate the welfare client with professional care ranging from prenatal medical aid to family therapy, "all of it provided by a corps of trained social workers. The poor were to be rehabilitated right up into the mainstream" (Chapman, p. 1). A limited number of test projects were conducted in various localities with multiproblem families. These projects were found to provide feasible and relatively effective rehabilitative methods, although they were not tried over a sufficiently long period to test the effectiveness of rehabilitation.

The service strategy was supported by a variety of professional training grants for a number of therapies and for other personnel in many graduate training settings. These grants provided stipends for students in training and, in many instances, for teachers as well. A few of these grants were also tied to employment obligations in public welfare agencies. Unfortunately, most of the graduates of these programs, when not otherwise obligated, went on immediately to employment in private sector social agencies, and those who were legally obligated moved on to nonpublic welfare agencies as soon as they could.

At the outset, the social work profession expressed considerable enthusiasm for the services-in-depth orientation, but few of the trained and skilled workers elected to work in public welfare. The small proportion who did work in such agencies, because of their higher status, became supervisors and administrators rather than workers with multiproblem welfare families. Those who did work with the clients (both multiproblem and others) were mainly untrained workers who were uninterested in welfare work as a career and who were only temporarily involved in it. Their service to the client consisted primarily of satisfying the regulations rather than seeking client rehabilitation goals.

Another problem with how the services-in-depth strategy was carried out was that the focus was not on the families most in need of service. On the contrary, whatever service was provided was spread through the clientele. Where the service was specifically directed toward the target group and in the few locations where professionally qualified workers were provided, an unfortunate mode of therapy was frequently offered. Much of the graduate training had a Freudian orientation and focused on preparing workers to serve mainly middle-class neuroses. This orientation was neither comprehensible to residual welfare clients nor suitable for directing them toward mainstream goals. The emphasis on affect and on helping the client to feel better rather than to do better probably reinforced the client's acceptance of dependency as a desirable life-style. Similarly, the worker's confusion as to the causes of residual poverty was quite evident in the pathology versus structural debate which was then, and still is, apparent (Handler). Obviously, few, if any, workers realized the interactive processes between a client who had probably never known self-sufficiency and a welfare system that was rapidly being converted into an income transfer system that put no obligations on the client and often reassured the client of regular, though limited, aid. Thus, few of the workers considered it their responsibility to break the symbiotic syndromic activity of client and system, which forever meant greater and deeper dependency. Few, if any, workers had the knowledge and skill to do such work as was described by Yelaja and others in *Authority and Social Work.*

In 1968, Moynihan (p. 17) stated that "the period of professional direction [of AFDC] appears to be coming to an end." Despite this generally supported viewpoint, the social work community, as late as 1969, was still concerned with services in depth. *Public Welfare,* the journal of the American Public Welfare Association, devoted an entire issue (October 1969, Vol. 27, No. 4) to the question "Can Public Welfare Deliver Services?" Articles on this question were included by such social work leaders as Richan, Lane, Bell and O'Reilly, Upman, and Williams. This question, even if answered in the affirmative, would not have helped very much because other equally important questions went unasked. The questions that should have been asked were: "Services to whom? To the temporary clients or the residual, multiproblem group?" and, more importantly, "Are these services effective in moving dependent clients into independence?"

By 1973, some questions were presented to the House Ways and Means Committee (Heffernan, p. 117) on deficiencies in the social services of welfare. The complaints included the following:

"Social services are too loosely defined." More definitive objectives for these
   services were sought.

"Services, even when specified, are offered without consideration of staff competencies."

"Little systematic research is done on ideal staffing patterns."

"Many services serve only a bureaucratic function." (Reference here is to voluminous case studies and social histories not directly related to client well-being.)

"Despite bureaucratic requirements, real accountability (for social services) is low."

"Limited client participation results in a self-defeating paternalistic pattern of service delivery."

The critical questions were asked by nonsocial workers. Aaron indicated that social services were often provided "because of their therapeutic value as perceived by welfare agencies rather than [by] recipients" (p. 5). Glazer commented that "social workers don't really know which services are useful or effective" (p. 113). He pointed to a variety of research studies showing that social services had no effect on the client's behavior. His contention was that social services, even if effective, were really not available to the clients who needed the service. When service was available, it was usually rendered by an untrained worker who had neither the requisite theory nor skills. Glazer also maintained that "it is hard to draw the line between advice which the client sees herself as *bound* to take to keep on welfare, *wise* to take because it keeps her in the good graces of the welfare worker, *good* to take because it is good advice, etc." (p. 114). As a result, he was concerned that the separation of services from eligibility would remove most of the motivation of clients to accept professional help when it was available and when it was directed toward a self-sufficient, nondependent life-style. In fact, Glazer went on record in support of professional services tied to eligibility supervision. Heffernan, too (p. 118), indicated that the classical model of social services may never have received a fair test.

The strategy of providing social services in depth was thus tried out from 1962 to 1969 and was found to have little significant effect on caseloads. By 1969, plans were underway to discontinue services in depth and to separate eligibility processing from services. Under this arrangement, families must now ask for social services in order to receive them. This plan is based upon the belief (according to Gilbert and Specht) that "the psychiatric model of casework services [voluntarily sought] would bring about a change in the economic dependency of individuals in poverty" (p. 47). It is also founded on the assumption "that services would thereby be improved because the client-worker relationship would no longer be tinged by the coercive overtones of the worker's [eligibility] authority."

According to Handler in *The Coercive Social Worker,* the philosophy behind the separation of services from eligibility was based upon a number of assumptions. The first of these assumptions is that the requirement that the client must behave in a particular manner or work toward a particular rehabilitative goal is a coercive and authoritative act which is inappropriate for a welfare program. Second, to tie service to eligibility is based on a pathology theory of welfare, which Handler views as incorrect and outdated. Handler further indicates that AFDC, prior to the separation of services from eligibility, imposed on the clientele a noncentralized administrative procedure that permitted each state, locality, and worker to be coercive. The separation of services therefore provided a condition-free situation wherein the client would be provided a regular, dependable grant without any obligation to strive for rehabilitation. Similarly, under the separation, the client was not required to make constructive use of the money or services given.

In addition, the separation of services was designed to minimize traditional forms of services such as counseling and guidance, the integrated approach toward multiproblem families, and the so-called soft services. Instead, its emphasis was on hard social services, including day care, abortion and birth control services, foster care, home management help, protective services, consumer protection, referrals to manpower agencies, family and marriage counseling, and temporary assistance with a specific problem or urgent need. Soft services are counseling, advice, guidance, and other relationship activities which can not be really measured or counted and where results are not easily apparent. Services could be rendered only when requested and imposed no obligation on the client.

It became apparent that when clients were free to accept or reject social services, fewer requested them. In general, the client group would rather not be advised in their use of welfare grants or in their style of life —no more than a child could be expected to ask for the increased parental constraints necessary for its socialization. AFDC has thus developed what Wilcox calls the assistance constituency (p. 243). In his view, "*there are women who are married to welfare,* [with] the public assistance check being the only income they have ever known." Wilcox asserts that "there are families in which a daughter brought up on public assistance has produced a second generation of children to be supported by the state."

In general, any program of income transfer, whether public assistance, social insurance, or otherwise, has both short- and long-term purposes. In the short term, these programs have social control (cooling off alienated sectors of the population) and humane purposes. As a short-term program, AFDC has met the needs of past decades, but no longer does so. In the long term, the program's responsibility is to preserve human resources for the sake of society's future values and stability. Apparently, AFDC effectively performed this function in the past, but no longer does so. The problem is therefore one of designing programs to match the contemporary needs of the society and its problem populations. This objective cannot be attained by further tinkering with the outdated and worn-out machinery of AFDC. Rather, certain basic foundations of public welfare, such as rehabilitation, must be recognized, and changes in relation to these purposes and foundations must be planned.

The first of the foundation principles is that of lesser eligibility. If AFDC is to be a precursor to reestablishing the poverty family in the mainstream community, then no grants should be made which provide greater security and support than the least remunerative available employment for that particular family. A second foundation principle relates to the issue of the minimum wage. Minimum wages create a lack of employment for those seeking to escape from the welfare system. Consequently, such statutes may have to be revised.

The problem of multiple benefits must be resolved if AFDC is to become a rehabilitative service rather than a permanent hiding place from society. It may be necessary to centralize the myriad programs so that each family will receive only one grant related to their needs and less than their potential earnings in the community. Similarly, the grant structure must be adjusted to prevent incentives for family breakup and to discourage multiple births within the welfare culture.

The fifty-four states and territorial administrations of AFDC may have to be federalized (as were OAA, AB, and ATD, which became SSI) in order to establish common norms for, and levels of, grants and policies. In this way, the legislative purposes of AFDC and simple equity and justice will not be negated. In connection with the above foundations, better programs for child care, employment opportunities, training and placement, and ancillary services may be needed if employment, schooling, self-respectability, and competence are to be encouraged.

Finally, the mythology of the 1960s regarding the assumed innate capabilities of all welfare clients must be amended to allow for a range of capabilities from high to low. A residual person on welfare is a person neglected by the society and accustomed to neglecting himself and his future. Money alone will not solve the problem. Only careful study, analysis, and social policy development, followed by intensive required services and constraints, can be expected to help resolve the problem.

Banfield recommends (pp. 100–101) that the philosophy behind the welfare system be revised. Rather than maintain a philosophy of income transfers, he states, the system should be considered a temporary service to persons who are in need because of unemployment or other causes beyond their control. If income redistribution is viewed as a fit matter for governmental action, then it would require mechanisms other than welfare. In Banfield's view, welfare should be retained as a limited purpose program, with a welfare bureaucracy directed to distinguish between the technically poor and the really poor, to keep the demand for benefits within manageable bounds, and to promote the clientele's return to self-dependence.

Miller states that four different categories of persons are in welfare poverty. In the first category are the poor who would be helped with money alone; these persons can easily resolve their difficulties. The second category includes those persons who might require some casework but who are primarily self-motivated to improve their family conditions and operations. For these persons, Miller recommends both financial assistance and limited professional services. In the third category, he places what he calls the stable copers. Such families, of course, need financial aid for a time and some practical help in regard to employment, relocation, or other concrete problems. Finally, in the fourth category are the unstable, the dependent, and those persons not motivated for change in their lives and who are often not even cognizant of such a possibility of change. He believes that specific programs aimed at this group, utilizing aggressive casework, supportive services, and a variety of direct and indirect interventions, are both necessary and important.

Morris suggests that, although social services alone cannot cure welfare poverty, resolution requires that social services become an integral part of the service rendered to the residual welfare poor.

It is easier to supply a child and its mother with additional food, housing, or security than to provide them with the opportunity to make some efforts in their own behalf. Without such an opportunity, a child may never grow beyond the elemental levels of emotional development necessary for his participation as a member of the society. Without a chance and motivational incentives to develop himself, he cannot be expected to reach adulthood unhampered by emotional dependence and the concomitant resentment of authority or fatalism.

Changes in public welfare are not required merely to conserve public funds. More importantly, it is the generations of children on welfare who need to be saved from misplaced good intentions, as is evidenced in a reluctance to establish and then adhere to standards and constraints.

We do not claim that AFDC is the *cause* of the gap between the classes. At the same time, it is not guiltless of perpetuating and widening that gap as well as reinforcing the cleavage between the residual poor and the rest of society. For the transitory poor, the effect is different in that people in temporary need are provided for until they can again begin to be self-sufficient. For the residual poor, AFDC can at best be seen as a concomitant factor in perpetuating dependency.

With the passage of time, the costs and generations affected will grow, thereby jeopardizing much of what Americans value most. Democracy, for one, cannot exist in a divided society in which a huge governmental entity grinds out new fodder daily for a war between the classes. The high crime rate, social unrest, and apparent anarchy reflect this divided society. The longer the society delays in shifting its focus to the foundation issues and the longer it ignores the implications of sociological legislative concepts, the more severe will be the problem and the more numerous will be those affected.

Food Stamps

Still another temporary project that "won't go away" is the Food Stamp program. The original program, initiated in 1939 as an experiment to increase food spending among participating families and to help absorb surplus food supplies, died in 1943. The current program started as a pilot program in 1961 and was passed as the Food Stamp Act of 1964. This program is funded entirely by the federal government and is administered by the states and the localities, with a 50-percent subsidy of administration by the federal government. Monthly food coupons redeemable for most food items and other specific necessities are distributed to eligible families on request. Families who are eligible are those on some form of public assistance (such as SSI, AFDC, and General Assistance) or those who have a net income after deductions for taxes, day-care costs, and work expenses of about $580 per month for a family of four. An assets and work requirement is also included in regulations; the exception is the adult who has an invalid or minor child at home. Currently, stamps are at no cost to the recipient (*Congressional Digest*). The Food Stamp program costs approximately $5.7 billion per year (Budget, fiscal 1977 and 1978).

The Food Stamp program was originally established as a means of supporting food prices for agricultural enterprises. Consequently, it originated in the U.S. Department of Agriculture. It continues to be located there, even though food stamps have become a major mechanism for providing aid to poverty families. As of March 15, 1978, an estimated 16.3 million persons were receiving food stamps, of whom approximately half were SSI or AFDC beneficiaries. The remainder qualified under the net income standards.

The Food Stamp Act of 1977 (Budget, p. 200) lowered the net income limits to the defined poverty line, simplified the food stamp eligibility application process, eliminated the purchase requirement, tightened the work requirement, and disqualified persons who have committed fraud.

Food stamps have been particularly helpful to families undergoing temporary unemployment. Most recipients do not find it embarrassing to use the stamps (Fishbein, p. vii). Most of the nonwelfare users of food stamps are regularly employed but are temporarily in difficulty because of structural or seasonal unemployment and because their earnings are insufficient for minimal family needs. In 1976 some 30 percent of users were found to be single individuals, living alone.

Although even today farmers receive some benefit from the program, its main thrust is to alleviate hunger and poverty. Its tie to agriculture, however, is not only economic but also political. Because it is located in the Department of Agriculture and is separately administered, it tends to overlap other aid programs in the Departments of HEW, Labor, and Housing and Urban Development (Fishbein, p. 64). At the state and local levels, the welfare departments administer food stamps and welfare and are thus required to deal with two national agencies that have different operational definitions, guidelines, and accounting procedures. One program may have a counterproductive effect on other programs. The multitude of sponsors for such programs even confuse statistical processes. Food stamps, Medicaid, and housing aid are not calculated in the government's measure of poverty, and it is therefore quite possible that the official estimate of poverty in the United States is somewhat overstated. A Congressional Budget Office report (p. 110) in 1977 indicated that the percentage of families in poverty in the United States could be reduced by 60 percent if these items were calculated in the estimates. The report emphasizes the value of food stamps in alleviating poverty. For example, it estimates that "about 30 percent of the pre-food-stamp [population] of poor persons would be lifted above the poverty line if the food stamp(s) were counted as income—[about] 4.2 million persons" (p. 31).

The Food Stamp program has considerable advantages as a welfare program. According to Fishbein (p. 67), the stamps "taper off gradually as income increases" and so "the work incentives are not as adversely affected." Food stamps do aid the working poor without adversely affecting their status as self-supporting, functioning, and participating persons in the community. The stamps are available to persons and families without children. Aaron believes that food stamps serve as a subsidy for the poor and is concerned that they will "lose some of their attractiveness if they induce [a] family to spend more for food than it would without a subsidy" (p. 17). This concern can be countered by the argument that having sufficient resources designated for food increases the probability that the nutritional needs of the family will be adequately met. Macdonald supports this position.

By and large, an in-kind program such as food stamps provides necessary aid to a poverty family. Because of the constraints inherent in the program, it does not foster as great a dependency as do the other available welfare mechanisms.

References

Aaron, Henry. "Financing Welfare Reform and Income Distribution." Speech and oral response to audience questions, UCLA Conference on National Welfare Policy, September 29, 1972.

Abrahamse, Allen F., David M. DeFerranti, Patricia D. Fleischauer, and Albert Lysson. *AFDC Caseload and the Job Market in California: Selected Issues*, R-2115-CDOBP. Santa Monica: Rand, 1977.

Allen, Henry L. "A Radical Critique of Federal Work and Manpower Programs, 1933–1974." Pp. 23–28, in Betty Reid Mandell (ed.), *Welfare in America: Controlling the "Dangerous Classes."* Englewood Cliffs, N.J.: Prentice-Hall, 1975.

American Conservative Union. "An Alternative Approach to Welfare Reform." Memorandum to Congress, 1969.

Banfield, Edward C. "Welfare: A Crisis Without Solutions," *Public Interest*, 16:89–101, 1969.

Bell, Carolyn Shaw. "The Carter Bill—Is It Welfare Reform?" *Journal of the Institute for Socio-Economic Studies*, 3(2):9-19, 1978.

Bell, Winifred, and Charles T. O'Reilly. "What About the Manpower Crisis in Social Welfare?" *Public Welfare*, 27(4):348–52, 1969.

Bishop, John. "Jobs, Cash Transfer and Marital Instability: A Review of the Evidence." Written testimony to the Welfare Reform Subcommittee of the Committees on Agriculture, Education and Labor, Ways and Means of the U.S. House of Representatives, October 14, 1977.

Brieland, Donald, and John Lemmon. *Social Work and the Law.* St. Paul, Minn.: West, 1977.

Budget of the United States Government. *Fiscal Year 1979.* Washington, D.C.: U.S. Government Printing Office, 1978.

Califano, Joseph A. "Special HEW Report on Welfare Reform." Washington, D.C.: U.S. Government Printing Office, 1977.

———. "Putting the Public into Public Policy Development," *Journal of the Institute for Socio-Economic Studies*, 3(2):1–8, 1978.

Chapman, William. "The Welfare Enigma: Despite All the Programs, Reforms and Billions, The Poor and Their Problems Will Not Go Away," *Manchester Guardian*, June 5, 1977, pp. 1, 17–18.

Comptroller General's Office. *Report to the Committee on Finance, U.S. Senate: Comparison of the Simplified and Traditional Methods of Determining Eligibility for AFDC*, B164031(3). Washington, D.C: Comptroller General's Office, 1971.

Congressional Budget Office. "Poverty Status of Families Under Alternative Definitions of Income." Background Paper No. 17. Washington, D.C.: Congressional Budget Office, 1977.

Cooper, Maudine. "Comment over National Public Radio," January 30, 1975.

Doolittle, Frederick, Frank Levy, and Michael Wiseman. "The Mirage of Welfare Reform," *Public Interest*, 47:62–87, 1977.

Durbon, Elizabeth. *Welfare and Employment*. New York: Praeger, 1969.

Durham, Eugene. "Have the Poor Been Regulated? Toward a Multivariate Understanding of Welfare Growth," *Social Service Review*, 47(3):339–59, 1973.

Feagin, Joe R. "Poverty: We Still Believe That God Helps Those Who Help Themselves," *Psychology Today* 6:101–29, November 1972.

Fishbein, Bette K. "The Food Stamp Program," *Journal of the Institute for Socio-Economic Studies*. Special Supplement, July 1977.

Freeman, Roger A. "Welfare Reform and the Family Assistance Plan." Statement before the Committee on Finance, U.S. Senate, January 27, 1972. Washington, D.C.: U.S. Government Printing Office, 1972.

Garmzey, Norman. "Vulnerability Research and the Issue of Primary Prevention," *American Journal of Orthopsychiatry*, 41(1):101–16, 1971.

————. *Vulnerable and Invulnerable Children, Theory, Research and Intervention*. Washington, D.C.: American Psychological Association, 1976.

Gilbert, N., and H. Specht. *Dimensions of Social Welfare Policy*. Englewood Cliffs, N.J.: Prentice-Hall, 1974.

Glazer, Nathan. "Beyond Income Maintenance—A Note on Welfare in New York City," *Public Interest*, 16:102–20, 1969.

Goffman, Erving. *Stigma, Notes on the Management of Spoiled Identity*. Englewood Cliffs, N.J.: Prentice-Hall, 1963.

Goldstein, Aaron H. *Interviewing for Eligibility Determination: A Management Aid for Enhancing Agency-Recipient Communication*. Washington, D.C.: U.S. Department of Health, Education and Welfare, 1975.

Goodwin, Leonard. "Welfare Mothers and the Work Ethic," *Monthly Labor Review*, 95(8):35–36, 1972a.

————. *Do the Poor Want to Work: A Social-Psychological Study of Work Orientations*. Washington, D.C.: Brookings, 1972b.

Griffiths, Martha. "Conference (With)," *Journal of the Institute for Socio-Economic Studies*, 1(2):40–67, 1976.

Hamilton, John A. "Will 'Work' Work?" *Saturday Review*, 53(21):24–27, 1970.

Handler, Joel F. *The Coercive Social Worker, British Lessons for American Social Services*. Chicago: Markham, 1973.

Harrison, Bennett. *Education, Training, and the Urban Ghetto*. Baltimore: Johns Hopkins Press, 1972.

Hartung, Frank. *Crime, Law and Society*. Detroit: Wayne State Press, 1966.

Hausman, Leonard. "The Potential for Financial Self-Support Among

AFDC and AFDC-UP Families," *Southern Economic Journal*, 36(1):63, 1969.

Heffernan, Joseph. "Public Assistance and Social Services." Pp. 109–20, in Joint Economic Committee of the U.S. Congress, *Studies in Public Welfare: Issues in Welfare Administration: Intergovernmental Relationships*. Washington, D.C.: U.S. Government Printing Office, 1973.

Hess, Robert D., Virginia Shipman, Brophy Jeref, and Roberta Meyer Baer. "The Cognitive Environments of Urban Pre-School Children, Summary of the Completed Project." Graduate School of Education, University of Chicago, 1969.

Hess, Robert D. "Educability and Rehabilitation; The Future of the Welfare Class." Paper presented at the Thirteenth Groves Conference on Marriage and the Family, Knoxville, Tenn., 1964.

Holden, Constance. "Teen Age Pregnancies Out of Control," *Science* 204 (4393): 597, May 11, 1979.

Jackson, Jacqueline J. "Where Are the Black Men? Scarcity of Males Upsets the Life Style of [Black] Women," *Ebony*, 27(5):99–102, 104, 106, 1972.

Johnson, Beverly L. "Women Who Head Families 1970–1977; Their Number Rose, Income Lagged," *Monthly Labor Review*, 101(2):32–37, 1978.

Klausner, Samuel Z. *Six Years in the Lives of the Impoverished: An Examination of the WIN Thesis*. Philadelphia: Center for Research of the Acts of Man, 1978.

Lane, Lionel C. "The Identity of the Public Social Service Worker," *Public Welfare*, 27(4):311–17, 1969.

Lawrence, William J., and Stephen Leeds. *An Inventory of Federal Income Transfer Programs, Fiscal Year 1977*. White Plains, N.Y.: Institute for Socio-Economic Studies, 1978.

Levinson, Perry. "How Employable Are AFDC Mothers?" *Welfare in Review*, 8:19, 1970.

Liebow, Elliot. "Fathers Without Children," *Public Interest*, 5:13–25, 1966.

Lyon, D. W., P. A. Armstrong, J. R. Hosek, and J. J. McCall. *Multiple Benefits in New York City*, R–2002–HEW. Santa Monica: Rand, 1976.

———, C. P. Rydell, and M. D. Menchik. *Welfare Policy Research: Findings on the Dynamics of Dependency*, P–5566. Santa Monica: Rand, 1975.

McCormack, Patricia. "A Report on Children Bearing Children: Lifelong Handicap Predicted," *International Herald Tribune*, August 22,:1978, p. 6.

MacDonald, Maurice. "Food Stamps: An Analytical History," *Social Service Review*, 51(4):642–58, 1977.

MacLatchie, Elizabeth B. *Simplifying Application and Investigation*

Processes. Chicago: American Public Welfare Association, 1968.

Maynard, Rebecca, Irwin Garfinkel, and Valerie Leach. *Analysis of Nine Month Interviews for Supported Work: Results of an Early AFDC Sample.* Mathematica Policy Research and the Institute for Research on Poverty. Madison, Wis.: University of Wisconsin, 1977.

Miller, S. M. "The American Lower Classes: A Typological Approach." Pp. 9–23, in Arthur B. Shostak and William Gomberg (eds.), *Blue Collar World: Studies of the American Worker.* Englewood Cliffs, N.J.: Prentice-Hall, 1964.

Minuchin, Salvador, Braulio Montalvo, Bernard G. Guerney, Bernice Rosman, and Florence Shumer. *Families of the Slums, An Exploration of Their Structure and Treatment.* New York: Basic Books, 1967.

Morris, Robert. "Welfare Reform, 1973: The Social Service Dimension," *Science,* 181(4099):515–22, 1973.

Moynihan, Daniel P. "The Crisis in Welfare," *Public Interest,* 10:3–29, 1968.

———. "One Step We Must Take," *Saturday Review,* 53(21):20–23, 1970.

Munnell, Alicia H. "Social Security: Public Financing for Human Needs," *The Pioneer,* October 19, 1978, pp. 6–7.

Nash, Jim. "Counter-Culture: A Bloodsucker on Our System," *Los Angeles Times,* July 26, 1978, Part II, p. 5.

National Center for Social Statistics. *Disposition of Public Assistance Cases Involving Questions of Fraud.* Washington, D.C.: U.S. Department of Health, Education and Welfare, n.d.

———. *Public Assistance Statistics.* Washington, D.C.: U.S. Department of Health, Education and Welfare, n.d.

———. *National Cross Tabulations from the 1967 and 1969 AFDC Studies.* Washington, D.C.: U.S. Department of Health, Education and Welfare, 1971.

New Republic, The. "Feeding a Hungry World." Comment. 171(1–2):5–8, 1974.

New York Times. "Goldin Audit Finds Fraud in Women on Welfare Not Reporting Marriages," October 30, 1977, Part I, p. 37.

Oblata, J.R. "The Blacks of Baldwin Hills: Worthy Models for Youth," *Los Angeles Times,* June 16, 1973, Part II, p. 7.

Office of Child Support Enforcement. "Good Cause for Refusing to Cooperate." Action Transmittal to State Agencies and Local Agencies, to Clarify Issues Concerning the Good Cause Regulation. Washington, D.C.: U.S. Department of Health, Education and Welfare, 1978.

Office of Research and Statistics. *AFDC 1975 Recipient Characteristics.* Washington, D.C.: U.S. Department of Health, Education and Welfare, 1977.

———. "Public Assistance: Comparison of Calendar Years 1975–1977."

Research and Statistics Note No. 10 (August 10). Washington, D.C.: Social Security Administration, 1978a.

———. "Public Assistance: Comparison of Calendar Years 1975–1977." Research and Statistics Note No. 10 (August 18). Washington, D.C.: Social Security Administration, 1978b.

Office of the Secretary, U.S. Department of Health, Education and Welfare. *Better Jobs and Income Act. HR 9030: A Summary and Sectional Explanation.* Washington, D.C.: U.S. Department of Health, Education and Welfare, 1977.

Piven, Frances Fox, and Richard A. Cloward. *Regulating the Poor.* New York: Random House, 1971.

Rein, Martin. "The Strange Case of Public Dependency," *Transaction,* 3(3):16–23, 1966.

———, and Lee Rainwater. *Patterns of Welfare Use.* Working Paper No. 47. Cambridge, Mass.: Joint Center for Urban Studies of MIT and Harvard University, 1977.

Rein, Mildred, and Barbara Wishnov. "Patterns of Work and Welfare in AFDC," *Welfare in Review,* 9(6):7–12, 1971.

Richan, Willard. "The Two Kinds of Social Service in Public Welfare," *Public Welfare,* 27(4):307–10, 1969.

Rush, Thomas Y. Letter to Ralph Segalman, August 8, with statistical table enclosures for SSI, 1978.

Rydell, C. P., T. Palmerio, G. Blais, and D. Brown. *Welfare Caseload Dynamics,* R–1441–NYC. Santa Monica: Rand, 1974.

Segalman, Ralph. "The Protestant Ethic and Social Welfare," *Journal of Social Issues,* 24(2):125–41, 1968.

Sheehan, Susan. *A Welfare Mother.* New York: New American Library (Mentor Books), 1976.

Smith, J. P. *Assets, Savings and Labor Supply,* P 5470–1. Santa Monica: Rand, November 1976.

Snee, John, and Mary Ross. "Social Security Amendments of 1977: Legislative History and Summary of Provisions," *Social Security Bulletin* (SSA) 78–11700, March 1978.

Social Security Administration. *A Chartbook: Aid to Families with Dependent Children.* Office of Research and Statistics (SSA) 78–11721, 1968.

———. *Public Assistance Statistics: October 1978,* U.S. Department of Health, Education and Welfare, HEW Publication No. (SSA) 79–11917, March 1979.

Social Security Information Items. "Trustees Report Social Security Financially Sound," No. 21, July 1, 1978.

———. "Effort Made to Increase Child Support Collections," No. 23, September 1978.

Staff Study (Subcommittee on Fiscal Policy of the Joint Economic Committee—Studies in Public Welfare). *Studies in Public Welfare: Public Income Transfer Programs: The Incidence of Multiple Benefits and the Issues Raised by Their Receipts.* Paper No. 1. Washington, D.C.: U.S. Government Printing Office, 1973.

———. *Issues in Welfare Administration: Welfare an Administrative Nightmare.* Paper No. 5, Part I. Washington, D.C.: U.S. Government Printing Office, 1974.

Steele, Paul D. "The Labelling Perspective of Deviance: A Critical Assessment," *Journal of Sociology,* 3:17–37, 1973.

———. "Exploration of the Labelling Perspective of Mental Illness in a Rehabilitation Situation." Ph.D. Dissertation, University of Texas at Austin, 1974.

———. "Exploration of the Labelling Systems in a Mental Health Rehabilitation Program." Paper given at the Midwest Sociological Society, Chicago, April 8, 1975.

Steiner, Gilbert. *The State of Welfare.* Washington, D.C.: Brookings, 1971.

———. "Reform Follows Reality: The Growth of Welfare," *Public Interest,* 34:47–65, 1975.

Stone, Robert C., and Frederic T. Schlamp. "Characteristics Associated with Receipt or Nonreceipt of Financial Aid from Welfare Agencies," *Welfare in Review:* 1–11, July 1965.

———. *Family Life Styles Below the Poverty Line.* A Report to the State Social Welfare Board. Institute for Social Science Research, San Francisco State University, 1967.

Thomas, Dorothea. "SSI Beneficiaries Medically Determined to Be Alcoholics or Drug Addicts." Research and Statistics Note No. 8. Washington, D.C.: Social Security Administration, 1977.

Tropman, John E. "Public Welfare, Change, Appropriations, Service." Mimeographed, 1971.

U.S. Bureau of the Census. "Poor Families Headed by Women Show Rise," *Los Angeles Times,* April 5, 1974, Part 1B, p. 3.

Upman, Frances. "The Changing Roles of Welfare Employee and Client," *Public Welfare,* 27(4):318–26, 1969.

van den Haag, Ernest. "Realistic Steps for 'Reforming' Welfare," *Journal of the Institute for Socio-Economic Studies,* 4(4):73–79, Winter 1979.

Waxman, Chaim I. *The Stigma of Poverty: A Critique of Poverty Theories and Policies.* New York: Pergamon, 1977.

Ways and Means Committee, U.S. Congress. "Hearings on H.R. 10032." Eighty-seventh Congress, Second Session. Washington, D.C.: U.S. Government Printing Office, 1962.

Weinberger, Caspar. "The Reform of Welfare: A National Necessity," *Journal of the Institute for Socio-Economic Studies,* 1(1):1–27, 1976.

Wilcox, Claire. *Toward Social Welfare*. Homewood, Ill.: Irwin, 1969.

Wilensky, Harold L., and C. N. Lebeaux. *Industrial Society and Social Welfare*. New York: Free Press, 1958.

Williams, Kenton. "Some Implications for Services," *Public Welfare*, 27(4):327–32, 1969.

Williamson, John B. "Beliefs About Welfare Recipients." Paper presented at the American Sociological Association, 1973.

———. "Beliefs About the Welfare Poor," *Sociology and Social Research*, 58(2):163–75, 1974a.

———. "National Income Insurance as an Anti-Poverty Strategy." Paper presented at the Annual Meeting of the Society for the Study of Social Problems, 1974b.

Winslow, Benjamin H. *Wage Record Clearance Systems: Colorado and Oklahoma*. Washington, D.C.: U.S. Department of Health, Education and Welfare, 1975.

Winston, M. P., and T. Forsher. *Non-Support of Legitimate Children by Affluent Fathers as a Cause of Poverty and Welfare Dependence*, P4665–1. Santa Monica: Rand, 1974.

Wishnov, Barbara. *Determinants of the Work-Welfare Choice: A Study of AFDC Women*. Boston: Boston College, Social Welfare Regional Research Center, 1973.

Yelaja, Shankar (ed.). *Authority and Social Work: Concept and Use*. Toronto: University Press, 1971.

INCOME MAINTENANCE PROPOSALS AND THE QUESTION OF POVERTY

5

CONTINUED dissatisfaction with AFDC has kept the issue of an income maintenance program at the forefront of public discussion. Tobin lists two basic strategies in the effort to control poverty; he labels these as structural and distributive. The structural strategy is represented by efforts to build up the capacities of the poorest segment of the population so that they may earn incomes that will provide an adequate living standard. The distributive strategy is represented by methods of income payments or arrangements to provide a base of financial support to ensure an adequate living standard for every family. The decentralized public assistance mechanism has been found to be ineffective, costly, and destructive for this purpose. As a consequence, it has been reorganized for all aged, disabled, and blind persons. Pressure to drop the public assistance mechanism for all others and to replace it with an income maintenance scheme for all has mounted in recent years. As a distributive strategy, the public assistance model has been considered a failure. The debate in recent years has centered on alternative models of income maintenance which are purportedly more effective and less destructive than public assistance.

Alternatives to public welfare which have been suggested generally fit four classes of options: (1) the model based on family income which sets a minimum floor under family income; (2) the children's allowance or universal payment (*demogrant*) in which all individuals receive grants, which are then retrieved by differential tax rates among the nonpoor as suggested by Greene and Handler; (3) the model based on categorical guarantees, providing a floor under the income of protected categories of the population; and (4) the model based on income and ownership policies that have underlying assumptions of basic changes in the economy which will eliminate or prevent poverty. A demogrant is a lump sum given to each person in the society to be used as he or she wishes. The government, hopefully, regains much of the money given to persons who do not need it by means of the income tax. In other words, the demogrant is income and must be reported. The word is derived from demos = people and a grant is a gift.

All of these options, and public assistance as well, are in reality transfer arrangements or transfer payments. Transfer arrangements do not use or change the total of material resources in the society, but they redistribute income from the nonrecipients to the recipients. Each of the four income transfer programs listed above is closely related to the governmental tax structure. If the transfer payments for the poor, for example, were to be increased without any substantial changes in the tax structure and its collection mechanisms, the burden of providing for the increase to the poor would fall upon the middle class and some working poor, who currently shoulder the burden of taxes in the society. Many of the proponents of income guarantees for the poor make their proposals without suggesting a concurrent plan for redesigning taxation patterns. Many income guarantee supporters assume that the additional revenue will come from smaller defense budgets, decreased farm supports, or more stringent tax collection from exempted categories.

Despite these assumptions, most income guarantee supporters pay little attention to the tax redistribution mechanism. The net effect of their position, therefore, becomes one of subsidy of the residual poor by the middle class and by some of the working poor. Many supporters of income guarantee undertake the effort in the interests of more equitable and just treatment of the less affluent population, but their activity, if fulfilled, may result in an injustice to those who cannot avoid taxation at the source. It is as if the affluent and exempted categories of the population, the military industries, the oil companies, the corporate farms, and the exempted bondholders are standing aside while fiery middle-class intellectuals design plans for further taxing the working poor and the middle class to support the residual poor.

Real Costs of Public Welfare

Social policy planners must attempt still another orientation to welfare reform—one relating to the real costs of a reform. The real cost is the reduction, if any, in the real income of the nation. If the reform causes some people to work less or keeps people from working, the real output of the nation is thereby diminished and fewer goods and services will be available for consumption or investment. A consequence of this cost, if not directly taxed, is usually apparent in the hidden tax of inflation.

Knowledge of how welfare really affects the supply of labor is sadly lacking (Aaron). The real costs of the AFDC program are unknown. The fact that most AFDC mothers are not available for the general job market because of the presence of young children in the family supports the view that to keep them on welfare does not increase the real costs to society. But in 1976 about 46 percent of *all* mothers with children under eighteen and 37 percent of all mothers with children under six worked (Grossman).

If AFDC did not exist, many current recipients would find jobs, although probably at very low wages (Aaron). This matter is a serious one for a society faced with a runaway inflation occasioned by too low levels of work productivity and with huge overspending, past and present, in nonsalable materials and activities such as a war in Vietnam, a heavy military budget, and a spiralling welfare program. Only when a welfare program becomes truly rehabilitative can it be viewed in a potentially productive sense.

The degree to which AFDC mothers do work is unknown, probably because most domestic employers do not report withholding.

The Office of Economic Opportunity and its successor programs in HEW and the Department of Labor conducted negative income tax experimental programs in areas of New Jersey and Pennsylvania, in Gary, Indiana, rural Iowa, and North Carolina, and in Seattle and Denver. These experiments sought to test the effects of a guaranteed income level on the families served and on the work effort of those in the families who were employable. Of the four programs, the Seattle and Denver units were the largest with 2,733 intact families and 2,035 families headed by mothers alone (see Albrecht, p. 76). All four units operated in a similar manner, although the financial constraints and supports were not all exactly the same. Guarantee levels of $3,800, $4,800, and $5,600 dollars to a family of four were combined with built in guarantee deductions of 50 percent, 70 percent, and 80 percent as outside income increased. A control group with no guarantees was matched to the guarantee group. The program began in 1970 in Seattle and in 1971 in Denver. The findings show that when such guarantees are made there is a 5 percent reduction of hours worked by the husbands and an 11 percent reduction for female heads of families. Extrapolated to the national labor scene the indication is that a 50 percent poverty line guaranteed income would reduce the participating husbands labor supply by 7 percent and the participating wives labor supply by 23 percent.

Even in these experiments, however, the findings show a greater incidence of marital breakup than was experienced in the control families not provided with the experimental income guarantee (Seattle and Denver reports by Spiegelman, Groenveld, and Robins). Similarly, from their reading of the Seattle/Denver data, Thuits and Hannan indicate that the low-income families with "an increase or stabilization of income may have a 'ripple effect'," causing other stressful life changes and increased distress levels. Middleton and Allen state that the income beneficiaries of the New Jersey experiment reported somewhat higher rates of psychosomatic symptoms than did the control groups. Distress was weakly (not significantly) but positively related to the levels of actual payments. Middleton (1976) also reports that a similar pattern emerged, statistically significant, in the rural income maintenance experiment. Furthermore, Jones reveals that, according to his reading of the New Jersey and Mississippi experiments, "the income treatment subjects seemed to be more convinced of their powerlessness, while control subjects were losing that negative conviction." Jones' explanation for this phenomenon is based on the shared "definitions of the situation" held by the client group. In Jones' opinion, even if the subject is influenced by the increased income to change his life-style and employment or nonemployment patterns, the limited increased income does not really alter his material circumstances; nor does it affect the influence of those in the social networks about him. Jones believes that the experimentally aided families experience frustration at the stagnancy of their low power and prestige status despite the increase in income. According to Jones, this reading of the data is consistent with both the culture of poverty and situational perspectives (p. 13).

The Rand Corporation has published a number of studies on the effect of income guarantees on the working poor. Greenberg and Kosters, in their evaluation of the Nixon Family Assistance Plan, found that the hours worked by the entire American work force would decline by about one-half of 1 percent, or about $1.4 billion in 1970 dollars. Pascal, on the other hand, suggests that a high guarantee tied to a high tax-earning welfare program would benefit the poor without substantially decreasing national output. Greenberg concludes that an attempt by New York City or State "to supplement proposed federal programs by supporting families headed by working males at existing city welfare standards would probably be very expensive, both in direct costs of assistance and the indirect costs associated with reductions in labor supply." Conversely, Lyon found that "lower benefit-loss rates tend to result in more AFDC women working."

The above research raises many questions about the advisability of instituting a minimum guaranteed income or similar income support program. There is a question not only of maintenance of work effort as a result of the program but also of the psychological effect of such a program. Even more critical is the effect of such a program on family stability.

Bishop questions the Seattle/Denver experiments based on four complementary hypotheses: (1) Husbands in the control group may have feared that the welfare department would pursue them for child support if they left their families but in contrast the experimentals were under no pressure for child responsibility. (2) Wives may have felt that AFDC was stigmatizing but that receiving payments from an income transfer program was much less so. (3) Many couples in the control group were aware neither of the wife's eligibility for AFDC if the marriage ended nor of levels of support available from AFDC, food stamps, and Medicaid. In the experimental group, a special effort was made to ensure that people knew benefits were available, even if the marriage were to dissolve. Thus, greater awareness made the advantages of a split a part of the people's lifespace. (4) In most working-class families, the husband has the primary responsibility for support. But the acceptance of an income-related transfer may have been seen as a signal that the husband was a failure. Anderson similarly questions the basic principle of income maintenance and opposes any similar plan such as the negative income tax because of its effect on labor supply.

Still another question about income maintenance plans is the degree to which AFDC women can be expected to choose between increased dollars from employment and continued and stable income payments. Appropriate employment-readiness detail about AFDC women (such as availability of child care, transportation, and job conditioning) as related to other relevant data (such as size of family, former employment experience, employment knowledge and skills, literacy achieved—rather than grades completed), plus other necessary information on factors that prevent AFDC mothers from taking employment, are all critically necessary if an employment-related income guarantee is to be considered. Even the AFDC mothers' pattern of spacing children or their lack of spacing or the feasibility of helping AFDC women engage in such family planning needs careful study, which without data is impossible. In examining the effect of income maintenance laws (programs) on fertility, Cain concludes that "the overall effect of IML's [income maintenance laws] is pronatal and there is not much scope for reducing this bias" (p. 350). Instead, he suggests that we should adopt programs that have antinatal positions. One such program would include employment opportunities for women which provide more attractive take-home pay than is provided by IMLs or welfare. He also suggests mechanisms such as eliminating the "first-baby bonus" in income maintenance by extending coverage to the childless, decreasing the size of allowances for children past the first, and increasing the allowance with the age of the child so that new babies will have very small grants (p. 351). Thus, the real costs of income guarantees or welfare reform are not currently available for determination.

Another cost conceptualization relates to the issue of long-range costs. If, for example, it became possible to develop an incentive plan which kept fathers at home in residually poor families and in the process allowed fathers and mothers to undertake gainful or marginally gainful employment, the children's esteem of their parents would probably improve and the new parental model would encourage middle-class aspirations for them. In one or two generations, as has occurred with America's immigrant population, these families, while still poor, would produce fewer children and these children would be more self-supporting and self-responsible. Hence, a plan that retains fathers at home would be less expensive to society in the long run, although quite expensive in the interim. To undertake such a long-range view is not customary for a society which budgets its funds from year to year and which is probably as shortsighted in its planning as the residual welfare family itself. The difference between the cost benefit data derived from short-range and long-range analysis can be considerable.

To take the example described previously, the immediate costs of keeping a father at home and providing incentives and opportunities for the family to become middle class in orientation would be great. Offsetting these costs would be the limited amount of taxes withheld by the father and others employed in the family. The long-run costs and benefits can be quite different. Among the benefits derived from the program are the taxes paid by the grown children during a lifetime of employment, the welfare costs saved by not having to support the families, and the tangential costs derived in a community where poverty-related problems are reduced or absent. Thus, the true aim of any welfare reform proposal is not the arrangement of more effective and equitable transfer payments to the poor. Rather, it is the development of arrangements whereby the residual poor would be transferred from the status of being assisted to that of being self-supporting, socially responsible taxpayers and participants in the mainstream of the society.

In order to understand income maintenance proposals, it is important to describe how employment relates to earnings in an AFDC family. If a family has no income other than welfare, and it receives $2,760 (which is still the payment minimum in some states), the family's total annual income is $2,760. If the family earns $600 in outside income and this amount is reported to the welfare authorities, the family's grant is not cut and remains at $2,760 per year, plus actual work expenses. (There is an earned income disregard of $30 per month, plus one-third income from outside work.) If the family earns $1,200, the total family income, after welfare grant deduction, is $3,960 per year. If the family earns $2,400, their annual income is $4,720, plus actual work expenses. If the family lives in a more generous state, the grant might be $6,726 per year. If the family earns $600, the total income is $6,876 per year. If the family earns $1,200, the total family income is $8,036 per year, plus actual working expenses. If the family earns $2,400, then it has a total income per year of $8,236, plus actual working expenses. In addition, the family is entitled to food stamps and Medicaid. That portion of the family's income that is from public assistance, food stamps, and Medicaid is of course exempt from income taxes. Thus, the equivalent of a salary to match this amount would be much larger. In addition to the income listed above, the family is eligible for an earned income tax credit of 10 percent of earnings up to $4,000 (and phased out gradually over $4,000) (Special HEW Report on Welfare Reform). To complete the picture of how employment affects the total dollars and resources of the AFDC family it is important to consider the contribution of food stamps. The amount of food stamps permitted in 1976 to a family with very little or no outside earnings is shown in Table 5.1.

TABLE 5.1   **Amount of Food Stamps Available**
            by Family Size in 1976

NO. OF PERSONS	AMOUNT PER MONTH	NO. OF PERSONS	AMOUNT PER MONTH
1	$50	5	$198
2	$92	6	$236
3	$130	7	$262
4	$166	8	$298

SOURCE: Fishbein, p. 15.

In the past, the deduction from AFDC grants for employment earnings was 100 cents on each dollar earned. This confiscatory deduction served as a disincentive for employment by AFDC families. It also served as an incentive for cheating on welfare as well as a disincentive for communication with welfare workers who had been putatively cast as advisors and helpers for these families under AFDC legislation and regulations. Hence, the welfare deduction on AFDC employment became counter-productive in helping the client attain self-sufficiency.

The reasoning behind the 100-percent welfare-employment deduction should be understood by anyone seeking to study welfare reform. Under the general principles of welfare law, the means test is a mechanism to prevent the granting of aid to families with adequate resources or income. Not to apply a means test might be unjust to self-supporting families who rely entirely on their own efforts to maintain themselves. To support a family that has sizable resources is a measure which plays favorites. It would be equivalent to helping those who apply at the expense of those who do not. To support *all* families that have sizable resources and income is probably beyond the ability of the society, and to provide assistance to those who do not need it would create social dissatisfaction and strain. Hence, some limits have to be set for the outside income and accumulated resources which a family may have and still be designated as needy.

Factors other than income and resources apply in terms of an analysis of need. A century ago, the considerations for assisting the poor often related to lack of land and access to land as a measure of need. In contemporary times, while money income is the basic element of family need, the needs of the residual poor are not always money. Biological endowment, family size, knowledge of how to get the most for their money and how to make the most of their life-chances, and environmental conditions affect the individual's access to opportunity. Any alternative to public assistance must go beyond income maintenance if it is to have long-range effects.

All options based on family income carry the same basic assumption—namely, that the family's primary need is for an income and that the causes of a lack of income are external to the family. An income-based option is therefore probably supportable for families that have inadequate income as a result of an external cause. For others, such programs may have to be supplemented by other plans related to individual family problems which have caused marginal incomes.

By definition, the option based on family income must provide an adequate income allowance to families with little or no earning capacity; reduce the disincentives to the individual to earn as much as possible without at the same time seriously disturbing the labor market; limit the cost to the society; and minimize payments to those who do not need them.

All of the income-based options are designed to be financed from general tax revenues. All operate on the simple principle that if family income is less than a breakeven amount, the family becomes eligible for a cash payment. If family income is more than a breakeven amount, there is no cash payment. The crucial question is what is the breakeven amount to be? If it is set high, then there will be more families supported at a higher standard of living and at a high cost to the society. In time, it will probably raise the cost of labor generally and provide even further stimulus for runaway inflation. If it is set too low, then it will provide inadequately for the poor and in the process cause further deterioration of their standard of living. In the process it would not serve the reform purposes sought.

Types of Income-Based Options

The negative income tax is one of the income-based options. Milton Friedman in his book *Capitalism and Freedom* seeks a program that will not only meet the parameters described above but will also satisfy a fifth requirement. This requirement is that the reform program not distort the economic market or impede its functioning. Because of this fifth requirement, Friedman prefers the negative income tax.

The negative income tax is based upon the arrangement whereby a cash payment is made to a family or individual whose income is less than the amount at which their income tax liability would begin. The payments to the poor are calculated on the basis of the unused exemptions and deductions to which these nontaxpayers would be entitled if they were actually paying income tax. If a family had before-tax income less than its basic income allowance from standard exemptions and deductions, that family would be entitled to a cash payment equal to a percentage of the difference between its basic allowance and its before-tax income. The percentage is called the negative tax rate. Friedman suggests a negative tax rate of 50 percent. If, for example, we were to use exemptions of $600 for each dependent and a standard deduction of $1,000 for the head of the house and $800 for the spouse, the basic allowance for the four-person family would total $3,000. That is the breakeven income for this family. If the family had no before-tax income, it would be eligible for a cash payment of $1,500 (or 50 percent of the difference between the basic allowance and before-tax income, which in this case is $3,000). Income tax liability begins when before-tax family income exceeds the basic income allowance. Thus, with an income of $4,000 a four-person family would have a $1,000 positive taxable income, and after a $140 income tax payment, the after-tax income for this family would equal $3,860. This plan would be particularly helpful to families with abnormal expenses such as deductible medical costs and tax-reportable losses.

Other economists have proposed more generous negative tax rates. In any case, Friedman's figures can easily be adjusted to meet contemporary standards. The higher the rate, the greater the cost in terms of less taxes collected and more negative income taxes to be paid out. Unrealistically low allowances for dependents in the negative income tax would serve as a depressant to the program. The program as a whole is understandable to an economist and would be understood by a tax accountant, but it would not be so clear to the residual poor. It is questionable whether the incentive to work contained in the proposal could be made clear to the residual poor, for they would not readily understand how the tax structure and government payments to them are related. The residual poor are usually poor planners and self-defeating taxpayers. Whereas the middle-class family keeps detailed records for tax deductions, the residual poor usually do not know of the deductions or they fail to keep records that make the deduction possible. Those of the residual poor who work do so in marginal employment in which income is not reported. Others have withholding taken from their paychecks on sporadic, irregular employment, and in many of these instances, they never collect on the income tax rebates for which they are eligible.

Alvin Schorr (1966b) points out other weaknesses in the negative income tax plan. He states that the incentive scale provided by the negative income tax is caught between opposing pressures. "Either the rate at which payments are made pushes downward and many people receive inadequate income or it moves upward and people with comparatively decent incomes receive assistance" (p. 117). Payments that push too far into the higher income brackets cost a great deal, and they undermine the credibility of a program supposedly designed to aid the poor. But payments that are too low at the bottom of the scale fail to assure income appropriate to the living needs of the residually poor families.

The advantage of the negative income tax over public assistance is that for the means test, which is applied only to the poor, it substitutes an income tax test, which is applied to all. For the middle class, this test is often a mechanical process involving not much more than the filing of forms that are examined at some distant office. For the poor, it may mean long waits in taxpayer assistance offices of the Internal Revenue Service, with family income and expense analyses that can be even more demeaning than is the current practice in AFDC. The fact that the test would be conducted by Internal Revenue rather than by a public welfare agency does not suggest that the test would be any more palatable or less humiliating. The fact that a test will be conducted by the Internal Revenue, whose job it is to secure accurate returns, and not by an eligibility worker in public welfare, whose job it is to complete the eligibility process without too much client trauma, may mean that the negative income tax may be even less popular with the residual poor than AFDC. Moreover, it would provide even less effective incentive for client self-help than is currently apparent in AFDC.

Robert Lampman suggests an alternate to the Friedman proposal: use of a graduated negative tax rate that would provide increased support for the lower income levels; and a shift of the basic income allowances from income tax exemptions and deductions to the poverty threshold income as established for the family size. Under this plan, a family of four would have the benefit of 50 percent of its income, if that income was equal to the breakeven income, and would not be benefited by the program if it earned more than the breakeven sum.

The Lampman proposal would be even more difficult to administer than the Friedman proposal, for it, too, would presumably be administered by the Internal Revenue Service with the presently available machinery. In addition, neither proposal, with their complicated formulas and irregular, confusing payment schedules, would be understood by the residual poor. Both, however, make possible the elimination of the complex AFDC machinery and the sizable costs of operating fifty-four different programs under national HHS direction. Neither requires more of the client than is required of the regular income taxpayer.

The Tobin proposal differs from the Friedman and Lampman proposals in that it is a guaranteed minimum income plan that makes additional cash payments an incentive to work. The result is that the breakeven income is twice the minimum payment received by the family in poverty. With an external income of $6,400, the cash payment is zero and the family's total after-tax income is $6,400. The more the family earns, up to twice the breakeven point, the less cash payment is made to the family. Presumably, here too the incentive to work is maintained. It is doubtful, however, that a proposal as complicated as Tobin's would draw the residual poor out of their poverty pattern of living.

Rolph and Break have proposed an extension of the family income maintenance concept by utilization of a credit income tax. With the credit income tax, a form of guaranteed income would be established, and public assistance would be woven into a simplified and reorganized system of taxation. Under this system, each person would be entitled to a flat sum of tax credit. There would also be a general proportional (but reformed) income tax, with no exclusions, deductions, or exemptions. As a result, the tax value of a dependent would not vary with family income. Under the plan, each taxpayer would pay income tax at the established proportional rate. Every individual would be entitled to a basic income allowance equal to the amount of the credit income tax multipled by the proportional tax rate. The result provides the level of the guaranteed income. Under the proposal, families could combine their income tax credits as they currently combine their present standard exemptions and deductions. The tax burden would fall mainly on higher income taxpayers and, among these, the taxpayers with income that is not now taxable.

The Rolph and Break proposal provides no special tax benefits for families which deduct large medical expenses, losses, property damage, and so forth. The sweeping removal of all deductions and exemptions may be quite threatening to families and others who have become accustomed to using these mechanisms to reduce their tax obligations. It is also doubtful that those interests in the society which currently benefit from tax exemptions and deductions would genially accept such sweeping tax reform without a struggle. Of all the plans, therefore, this one is probably least likely to be seriously considered for adoption. Moreover, even though the plan does preserve the work incentive, at least in terms of money received by the family, the residual poor would not adequately understand the plan.

The Nixon administration proposal (Moynihan, 1973, p. 12), later designated as HR 1, was offered in the fall of 1969. It has since been examined in depth in the Senate, and according to Moynihan (1969), it fell at the hands of a "coalition of Congressional conservatives, welfare-rights radicals and social work professionals frightened of losing their jobs and status." This plan sought to put a base under family income, while at the same time retaining the work requirements of public assistance. In this respect, it differs from the plans previously presented in this chapter.

Under HR 1, for the first time, one set of rules for eligibility would be applied on a nationwide basis. This innovation has subsequently been adopted for the aged, blind, and disabled needy under the SSI program of the Social Security Administration. The plan also called for a national minimum payment for all eligible families, just as already applies to SSI. Adults would be required to register for employment and to accept training and suitable work, if offered. The question for most realistic scholars on the work issue is whether or not a work requirement as a basis for benefit eligibility is an appropriate and effective means of encouraging meaningful employment for this population segment.

The plan also provided for a cost of working allowance, so that involvement in employment would not create an additional financial burden on the family's finances. Under the plan, an eligible family could have a male or female head. It would no longer be necessary for fathers to be absent from the home in order for a family to be eligible for inclusion in the program. Couples without children and single adults, however, would not be eligible.

Before families could become eligible for inclusion in the program, HR 1 required that they meet a resource and income criteria. This means test would determine whether the family could manage financially without having to enroll in the program. Eligibility for the plan was so constructed that a family could not have resources of more than $1,500, nor could their income be above the established breakeven level of $3,920 for a family of four. In the legislative hearings, it was understood that these financial levels would be readjusted from time to time based on economic reports. Property essential to the family's means of support or to family life, such as a home, household goods, personal effects, and a means of travel necessary for employment, was exempted from the resource limitation. In the calculation of payments to families, counted income would be subjected to a 50-percent negative deduction rate. Payments such as survivors benefits under Social Security, earned pensions, proceeds from life insurance, and similar nonwage income would be exempt from any tax and would not affect eligibility. (This practice is a variance from the current one in public assistance in which such income is deducted from family grants.) Also exempted as uncounted income would be all earnings by a student in the family, any tuition paid by scholarships, contributions from private charity, and the value of home-produced and -consumed food. The exemption of private charity as uncounted income was an innovation. In the past, when such gifts were reported or discovered, they were deducted from the grant, even though charity gifts were often given as part of a plan to provide opportunities to the families to make productive and useful changes in their lives. Income analysis for families was to be conducted on a quarterly basis. The applicant would submit his wage stubs for each quarter, and the payments made during the next quarter would be based upon the calculations derived from this data.

Problems were raised about the workfare requirements of the proposal. When any adult member of an eligible family refused to register for employment or training or refused offers of employment, he would have his portion of the family's grant deducted from the total. It was therefore assumed that this individual rather than the whole family would suffer for his recalcitrance. Mothers of preschool-aged children for whom day care was not available were exempted, as were adults required in the home for the care of invalids.

Some problems were raised as to the definition of suitable employment. It was feared that HR 1 would ultimately subsidize marginal employers who could not afford to pay standard wages. Many were also concerned that adults would be forced into employment without obtaining adequate, safe day care for their children. This was viewed as a hazard to child safety and as a violation of the principle that young children should not be separated from their mothers. (Such principles are violated regularly in the middle class, where working mothers make up a sizable proportion of family wage-earners. The issue here is whether the government should be a party to a forced separation of mother and child. In justice to the middle-class mother, however, equal consideration might be given to subsidizing her day-care costs.)

The program was to have been administered by the fifty-four states and territories under federal supervision, but this system was considered unwieldy and inefficient. The plan contained proposals for transfer from state to federal administration over an unspecified period of time.

It was openly acknowledged that HR 1 was not designed to eliminate poverty. Rather, its intent was to keep the poor working man working and to reduce the incentive for husbands to stop working and to separate from their families.

The HR 1 program was criticized for many of the same reasons as other complicated graduated income programs. First, the plan would not be easily understood by the poor. In addition, it made no provision for childless couples. For some less employable women who might be without children because they remained single or as a result of divorce or desertion, the effect could be particularly severe. The criticisms of too low a minimum payment and too low a breakeven level could be countered by raising them, but this step would raise the cost to the taxpayer to such a level as to make the program unfeasible. The difficult problem of making employment available and easily accessible to families eligible for assistance was not considered in the plan. The limited availability of adequate day care and its limited accessibility to the poor were also not considered. Some viewed workfare without adequate day care as a trap to force mothers to leave their children with each other as sitters while they undertook employment that held little promise to themselves or their families.

A review of the proposals presented thus far shows that the Friedman, Rolph and Break, and Nixon administration plans were not designed to eliminate poverty, while the Lampman and Tobin plans were so intended. Both Lampman and Tobin tried to design plans that, by their economic gradations, would encourage people to move from receiving assistance to self-support. They also attempted to create a system whereby people would respond to the society's attitudes toward work. Each plan was necessarily tuned to variable payments based upon annual earned income and family size. These plans all focus on the fact that the common denominator in all poor families is their lack of income. On the assumption that their lack of income is a cause and not an effect of their poverty, these plans seek to transfer funds within the society to provide for a more equitable distribution between the affluent and the poor. The issue of lack of income as an effect rather than as a cause of poverty remains to be discussed. It is a basic concern underlying questions of effectiveness for guaranteed annual income plans.

Alternatives to Public Welfare Proposals

Another alternative to public welfare is the children's allowances proposal. Children's allowances, sometimes called family allowances, are systematic payments made to families with minor children, primarily to promote the welfare of such children. Eligibility for such allowances is not based on whether the parents are deceased, widowed, divorced, separated, married or not married, nor is it based on family income. An eligible child would be one under a specified age, usually age eighteen. Some plans provide for extensions of payments beyond age eighteen for students or for sick or handicapped children. Children's allowances would be financed either by a tax on employers or out of the general revenue. (In some countries, the children's allowance is subject to taxation.)

Children's allowances were originally developed in nineteenth-century France, with a special allowance required of employers over and beyond regular wages to be paid to workers with large families. Countries that had to rebuild their populations after devastating wars were particularly interested in such programs. Many nations adopted the plan after World War II and financed it by payroll taxes or income taxes. The basic theory underlying the children's allowance is that the entire nation should have to carry the cost of rearing the next generation. If a worker and his wife have more children than others, then they are presumably doing a service to the society and should be at least partially reimbursed, much as a foster parent is subvented for rearing a homeless child. An important issue relating to children's allowances is the question of whether all children are equally valuable to the society and equally subvented by the society. A family with eight children will probably not be able to provide each child with the same level of socialization, preparation, and equipment for personal competency as a family with two or three children. If this view is accepted, then family allowances should be larger for the first few children and scaled down as the number of children in the family goes up. In a pronatalist country, stipends per child increase with the number of children; in an antinatalist country the reverse is the case.

Another concept underlying children's allowances relates to the issue of equality of opportunity. If there are many children in a family, the opportunities of each is diminished unless an offsetting factor is present. Thus, a children's allowance for all would presumably benefit these children, while only minimal benefit would accrue to children in small families where the allowances could be regained by income tax.

Various plans for children's allowances have been proposed for the United States (Schorr, 1965, 1966a). One plan would remove income tax exemptions for children, would make allowances taxable, and would provide $50 per month to each child under age six and $10 per month to each child in the six- to eighteen-year-old group. Another proposal would make a monthly payment of $15 for each child under the age of eighteen. Yet another proposes a children's allowance of $10 per month for all children under age eighteen as long as there is satisfactory school attendance. Payments for the care and education of the children would go to the mother. Benefits would be taxable, and present exemptions would continue. Each of these plans presumably provides for scaled adjustments under changing economic conditions.

Children's allowances could be easily administered, and no major change would be sought in existing programs. These programs do not, however, provide any added service to needy single persons without children, childless couples of all ages, and middle-aged couples without children. Nor do they provide any help to the working poor who have no children. Although children's allowances have the advantage of not affecting wages, they are believed to be an inefficient way of helping the poor. Where the grants are sizable and where they are subject to taxation, recovery of such allowances from those who have no need for allowances would be highly inefficient. Unless there is a severe restructuring of the income tax system of exemptions and deductions, the provision of children's allowances to the nonpoor would be wasteful and without purpose. The possibility of reform of the tax structure is doubtful. Unless the allowances were sizable, they would not make possible the elimination of the AFDC program with all of its problems. If allowances were sizable, the costs of the program would be so large as to be prohibitive. Because most allowance schemes are not designed to graduate in size on the basis of family income, they would not be particularly helpful to the very poor unless they were so sizable as to make the costs prohibitive. Demogrants, the expanded version of family allowances, presents the same drawbacks as family allowances.

Another alternative to public assistance is the national income insurance plan as proposed by Etzioni, Williamson, and Jencks. This program would provide social insurance benefits for any family whenever the family income fell below a specified level. Under the Jencks et al. plan, the government would guarantee a worker an income equal to half the income he could be expected to earn as determined by careful actuarial projections, taking into account family background, level of education, occupation, and other appropriate characteristics. When the employee earned less than his predicted income, the government would make up half the difference. When he earned more than his predicted income, he would pay the government half the difference.

The Williamson plan would be financed by a payroll tax, with half paid by employers and half by employees. The guaranteed minimum income would be established solely on the basis of family size. The guaranteed minimum income would be initially set at a low level, at first equal to about 25 percent of the median American family income. If the 1973 median income was approximately $10,000, then the guaranteed minimum income would be $2,500 for a family of four. This guarantee would be made available to all families and single individuals, but it would be adjusted to family size. It is substantially below the poverty line for a family of four, which was set at $4,550 for mid-1974. The level chosen for the minimum of $2,500 initially would increase the political feasibility of the proposal. The higher the level of the minimum, the greater the number of recipients and the higher the cost of the program. The choice of a level of 25 percent as the minimum would minimize the impact of the program on labor force participation. With a higher minimum, an increase in voluntary unemployment would be possible, and people without jobs would be under less pressure to find employment.

Some workers would probably leave jobs with low wages. The resulting drop in the labor force might create so much public concern that such a program would not be established. Williamson's strategy is one of incrementalism: there would be an automatic increment in the level of the minimum up to an eventual level of 50 percent of the median income in ten years. This plan would presumably lead to a gradual reduction in the economic gap between the poor and others. It calls for a 50-percent marginal tax rate on all sources of income up to the breakeven point, that is, the income at which the tax on other sources of income equals the guaranteed income. The tax rate is high relative to what those in the low-income brackets currently pay. A lower tax rate was avoided in order to keep the total program cost down.

The plan would be financed by a federal tax on all sources of income above the breakeven point. The tax would be progressive and so calibrated as to raise the revenues needed to cover the program. The tax would initially raise about $7 billion, and within ten years the total raised would be approximately $50 billion annually. As the minimum increased, so would the tax.

Williamson's plan does not take into account differences in the size of family assets, for to do so would be administratively unfeasible and cost-prohibitive. At first, the plan would not provide a minimally adequate standard of living for the poor. In time, the minimum guarantee would rise to the level that it would be able to replace the AFDC welfare program. In addition, the plan would make no provision other than financial for making recipients self-sufficient. It would merely strive to maintain an income base under all families. While the plan could be exceedingly inflationary, the sizable AFDC expenditures which, in themselves, are continuingly inflationary, would be eliminated. Under the plan, employees and employers would pay the premiums for a social insurance program to be provided to others. As such, it can hardly be viewed as attractive to the taxpayers of America, nor can it really be categorized as insurance in that it taxes one group to serve another.

The entire spectrum of such income transfers deserves careful analysis. Is it income transfer or aid to the poor which we seek? Brittan and Lilley (p. 210) sharply criticize the proponents of income transfer who seek to equalize the rich and the poor. They indicate that "equalitarianism in the sense of making the pips of the rich squeak louder has nothing to do with helping the poor." They suggest an imaginary stock market and real estate crash, so that those in the top 1 percent would be moved down to the level of the 10 percent. The degree of equality, they state, would have increased under almost every definition, particularly under the definition of relative deprivation which is the favorite of those who seek income redistribution. But, ask Brittan and Lilley, "would the condition of the poor have improved?" Their answer is that there would have been no perceptible change in the condition of the poor. This, the authors maintain, is the effect of enforced income transfers.

The moral of [the data presented] is emphatically not that we have come to the limits of redistribution toward the poor and unfortunate but [that] the only sizable funds for redistribution [in England and presumably the Western world] is the broad mass of middle taxpayers who are neither very well off nor very poor (p. 209).

Concern for the underdog and envious egalitarianism are not the same and may even be in conflict. Presumably these authors believe that there are two groups pressuring for equalizing societal incomes. Some (the liberals supposedly) take the position that incomes can be equalized by taxing the people in the top income brackets to serve those in the lower brackets. Others, at the lower level of income presumably, are the envious egalitarians, who seek to equalize all income, including the sharing of middle-class incomes with the poor. Therefore, one can suppose, when the income from the affluent group does not suffice to bring the poor up to middle-income levels, then those concerned for the underdogs and the envious egalitarians would come in conflict. To equate the two presents social policy planners with a false dilemma.

A very different plan to replace AFDC has the support of the American Conservative Union. This plan is based on making "the sharpest possible distinction between the working poor and the non-working poor for the simple reason that it is bad policy to involve an industrious, hard-working group of families . . . with the problems of a very specialized and very troubled poverty substratum" (American Conservative Union, p. 2). Thus, the organization supports a plan to expand the concept of free food stamps to most or all welfare recipients. Under their plan, based on a proposal of Edward Banfield, housing and medical stamps as well as food stamps would be given to current AFDC clients, and the system would be so carefully regulated that the stamps could be used to buy only the goods designated for the particular stamp. There would be tough penalties for black market stamp exchanges. The present Food Stamp program would be continued. Hence, the incentive would be created for getting money, which a family could secure only by accepting employment. No family would be denied food, shelter, medical care, necessary transportation, and other essentials; they would be denied only the right to buy many inessentials.

The American Conservative Union (ACU) opposes the work requirement because it has seen no evidence of possible enforcement by the welfare bureaucracy. Under this plan, the working poor could have food stamps if they needed them, but they would also have money from earnings. In ACU's view, their proposal for an in-kind goods and services program presents a new concept for welfare that should be considered.

Carter's Welfare Reform Proposal

President Carter's welfare reform proposal of 1978, which he called the Better Jobs and Income program, requires very careful study. The decision to opt for an overall reform of welfare rather than to seek incremental changes on a piecemeal basis was pressed by Henry J. Aaron, then assistant secretary of HEW. He said that "it is possible, in principle to identify one-by-one the shortcomings of the present programs . . . [but] it is not possible to cure them one-by-one" (Weil, p. 13). The incremental approach would make administrative simplification and fraud reduction impossible, and would be very expensive, according to Aaron. On the other hand, Richard Nathan of the Brookings Institution (Weil, p. 12–13) believes that attempts at overall reform are doomed because they involve issues that are bound to raise the discussion (and controversy) to a high emotional pitch, making change unattainable. Senator Howard Baker of Tennessee supports Nathan, stating that with incrementalism it is always possible to proceed even if everyone involved is not in full agreement on the final design. The Carter administration has chosen the total reform approach and has proceeded to design and present a program of total reform to the Congress (Office of the Secretary, HEW: Summary).

Under the Carter plan, "food stamps, AFDC, SSI would all be replaced by a single cash grant indexed to the poverty level and the cost of living" (*Congressional Digest*, p. 1): "A work requirement would be imposed on major categories of recipients. Job training and employment assistance would be intensified and tightened eligibility requirements and their enforcement would be mandated." The existing Medicaid program would be continued for the present (probably until a universal health program is established with the Medicaid services included in it). Administrative reforms, however, would be installed in Medicaid parallel with welfare reform.

Under the Carter plan, a child in foster care would be filed for as a separate unit. Related individuals living together at one residence would apply as a unit. Exceptions would be the aged, blind, or disabled adults and their families, who would apply separately even if they were living in the same house with other related welfare applicants. Payments would be made to aged, blind, or disabled persons in group homes of less than sixteen residents as if they were living alone, as is the current practice under SSI. A nuclear family would file separately even if living with relatives. Single adults under twenty-five years of age with no children and not blind or disabled, regardless of where they live, would be required to apply with their parents, if the parents were alive and available (those not in institutions or whose whereabouts are unknown). This provision was apparently added in reaction to the actions of thousands of young people, many of them from middle-class or affluent parentage, who secured aid from public sources by declaring themselves no longer attached to their parents. Thus, parental approval of their applications for aid was not needed, and the parents could not be pressed to maintain their children. This situation was evident in student aid programs as well as in several General Assistance programs.

Every adult under the Better Jobs and Income program would be subject to the work requirement except for the following: (1) the aged, blind, disabled, or temporarily incapacitated, (2) an adult other than the principal family earner in a family of two or more adults and at least one child, (3) the only adult member of a family which includes either a child under seven years of age, a child over six who has a specific condition requiring close parental supervision (such as a physical, psychological, or other handicap or illness), or an adult who is aged, blind, disabled, or so incapacitated as to need a caretaker at home; (4) any person under twenty-one years of age who is enrolled in primary or secondary education, and (5) any person who is enrolled as a full-time student, if his monthly earnings equal the federal hourly minimum wage for twenty hours per week, or if he is the only adult in the family with a child seven to thirteen years of age. This exemption from the requirement to work is made to encourage persons on welfare to go to school and thus move out of poverty while working their way through school by part-time employment. It also encourages efforts at self-support for welfare mothers with children of school age. Mothers of preschool children would not be required to work, but they would be allowed to do so if that was their desire. The only adult in a single-parent family with school-aged children would be required to accept available work if it allowed her or him to be at home when the children were not at school. As is the current requirement under SSI, blind, disabled, or incapacitated persons under sixty-five years of age would be required to register for and accept appropriate vocational rehabilitation services.

The cash grant levels of the reform proposal for people without income or assets as established by regulations would be as follows:

Aged, blind, or disabled person	$2,500 per year
Aged, blind, or disabled couple	$3,750 per year
One- or two-parent families making up a family of four	$4,200 per year
Single individuals	$1,100 per year
Childless couples	$2,200 per year

In comparison, the current AFDC grant in the minimum payment states is $2,760 per year, plus food stamps. In addition, the family would still receive Medicaid under the reform proposal but would not receive food stamps. Thus, the $4,200 cash grant plus Medicaid under the reform proposal is somewhat less generous than a $2,760 grant plus $1,992 in food stamps, making a total of $4,752 plus Medicaid under AFDC.

Under the Carter plan, grants would increase with the size of the family up to a family of seven. Where an eligible family shares a household with an ineligible unit, there would be a reduction of $800 a year paid to the eligible family, except where that family paid a reasonable rental or $800 a year or more toward the joint household maintenance. For an individual or a childless couple this rule would not apply (Committees on Agriculture, Education and Labor, and Ways and Means, Explanatory Material on HR 10950.)

A five-week job search is required for each applicant who is subject to the work requirement. During that five-week period, the cash grant for two-parent families with children or single-parent families without children under fourteen years of age would be $2,300 (and not $4,200 as above). If, however, the adult were adjudged to be incapacitated or lived in an area where there was no reasonable prospect of employment (based on local unemployment rates), then the cash grant would be established at the regular figure. If, after the five-week search, no employment or training was found to be available, the cash grant would be reset at the higher figure. The temporary low-grant figure is used to motivate the search for employment or placement, following which a higher grant, or grant plus earnings or training stipend, becomes available.

Failure to comply with the work requirements would result in the following grant reductions: for a family of four, $2,300 annually instead of $4,200; for a family without children, $1,100 per year instead of $2,200, if one adult did not comply and zero if both did not comply; and for a single individual, zero. The basic cash grant schedule would be indexed to the Consumer Price Index annually so that grants would be increased in relation to the inflation rate. No food stamps would be available to persons considered eligible for the welfare reform program.

With regard to income, the basic monthly cash grant would be reduced, dollar for dollar, for any funds received from other federal means-tested programs. This stipulation would resolve the multiple benefits problem. Eighty percent of all nonemployment dollars received as income, such as OASDI, unemployment compensation, veterans compensation, workers' compensation, and retirement or disability benefits, would be deducted from the basic monthly cash grant. Finally, 50 percent of all earned income would be deducted from the cash grant. This provision would leave the client with sufficient motivation to work as much as he could.

Some types of nonearned income would not be deducted from the monthly cash grant. These would include in-kind support from a person with whom the client was living, housing subsidies, emergency aid, and the value of social services rendered by a public or private nonprofit social agency. Inheritances or other nonrecurring income would be treated as assets rather than income. Similarly, food received under a federally funded nutrition program and foster care payments for care of children would not be treated as deductible income. In addition to the above, a base monthly amount from earned income would not be deducted from the monthly cash grant for:

(1) families with two parents with children or for single-parent families with children under age thirteen. The first $316.67 of monthly earnings would be excluded if the family member expected to work had a job. For single-parent families, child-care costs for a child up to fourteen years of age, up to a maximum of $150 per child and up to $300 per month per family, would be excluded.
(2) aged, blind, or disabled persons. The first $65 per month of earned income would not be deducted. In addition, earned income needed to achieve self-support for a blind or disabled person, to pay a blind person's work-related expenses, or to cover attendant care costs for a severely physically disabled person would not be deducted.
(3) a student under age eighteen. All earned income would not be deducted. For a student eighteen to twenty-five years of age, all earned income up to an amount equal to the student's educational costs would not be deducted.
(4) a stepparent who is not legally responsible for the children in the household where he lives. If a stepparent were to file an affidavit stating that he or she did not contribute to the children's support and indicated that he or she was not legally responsible to do so, provisions would be made under this plan to provide additional assistance for the stepchildren. Thus, the stepparents would not be financially penalized for remaining in the home and continuing to serve as a stepparent.

Under the reform act, assets would be limited in relation to eligibility. For single persons, up to $1,500 in assets would be permitted, and for larger families, up to $2,250. Excludable assets (which would not be counted in the above amounts) would include a home, household goods, personal effects, vehicles (in value as permitted by the secretary of HEW), employment-related tools, burial expenses, business assets needed for self-employment and small amounts (as defined by the secretary of HEW) of life insurance. State supplementation would be permitted in states that chose to do so, as is currently permitted under SSI, through the established unit administering the reform program and subject to maximum amounts to be set for each recipient category. State fiscal participation would be at a rate of 10 percent of the cash grants paid within each state, but this amount would not exceed 90 percent of the state's 1979 expenditures for AFDC, SSI, emergency assistance, and General Assistance.

Administration of the Welfare Reform Program

The Carter welfare reform proposal includes a set of administrative plans. For the SSI programs, administration would continue as at present, with the Social Security Administration carrying out the payment procedure and state-federal contracts operated in each state for supplementation and special services. For other recipients, the federal government would either administer the cash program, including state supplementation funds, or the particular state could elect to carry out this function. As an alternative, a state would be allowed to perform the intake procedures only and have the federal government administer the cash payments.

Administrative arrangements would include procedures to correct overpayments and underpayments, penalties for fraud, promptness standards for eligibility determinations, check issuance, hearings and appeals, notification requirements, safeguards regarding use, disclosure, and verification of applicant information, and restrictions on the use of applicant information for income tax purposes.

The welfare reform proposal would also allow for an emergency assistance program for emergency food and shelter for eligible applicants. A prohibition would restrict use of such funds for individuals or families whose gross monthly income was more than twice the maximum cash payment payable in the particular state. Emergency assistance would also be available for victims of natural disasters and similar occurrences when certified by the HEW secretary.

Unlike the present arrangement under AFDC, a client's earned income would not entitle him to earned income credit under the proposal plan, and cash payments made would be included in the adjusted gross federal income tax calculation. This restriction is offset by calculation of an earned income credit allowance into the tax schedule for families with regular earnings from nonpublic-created jobs in the range of $4,000 to $15,620 per annum. For a family of four, for example, the maximum credit (or rebate) would be $654 for $9,080 of earnings. This credit would be limited to families with children, and some caution might be advisable in that it might serve to have a pronatalist effect. The foster care program of AFDC would be continued under the proposed reform plan.

In addition to the aid program described above, the Carter reform proposal includes an employment and training program as well. Persons who have completed the five-week job search would be assigned by the secretary of labor to training and employment programs under Comprehensive Employment and Training Act (CETA), as described in Chapter 8. Clients would receive pay equal to that paid other workers and would receive at least the state or federal minimum wage, whichever was higher. Eligible clients would also be enabled to participate in job search assistance programs. Refusal of an offered job could make a client ineligible unless the pay was less than that as noted above; the conditions of work were unacceptable because of hours, health, safety conditions, or geographical factors; the job offered interfered with the presence of the parent of a minor child when he was not in school; the job provided weekly earnings not adding up to a forty-hour week at the minimum wage;

the job was one created by a strike, lockout, or other labor dispute; or the individual was enrolled in an approved training program.

Analyses of the welfare reform proposal have been offered from many quarters. Danziger, Haveman, and Smolensky believe that under the reform proposal certain gains are to be noted. Welfare would be integrated with earnings, and both would be coupled with the tax system. The system would be consolidated, and thus administration could be streamlined. Family stability would be enhanced by allowing married couples with children to be aided in the same manner and to the same extent as single-parent families. The generally high national minimum grant would discourage migration from low- to high-grant states. Finally, states and localities would be relieved of much of the welfare burden.

Danziger, Haveman, and Smolensky indicate that the total income of families at every earnings level would be higher under the proposed system than under the current system. They also claim that the program would induce more work effort and more income, but in return the single-parent family would have to sacrifice her child-care and home production activities as well as her leisure. This consideration is not so important inasmuch as more than half of all mothers in the United States work. Indeed, it is probably a gain if the children are put into more constructive day-care activities and if the mother gains mainstream experience at her work which can enrich the lives of her children.

Danziger, Haveman, and Smolensky believe that the state supplementation permitted under the proposed plan would offset the horizontal equity offered by the universal grants and earned income. Thus, the very advantage of uniform grants and procedures would be lost, and migration to higher payment states would again be built into the system, as is the case with the current SSI and AFDC programs. Allowing the states to supplement the wage rate on the public service jobs would raise the costs per job and would cut back on the number of jobs to be offered. Thus, Danziger and his associates maintain that the plan would offer the advantages of including the working poor, increase work among the poor, help encourage intact families to remain so, increase family income for the poor, and discourage migration between states, if supplementation were not included in the plan.

Danziger, et al., have a variety of concerns about the proposed program. They believe that it would be impossible to shift the 1.4 million jobs from the current CETA program (see employment section, Chapter 8) to public service or low-income workers. The emergency employment CETA program could therefore be expected to continue and the additional costs to be much more than the $2.8 billion estimated by the Carter administration. The so-called savings expected by reduction of fraud built into the program could also either be discounted in the budget or be utilized in cost reduction of any alternative program, including the present system. The administration's estimate of the savings from the more restrictive child-care expense deductions may have been overestimated. The full reduction in tax revenue deriving from the broadened earned income tax credit should also be charged to the welfare reform plan. Danziger et al. have noted other underestimates of costs. Danziger and his associates also call attention to the fact that the probable work disincentive may be substantial for some recipients under the plan, especially after state supplementation.

The proposed enactment of national health coverage and tax reform may also impinge on the welfare reform proposal in that both programs may have undesirable effects on the cumulative grant reduction rate. They would reduce work incentives, just as Medicaid currently tends to reduce work incentives for families who are afraid to make themselves ineligible for these services.

Danziger, et al., also raise questions regarding the feasibility of creating a mass of public service jobs for low-wage, low-skill workers. In a sense, to do this without previous experience is analogous to a commercial firm's entrance into the production of a new product before the technology has been developed. Such problems as judgment of the competency and honesty of prime job sponsors, the effect of their locations, the inequities arising out of the diversity of such sponsorship, and the question of differential job-slot allocations are raised. Similarly, the critical question of whether sufficient nondemeaning and non-deadend jobs can be created has yet to be answered. Another question relates to the training component: can it be effectively designed and implemented within the $1,600 budgeted for each job? What about competition between the jobs and the employment marketplace? How can the transition from public to private job be effected for the clientele? What would happen to employment opportunities for the ineligible low-skill, low-wage candidates, such as inexperienced youths and wives? Would public employees be displaced under the plan, as is now frequently apparent in many CETA locations?

Danziger et al. believe that the administrative work load involved in monthly recertification, a six-month accounting period, discretionary actions in relation to the filing units, the decisions on who fits the category of being expected to work, the decisions as to who is incapacitated according to the legal definitions, and the required periodic determinations of reclassification and their administration would be overwhelming. As individuals in a family are born, grow, added, leave the unit, or move into or out of work, the number of necessary reclassifications would be so onerous as to be administratively unfeasible. Discretionary actions in relation to family units indicate determination of who is to be counted in the family to be aided. There are different family allowances that relate to who is in the family and their ages; who is expected to work and does or does not; who is not expected to work due to incapacitation. These discretionary decisions are often complicated, especially when psychological components are involved in determining work ability or when there is a person in the home who needs care and is presumed, therefore, to be incapacitated. Appeals from discretionary decisions will apparently be directed to appellate and judicial processes that have not yet been determined.

Will the program gain any administrative efficiency by converting the three programs of AFDC, SSI, and food stamps into three tracks—a jobs program, a program for those expected to work, and a program for those not expected to work, with different grant levels for the disabled, blind, and incapacitated, and for others? Would the computer system and staff be able to handle the more complex procedures? In the Danziger, et al., view, the Better Jobs and Income program requires considerable refinement.

Bell questions whether all the effort in creating the reform plan in order to deal with AFDC is justified inasmuch as she believes AFDC accounts for only 5 percent of all assistance programs and income transfers. Bell errs, however, in equating AFDC with massive social insurance programs, which in reality are merely the return of funds to persons who have invested in the system. Bell's error, a common one among social policy analysts, is based on the false assumption that because a person pays into the Social Security fund in his youth and receives the benefits several decades later, and because he is not receiving the same dollar he put in, he is, in actuality, dependent upon the payments of the next generation. While it is true that many put into the system much less than they receive and vice versa, that inequality derives from the shared risk insurance principle and other intrinsic patterns in the Social Security system.

Bell's criticism of veterans' pensions, which she believes also constitute welfare, is also erroneous. The veterans' pension is based on an economic consideration for military service at a lower pay scale than civilian jobs and under hazardous circumstances. As such, veterans' pensions can be considered a form of deferred payment, something not at all comparable to AFDC.

Neither the social insurances nor veterans' pensions are pathogenic in nature. Neither program results in critical social costs in terms of perpetuating dependency in ensuing generations. Neither presents a potential threat to the economic survival of the society deriving from a biological process with strong dependency and antiwork incentives.

Bell makes the important point that the typical family in America does not consist of a breadwinner-father, his homemaker wife, and children (p.17). The typical family now consists of two married wage-earners and their children. The two-worker family would probably be living in poverty if it were converted to a one-worker family. Thus, the homemaker has become a luxury which only the few can afford.

According to Bell, most children who are in single-parent families live with their mothers. Thus, poverty cannot be measured on the basis of calculated individual earnings without considering family size and constituency. To attempt to "deliver from poverty every family with one adult working member by supplementing individual wages . . . flies in the face of recent experience." Bell states that between 1959 and 1975 poverty was halved among families headed by men, and the number of people in poverty fell from 30 million to 13.5 million. "Families headed by men can contain two parents with paid jobs [but] families headed by women cannot."

Bell criticizes the plan for not making it possible for mothers of small children to receive training and employment as well. She questions a plan which does not take the two worker per family model into consideration and which views poverty on the basis of too low an income rather than on the basis of too large a family.

Jerry Wurf, president of the American Federation of State, County and Municipal Workers, which represents the employees of many local and state welfare departments, has also criticized the plan. He states that the basic flaw of the proposal is its failure to focus on the problems of the urban areas where many of the poor live (*Congressional Digest*, pp. 141, 143, 145). Its weakness is most apparent, he says, in its jobs component which is based on "unrealistic assumptions" and "relies on temporary employment programs [that] have dismal track records of downgraded employment standards." "It will create a second-class workforce," in his opinion. Wurf attacks the idea that work can be forced on welfare clients, and he instead suggests the promotion of private employment. He claims (with the support of considerable data) that the jobs component will replace public employees with welfare grantees. He questions the effectiveness of a work requirement in any welfare program.

Maggie Kuhn of the Gray Panthers criticizes the proposed program for requiring a sixty-two-year-old widow to work, but not a sixty-five-year-old widow, and for not making it possible for either to be eligible under the jobs component (*Congressional Digest*, pp. 147, 151). For his part, Bob Cheeks of the Baltimore Welfare Rights Organization questions the use of a jobs program that makes no provision for unskilled low-wage workers to enter into careers (*Congressional Digest*, pp. 151, 153, 155).

Nathan of the Brookings Institution (*Congressional Digest*, pp. 155, 157, 159) sees little need for the wholesale restructuring of the welfare programs. He believes that the SSI and Food Stamps programs are now relatively functional and effective, fulfilling the purposes for which they were created. The strong work requirement is already in the law; it needs only to be adequately enforced. There is a striking improvement in the AFDC error rate. The real improvements needed, Nathan believes, and at much less cost than the Better Jobs and Income proposal, are a national minimum grant standard; uniformity in eligibility standards; addition of working families to AFDC eligibility; a move toward full state administration; increased fiscal relief to the states; and improvement of AFDC management through legislative and administrative actions.

Others contend that the program has not gone far enough. Moynihan (Weil, p. 41) believes the $4,200 grant to be too low, as does the AFL-CIO. The U.S. Catholic Conference, the National Association of Social Workers, the Center on Social Policy and Law, and the National Welfare Rights Organization also support this view. Opponents (Weil, p. 43) claim that the two-tier payment system would harm family life. Moynihan believes that the plan does not provide adequate incentives for a family to stay together. In a two-parent family, he states, only the primary wage-earner is eligible for a public job. If a father secures a private sector job, he can desert his family (or fiscally abdicate from it while still quietly staying on). The wife thus becomes eligible for a public job, and this can significantly increase total family income in a manner not intended under the program. A single-parent family of four has a base grant of $4,200, and a two-parent family of four has one of $2,300. Isn't this an incentive for a father to desert or play absent, just as under the current AFDC program? If there are more children, then the incentive to desert or be absent is increased commensurately.

A two-parent family of four with both children under the age of seven and with the father earning a minimum wage receives $5,512 in wages and $1,444 in cash supplement, making a total of $6,956. But if the father leaves, the supplement goes up to $3,600, making a total of $9,112. If, however, the father leaves and the mother takes a public job, then the family has not only the father's income of $5,512, the mother's income of $5,512 but also the cash supplement, after a child care deduction of $3,-244, for a total of $14,268. Without adopting expensive and destructive investigative methods, it is almost impossible to prevent the fiscal abandonment of families such as is possible under both the AFDC and the Better Jobs and Income programs.

The jobs-income question also has had its critics. Representative Dave Stockman of Michigan has attacked the high grant-reduction rates. When welfare grants (plus work income) become higher than net income earned by persons in low-paying jobs, Stockman contends that family breakup is encouraged. "By leaving his family" (*Congressional Digest*, p. 48) "or by appearing to do so—a father continues to collect his earnings, while the mother and children now become eligible for full grants." Stockman says that since child support payments from an absent father impose a reduction on the mother's government grant of 100 percent, there is no incentive for a father to contribute.

Similar questions were raised in the Joint Economic Committee study (*Congressional Digest,* p. 54). "A father in a two parent family with children who refuses to work, suffers no penalty while there is a loss in benefits for a parent in a one parent family." "Only individuals without children lose benefits completely for refusing to accept a job. Yet childless individuals cannot receive created jobs."

Garfinkel (1978) believes that the Better Jobs and Income program would modestly improve income supports for the poor. His primary complaint is that the changes are too modest. He suggests that guaranteeing the poor an opportunity to work and to be self-reliant is only a beginning in improving the self-esteem of the poor. It would raise the level of grants in twelve of the poorest states, provide some fiscal relief to all states, and lay the groundwork for the federalization which Garfinkel seeks. He welcomes the "cashing out" of food stamps, which will cut down on the number of beneficiaries and required administrative procedures, and raise the earned income credit of earnings by the poor. On a more negative note, Garfinkel asserts that the program seeks to embark on a massive job program without the required experience or pretesting. It also locks out individuals and childless couples from earned income tax credits and subsidized jobs, and does not offer jobs to all adults in each family rather than limit them to one. He believes that the cash grant levels are too low and that for SSI beneficiaries, they constitute a step backward.

Garfinkel openly states that he seeks to avoid a discussion of program costs. He believes that the more adequate the program, the higher the cost, and vice versa. Danziger and Plotnik (1977) agree. They contend that the elimination of poverty can be achieved only at the expense of Carter's first principle of welfare reform which is the holding down of costs. In their view, the reform program raises the incomes of the poor but does not eliminate poverty for those who do not work. In its favor, it does provide a work opportunity above the poverty level for family heads who cannot find a regular job.

Anderson maintains that a tolerable welfare plan must support the needy at decent grant levels, provide powerful incentives to seek gainful employment and get off welfare, and entail total costs that are politically acceptable to Congress and the public. Apparently, the Carter reform plan has met the first of these objectives, but not to the satisfaction of Garfinkel, et al. Many have questioned the effectiveness of its incentives for employment and it was never even reported out of committee to the Ninety-fifth Congress.

Walker and Hunt offer an intriguing comment on the plan. They believe that if the welfare reform plan were to be passed, blacks in Mississippi, for example, would want to remain there because their grants would be the same there as elsewhere and prices of food and housing in that state would be more advantageous. Thus, blacks would remain in or return to that state and white paternalism would shrink. Walker and Hunt did not, however, take into account the effect of state supplementation which would still make such states as New York and California financially attractive to welfare clients, depending on the degree of supplementation provided.

Haveman and Smolensky (pp. 12–13), who have also done an analysis for the Joint Economic Committee, conclude that the provision of cash assistance creates an incentive to work less. This affects not only those who are not usually in the work force. It also affects marginal and perhaps even regular workers at the low-income levels. Haveman and Smolensky offer two alternatives, each of which are costly and difficult to implement. The first alternative is to enforce a work test through tough administration. The second is to create many effective remunerative opportunities for employment, made work programs, and to keep financial assistance (at least for the employable) at rates which will make employment more attractive. Apparently, the BJI program opts for this alternative. Thus, under the Better Jobs and Income program, "when work is refused by those expected to work, not only are earnings sacrificed but the family sacrifices $1900 per year in cash assistance. . . . [The] special [created] jobs are intended to temporarily supplement private sector jobs." The special jobs are not intended to substitute for private sector jobs. The combination of "cash assistance, financial work opportunities, financial incentives to seek private sector employment and maintaining budgetary restraint make for a complicated program." A further complication is that fiscal relief must be provided to the states, and current assistance levels must be sustained for welfare recipients in such a way as not to jeopardize other objectives. "Balancing all of these objectives involves a multiplicity of tradeoffs." With all this intricate machinery, supposedly in delicate balance, the questions are asked: Will all people in equal need receive equal treatment? Are the incomes of some beneficiaries raised above the incomes of some nonbeneficiaries? Is HEW the most appropriate agency to administer the program (the one most likely to attain and retain the necessary balance)? What will be the cost and distributional effects of the program if the unemployment rates go above or below the posited rate of unemployment around which the program is based?

Bishop (1977) raises questions about the entire issue of jobs and cash transfers as they relate to marital instability, and therefore as they relate to dependency for female-headed families. He indicates that the president's plan for welfare reform was ostensibly established (in the White House message of August 7, 1977), "to provide strong incentives to keep families together . . . (1) by offering the dignity of useful work to family heads and (2) by ending rules which prohibit assistance when the father remains in the household" (p. 1). Bishop holds that "while there is strong empirical support for the first claim (providing jobs will reduce family instability), there is no [support] for the second. In fact, the best available evidence is that expanding welfare eligibility to include two parent families will increase marital splits rather than decrease them" (p. 1).

Such an increase in marital disruption is likely to be followed by an increase in female-headed families on welfare. Furthermore, the "cashing out" of food stamps makes the program very much like the negative income tax plans used in the experiments and thus may be expected to create a substantial increase in family breakup. Bishop suggests that any plan for regular sizable cash grants should therefore be approached with caution and that instead the focus should be on jobs. He believes, however, that jobs for unskilled men will have to provide more than a minimum wage. He points out that men who cannot support their families lose respect in the families, but they are reluctant to accept jobs at the minimum wage because they reject the low status such jobs provide. The dilemma here is that provision of a higher wage for the unskilled, even though it is accomplished by providing for many jobs at that level, would also result in higher wages for skilled and professional workers and thereby create an even greater inflation rate.

Another of Bishop's suggestions is to segregate programs serving two-parent families from those serving one-parent families. In his opinion, the first priority of government policy should be to help the father in the family retain his dignity and family status by providing job opportunities.

The Better Jobs and Income program has the advantage of adding the working poor to the grant system without unduly disturbing the work efforts and labor market, because the total income for mothers and children comes to much less than the total of the man's earnings plus the cash grant supplement. It also adds childless couples to the grant system. In the past, such people have had to depend on General Assistance and food stamps in programs that were spotty, limited, and varied in terms of local or state patterns. Moreover, the plan provides a clear work requirement. It does provide grants to intact families so that the father is not locked out of the grant, as is often the case in AFDC. Furthermore, there is a large differential between grants to families without a worker and those with a worker.

The plan has far more disadvantages, however. It does not provide for work experience for the mother with small children where there is no one else in the home. Thus, there is no working role in the home, and no model for the child who needs to know that most functional persons work. This problem is especially critical in a family where pregnancies occur every five years or less, so that the mother is never expected to work during the years while the children are growing up at home. The plan may even provide incentives for additional pregnancies for those who seek to avoid the work requirement. Another disadvantage is that its work requirement may turn out to be as ineffective in practice as the present one. Nothing new has been added in this regard in order to ensure effectiveness.

While the plan does allow for day-care costs, it does not provide for organization support and direction of adequate day-care programs where children could be prepared for a life-style of educational gains and employment relating to self-sufficiency. Nor does it provide for the required counseling of mothers relating to their life-goals and those of their children. Counseling is particularly important for the very young mothers and the residual poor. If vocational rehabilitation counseling and treatment can be required for the disabled, why not counseling about family care and direction for those who are apparently handicapped by disorganized life-styles?

The plan makes no provision for the financially disorganized who usually neglect to pay their landlords and often spend rent funds for something of lesser priority. They thus face one eviction after another and usually have to fall back on the worst living quarters. Why not careful, required budgetary counseling for such families, plus two-party checks (landlord and client for the rental portion of the grant) where appropriate, as suggested by Moynihan (1978)?

The plan is not clear as to what is intended for large families. It might be reasonable to require two persons to work, rather than have one worker, and to supplement the family with a "supergrant." The plan does not, as Bell suggests, base its assumptions and regulations on a two-worker family as the answer to poverty. It does not answer Bishop's criticisms about the drawbacks of such substantial grants in promoting familial dissolution and thus promoting further one-parent family dependency. It does not answer the questions raised by Moynihan (Weil, p. 43) about the father who leaves or fiscally disappears so that the family gains substantially from a combination of incomes and assistances. If no mechanism is established to prevent the father's desertion, the plan would merely become an expansion of AFDC and its problems. The plan is unclear as to how the mass job creation project will be carried out without prior experience in this area of implementation. It does not clarify whether all people in equal need will be treated equally, or if the incomes of beneficiaries will not be raised above those of nonbeneficiaries. If beneficiaries do gain such supported incomes, what will that do to the economic marketplace?

It is not certain that the expected costs of the plan could be kept within the limits permitted by an economy already in danger of runaway inflation. Nor does the plan show how the administrative units will be related to one another. Will this plan provide any better integration and controls than currently exists in SSI, AFDC, the Food Stamp program, the WIN program, and CETA?

The general criticism that could be directed at all of the programs discussed in this chapter is that they would provide additional supports to the working poor and in the process change their life-patterns from self-reliance to growing dependency and thus further enlarge the dependent population. Simmel states that people emerge as poor only when society recognizes their condition as poverty and directs specific assistances to them. He believes that "the fact that someone is poor does not mean that he belongs to the social category of the 'poor.' It is only from the moment that [the poor] are assisted . . . that they become part of a group characterized as poverty" (pp. 138–39). In this regard, all of these plans can be viewed as potentially destructive.

In general, many of the plans (especially negative income tax and minimum guaranteed income) depend in great part upon some significant changes in existing income tax law. Such changes are not currently on the political horizon, however. All of these programs inherently define poverty as a condition caused primarily, or even exclusively, by lack of funds rather than as a complex condition in which a lack of funds may be an effect of poverty. To the extent that poverty is caused only by a lack of funds, such proposals may solve the problem of poverty. To the extent that poverty is caused by individual inadequacies and handicaps, it is doubtful that any income transfer plan alone would make any inroads into the problem. Alternately, where poverty is occasioned by an interaction between a lack of funds and personal handicaps or life-style, the provision of an income floor can be expected to serve only as a palliative and not as a solution to the problem. In fact, from the data presented previously, one may consider such a program deleterious.

Neither an improved welfare program nor an innovative income transfer program alone can solve the problem of how to deal with dependent people who cannot, without external motivation and aid, move out of poverty into self-sufficiency. It is true that an innovative transfer program may help resolve the problem for those who need income support only. Such a program may serve to speed those who are in transitory poverty back to self-sufficiency, just as past welfare programs during the Depression helped the temporary poor. Those remaining were people who stayed in poverty for reasons other than a lack of income or who may have fallen into poverty and could not or were not able to extricate themselves, again for reasons other than an income lack.

As the above discussion indicates, another approach to the problem of welfare restructuring is in order. We propose that such a restructuring be based upon a further transfer of eligible cases (as is defined below) from AFDC to SSI, as was done for aged, blind, and disabled dependents. Under such a plan, people currently dependent upon AFDC would be identified according to various factors. This identification could be effected by a process of separating those who need only temporary financial support from those who need much more than financial support if they are to be moved out of poverty.

The program could be facilitated in a number of ways. All AFDC families where the head of family is a totally disabled person would be assumed to be dependent as a result of his disablement. Such a family would be transferred to the jurisdiction of the Social Security Administration, in the Supplementary Security Income Division. The assumption here is that the children in this family would be brought up to become self-sufficient because the family is in poverty only during the disablement of its key wage-earner. The family would remain in the SSI category as long as the children made progress in school or in their preparation for a gainful career.

The second category to be transferred to the SSI group would be widows (and their children) currently on AFDC, who have not remarried since the death of the husband (and father of the children) and who have not conceived any additional children since the death of the husband. The transfer of this category to SSI would not be based on moral grounds. This action would be logical if the family is found, on the basis of their history and current behavior, to be so imbued by middle-class behavioral patterns that we could expect them to move out of the assistance program as soon as they could and at least within one generation. For history and current behavior related to this decision it would be necessary to check such items as work experience in the family, and particularly the parents, past employment, family stability, career planning for the children, school progress and performance, family money management patterns, and the family's ability to plan and carry out goals related to self-sufficiency. The family would remain in the SSI category as long as there were no additional children from a liaison outside a legitimated marriage. If additional children were to be born, the family would be transferred back to the residual AFDC category as an indication that it was probably falling into behavior that would hold them in poverty.

The third category would be made up of divorced women with children whose family life had become stabilized. If there were not further divorce experiences and no children added other than from a legitimated union, and if the children showed continuing progress in school and/or preparation for gainful employment, the family would be transferred to SSI support.

Finally, families that remained in AFDC for a year or more and made no progress toward family stability and self-sufficiency would be designated for an AFDC intensive service category. This group would be provided with an intensive service program in addition to an AFDC financial support program. With this category a careful case plan would be developed with each individual family. Here the emphasis would be placed not on the adult in the family but on antipoverty programming for the children. With such families, the program would concentrate on motivation for achievement in school, gainful career or occupational counseling, tutorial services, development of upward-directed expectations, provision of birth control services where appropriate, provision of quality day care, and special grants to children making progress toward gainful occupations. The program would conceivably provide a continuing "significant adult" to work with the family. Poverty in the residual AFDC category would be regarded as one that is not focused on income inadequacy only. Poverty in such cases would be viewed as a syndrome of social-psychological, economic difficulties that are transgenerational unless diverted by strongly focused intensive services.

The service orientation to poverty has failed in the past probably because it has been diluted, being provided as a service to all rather than to that population segment for which service is most appropriate. The service strategy apparently failed because it did not concentrate its efforts on the socioeconomic upgrading of those who were most likely to remain in poverty unless otherwise served. It also failed because quick solutions for poverty were sought in families where the problem had developed over generations.

Robert M. Ball, former commissioner of Social Security, once described the policy of that organization in regard to the independence of its beneficiaries:

We jealously guard the right of beneficiaries to spend their money [and live their lives] without interference from us. Fortunately, our beneficiaries are preponderantly able to manage their own affairs . . . [but] the incapable and incompetent require from us a different kind of responsibility . . . [which is not provided under the law] (p. 1).

Obviously, a family that has been in poverty for a generation or more is unable to understand what havoc its life-style and its way of looking at opportunities, education, and society confer on the life-chances of its members. Selective intensive services for the few may keep them from becoming many, while permitting the many to make their own way in society or back to participation in society.

For the aged, the blind, and the disabled whose life-chances are already defined, a minimum guaranteed annual income is humane and probably necessary in a civilized society. For the working poor with and without children, a graduated guaranteed income which is designed not to be a disincentive to employment and economic upgrading is probably also humane and appropriate for a civilized society. For children and their parents, however, who have not yet achieved some semblance of competent participation in the society a minimum guaranteed income or a similar transfer program prevents transgenerational escape from a life of poverty. As such, an income maintenance plan or an AFDC becomes stifling and disturbing, despite their aura of humaneness and concern for the needs of the poor. Any program that deals with poverty only as an insufficiency of funds without regard to its diverse causes can lead to a depressive and enslaving life-style for some.

Social legislation is highly useful in redressing imbalances in the society. However, any social legislation that further interferes with the viability and functionality of the society by creating disincentives to employment and/or to involvement of people in the maintenance and operation of that society would be counterproductive. Any social legislation that draws potentially employable people and future workers out of the employment market as long as the society has urgent work needs would be antisocial. A society with inadequate public transit, deteriorated railroads, too many children in crowded urban school classes who need small-group attention, inadequate day-care facilities, deteriorated and dilapidated housing, and other urgent needs must necessarily forego planning for a guaranteed annual income. Instead, it must consider the use of its resources for community needs that may serve both the potential dependent population at risk and the society in general. A decision to undertake a minimum guaranteed income must be made only with full knowledge of its costs and its potential effect on the functionality of other economic and social processes in the society.

By the end of the Ninety-fifth Congress in the fall of 1978, it became clear that the Carter welfare reform proposal would not become legislation that year. Hopes for 1979 were somewhat obscured when the administration shifted its focus to other critical issues. Generally, the American public does not approve of welfare. Lerman and Skidmore reported in 1977 that "welfare's unpopularity with the public seems to stem from beliefs that the system rewards the wrong behavior (including fraud) and the wrong people." The public also seems to agree with Danziger and Lampman that "income inequality has not increased, and poverty and intergroup income differences have declined" (p. 23). The public view of poverty is generally congruent with the Danziger and Plotnik (1977) view that "poverty has been significantly reduced in the recent past, if measured by the official definition or almost eliminated, if income is defined to include in-kind income (such as food stamps). [Only] if we adopt a relative measure of poverty [then] this downward trend is replaced by a near constant level" (p. 13).

Public opinion polls about welfare and government spending on welfare also reflect this view. Yankelovich, Skelly, and White's report shows that a majority of the respondents thought welfare and foreign aid were getting too much money (72 percent for foreign aid and 51 percent for welfare). Funding for defense, education, health care, and crime control all received much less criticism, ranging from 27 percent to 9 percent. In an earlier report on public opinion on taxation, Yankelovich (September 25, 1978) explained taxpayer views of welfare: "There is a raging debate in the society over two competing conceptions of fairness. One is the concept of need as a right. . . . The other concept of fairness [is] based on an older proposition—I get what I deserve. I worked hard for my [money] and so I deserve it" (p. 60). According to Yankelovich, the majority backs the concept of fairness "based on getting what you deserve and opposes the notion that need constitutes a right." Eighty-seven percent of his respondents said they supported the notion that "those who are able to work but choose not to, have no right to expect society to back them financially."

In such a political climate, Weil reports, "no legislators wanted to face the electorate in November after having voted on some provisions of the bill" (p. 99) without some guarantee that final action on the bill would not place them in an embarrassing light before their voters. Except for the legislators from heavy welfare districts, most legislators could not vote on a bill that the home voters might consider more costly than the current welfare plan. The welfare bureaucracy in Washington might have some influence over legislation between elections, but not in an election year, particularly when welfare reform is involved.

In addition to this resistance to act, the legislators were being pressed from two directions. Because the Carter plan (as was HR1) was a compromise, pressure came from both sides with the conflicting claims that the bill was both too lenient and too restrictive. Much of the pressure had an ideological rather than rational basis. Those who sought liberalization of welfare were fundamentally hoping to use the Carter program as a first step in their chosen direction of income equalization. Those who sought a more restrictive plan saw it as perhaps a first step in making AFDC a welfare program again, based on client need deriving from widowhood or other acts of God rather than from a life-style. Few thought the proposed revision was necessary to bring better integration and purposeful functionality into the welfare program, and to cut back on the social waste of welfare. Without a broad coalition of interest, welfare revision was doomed in both the Ninety-fifth and Ninety-sixth Congresses.

The immediate problem is what to do with AFDC until welfare can be changed. Obviously, wholesale reform is politically impossible for the present. Street suggests that "significant changes in welfare—if any transpire—may occur less through contemporary reforms than slowly and somewhat unpredictably through a foot-in-the-door process that pleases neither proponents nor opponents of reformist proposals'' (p. 21). Neither the Carter reform plan nor the AFDC as it is currently constituted and operated offers much of a solution to the social problems deriving from residual welfare. Whether by piecemeal changes or by wholesale reform, no change can be achieved until American society reaches some kind of consensus on the philosophy, purposes, and goals of welfare.

Sociologists have observed that no society in which social stratification has been fully eliminated has ever existed and functioned continuously. The existence of an imbalance in rewards, status, and power provides the necessary dynamics not only for such social stratification but also for the motivation of individuals to move from one stratum to another. To equalize all, economically or otherwise, may remove incentives for any social components to function and in the process to keep the society going.

The entire concept of a guaranteed annual income or equivalent rests upon a number of concepts that are quite foreign to American belief. Fishbein (1975) points out that whereas European social policy focused on a pooling of the social risks and lodged them in a welfare state, American philosophy has sought a policy whereby each individual who can should take care of himself. Under this philosophy, equal opportunity rather than equal provisions is the primary goal. Thus, in the American view, each person shall be equally free to seek the benefits of the fruits of a society and shall be left free to enjoy them. If someone, by misfortune or by self-action, whether intended or otherwise, fails to take advantage of his opportunities or does not use them, the American view is to provide help to that person only until he can again become self-supporting and only to the extent that it will make it possible for him to survive during that period. At no time has any consideration been given to make it unnecessary for people to strive and to be as self-supporting as possible.

Much of the guaranteed annual income discussion is openly directed toward redistributing income, even to the point of creating equality at all levels in society. Erich Fromm provides much of the rationale for this idea in his article ''Psychology of a Guaranteed Income.'' According to Fromm, new scarcity and disparity of income produce anxiety, envy, and other emotions which are destructive to the individual's sense of comfort. Yet, much of the economic marketplace operates primarily in response to such motivation. It is true that a guaranteed annual income might be helpful in enabling a woman to leave her husband and yet be assured of surviving. According to Eleanor Garst, it would also make it possible for women to leave their children, never to marry, to revert to ''dormitory arrangements,'' and to make their progeny the foster children of a communal society. Garst views the guaranteed annual income as the beginning of "the disappearance of our humane [life]," and she complains that no one seems to be discussing the alternative possibilities for good and evil in such a development. Iyer also views the guaranteed annual income as a potential destroyer of the humane, individualistic society. In his opinion, any philosophy that strives for the extreme equalization of all is ultimately led to further inequality at yet another level. An example of the futility of such egalitarian effort already exists in some countries where salaries are so much alike that competitiveness in society is maintained only through the hidden perquisites of the job and the political positions of power.

The futility of the extreme equalization position is epitomized by Schorr (1966) who objects to Tobin's plan not only because it is inadequate but also because "almost as important as not *being* poor is not *feeling* poor. Only income-by-right achieves that." Schorr forgets that if people do not feel poor any more or if people do not fear becoming poor, few people, other than those fortunate enough to have creative work closely suited to their talents, would have a motive for regular work. Our society is not yet so affluent, so abundant in resources and energy, and so mechanized as to be capable of providing the necessities and supports of an entire population, all operated by the few who supposedly enjoy their work. If all are subsidized without work, those who do work will ask to be paid more or will ask for other forms of payment. In either case, we will be substituting either inflation or psychic blackmail for our current arrangement, and some would still be poor.

One may conclude that the guaranteed annual income plan is built more on a romantic notion of man as he ought to be, or as many planners wish he would be, rather than on man as he is. Thus, the plan or a similar one is flawed not so much in its format as in its preconceived wishful notions about man and his behavior. Because of the nature of man, the guaranteed annual income is probably ineffective as a means of resolving poverty when poverty is defined as more than a lack of funds.

By and large, income transfer programs, whether of the AFDC or the guaranteed annual income type, can necessarily focus only on transitional populations in need or at risk. Transgenerational, multiproblem families will need much more.

Residual welfare is therefore a result not of social structure but of the way in which a welfare institution has been reshaped over a few decades. From a service to the unfortunate needy it has been transformed into a subsistence program for those who have withdrawn from the socialization processes required for entry into mainstream employment and its benefits. As Kristol puts it, "a liberal and compassionate social policy has bred all sorts of unanticipated and perverse consequences."

"Welfare," says Kristol, "does nothing to hold a poor family together." But neither will a guaranteed annual income, a negative income tax, or a graduated employment/welfare grant incentive plan. Kristol's belief in 1971 was borne out by the research of 1977 and 1978 showing that "the existence of a liberal welfare program . . . [was] responsible to a considerable extent for family disorganization."

If the Irish immigrants in the 19th century had had something comparable to our present welfare system [or a guaranteed annual income?] there would have been a "welfare explosion" then, and a sharp increase in Irish family dissolution, too. . . . Welfare robs [the family] of its function. . . . Welfare robs the head of the household of his economic function . . . and [makes] him a "superfluous" man. Welfare competes with his usually low earning ability—the more generous the welfare program, the worse [the husband] makes out in this competition [with welfare] (p. 242).

One wonders how many white middle-class families would survive if mother and children were guaranteed the father's income or more without the father's presence? And how many fathers would persist at their not-always-interesting jobs? (p. 242).

Kristol sees welfare as a vicious circle in which the best of intentions merge into the worst of results. Welfare and its residual clients operate in a dreary symbiotic interaction that can be resolved only by restating the limited purposes of welfare and by reinstituting social services that lead to rehabilitation. If not in one generation, this change should come within two or three. This type of reorganization cannot be expected to come quickly. Only if the general public attains an improved understanding of residual poverty and its problems will a decision for change come.

References

Aaron, Henry J. *Why Is Welfare So Hard to Reform?* Washington, D.C.: Brookings, 1973.

Albrecht, James W. "Negative Income Taxation and Divorce in SIME/DIME," *Journal of the Institute for Socio-Economic Studies,* 4(3):75–82, Autumn 1979.

American Conservative Union. "An Alternative Approach to Welfare Reform." Memorandum to Congress, September 1969.

Anderson, Martin. *Welfare: The Political Economy of Welfare Reform in the U.S.* Menlo Park, Calif.: Hoover Institution Press, 1978.

Ball, Robert M. "Principles of Representative Payment," *Oasis,* August 1967.

Bell, Carolyn Shaw. "The Carter Bill—Is It Welfare Reform?" *Journal of the Institute for Socio-Economic Studies,* 3(2):9–19, 1978.

Bishop, John. *Jobs, Cash Transfer and Marital Instability: A Review of the Evidence.* Special Report No. 19. Institute for Research on Poverty, University of Wisconsin at Madison, 1977.

———. "The Welfare Brief," *Public Interest,* 53:169–75, 1978.

Brittan, Samuel, and Peter Lilley. *The Delusion of Income Policy.* London: Meyer Temple Smith, 1977.

Cain, Glen G. "The Effect of Income Maintenance Laws on Fertility in the U.S." Pp. 329–73, in Robert Parke, Jr., and Charles F. Westhoff (eds.), *Aspects of Population Growth and Policy: U.S. Commission on Population Growth and the American Future.* Research Reports, Vol. 11. Washington, D.C.: U.S. Government Printing Office, 1973.

Committees on Agriculture, Education, Labor, Ways and Means. *Explanatory Material to Accompany HR 10950, Better Jobs and Income Act: Comparison of Title I with Present Law.* Washington, D.C.: U.S. Government Printing Office, 1978.

Congressional Digest. "Congress and the Welfare Reform Controversy," 57(5):131–60, 1978.

Danziger, Sheldon, Robert Haveman, and Eugene Smolensky. *The Program for Better Jobs and Income: A Guide and Critique.* Washington, D.C.: U.S. Government Printing Office, 1977.

———, and Robert J. Lampman. "Getting and Spending," *Annals of the American Academy of Political and Social Science,* 435:23–39, 1978.

———, and Robert Plotnick. "Poverty Today: Does It Persist or Has It Been Eliminated?" Paper prepared for the Center for the Study of Democratic Institutions, 1977.

———. "Can Welfare Reform Eliminate Poverty?" Paper presented at the Annual Meeting of the American Sociological Association, San Francisco, 1978.

Etzioni, Amatai. "Anti-Poverty Insurance: A Mode of Private Sector Participation," *Public Administration Review,* 29(6):614–22, 1968.

Fishbein, B. K. *Social Welfare Abroad: Comparative Data on the Social Insurance and Public Assistance Programs of Selected Industrialized Democracies.* White Plains, N.Y.: Institute for Socio-Economic Studies, 1975.

———. "The Food Stamp Program," *Journal of the Institute for Socio-Economic Studies:* Special Supplement, July 1977.

Friedman, Milton. *Capitalism and Freedom.* Chicago: University Press, 1962.

Fromm, Erich. "Psychology of a Guaranteed Income," *The Nation,* 201(19):439–42, 1965.

Garfinkel, Irwin. "Income Transfer Programs and Work Efforts: A Review." Pp. 1–32 in *Studies in Public Welfare.* Subcommittee on Fiscal Policy, Joint Economic Committee. Washington, D.C., 1974.

———. "What's Wrong with Welfare?" *Social Work,* 23(3):185–91, 1978.

Garst, Eleanor. "The A-Sexual Society," *Center Diary,* 15:43. Santa Barbara: Center for the Study of Democratic Institutions, 1965.

Greenberg, D. H. *Income Guarantees and the Working Poor in New York City: The Effect of Income Maintenance Programs on the Hours of Work of Male Family Heads,* R–658–NYC. Santa Monica: Rand, 1971.

———, and M. Kosters. *Income Guarantees and the Working Poor: The Effect of Income Maintenance Programs on the Hours of Work of Male Family Heads,* R–579–OEO. Santa Monica: Rand, 1970.

Greene, Leonard M. *A Plan for a Demogrant Financed by a Value-Added Tax.* White Plains, N.Y.: Institute for Socio-Economic Studies, 1976.

Grossman, Allyson Sherman. "Almost Half of All Children Have Mothers in the Labor Force," *Monthly Labor Review,* 100(6):41–44, 1977.

Handler, Joel. "Federal-State Interests in Welfare Administration." Pp. 1–35, in *Studies in Public Welfare: Issues in Welfare Administration: Intergovernmental Relationships.* Part 2. Joint Economic Committee of the U.S. Congress. Washington, D.C.: U.S. Government Printing Office, 1973.

Haveman, Robert, and Eugene Smolensky. *The Program for Better Jobs and Income: An Analysis of Costs and Distributional Effects.* Reprint No. 275. Institute for Research on Poverty, University of Wisconsin at Madison, 1978.

Iyer, Raghaven N. "The Social Structure of the Future." P. 16, in Walter A. Weiskoff (ed.), *Looking Forward: The Abundant Society.* Santa Barbara: Center for the Study of Democratic Institutions, 1966.

Jencks, Christopher, Marshall Smith, Henry Acland, Mary Jo Bane, David Cohen, Herbert Gintis, Barbara Heyns, and Stephen Michelson. *Inequality.* New York: Basic Books, 1972.

Jones, Brian J. "Change for Money? An Analysis of Welfare Failure." Paper presented at the Annual Meeting of the Society for the Study of Social Problems, San Francisco, 1978.

Kristol, Irving. "Welfare: The Best of Intentions, The Worst of Results," *Atlantic Monthly,* 228(2):45–47, 1971.

Lampman, Robert. "Approaches to the Reduction of Poverty," *American Economic Revolution: Papers and Proceedings,* 55:521–29, 1965.

Lerman, Robert, and Felicity Skidmore. "Welfare Reform: A Reappraisal of Alternatives," *Tax Notes,* 5(17):3–19, 1977.

Lyon, D. W. *Welfare Policy Research for New York City: The Record of a Five Year Project,* R–2119–RC. Santa Monica: Rand, 1976.

Middleton, Russell. "Psychological Well-Being." Chapter 7 in *Final Report of the Rural Negative Income Tax Experiment.* Vol. 5. Madison, Wis.: Institute for Research on Poverty, University of Wisconsin, 1976.

———, and Vernon Allen. "Social-Psychological Effects." Chapter 8 in H. Watts and A. Rees (eds.), *The New Jersey Income Maintenance Experiment.* Vol. 3. New York: Academic Press, 1977.

Moynihan, Daniel Patrick. *The Politics of a Guaranteed Income: The Nixon Administration and the Family Assistance Plan.* New York: Free Press, 1969.

———. "The Rocky Road to Welfare Reform," *Journal of the Institute for Socio-Economic Studies,* 3(1):1–10, 1978.

Pascal, A. H. *Enhancing Opportunities in Job Markets: Summary of Research and Recommendations for Policy,* R 580–OEO. Santa Monica: Rand, 1971.

Rolph, Earl, and George Break. *Public Finance.* New York: Ronald Press, 1961.

Schorr, Alvin. "Income Maintenance and the Birth Rate," *Social Security Bulletin,* 28:22–30, 1965.

———. "The Family Cycle and Income Development," *Social Security Bulletin,* 29:14–25, 1966a.

———. "Against a Negative Income Tax," *Public Interest,* 5:110–17, 1966b.

Simmel, Georg. "The Poor." (Claire Jacobson, trans.). *Social Problems,* 13(2):118–39, February 1965.

Special HEW Report on Welfare Reform in *Administration's Welfare Reform Proposal.* Joint Hearings before the Welfare Reform Subcommittee of the Committee on Agriculture, the Committee on Education and Labor, and the Committee on Ways and Means. House of Representatives, Ninety-fifth Congress, First Session on H R 9030. September 19, 20, and 21, 1977. Serials 95–47. Washington, D.C.: U.S. Government Printing Office, 1977.

Spiegelman, Robert G., Lyle P. Groenveld, and Philip K. Robins. "The Work Effort and Marital Dissolution Effects of the Seattle and Denver Income Maintenance Experiments." Menlo Park, Calif.: SRI International, 1978.

Staff Report, Subcommittee on Fiscal Policy of the Joint Economic Committee of the Congress of the U.S. *Studies in Public Welfare, Paper No. 15. Welfare in the 70's: A National Study of Benefits Available in 100 Local Areas.* Washington, D.C.: U.S. Government Printing Office, 1974.

Street, David. "Welfare Administration and Organization Theory." Paper presented at the Annual Meeting of the American Sociological Association, San Francisco, 1978.

Thoits, Peggy, and Michael Hannan. *Income and Psychological Distress: The Impact of an Income Maintenance Experiment.* Menlo Park, Calif: SRI International, 1978.

Tobin, James. "The Case for an Income Guarantee," *Public Interest,* 4:31–41, 1966.

Walker, Lewis, and Chester L. Hunt. "Welfare Reform and the Possible Demise of White Paternalism: Black Flight in Mississippi." Paper presented at the Annual Meeting of the American Sociological Association, San Francisco, 1978.

Weil, Gordon L. *The Welfare Debate of 1978.* New York: Institute for Socio-Economic Studies, 1978.

Williamson, John B., et al. *Strategies Against Poverty in America.* New York: Schenkman, 1975.

————. "National Income Insurance as an Anti-Poverty Strategy." Paper presented at the Annual Meeting of the American Sociological Association, 1973.

Yankelovich, Daniel. "The Revolt's Deeper Roots," *Time* Magazine, 112(13):59–60, 1978.

————, Skelly and White. "Wishing for More for Less," *Time* Magazine, 112(17):26, 28, 1978.

MEDICAL SERVICES
FOR THE POOR

6

Socioeconomic Status or Discrimination

TWO prevailing assumptions underlie most contemporary discussions of medical services for the poor in America. One is that the poor population receives less medical care because they are poor—a systemic discrimination. The other is that because the poor lack medical knowledge and have less education than other social classes, they have impaired health—a class condition. The current debate over national health insurance bills introduced in the Ninety-fifth Congress, which propose to remedy the needs of the poor for improved care and to aid those who have no medical assistance, focuses on these two assumptions.

Lefkowitz (1970 and 1973) has undertaken a careful analysis of data relating to questions of poverty and health. He has found that the correlation between poverty and poor health usually disappears when education is taken into account. The correlation can also be considered less than significant because both income and medical deprivation appear to be consequences, at least in part, of education. The claimed assumptions of poverty and ill health have corollaries. One is that the poor receive less medical care and lower quality care than others. Lefkowitz's examination of the data indicates that there is little correlation between the average number of physician visits per person per year and family income. In terms of quality of care, Lefkowitz has found that education rather than income is related to medical care utilization. Leveson has also found that when other factors are held constant education is the key factor in medical care utilization. Lefkowitz's study, however, omits the distinction between perceived poor health and poor health as verified by objective clinical findings.

In terms of clinic care versus private physician care, Lefkowitz (1970 and 1973) also found that the proportion of one to the other is the same among the poor and other populations. He says that the image that the poor are at the mercy of public clinics is overdrawn.

There are other questions about the health of the poor. If the poor are less healthy than others but utilize medical care facilities in much the same way, then it seems that the poor have a greater need for medical care. This would indicate that some kind of inequality exists, but to a considerable degree, the apparent condition is also based on mixed and equivocal data. After controlling for the factor of age, Lefkowitz (1970 and 1973) found little relationship between income and chronic diseases.

Langer presents the general view of the poor in relation to health services. She quotes a pre-Medicare and pre-Medicaid report on residents in a public housing project in Boston which lists persons suffering from undiagnosed chronic bronchitis and chronic nervous disorders (self-diagnosed) at 20 and 25 percent, respectively, and from visual disorders at 12 percent. Langer reports that 40 percent of these persons were not receiving treatment. She describes some of the problems the poor experienced before Medicaid went into effect, for example, the presumed personal humiliation of charity medicine. She also discusses the problems of the poor in securing medical care which is overspecialized and so geographically scattered that much time and travel are involved. The middle class, she indicates, is apparently better equipped to deal with such a medical care delivery system; for the poor, it is exhausting and debilitating. She suggests that the structure of the medical delivery system for the poor adds to the overall consequences of poverty and medical care.

McKinney lists the particular health problems of blacks. The U.S. Bureau of the Census classifies 26 percent of all blacks age sixteen or over as poor (*Current Population Reports,* Series P-60, No. 107). They have particular health problems, notably birth of premature babies or babies of low weight at a rate two to three times the national average; a childhood disease (such as measles) rate twice that of white children; lead poisoning of black children because of the presence of lead paint on the walls remaining in the homes in which many blacks live; decayed or untreated teeth; a rate of hypertension estimated as one in seven; a high incidence of the Sudden Infant Death Syndrome; and a large number of children and adults who have not recently undergone a physical examination.

It is difficult to determine whether these medical problems can be attributed to the inadequacies of the health care delivery system, or to how this population group deals with its health problems or interacts with the current health delivery system available to it. The incidence of premature and low birth weight babies is known to be directly connected with the mother's prenatal care, the degree to which she follows her physician's program during pregnancy, and other factors, such as how many women do not use the medical supervision available to them. In general, in the large cities where most of the black population resides, such care is now available to the poor under the Medicaid program, with service provided by a physician of choice.

Similar questions can be raised about the high incidence of childhood diseases among blacks, many of which are preventable by immunization. Here, too, pediatric care is available under Medicaid, but McKinney does not indicate the degree to which this population uses these facilities. Lead poisoning of children has been a continuing concern of health authorities. In recent years, much of the wall paint hazard has been removed, although the ingestion of lead by inhalation remains a problem. The question of decayed, untreated teeth falls in the same category as premature births and childhood diseases in that dental care is available under Medicaid. In fact, Medicaid is the only such program to include dental care, unlike Medicare, Blue Cross, Blue Shield, and most health insurance programs available to the nonpoor. Little is known about the causes of the Sudden Infant Death Syndrome, and there is no indication that medical care can do much about it at present. Hypertension is a problem which generally cannot be treated by the physician but can only be alleviated. McKinney does not elaborate on what proportion of blacks with hypertension is being treated, although Medicaid does make full medical service, including prescriptions, available for such conditions. The high percentage of blacks who do not have regular physical examinations also raises the question of how much available services under Medicaid are being utilized. The work of Lefkowitz (1970, 1973) and Leveson shows that health care is probably dependent more on the way the person lives and sees to his health needs than it is on the structure of the available medical care delivery system. In any case, Leveson concludes that income is only one factor in the utilization of medical care along with general health status, education, price variables, and travel distance. Color, Leveson found, is not an important determinant in health care utilization.

Health Care and the Disadvantaged

Brooke and Williams have examined the research literature on the health care of the disadvantaged. They have found that the differentials in health status between the disadvantaged and the nondisadvantaged persist; that the differentials in the overall amount of health care received are less dramatic than in the past, although standardization by need demonstrates discrepancies in health services provided; that the quality of health care in general has demonstrable shortcomings, but the technical quality of care for the disadvantaged is not strikingly poorer; and that efforts to improve the quality of care for the disadvantaged through either traditional or new means have not been very successful. They suggest further research, especially in testing out the feasibility of increased patient responsibility and consumer knowledge of this population and of greater financial accountability for those delivering health care services to this population.

Taylor, Aday, and Andersen conclude that "non-whites, rural farm people, the poor and those who do not have a regular place they can go for medical advice and treatment [have] less medical care than they should" (p. 47). This finding corroborates our earlier premise, namely, that the issue does not relate to being poor as much as it does to social or physical distance from the health care delivery station or lack of knowledge about self-care, availability of medical care services, and motivation to follow up on prescribed treatment plans.

A report of the Congressional Budget Office in late 1977 as summarized by Scott indicates that the medical system still provides better care to whites than to nonwhites, "despite important gains over the last 20 years." The reasons for this problem were listed as high costs combined with low incomes (apparently for the working poor who had not applied but were eligible for Medicaid in the medically indigent category); nonfinancial barriers, such as discrimination or localized shortages of physicians; lack of followup care; and "too little emphasis on some conditions affecting non-whites" (p. 1). The study found that health services which government programs give directly to nonwhites are more effective than programs which contract for medical care with private health service facilities. The report lists a 70-percent higher infant mortality rate for nonwhites, a 50-percent higher bed disability rate, and a life expectancy six years shorter than that of whites. Nonwhites were four times more likely to die of heart disease and chronic kidney failure, three times more likely to die of high blood pressure, five times more likely to die of tuberculosis, two times more likely to die of diabetes, and seven times more likely to be victims of homicide. Black women were found to be five times more likely to die of complications in childbirth, a figure which, when added to the infant mortality rate, indicates an inadequate involvement in prenatal care.

These problems, it must be emphasized, should not necessarily be traced to a lack of medical care. Rather, they relate more to the life-style of the population, their involvement with and commitment to personal health, their knowledge about the health and disease processes and health facilities, and their pattern of use of such facilities. The available health care system can be blamed to the degree to which such health care delivery systems are physically, culturally, and socially distant from that population. These disease problems can be said to be self-inflicted to the extent that the population at risk does not seek the services of the system, does not follow up on the recommendations of the health care facilities, and pursues a life-style that is destructive to health.

June Christmas, commissioner of the New York City Department of Mental Health and Mental Retardation Services, believes that the system fails minorities because of systemic defects. She also believes systemic discrimination is present. While she agrees that the systemic defects affect both the rich and the poor, she points out that the poor are least able to deal with them. In her view, the poor of the inner city have a choice only between the overcrowded, impersonal public hospital emergency room and the "Medicaid mill." The "Medicaid mill" image is easily negated, however, by Medicaid reports revealing the distribution of thousands of physicians throughout every city, including the inner city, whose Medicaid billings do not reveal them to be operating "mills."

Christmas's complaints that hospitals, both private and public, tend to offer episodic service and fail to provide continuity of care are valid, but this problem applies to both the rich and the poor. Only those families who consistently utilize the same physician can expect to develop a relationship of preventative care. Furthermore, the patient has to initiate and maintain the relationship because physicians see only those patients who come to them. Christmas also indicates that whites more easily find someone to care for them at home during illness or upon hospital discharge. Here, too, the problem is not within the medical care system, but within the patient family care system. Christmas is correct in her complaints against those states which restrict certain types of care under Medicaid because of the complications of billing and the often inordinate wait for payment.

What Christmas perceives as racial discrimination against the poor in the way they are handled in a physician's office or clinic may be more reflective of the culture of medicine and scientific medicine than a particular resistance to serving the poor. As cited earlier, the misunderstanding between medical personnel and the poor is often related to educational level. Just as the poor have trouble with the employment market until they have achieved an adequate comprehension of mainstream communication, culture, and skills, so they have problems securing an adequate degree of service from the medical system.

Beverlee Myers, reporting on the health problems of California, states that the usage of health facilities varies widely between poor and nonpoor. She claims that the poor have more severe health problems, and so the equal use of physician services means that the needs of the poor are not being met. There is a sizable difference, she states, between the poor and others in the use of hospitals and dentists. The lowest income groups have twice as many hospital admissions as others, which Myers suggests indicates that the poor have greater needs for ambulatory care which are unmet. Unlike the nonpoor, the poor tend to seek care only when they suffer severe pain rather than when they notice certain symptoms. They often discontinue medical visits when the symptoms disappear. The poor also do not generally undergo periodic physical examinations. Thus, the poor usually come for care when the illness has reached a critical stage or when hospital admission is indicated.

Monteiro has also reported on the pattern of utilization of physicians by low-income and other patients. She asserts that, although both groups show an equal tendency to visit physicians when ill, the low-income group reports more days of illness for each incidence of sickness. "Low income persons not only have a higher need and therefore a higher use, but also the availability of publicly financed care seems to stimulate use even when need, as measured by restricted activity days, is not present." Thus, an inverse trend in physician use may be developing when compared with income.

The Sudovar and Sullivan report that "the average American's health experience is primarily related to life-style" supports this view. The problem, however, in assessing health care services for the poor is compounded by the fact that "there is no widespread consensus on the range of services or benefits which constitutes an 'adequate' level of care." In terms of the reported gap in medical services between low-income and other populations, Ginsberg states that "recent data indicate that Medicare and Medicaid have gone far to narrow the gap in access [between the poor and others to medical care] though not necessarily in quality. The rates of utilization of medical service are no longer conspicuously different for rich and poor" (p. 39).

Upon closer examination, the problem in the utilization of medical services can be attributed more to the personal health care patterns of the poor than to the medical services delivery system. Davis and Schoen (p. 10) have commented on this problem:

[T]he health problems of the poor and disadvantaged tend to be both more numerous and . . . complex. Poor nutrition, inferior housing, inadequate sanitation and the physical and psychological stresses of unemployment and deprivation all interact to intensify the health problems of the poor. An attack on poor health that focuses exclusively on the medical treatment of illness will not be [as] successful as one that deals with both the causes and symptoms of poor health.

Enos and Sultan (pp. 139–44) accept the view that there is a subculture of poverty which negatively affects the residual poor both in terms of their health and their life-patterns as they relate to health and in terms of their ability to comprehend, utilize, and cooperate with the health services. Cassell (1973) has also examined the problem of disease as a way of life. In his opinion, "there is little evidence to support the assumption that the health of a population is primarily a function of the medical services and [there is] much to contradict it" (p. 80). He points to the example of the Navajo Indians, who were provided with in-depth medical care but who made no change in their general environment. After five years, there was no evidence of any real change in the pattern or prevalence of disease among them. Cassell points out that disease among the Navajo is a function of the way they live and raise their children. Medical care alone—no matter how modern, well delivered, or technically complete—cannot be expected to lift the continuing burden of sickness deriving from dysfunctional health activity.

In examining the reasons, Cassell (1973) says that over the past forty years profound changes have occurred in the patterns of American disease. The demise of the common infectious diseases and the development of modern scientific medicine are not responsible for these changes, however. Rather, changes in the quality of life brought about the dramatic improvement in American health. The high rate of mortality in the past was in part directly the result of urban conditions caused by the Industrial Revolution. Mass movements from rural to urban poverty, crowding, and inadequate or pestiferous housing (which are discussed in the next chapter) all contributed to the transmission of disease. The decline in mortality rates occurred in the 1950s when improved living conditions and better nutrition became available to major sectors of the population. During this time, the clinicians knew of few specific decisive therapies or preventatives. At the same time, because of economic rather than health considerations, new methods of packaging and distributing food were developed. Contamination and spoilage were considerably reduced. These innovations produced tangential and unintended benefits in disease control. Thus, our present pattern of reduced mortality springs from changes in the way of life of the masses rather than from the quality or delivery patterns of medical care.

The level of mortality among American infants has been compared unfavorably with that of other countries. (See Langer, Myers, et al.) Similar concern has been expressed for the higher infant mortality rate among black infants in the United States. The implication of these criticisms is that the higher rate of infant mortality follows from an inadequate medical care delivery in the United States. This conclusion does not stand up under examination, for here again, according to Cassell, the matter can be traced to the different life-patterns of the populations involved. The infants' home environment is the crucial factor, specifically as it relates to prevention of the diarrhea-pneumonia complex. A program of health education will not solve the problem. To teach the procedure of hand washing without explaining the germ theory will not change child care and life-patterns. The less educated carry the greatest burden of mortality, and ignorance of health matters occurs mainly among the poor. When a family's income rises above $5,000 per year (1973 dollars) and when both parents are at least high school graduates, the infant mortality rate falls. Thus, poverty, as it relates to health, means more than being without the money to purchase medical care. In the British experience where medical services are readily available to all, the lower social classes still have a greater incidence of illness. Among the American military where the same medical facilities are available to families at all ranks, prenatal mortality increases with the decreasing military rank of the husband.

The simple fact is that poor health and poverty are related in many ways. Illness and the quality of medical care have more serious consequences for lower income populations than for others (Langer p. 331, Eitzen p. 99, Enos and Sultan pp. 142–43, Duval p. 187, Wildavsky p. 119, Ginsberg pp. 205, 207, Anderson p. 378). The costs of disease are inequitably distributed among the socioeconomic classes (Richmond pp. 254, 257, Knowles pp. 74, 79, Rogers p. 85, Enos and Sultan p. 144, Kotelchuk pp. 6–13, Wildavsky p. 119, Langer p. 331, Eitzen p. 99, Lefkowitz p. 170). Disease may cause or increase impoverishment among the lower classes more readily than among the wealthier classes (Kotelchuk pp. 10–13, Anderson p. 376, Langer p. 331).

The relationship between poverty and health must be understood because many incorrect social policy implications have been drawn from that relationship. People who have chronic conditions that limit their activity are more likely to have low incomes. These families lose a greater portion of their salary as a result of illness than do other families. The reason is that people in higher income occupations are more likely to have paid sick-leave job benefits, adequate medical insurance, and other informal arrangements that make illness less of a loss in income. In contrast, for lower income people, illness can mean a proportionately greater out-of-pocket cost. Hence, illness does have a greater financial impact on the poor than on any other social class. The Medicare and Medicaid programs represent attempts to correct this inequity.

The report *Expenditures for Personal Health Services* (Anderson, et al., 1973) bears out the Lefkowitz and Cassell positions. It indicates that medical care payments increased steadily during the 1960s, but that after adjustments were made for family size, the difference in medical care expenditures between lower income groups and others was small. The report also points out that the poor spend a greater proportion of their income on health care than do the nonpoor, and that this proportion has been rising despite the enactment of Medicare and Medicaid. Even though Medicare and Medicaid pay for approximately one-half of the medical services received by the lowest income families, these programs have not reduced the proportion of their incomes which the poor spend for medical care.

Health Services Use (Anderson, et al., 1973) reports that the gap between the percentage of low-income and high-income people seeing a physician during the year narrowed considerably between 1963 and 1970.

The percentage of low-income children and young adults who regularly see a physician has definitely increased, and once they do see a physician, they average more visits than others. The mean number of visits by nonwhites is almost as great as that by whites. The mean number of visits to a physician by central city residents exceeded the national average. By 1970, the mean number of dental visits per person did not differ greatly according to income and race. The 1978 report from HEW on *Health-US* indicates that persons in families with low incomes are generally hospitalized more often. Once hospitalized, they remain in the hospital longer than people with higher incomes. This is most pronounced for people under age 65. On average people 45–64 years of age with an income under $5,000 spent more than three and one-half days longer than people with larger incomes (p. 8) (see Nation, Center for Health Services Research).

Despite the increase in the use of medical services by the poor in 1977 the *Health-US* report indicates that the gap in health status between the poor and nonpoor as measured by morbidity, disability, and mortality has actually widened. This report points to the differential use of preventative health efforts made by the poor and other income groups and indicates that prevention and lifestyle may be a central factor in health maintenance (pp. 21, 25–26).

Poverty and Health

Glazer (1971) discusses the paradoxes of health care as they relate to poverty. With regard to the comparative crude mortality figures of the rich and the poor, he concludes that there is only a slight difference between them, but that the people in poverty areas are younger. "If it had been possible to compute age-specific rates [in the study] the differences would have been much greater" (p. 68). In the case of infant mortality, the rates were much higher in poverty areas, but Glazer does not indicate whether poverty and infant mortality are caused by a common factor or whether they are a matter of cause and effect. In his view, the best evidence of poorer health among those in poverty is the number of days of disability they experienced. Here he reports differences on the order of two to one. Although the poor may be sicker, their patterns of utilization of health care are not as different from those of other people as one might expect. For example, the correlation between hospital admissions and income was greater in 1928 than it was in 1952; by 1952–1953, no association between the two was apparent, and this, it should be noted, was a decade or more before Medicare and Medicaid programs made hospitalization much more accessible for all.

Glazer finds "striking evidence of the increasing utilization of health resources among different income groups" (p. 67). This pattern, he believes, can be attributed to the elimination of financial barriers to the poor's use of health resources. He concludes that economic barriers to medical care are either nonexistent or minor for the poor. In fact, he claims that the poor face fewer economic barriers to health care than do most of the nonpoor, who are limited by the terms of their health insurance. The difference in the health care given the poor is that they see specialists less often than do other people, inasmuch as they make medical visits primarily for acute conditions in clinics and emergency wards where medical specialists are less available. But whether there is a difference in the quality of care between generalists and specialists is an issue still being fought in medical circles. Glazer supports the view that medical costs and medical care are less important factors in health maintenance than what people do and don't do, to and for themselves. If there is a possible basic difference between the health of the poor and the nonpoor, it probably can be found in this set of factors.

The Anderson, et al., conclusions of 1973, and the Lefkowitz and Cassell views are generally supported by the data in the staff report's *National Health Insurance Resources Book* (pp. 88, 89).

Isaccson has done a careful review of the studies on poverty and health. He challenges the assumption that "because health care is expensive it doesn't reach the poor who therefore get sicker and die at a higher rate" (p. 15). Furthermore, he argues against the belief that "medical technology and skills are [now] superb" and that "we lack a system of health capable of delivering care to everybody" (p. 15). In essence, he examines the assumption that poverty causes poor health as well as similar assumptions that inadequate medical care among the poor leads to more illness and that inadequate medical care among the poor is related to high infant mortality. These views may have been tenable when infections were the most prevalent causes of infant mortality. In contemporary times, no single variable can be isolated as the cause of illness among the poor. In Isaccson's view, "poverty has a set of associated characteristics and they travel together" (p. 16). At best, most of what medicine can provide to the poor is secondary prevention of disease, that is, the treatment of illnesses as soon as their early signs appear. Except for immunizations, there are "disappointingly few examples of primary prevention [which] can be applied in the usual medical setting" (p. 17). Even secondary prevention is more an act of faith than a matter of proven fact. Thus, being poor and sick at the same time is not definitely the result of deficiencies in the quality, type, and amount of medical care available (pp. 15, 16, 17). Brian Abel-Smith, in his international study of health expenditures, has shown that there is no correlation between the level of medical expenditures and identifiable needs for health care.

The weak relationship between medical care and health is not a new discovery. Dubos in his *Mirage of Health* presented this view as early as 1959. Isaccson makes a sharp distinction between public, as opposed to personal, health efforts. In his view, programs designed to supply second-ary preventative efforts cannot become primary preventative foundation programs for the general population. Thus, if the health of the poor is a social policy goal of the society, then it must be approached by programs that are not locked into personal care settings. Isaccson emphasizes that the system of paying for sick care in the United States is "in bad shape," but this fact must be kept "conceptually separate from the problem of keeping a society [and its poor] healthy."

Medical care for the poor has often been discussed as a "right to health." Szasz (pp. 100–102) takes issue with this position. He states that "every important human need and satisfaction [are related] to the self-evident fact that the poor will always have more needs than the rich and the rich more satisfactions than the poor." Szasz calls this view—that a person, regardless of personal effort or self-care, has the right to have all needs met—naive and plaintive. He asserts that "except in the eyes of the utopian social reformer who views all social differences as contagious diseases there is no paradox about this pattern of distribution." He ex-plains that the concept of medical treatment as a right rather than a privilege is negated by the problems of how to distinguish between ine-qualities and inequities and how to determine which government policies are best suited to the securing of good medical care for the maximum number of persons. Szasz asks: "(1) Which inequalities shall be consid-ered as inequities? (2) What are the most important means for minimizing or abolishing the inequities we deem unjust?"

Despite these questions, American society has provided medical care for the poor in a series of programs that are part of the general nonsystem of American health care (Levin, Enos and Sultan, Friedson (1970), and Mechanic). The system of providing sick people with care is, of course, an important matter. Such care is paid for in a number of ways: by federal funding in the form of Medicare; by matched federal and state funds in the form of Medicaid; by third-party funds from private insurance car-riers and Blue Cross and Blue Shield; and by private payments.

A Closer Look at Medicare and Medicaid

MEDICARE

Medicare was established in 1965 as a health insurance program for persons sixty-five years of age or over. Medicare patients who meet low-income or other eligibility requirements may also be eligible for Medicaid help to pay costs not covered by Medicare (Myers, McCormick).

The benefits and specifications of Medicare are uniform throughout the United States; hence, a person's deductibility and co-insurance status is the same everywhere. Payments for medical care are made from the Social Security trust funds deducted from payroll taxes and from premiums paid by individuals who are covered but who elect to have the optional supplemental coverage. (See Social Security Administration, Chapters 21–24.)

Included in Medicare's basic program are inpatient hospital care, posthospital extended care, and posthospital home health care (up to a specified days-care-per-year limit). An optional supplemental medical care program is available if the person enrolled pays a nominal monthly amount that is matched by a federal contribution. The optional program provides protection against costs of physicians' services, medical services and supplies, home health care services, outpatient hospital services, various therapies, and other services. The basic portion of Medicare is, in practice, a hospital insurance program. Except for the first $160 in each benefit period, the full hospital costs are paid. The optional program pays 80 percent of medical costs after the established deductible in each calendar year (*Social Security Information Items*).

The Medicare program is essentially a companion program to the Social Security Old Age Annuities program. By the end of 1970, approximately 10 percent of the population was covered by the basic Medicare plan, and about 95 percent of these people were also covered by the optional or supplementary program. By 1970, the program paid medical bills for approximately 10 million elderly people in the United States (about 50 percent of those covered). By 1973, Medicare covered 21 million aged insured and 1.7 million disabled insured persons. Hospital services for 1973 represented $4.7 million, and physicians' services, $10.5 million (Martin Anderson). For fiscal 1978, $25.6 billion were estimated for Medicare in the national budget. This sum was expected to grow to $29.4 billion in 1979.

The Medicare program is administered by the Bureau of Health Insurance of the Social Security Administration. Unlike other Social Security Administration programs, payments are usually made not to the beneficiaries but to the vendor (for example, the hospital, physician, nursing home, or medical laboratory). The Bureau of Health Insurance contracts with a health care administration corporation in each state (usually the Blue Cross-Blue Shield organization or some health insurance company) to deal with claims, to verify services, and to make payments to vendors. Although Medicare is social insurance, because of this administrative process it could be inferred that private enterprise is intricately involved in the process. Hospital associations and medical groups that are closely bound to the policies of Blue Cross and Blue Shield are also tied to Medicare by reason of their connection with these companies. Blue Cross, Blue Shield, and private commercial health insurance programs are also connected with Medicare by a variety of medical insurance plans which provide further supplements to the Medicare program for those who wish to purchase such coverage.

Two years after Medicare was established, it became clear that the program had a built-in propensity to raise medical fees, not just for the aged covered by Medicare but for all medical clients. Marmor found that the federal government could not avoid paying physicians increased and increasing fees under Medicare on a fee-for-service basis. In the design of Medicare, the choice was between a reasonable (undefinable) fee system or one based on costs and pro rata professional time spent. The AMA fought for the former, and that opened up the door to unreasonable, seemingly organized gouging of the government under the guise of arriving at a "reasonable" fee structure. As a result of the law of supply and demand in a situation of increased funded demand on a relatively inelastic quantity of supply, all medical fees were raised and the volume of physician services at higher fees increased. According to Marmor, "When governments pay doctors by a method the doctors prefer, governments should be certain that reforms in medical practice accompany such concessions" (pp. 18–19). In view of the lack of any incentives to improve practice and of the fact that intermediaries, and not the government, are responsible for the primary review of fees and quality of services, "There is little reason to believe that higher prices paid to doctors by private citizens and Medicare [do] result in improved medical practices" (Marmor).

Similar reports on the Medicare experience have emanated from other sources. Schechter, for example, writing on "Medicare on Its Fourth Birthday," declared it to be "Alive But Not Well." He points out that private health insurance and Medicare and Medicaid distort comprehensive medical practice by the benefit or coverage structure, which is biased toward the coverable rather than toward the necessary for the patient's health maintenance. As a result, Schechter believes that almost a 25-percent wastage was apparent in what was then a $60 billion a year industry. As one program "reimburses better than other programs, it draws off scarce manpower [and services] and promotes higher prices" (p. 17). At that point, Schechter believed that Medicare (and later Medicaid) was a drastic distortion of health care delivery rather than a service to those in need of health care.

George Melcher of Group Health Insurance, Inc., of New York, discussed the problems of Medicare utilization controls for the intermediary fiscal agents in the testimony he gave to the Subcommittee on Medicare-Medicaid of the Committee on Finance, U.S. Senate, in early 1970. He indicated that for every $100,000 he paid out for the government on Medicare medical bills, his agency was paid $10,000. If, however, by careful utilization analysis, his agency was able to disallow $10,000, they would then dispense only $90,000 and his company would be paid $9,000. In other words, his company was rewarded for the amount of money paid out rather than for the time, effort, and costs of voucher checking and utilization control. Under such an arrangement, Dr. Melcher reports, "it is much easier to pay claims rather than to try to control program costs." The incentive for the Medicare payment to agents is therefore structured to pay more rather than less for medical and hospital services.

Lowell E. Bellin, first deputy commissioner of the New York Department of Health, before the same subcommittee on June 2, 1970, categorized some of the control problems of Medicare and Medicaid. His first category listed as "fraud" the act of billing the government for a service that never took place. His second category of abuse was "poor quality" which also cheats the public because the quality of care paid for is not delivered. The third abuse he listed as "overutilization," that is, the provision of health services that are justified for neither preventative nor therapeutic reasons. Bellin described a study of 1,200 Medicaid dental patients who responded to a followup letter sent to 6,000 patients. Of the 1,200 patients seen in the followup, 9 percent did not have the dental work done for which the government had paid. Another 9 percent had work of very poor quality, not at all up to the prescribed standards. Overutilization (for example, the provision of dental work not necessary for preventative or therapeutic care) represented still another 25 percent. If these 1,200 patients represent the kind of work done under Medicare and Medicaid, it would appear that 43 percent of what the government pays is fraud or overutilization.

Bellin also reported that medical organizations resented the Medicare and Medicaid audits by his staff to check patients' medical records. These audits sought to determine whether a Medicare or Medicaid physician, in his private office, routinely recorded a patient's chief complaint and pertinent case history, performed a physical examination and recorded it, recorded all laboratory tests and x-rays ordered and their results, developed and recorded a plan of therapy, and followed a proper plan of diagnosis, prevention, and treatment. He indicated that the audit caused resentment largely because in many of the cases such records were lacking where services were billed to the federal government. In such matters, he concluded " a peer society cannot by itself dispassionately audit the professional activities of its membership" (p. 529). Only through an external mechanism can such problems be uncovered and dealt with. Fraud and abuse legislation planned for 1979 were aimed at reducing payment errors by $400 million in the 1979 federal budget.

Berkeley Bennett of the National Council of Health Care Services appeared before the same subcommittee on June 3, 1970. His organization attempted to make a case for incentives to control skyrocketing

Medicare and Medicaid costs by a system that sought a "best combination of quality and costs." The system would utilize incentives for more economical operation and costs for providers, consumers (co-insurance and deductibles), and mechanisms for limits on costs. A careful study of these proposals shows little in the way of effective mechanisms to control abuses, overutilization, and waste in Medicare and Medicaid. Our reading indicates that these proposed mechanisms are merely a change in procedures, with more controls. The key to medical cost and utilization control apparently lies in finding the means of motivating the patient to exercise restraint on medical expenditures (for example, avoiding useless visits to a physician) and of equipping the patient with the knowledge necessary for this purpose. This problem is particularly difficult with the residual poor, who lack the communication skills, knowledge of human biology, and academic background needed to understand the medical explanations of their conditions.

The staff study of the Ways and Means Committee in *The National Health Insurance Resources Book* reports that the growth of the Medicare program was matched by a long-term rise in physicians' net incomes (pp. 54–55). This rise reflected an increase not only in fees charged, but also in productivity caused by "seeing more patients in the same amount of time," by cutting back on house calls, by using more capital equipment and auxiliary personnel, and by improving collection rates as made possible by third-party payments. Medicare and Medicaid have raised physicians' incomes even further "because of the payment of customary charges under the program; many physicians previously charged their aged [and needy] patients on a sliding scale and thus [previous to Medicare] were paid less than their customary charge or nothing at all" (Staff, Ways and Means Committee). The shift to Medicare enabled doctors to be paid for work they previously did for little or no pay. In less than a decade, Medicare has effectively removed all semblance of the humanitarian worker image from modern medicine. It has also, to a considerable extent, made legitimate medical service consumers of many former charity patients.

Klarman's study of the effects of Medicare on medical services indicates that the number of visits to physicians per capita has declined in the past decade among all patients, including the aged. There has been a tendency for more equal use by all income classes, especially among adults under sixty-five years of age.

Scitovsky and Snyder found that older people now make more demands for general care than for specific medical care in their visits to medical offices. This trend is seen as a request for personal services, "an appeal for attention from others." "In the absence of any other source that can meet this demand, this appeal becomes translated into a demand for medical care. A misallocation of resources results" (p. 25). Medicare, and probably Medicaid, end up paying for substitutes for the care and concern that were provided by the extended family and friends in earlier generations. The friendless aged person with no one to be close to can easily invent a medical complaint by which he can gain legitimate entry into medical care facilities. The Scitovsky and Snyder study, which is based on data more recent than those used by Klarman, shows that aged people in residential settings with middle-class standards of health care "seem to have a very high demand for physicians' services when given free and easy access to [them]."

Medicare thus distorts the nature of medical services for the lonely aged. Rather than solve the problem which is at the base of their complaints (a problem which is familial, social, and interpersonal), it distorts the nature of the expressed complaint and the role of a physician, causes useless expense, and does not really resolve the patient's underlying problem.

Klarman also reports on the distortion of hospital fees by Medicare. He states that Medicare "perpetuates a dual set of prices—a gross price paid by the provider and a much lower net price paid by the consumer out-of-pocket at the time of the illness." It distorts reality for the consumer and encourages the provider to enhance and elaborate the quality of care, even at a higher price. An alternate effect also occurs in the relationship between Medicare funding and hospital costs. As Medicare and Medicaid become more available, a hospital administrator "can no longer deny requests for higher wages or more supplies on the ground that money is lacking; to get money, he need only spend more [and bill more]" (p. 110). Thus, just as the physician's behavior changed after Medicare, so did the behavior of the hospital administrators. This change is particularly evident in Klarman's explanation of Roemer's law which states that "under conditions of [guaranteed] prepayment, hospital beds, if built, will be used" (p. 118). Medicare and Medicaid have therefore been responsible for an expansion of hospital beds—in many instances, where they were not really needed.

Deborah Shapley, in a report on national health insurance, raises the issue of whether any further provision of funding on a cost-per-service basis will promote costly technology, just as Medicare and Medicaid have already done in their attempts to provide care for 50 million aged and poor people. She concludes that the cost and ineffectiveness problems of the current programs, let alone any expanded programs, cannot be resolved until the fees-for-service problem is resolved.

Still another critique of Medicare was made by the Comptroller General's Office in 1971. As a result of its analysis, review committees of physicians have been established in each hospital to reduce the number of hospital days or extended care days chargeable to Medicare for aged patients. Thus, when a patient becomes ready for a less costly type of service, whether extended care, custodial care, or outpatient care, he is quickly transferred to a less expensive nursing facility or put on his own financing. These review committees pose several problems of their own, however. Such intensive and continuous study of records by professional staffs means added costs, and the physician who must rule against a colleague's request to retain a patient in the hospital faces a potential conflict of interest.

MEDICAID

Medicaid is a form of public assistance for generally indigent persons and the medically indigent. Medically indigent persons are those not financially eligible for public assistance who are in financial difficulty because of their medical needs. Medicaid enables the states to furnish medical assistance for families with dependent children, the aged, and the blind, or totally disabled persons who do not have sufficient income and resources to meet the costs of medical care. It also allows the states to provide rehabilitation and other services to help such persons attain or retain capability for independence and self-care. The program is financed through shared funding by federal and state contributions.

Medicaid gives broad leeway to the states to set the payment levels of the program. It uses federal, state, and local tax funds to pay for medical care for eligible persons. The states design their own Medicaid programs within federal guidelines, and in most instances, the programs are administered through state welfare or state health agencies. The federal share ranges from 50 percent of total Medicaid costs in states with high per capita income to 83 percent in low-income states. Only one state (Arizona) has opted not to provide Medicaid to its indigents. By 1970, the program had paid medical costs for 17 million persons, mainly public assistance clients. By 1978, according to the 1979 federal budget, costs amounted to $11 billion for 21 million recipients and were budgeted for $12.1 billion for 1979.

Medicaid covers inpatient hospital care, outpatient hospital services, laboratory and x-ray costs, nursing home care, physicians' services, screening, diagnosis, and home health care services. In a number of states, Medicaid covers dental care, drugs, eyeglasses, and extensive diagnostic, preventative, and rehabilitative services. Medicaid was designed as an open-ended program so that a state government could provide health services in depth to those in poverty.

Under Medicare, the limits of costs per patient are set nationally, but under Medicaid, there are no federal limits for the individual patient.

Thus, a person who uses up his Medicare health benefits and who can pass a public assistance means test can be served indefinitely under Medicaid.

Eligibility for Medicaid resembles categorical assistance in public welfare. If a person falls into a particular category, he is thereby eligible. The subcategories eligible include recipients of AFDC (adults and children); public assistance recipients under the SSI program (needy aged, disabled, or blind); and General Assistance recipients (persons or families receiving local relief who are without funds for medical care). Each of these subcategories provides automatic eligibility for Medicaid. Under this arrangement, the proof that a person is unable to support himself through his own resources (the means test) is matched with a logical assumption that he cannot provide for his own medical services.

The next category, the medically indigent recipients, is different in this respect. The medically indigent person can provide for his own care but cannot pay for an essential medical need. Such a noncategorically related needy person must be processed by a local public assistance agency for means test purposes. Generally, the same standards exist for this application as for an AFDC application. This requires a signed statement of facts that may be used as a basis for the eligibility determination. The local public assistance staff usually makes the determination of eligibility. A face-to-face interview is required in many states at the time of the application. Eligibility factors such as actual residence in state and county, legality of admission into the United States, financial resource limits of the family, and availability of co-payment individuals (such as married children with income resources beyond their adjudged needs), must all be evaluated. Many of the requirements differ in each state or territory. Many states severely limit coverage and reimbursement rates to vendors (Fox, p. 5).

In the more liberal Medicaid states, such as California and New York, the medical indigent category has provided a form of medical catastrophe insurance for middle-class families who have drained their resources to pay for extremely expensive medical care for one of their members. In such instances, if the family can qualify by indicating the extreme disparity between its income and the medical demands made upon it, Medicaid becomes a last resource mechanism to provide continued medical services that would otherwise not be available to the family. In other instances, Medicaid has become a means by which elderly middle-class relatives who have otherwise disposed of their funds can be taken care of without much pressure on their grown children. This practice also occurs, to some extent, with Medicare and Social Security retirement funds, except that these losses to the system have been offset by prepayments made in earlier years. In the case of Medicaid (and SSI), each recipient and each otherwise able and grown member of his family becomes dependent upon others in the taxpaying population. In the case of the catastrophically medically indigent, dependency is less evident because such families have been self-supporting prior to the catastrophe and usually have supported others by their tax contributions.

Medicaid was not invented *de novo*. It was preceded by special medical allowances included in the family budgets of AFDC, OAA, ATD, and AB. In these programs, the payments were made to the recipients rather than to the vendors of the services. This means of paying for medical care was important because the client who received and forwarded a payment for medical care to his physician was necessarily informed of the amount charged and the amount paid. This mechanism also contained its own problems, one of which was that a client who did not manage money too well could neglect to forward funds received for his doctor, especially if these funds were part of a larger monthly subsistence check. The advantages of direct payments to clients were not only the control by the client of unreasonable medical expenditures, but, more importantly, the development of responsibility on the part of the client. To make a client part of the payment process indicated to him that payment was his responsibility as well as that of the funding agency.

By 1950, Congress authorized vendor payments for medical care, to be paid to physicians, health care institutions, and other providers of medical services (*National Health Insurance Resources Book*, pp. 487–95). By 1960, 80 percent of the states had made provisions for medical vendor payments. In 1951, these had amounted to $100 million, but by 1960, they had risen to over $500 million. In 1960, Congress authorized the medically needy aged category of recipients for cases in which usually self-sufficient old people were faced with medical costs beyond their resources. Under the Kerr-Mills Act, the federal government became responsible for 50 to 80 percent of the costs of such medical services. Between 1960 and 1965, total vendor payments increased from $500 million to $1,300 million. Most of this increase was occasioned by vendor payments for OAA and the Kerr-Mills program. By 1965, it became clear that a more sophisticated and comprehensive medical assistance program was required in the United States. In that year, the Medicaid program was enacted into the Social Security Amendments. This program substituted a single program of medical assistance for the vendor payments of the different categorical assistance programs and the medical assistance for the aged programs. In addition, Medicaid made possible medical services without prior authorization by a public assistance agency on the voucher system. Thus, a client could visit a physician and the physician could order whatever he needed for the client without reference to the public welfare authorities.

By January 1970, federal sharing of costs with states and localities in public assistance medical vendor payments was no longer permissible, except under the Medicaid program. The program offered a higher federal contribution to vendor payments for medical care than had existed under the cash assistance categorical programs. All states enrolled in the Medicaid program were required to cover all persons receiving public assistance. The states were thus able to include medically needy aged, blind, and disabled persons, as well as dependent children and their families at their option. All states were required to include inpatient and outpatient hospital services, other laboratory and x-ray services, skilled nursing home services, and physicians' services. Other types of services were also authorized at the states' options. Of the 28 million recipients of Medicaid in 1975, 7.9 million were adults in AFDC families, 12.9 million were other children under age twenty-one, 5.1 million were aged, and the balance were blind and disabled

Some of the payments under Medicaid have grown to such an extent that "on a crude estimate the Medicaid patient in New York City costs at least twice as much to provide with health care as the average American" (Glazer, 1973). A number of reasons may be hypothesized for this extraordinary cost. First, the needy person may be sicker than others, or has so delayed arrangements for his health care that to serve him medically is twice as expensive as serving less ill persons. Second, the difficulties of delivering health care to the needy may be so much greater that the costs for their care are twice that of care for others. Third, the mechanism of Medicaid may be so structured that purveyors and consumers of medical services under Medicaid provide for a volume of service beyond that which is fundamentally necessary for a person's full functionality. Fourth, the condition of poverty may be such that an assisted person with an emotional need deriving from his dependent condition will tend to ask for and receive more medical care than will others who are not dependent. As one ghetto inhabitant put it in the Louis Harris survey (1969), "When you're living sick all the time (which includes being on public welfare) you're living sick all over from head to toes." Hence, a public assistance client who is disturbed by his situation and who has a need to do something about it will tend to translate his disturbance into medical symptomatology because this is more acceptable and the service is more available at a medical level. Fifth, it may be that most persons who are fully functional and self-sufficient do not have the time or motivation to obtain the degree of medical care available to the poor under Medicaid. Finally, the structure of Medicaid may be so arranged that medical service billings are less controlled by circumstances and persons than in cases where the client pays directly for the service, or where the client makes partial payment for the service as under most medical insurance programs (and therefore is more concerned about medical expenditures), or where the client's services are controlled by the health maintenance organization. These three conditions account for most of the medical payments in the United States other than Medicare and Medicaid.

A number of Medicaid practitioners in the ghettos have been known to expand their incomes inordinately by using Medicaid billings. These mechanisms include providing services to the Medicaid patient over and beyond his medical complaint and billing Medicaid accordingly. This is analogous to doing an overhaul of a customer's motor when he drives in to have his carburetor adjusted. The customer can probably get by with a carburetor adjustment, but if both the garage owner and the customer know that someone else will pay for the more comprehensive job, and for other services as well—then, why not?

A second mechanism is providing services not only to the Medicaid patient with the medical complaint but also to everyone else in his family who accompanies him. This practice has sometimes been called family ganging. The entire family is served assembly-line fashion as long as any one person in the family needs a visit to the physician. A third mechanism is operation in tandem, with two physicians serving everyone at the clinic. One physician is listed as the primary provider of the service and the second as consultant, even when neither the patient nor the physician would have called for a consultation if the patient, and not Medicaid, were paying for the service.

Glazer (1971) states that "one aspect of American medicine unfortunately . . . seems to stand out as unique: the corruption practiced by many . . . doctors." This aspect seems most apparent in many of the 1970 congressional hearings on Medicare and Medicaid. Glazer speaks of his concern for activities that are "barely legal" and can only be described as "profiteering at public expense."

It is useful to examine each of the possible reasons for the inordinate costs of Medicaid. That the poor are less healthy than others is clear, if we define less healthy as a condition of perceiving oneself as such. In the Harris poll (1969), respondents were asked if "some immediate member of the family now has a serious illness." The reported incidence for the poor was two to three times higher than for the population as a whole. According to the reports of the poor, they have more heart trouble, high and low blood pressure, and nerve ailments than do others. The possibility should be considered, however, that complaints of illness among the poor may be more an expression of unhappiness with one's lot in life than a somatic medical complaint. This theory can be tested in individual instances by offering the individual an opportunity for an activity not previously available to him. If he forgets his medical complaint in the process, only then can one judge the complaint to be situationally related.

The Harris poll in 1969 reported an inordinate incidence of psychosomatic conditions such as "worried and nervous" or "too exhausted to get up." It may be that the cause of a person's dependency may also serve as a medical complaint and that to continue to fund medical care for such conditions may perpetuate both the dependency and the medical complaint. If so, then both Medicaid on demand and public assistance may be countertherapeutic for the client's well-being and life-chances.

Part of the answer to the question of why Medicaid is so expensive lies in the answers given to the Harris poll. The findings indicate that the affluent are usually most prone to suffer from psychological concerns and to keep them to themselves rather than bring them to a physician's attention. The poor usually sense that whenever they feel ill, whether from a serious illness or a psychosomatic problem, the doctor should be seen. More than any other social class, the poor see the medical profession as a source of corrective action; they tend to view medicine unrealistically in terms of its competencies and scope.

For the affluent, medical care involves some amount of waiting time and cost. For the poor, medical care involves even more waiting time because clinics and other health providers for the poor tend to have given up on making appointments for their clientele. Thus, the poor expect to wait, do not expect to be given appointments, are not expected to structure their lives by appointments. They therefore wait even longer for care than do other medical customers. With the poor, the crisis approach to health is well entrenched.

Other reasons for the size and volume of Medicaid costs are listed in two comprehensive reports on Medicaid made by the comptroller general of the United States. The first, dated May 11, 1970, covers *Questionable Claims Under the Medicaid Program for the Care of Persons in State Institutions for the Mentally Retarded in California*. In this report, the comptroller general indicates that claims were questionable in that they "were not made on the basis of the person's need for skilled nursing care but simply on the basis of their presence in institutions certified as skilled nursing homes" (p. 1). An entire population that had been previously supported by local or state governments or charities or private family funding was dumped on Medicaid by certifying custodial programs for the mentally retarded or elderly as "necessary skilled nursing institutions" (p. 1). This is another way in which Medicaid has distorted a social or biological condition, namely, mental retardation, and redefined it as a medical condition in order to better suit the financial needs of the providers of services.

The second significant report by the comptroller general, dated July 28, 1971, is titled *Ineffective Controls Over Program Requirements Relating to Medically Needy Persons Covered by Medicaid*. Here the comptroller general found a serious weakness in the quality controls of the two states studied (p. 2). The states were not adequately assured of the validity of the billings made and of the propriety of having the billings charged to

Medicaid rather than to other responsible persons. As a result, by March 1974, Richard D. Godmere of HEW reported the establishment of a Medicaid Management Information System which ties state Medicaid control systems and entries into a national computer network to trace issues and questions of control.

This job will be a sizable one if the Colombotos study on Medicaid is generally valid. In a 1969 study of Medicaid in New York State alone, he found that Medicare covered less than 2 million people, but Medicaid covered up to 7 million people in New York alone, according to 1966 estimates. Medicaid also provided a wider spectrum of services than Medicare and affected the physician's practice more directly since it covers a larger share of his clientele. The controls set by Medicaid and the procedures set up by the physician for his Medicaid patients become the standard for his practice. In this way, the physician often becomes a captive of Medicaid, and his practice tends to service Medicaid more than it services the clients.

Colombotos also showed that Medicare's reimbursements and standards are generally uniform throughout the country but that Medicaid varies from state to state. The more ambitious and liberal the Medicaid program becomes in a state, the more the physician becomes tied to Medicaid funding and procedures. The physician who refuses Medicaid patients may have to deprive himself of a sizable portion of his potential practice, which most physicians cannot afford to do.

Thus, the inordinate costs of Medicaid can be traced to a number of factors: the illness of the poor; their illness-oriented, social-psychological condition; the structural weaknesses of Medicaid; the difficulties in fiscal and quality control; and the tendency of Medicaid to take over a physician's practice and to convert him from a vendor of services into another form of public assistance dependent, which hardly makes for quality medical care.

Medicare and Medicaid differ in more ways than in the volume of services they cover. These differences are presented in Table 6.1.

The original purpose of Medicaid was to provide medical care to the nonaged poor. (Presumably most of the elderly were covered by Medicare—see Doolittle, Levy, and Wiseman, p. 67.) For an AFDC recipient, Medicaid operates in a straightforward manner. Each month the recipient automatically receives a Medicaid card. If a recipient believes he needs medical care, he goes to a physician, clinic, or hospital of his choice and presents the card in lieu of payment. In California, Medicaid is generally offered on a more generous basis than in the rest of the nation under the designation of MediCal. The MediCal card has been called the Magic Kingdom card by drug addicts who are enrolled in one or another public assistance category which makes them eligible for MediCal. The vendor

TABLE 6.1 **Differences between Medicaid and Medicare**

	MEDICAID (*Public Assistance*)	MEDICARE (*Social Insurance*)
Eligibility threshold	(1) By virtue of means test processed under AFDC or SSI, General Assistance categories. (2) Means test operative under medically needy category.	By virtue of benefit eligibility earned under Social Security-covered payments.
Category of clients	Unlimited for persons in included categories of public assistance	Limited, based upon benefits available under coverage.
Factors to which grants or benefits are related	(1) Principle of lesser eligibility is nonoperative because of general consensus that medical needs should be exempt from the usual aid limitations. (2) Principle of husbanding of resources. Aid to medically indigent given only to the degree to which own resources are unavailable.	Benefit ceilings are fixed and unrelated to income.
Construction of allowances of benefits	(1) Varies from state to state. (2) Payments made to vendors, not clients.	(1) Generally uniform over the United States. (2) Although payments are paid to vendors, reports regarding coverage are made to the clients.
Outside income	Deducted where applicable.	Not deducted on Medicare.
Family financial responsibility for children and aged parents	Applicable only in some states. No longer applicable in most.	Grown children are not financially involved.

Table 6.1—*Continued*

	MEDICAID (*Public Assistance*)	MEDICARE (*Social Insurance*)
Cultural stigma	Occurs but is less important than in other public assistance because of cultural view of illness.	Not applicable.
Benefits as a right	Not by legislative intent, but fast becoming so by accumulating court decisions.	He who has credits in the system is eligible for benefits as a right.
Co-payments required	None (assumption is that client has no funds for them). (This is a considerable problem in designing incentives for control.)	Required for a number of listed benefits.
Policies	Constraints and entitlements are decentralized and discretionary in the states.	Centralized, nondiscretionary, highly developed procedures, constraints, and entitlements.
Funding	A grant program financed federal and state programs, derived from taxes.	Medicare hospital insurance financed by a separate Social Security payroll contribution paid by employee and employer. Federal government pays half the monthly premium and the insured person pays the other half. (Medicaid can pay this monthly fee for a person who has limited assets and income but who is otherwise covered by Medicare.)
Administration	By individual states (who may designate a payment agency such as Blue Cross for processing of bills). Operations must meet the regulations of the federal government for Medicaid in order for states to receive reimbursement.	By the federal government. (In most instances, the payment process is managed by an agent, such as Blue Cross, by contract).

then bills the contract payment agency, such as Blue Cross, which, in turn, bills the state government (which is then partially reimbursed by the federal government). If the physician cannot wait for his money or does not care to wait, and because such payments may take as long as six months for reimbursement, many physicians offer their bills to factoring companies which pay the physician minus, of course, a percentage charge for the service. The factoring company is paid in the end, but many physicians have learned to offset the factoring costs by setting their initial bills even higher. This practice is common in New York City.

Because a recipient must be covered by AFDC in many states, or by some other assistance program in order to receive a Medicaid card, Doolittle et al., believe that AFDC became even more attractive to beneficiaries after 1965. These authors believe that Medicaid has therefore been directly responsible for much of the growth of AFDC since its inception.

Culliton also believes that Medicare and Medicaid have been "among the most expensive pieces of social legislation of the 1960's," because Medicare and Medicaid "brought into the health care system millions of persons who previously had no access to care. This was done without any serious cost control measures."

Freymann (pp. 107–108) comments on the high costs of the Medicare and Medicaid programs:

Medicare and Medicaid were launched in 1965 in the naive belief that the only barrier separating the aged and the poor from equal access to health care was inability to pay. In retrospect, it is hard to understand how we could have ignored the elementary economic principle that pumping billions in the demand side of the system without increasing supply would inevitably balloon costs.

The cost of the program, Freymann explains, doubled in the first year because the government underestimated the number of physician-visits which beneficiaries expected to be made per year and because the projected annual increase in hospital costs was underestimated (7 percent versus 15 percent). The underestimation was prompted by the two programs providing most of the new money the federal government was able to allocate to health.

The net result, says Freymann, was the virtual failure of the federal government's original resolve to create one class of care. It then reverted to the eighteenth-century practice of expecting doctors and hospitals to care for the poor at less than cost as charity patients. Freymann believes Medicaid has thus deteriorated into "a grudging, vindictive welfare system which squeezed out the bare minimum for care which could not otherwise be avoided."

Frieden states that Medicare and Medicaid were designed to help people pay their medical bills, but not to address the size of those bills (p. 86).

The Medicare and Medicaid programs were enacted in 1965 in response to the states' general failure to deal with the health problems of their aged and poor. As mentioned earlier, prior to 1965, the poor and aged were served by the generosity of physicians and hospitals who usually viewed their roles as something more than earning a profit. Ginsberg describes how physicians gave their free time for the care of the poor in hospitals in return for the hospital's provision of a secure work environment and a chance to optimize the physician's income by the economical use of his out of office time. The hospitals thereby provided a large support system free of charge to the physician, including expensive technical equipment and staff in return for his free services to some patients. Since 1965, the physician has not been called upon for free time at the hospital. He receives the support of the hospital at no cost, while the hospital is subsidized for such services by federal grants and, more importantly, by "costing out" such charges via commercial insurance, Medicare, and Medicaid additions to regular billings. The changes which Medicare and Medicaid have wrought in the medical care delivery system since 1965 have been so overwhelming that Enos and Sultan describe them as "two mice that roared." In a discussion of American housing policy, Welfeld has said that "the logical fruit of an ill-perceived problem is a misconceived solution" (p. 141). Obviously, his observation applies particularly to Medicare and Medicaid.

CONTROL MECHANISMS FOR HEALTH CARE QUALITY AND COST

Medicare, Medicaid, Blue Shield, Blue Cross, and other insurances contribute to the rising cost of medicine. Once a service has been paid for, whether by the individual, an employer, or by the government there is no incentive not to use the service. The provision of health insurance to the employee by his employer or to the recipient by a government entity levies no increased tax or appreciable direct cost on the patient. Without established limits in the number or frequency of services rendered, the patient is tempted to demand what is available and since the vendors are paid by the service, the vendors are also motivated to provide all the services the patient is willing to accept. Recently, the government has initiated a number of quality and cost control mechanisms, most of which affect all medical clients. Some of these mechanisms have direct implications for the poor. The most noteworthy of these methods has been the federal government's effort to increase the number of poor served by health maintenance organizations (HMOs). These programs charge their members (or Medicaid) a monthly fee, for which they receive unlimited medical and hospital care as long as it is prescribed by a physician of the organization. This type of group practice benefits from the savings derived from preventative programs which are more feasible under the HMO structure. It also benefits from the usually more efficient organization made possible by this form of medical service delivery.

If the programs are well organized, they provide built-in incentives for physicians to keep their patients healthy and out of hospitals. Because these plans have to compete with the fee-for-service practitioners in negotiation with organized patient groups (such as labor unions), the quality, convenience, and costs of such care must be kept comparable, if not better. Only those tests and treatments are provided which are deemed necessary (by the physicians) to deal with the illness rather than to satisfy the patient's psychic needs or to increase the physician's earnings. It should be noted that the physician is paid a salary, and his retention, increases, and tenure in the HMO are based on peer review of the quality and volume of his patient services. The HMO also is economical in that it does not have to compete with other institutions in the acquisition of new glamour equipment and buildings that characterize the most modern medical center. Thus, sizable building and equipment expenses do not have to be costed out by increased charges to all its consumers. (See Clairborne.) Still another saving of the HMO is the usual practice of requiring all members to agree in advance to submit all malpractice disputes to compulsory arbitration, which eliminates the need for the many tests found in the defensive medicine mode of many fee-for-service practitioners.

Many HMOs operate their own pharmacies, buying generic medicines in large quantity and providing prescriptions to members at low cost. HMOs also effect savings by use of paraprofessionals where appropriate to the health needs of the patients. Usage of paraprofessionals is generally not possible in fee-for-service practices where the patient feels justified in asking only for the physician or even for the specialist for every service as long as the fee is paid for by a third party.

The problems of integrating the poor into the HMO service format are considerable. An employed population is usually a more healthy population than the unemployed or never-employed poor. An employed population and dependents cover an age spectrum which includes a higher percentage of healthy people. An HMO organization benefits in efficiency by serving a usually literate, busy population which is better educated and better equipped for health maintenance and disease control and treatment. The industrially and bureaucratically alert populations such as are found in employed groups are more apt to follow up on their physicians' directions and to keep scheduled appointments (often made far in advance) and less apt to get lost in "the medical maze." This patient population of the HMO can also be a vocal population when dissatisfied, and complaints are seldom lost on their way up through the labor union or other board channels in the HMO. The dissatisfied patient on a fee-for-service basis can either go elsewhere or entirely stop going to physicians (a pattern often found among the poor), but the HMO member can usually be depended upon to find a responsive answer without increased medical costs.

Conversely, HMOs have a tendency to underserve some populations, especially undereducated patient groups. Those patients who do not know how to secure a regular place on the panel of a physician of their choice and who do not plan ahead for health maintenance needs end up being cared for episodically by whichever physician may have an open time slot on the day they come with acute problems. Such patients seldom enjoy the medical record review which many HMO physicians give their regular patients.

HMOs have expanded at a slow rate, partly because of the resistance of medical societies to the HMO concept. This resistance is reflected in the societies' association policies and their lobbying efforts for restrictive legislation in state capitals. Another reason for the slow expansion has been the lack of knowledge about the availability of HMO care by the American public.

The HMO is an attractive and economically viable program for many informed subscribers, but it is not a panacea for the poor's health care problems. An HMO without an adequate mix of self-sufficient, health-responsible subscribers might be weakened by having too many people without the health skills required for HMO membership.

Other mechanisms for cost and quality control of health care are the Professional Standards Review Organization (PSRO), the Health Services Agency (HSA), and the threat of imposed cost ceilings. The PSRO mechanism establishes standards for length of hospital care for specific illnesses and conditions at each hospital. This peer review mechanism hears appeals from physicians who seek to utilize hospital and special equipment beyond the accepted standards. These appeals are judged on the basis of the particular complications or problems of the patient under consideration. This mechanism is designed to keep down equipment and hospital bed use and thereby prevent overutilization and unnecessary costs. Culliton questions the effectiveness of this mechanism because the number of days per illness has been set high enough to serve the patient who needs the maximum number of days. The result is that many who do not need the maximum number of days still stay the maximum because it is routinized, it is in the interest of the physician for the patient to stay on, it is in the interest of the hospital to keep the beds filled, and it is in the patient's interest to be cared for as long as possible before he has to start caring for himself. Culliton also believes that the peer review method and the establishment of standards by a peer group becomes a mutual protection process. Another failing of the PSRO mechanism is that its standards are set without consideration of the differing capacity of poverty and middle-class homes to provide care for discharged patients. A case could be made for longer hospital stays for poor patients who have limited home care facilities and no one to help them during convalescence.

The HSA is supposedly a health resources planning organization at the local level, established for the purpose of preventing the adding of unnecessary hospital beds in each neighborhood and unnecessary duplication of very expensive medical diagnostic and treatment equipment. (Extra beds and limited use equipment are paid off by costing out additions on all other items charged to hospital patients.) The HSA, created under Public Law 93–641, can grant or refuse a certificate of necessity for all sizable medical construction or equipment additions. Unfortunately, the jockeying to get in on the ground floor of HSAs throughout the United States has led to strong competition between hospital representatives and other providers, medical associations, political entities, labor unions, and, to a lesser extent, consumer groups. According to Cronkhite, the HSA is equivalent to adoption of a policy of public franchising for health care delivery services. The entry of the HSA on the local medical care scene has led to the engagement of expensive planning, public relations, and legal specialists by hospitals. All of these costs have been added to all hospital charges, whether Blue Cross or Medicare or Medicaid, without in any way improving or increasing the health care delivered to the patient population, including the poor. Schwartz believes that the HSAs will ultimately raise the cost of medical care by adding the extra costs of policing medical care planning and programming. Ginsberg also questions the potential effectiveness of the HSA mechanism.

The only other mechanism proposed for health care cost controls is represented by the wage-price pressures of the Carter administration, which is seeking to keep increases in costs in line with the labor and service charge increases of other industries. Until now, this approach has shown little effectiveness.

Pressure for a national health insurance program has been slowly mounting in the past decade. The Carter administration has decided to postpone establishment of a comprehensive program until medical and other inflationary pressures are reduced. Meanwhile, a series of bills were introduced in the Ninety-fifth Congress (*Congressional Digest*). The salient proposals submitted thus far are summarized below.

Health Security Act (Kennedy-Corman Bill) (S3, HR21, and companion bills HR 4900 and 4011).

Supporting Groups: AFL-CIO, Committee on National Health Insurance, and others.

Basic Orientation: Establishes a universal, federalized, comprehensive health insurance plan. Includes arrangements for reorganization of health care system and provisions to develop health resources.

Clientele Coverage: All U.S. residents.

Medicare: To be repealed and supplanted.

Medicaid (MediCal in California): To be retained in part to cover services beyond benefits provided.

Benefits: Covers the entire range of personal health care, including full prevention services; early detection of disease.

Deductible: No waiting period, no co-insurance, no deductibles.

Limitations: Some initial limitations on adult dental care, psychiatric care, and long-term nursing care, but all with a planned phase-in for the above.

Financing: 50 percent from general tax revenues and 50 percent from a 3.5 percent tax on employer payrolls, plus a 1 percent tax on the first $24,750 of annual wages and a 2.5 percent tax on the first $24,750 of the self-employed.

Administration: By a Health Security Trust Fund operated within HEW —five-member Health Security Board plus 10 regional and 200 subregional advisory councils.

Private Insurers: All payments by employers and individuals to be eliminated.

Cost Control: By an annual national budget, regional budgets, prospective budgets for hospitals, and the like. Negotiated budgets for prepaid group practices. Negotiated payments to practitioners on a fee-for-service basis. No additional charges permitted to be laid on patients.

Quality Control: By a quality control commission and by accepted national standards for participating professionals and institutions. Regulation of major surgery and other specialist services. National licensure standards, with requirements for continuing education.

Additional Provisions: Increased health resource promotion via companion bills.

Health Services Act (Dellums) HR 6894 (The "Health Bill of Rights").

Supporting Groups: Not known at this time.

Basic Orientation: Guarantees access to all health services, choice of facility, provider, and an explanation of all procedures in the person's own native language. Ensures specific protections for health needs and services for women, children, and institutionalized persons.

Clientele Coverage: All U.S. residents, without charge.

Facilities: To be provided by and maintained by a National Community Health Service.

Benefits: Full range of medical, dental, and psychiatric services as well as home health, midwifery, occupational health, and health education.

Financing: By a special health services tax on individual and corporate incomes, plus federal revenue subsidy of deficits. A steeply progressive income tax. General revenues would also reimburse current spending on health services by federal, state, and local organizations.

Facility Operations: Providers of health care services to be given funds on a uniform, per capita basis, but special funds to be allocated for communities of care for persons over sixty-five years or with special conditions.

Administration: By district health boards to divide funds at district and community levels, based on a majority of community health board members. Similar divisions at regional and national levels.

Quality Control: Provides an elaborate system of checks and balances. Health board members held accountable to those who elected them or appointed them, and regional boards empowered to investigate complaints regarding mismanagement and to develop advanced specialty programs.

Additional Provisions: Sets a first priority for health research in the National Community Health Service to prevent and correct the leading causes of illness, including environmental, occupational, and social factors. Research to be promoted under community and district boards, to make it responsive to individual segments of the population. (Includes provision to decentralize National Institutes of Health.)

Distribution of Services: Primary care via community facilities and Health Service Board. District boards to operate or supervise hospital and health team schools to educate all health workers. Regions to operate specialized medical services. National Board to operate national administration and research.

The National Health Care Act (Burleson and McIntyre) (HR 5 and S 5).

Supporting Groups: National Health Insurance Association of America.

Basic Orientation: Utilizes a voluntary approach based on federal income tax incentives for employees and employers to encourage a minimum package of health insurance (private and commercial or nonprofit). To be effected through employer-sponsored health coverage; individual coverage plans; and grants to the states to purchase insurance for the poor (the state plan) and to cover the uninsurables through a state insurance pool. Provides limited provisions to improve health care delivery. Program voluntary for all U.S. residents, but noncitizens not eligible.

Medicare: To be continued.

Medicaid (Medical): To be continued for services beyond provided benefits.

Benefits—Two States: A maximum deductible of $100 and co-insurance of 20 percent with a maximum annual out-of-pocket expense per family of $1,000, except for mental health and dentistry. In 1978 (or whenever enacted—first years), benefits to encompass unlimited hospital inpatient and outpatient care, including psychiatric care, full physician's services, twenty outpatient mental health visits, prescription drugs, and contraceptive devices, 180 days of skilled nursing, 270 days of home health care, some oral surgery, and well-child care. In 1985 (or eight years after enactment), coverage for specific dental care, physical and speech therapy, eyeglasses, and periodic physical exams.

Financing: Through purchase of private insurance with three classes of beneficiaries: employees and dependents, individuals (nongroup plan purchasers), and state-covered persons (the poor, near poor, and otherwise uninsurables). Under employer plan, both employer and employee to share premium cost for commercial or nonprofit insurance, but low-income employee contributions limited in proportion to wage level. Under individual plan, employee to pay full premium. Under both plans, a federal income tax deduction allowed for employers and enrollees (they have that now) equal to full cost of premiums for approved insurance only. Under state plan, enrollee premium contributions to be based on income and family size, with balance paid from state and federal general revenues through a state insurance pool, with federal share between 70 and 90 percent.

Cost Control: Payments to institutions based on prospectively approved rates, by category of institution (as per current practice under such insurances and Medicare and Medicaid). State health commissions to approve budget and charge schedules on basis of reasonable charges, subject to HEW review. HMOs to be paid on a per capita basis. Physicians paid reasonable charges "not exceeding customary and prevailing rates" (as per current practice).

Quality Control: None other than Medicare standards and HMO regulations as set by HEW et al.

Administration: At state level, by state insurance department, to approve policies, monitoring of private and nonprofit insurance carriers. For state plans, HEW to set standards, policies, and operational constraints. State insurance departments to supervise state plans.

Comprehensive Health Care Act (Carter, Duncan, Murphy, and Hansen) (HR 1818 and 5.218).

Supporting Groups: American Medical Association.

Basic Orientation: Mandates that employers offer qualified private (and nonprofit) health insurance to employees and families, with federal tax credits or cash subsidies to employers if the program increases payroll cost by 3 percent or more. Federal government to arrange for tax credits for the nonemployed and self-employed to help provide their coverage.

Unemployed to have health insurance provided by federal government.

Clientele Coverage: All employees, nonemployed, and self-employed, but only with voluntary acceptance by employees.

Medicare: To be discontinued, but present Medicare population to be eligible for benefits equal to those provided for above groups.

Benefits: Inpatient and outpatient care, 100 days in a skilled nursing facility, diagnostic, therapeutic and preventative medical services, home health services, dental care for children ages two to six, emergency dental services, and oral surgery for all.

Deductibles: None but 20 percent co-insurance for all services, with limits based on family incomes. A ceiling of $1,500 per person or $2,000 per family.

Financing: By premium payments of at least 65 percent by employers, balance by employees.

Administration: By a fifteen-member Health Insurance Advisory Board made up of the secretary of HEW, the commissioner of Internal Revenue, and eight members from the medical profession and five from the general public. Board to prescribe regulations and federal standards for state insurance departments and to review program effectiveness.

Cost Control Provisions: None.

Quality Control Provisions: None except for Advisory Board action.

Catastrophic Insurance Act (Long-Ribicoff) (Number not yet announced in Senate) (a rewrite of S 2470 and HR 10028 of ninety-fourth Congress).

Basic Orientation: Three-part program: catastrophic coverage for all, medical assistance plan with basic benefits for the poor and medically needy, and voluntary program for certification of private insurance to cover basic benefits.

Benefits: Catastrophic coverage—all medical costs after expenses of $2,000 per family and all hospital costs after sixty days per person for all U.S. residents covered by private carriers or by Social Security (under Medicare).

Medicare: To be continued.

Medicaid (MediCal): To be continued, federalized, and applied to additional classes of the medically needy.

Benefits: Besides those under catastrophic part of the plan for Medicaid population (expanded Medicaid plan), includes hospital, skilled nursing, and intermediate facility care, home health services, physician's services, x-ray, lab work, medical appliances, prenatal and well-baby care, family planning, periodic screening, diagnosis and treatment to age eighteen, and inpatient mental health care in community health centers. Co-payments of $3 required for each of the first ten visits to a doctor per family per year.

Cost Control: Loose guidelines, as presently under Medicare. Payments for Medicaid must be accepted as payment in full.

Quality Control: Same as under Medicare, with PSRO panels.

Administration: Through Social Security Administration. HEW secretary to certify private plans in the voluntary program based on adequacy of coverage, conditions of eligibility, and availability. Insurers not offering certified policies ineligible to serve as Medicare carriers or intermediaries.

References

Abel-Smith, Brian. "Value for Money in Health Services," *Social Security Bulletin:* 17–19, July 1974.

Andersen, Ronald, and Odin W. Anderson. "Trends in the Use of Health Services," in Howard E. Freeman, Sol Levin, and Leo G. Reeder (eds.), *Handbook in Medical Sociology.* Englewood Cliffs, N.J.: Prentice-Hall, 1979.

Anderson, Martin. *Welfare: The Political Economy of Welfare Reform in the U.S.* Stanford: Hoover Institution Press, 1978.

Anderson, Odin W., Ronald Andersen, Joan Daley, and Johanna Kravitz. *Expenditures for Personal Health Services: National Trends and Variations, 1953–1970.* Washington, D.C.: U.S. Department of Health, Education and Welfare, 1973.

————, Ronald Andersen, Rachael McGreely, and Johanna Kravitz. *Health Services Use: National Trends and Variations.* Washington, D.C.: U.S. Department of Health, Education and Welfare, 1973.

Bellin, Lowell E. "Statement before the Subcommittee on Medicare-Medicaid of the Committee on Finance." Pp. 511–38, in *Hearings Before the Subcommittee on Medicare-Medicaid,* Part 2, June 2. Washington, D.C.: U.S. Government Printing Office, 1970.

Bennet, Berkeley V. "Statement Before the Subcommittee on Finance." Pp. 565–617, in *Hearings Before the Subcommittee on Medicare-Medicaid,* Part 2, June 3. Washington, D.C.: U.S. Government Printing Office, 1970.

Brooke, R.H., and K.M. Williams. *Evaluating Quality of Health Care for the Disadvantaged: A Literature Review.* Santa Monica: Rand, 1975.

Budget of the United States Government. *Fiscal Year 1979.* Washington, D.C.: U.S. Government Printing Office, 1978.

Cassell, Eric J. "In Sickness and Health," *Commentary,* 49:59–66, 1970.

————. "Disease as a Way of Life," *Commentary,* 55(2): 80–83, February 1973.

Christmas, June Jackson. "How Our Health System Fails Minorities: Systemic Defects and Systemic Discrimination," *Civil Rights Digest,* 10(1):2–11, 1977.

Clairborne, Robert. "The Great Health Care Rip-Off," *Saturday Review*, 5:10–13, 16, 50, January 7, 1978.

Colombotus, John. "Physicians and Medicare: A Before-After Study of the Effects of Legislation Attitudes," *American Sociological Review*, 34(3):318–34, 1969.

Committee for Economic Development. *Building a National Health Care System: A Statement by the Research and Policy Committee.* Washington, D.C.: Committee for Economic Development, 1973.

Comptroller General's Office. *Questionable Claims Under the Medicaid Program for the Care of Persons in State Institutions for the Mentally Retarded in California.* Washington, D.C.: Comptroller General's Office, 1970.

———. *Improved Controls Needed Over Extent of Care Provided by Hospitals and Other Facilities to Medicare Patients.* Washington, D.C.: Comptroller General's Office, 1971a.

———. *Ineffective Controls Over Program Requirements Relating to Medically Needy Persons Covered by Medicaid.* Washington, D.C.: Comptroller General's Office, 1971b.

Congressional Digest. "Main Health Insurance Proposals Pending in the 95th Congress," 198–99, 224, August-September 1977.

Cronkhite Leonard. "Control and Regulation of the Health Industry," *Journal of Medical Education*, 49(1):14–18, 1974.

Culliton, Barbara. "Caspar Weinberger: Beware of an 'All-Pervasive' Federal Government," *Science*, 189(4203):617–19, 1975.

Davis, Karen, and Cathy Schoen. *Health and the War on Poverty: A Ten Year Proposal.* Washington, D.C.: Brookings, 1978.

Doolittle, Frederick, Frank Levy, and Michael Wiseman. "The Mirage of Welfare Reform," *Public Interest*, 47:62–87, 1977.

Dubos, Rene. *Mirage of Health, Utopias, Progress and Biological Change.* Garden City, N.Y.: Doubleday-Anchor, 1959.

Duval, Melvin K. "The Population, The Government and The Consumer," in John H. Knowles (ed.), *Doing Better and Feeling Worse: Health in the U.S.* New York: W.W. Norton, 1977.

Eitzen, D. Stanley. *Social Problems.* Boston: Allyn and Bacon, 1980.

Enos, Darryl D., and Paul Sultan. *The Sociology of Health Care: Social, Economic and Political Perspectives.* New York: Praeger, 1977.

Fox, Peter D. "Options for National Health Insurance: An Overview," *Policy Analysis*, 3(1):3–24, Winter 1977.

Freymann, John Gordon. *The American Health Care System: Its Genesis and Trajectory.* New York: Med Comm Press, 1974.

Frieden, Bernard J. "The New Housing Cost Problem," *Public Interest*, 49:70–87, 1977.

Friedson, Elliott. *Profession of Medicine.* New York: Dodd, Mead, 1970.

————. "Professionalism: The Doctor's Dillemma," *Social Policy,* 1(5):35–40, January-February, 1971.

Ginsburg, Eli. "Health Services, Power Centers and Decision Making Mechanisms," in John H. Knowels (ed.), *Doing Better and Feeling Worse: Health in the U.S.* New York: W. W. Norton, 1977.

————. *The Limits of Health Reform.* New York: Basic Books, 1977.

Glazer, Nathan. "Paradoxes of Health Care," *Public Interest,* 22:62–77, 1971.

————. "Perspectives on Health Care," *Public Interest, 31:110–25, 1973.*

Godmere, Richard C. "Medicaid Management Information System," *Social and Rehabilitation Record,* 1(3):30–33, 1974.

Harris, Louis. *Living Sick: How the Poor View Their Health Sources.* New York: Blue Cross Association, 1969.

Isaccson, Peter. "There's Only So Much That a Doctor Can Do: Poverty and Health," *New Republic,* 171(24):15–17, 1974.

Klarman, Herbert F. "Major Initiatives in Health Care," *Public Interest,* 34:106–23, 1974.

Knowles, John H. "The Responsibility of the Individual," in John H. Knowles (ed.), *Doing Better and Feeling Worse: Health in the U.S.* New York: W. W. Norton, 1977.

Kotelchuck, David. "The Health Status of Americans," in David Kotelchuck (ed.), *Prognosis Negative: Crisis in the Health Care System.* New York: Vintage, 1976.

Langer, Elinor. "The Shame of Medicine," *New York Review of Books,* 6(9):6, 8–11, 1966.

————. "The Shame of American Medicine," in Rose Giallombardo (ed.), *Contemporary Social Issues.* Santa Barbara: Hamilton, 1975.

Lefkowitz, Myron J. *Poverty and Health.* Discussion Paper 71–70. Madison, Wis.: Institute for Research on Poverty, 1970.

————. "Poverty and Health: A Re-examination," *Inquiry,* 16(1):3–13, 1973.

Leveson, I. *The Demand for Neighborhood Medical Care.* Santa Monica: Rand, 1968.

Levin, Tom. *American Health: Professional Privilege Versus Public Need.* New York: Praeger, 1974.

McCormick, Harvey L. *Medicare and Medicaid: Claims and Procedures.* St. Paul, Minn.: West, 1977.

McKinney, Edward A. "Health Crisis for Whom?" *Health and Social Work,* 1(1):101–16, 1976.

Marmor, Theodore R. "Why Medicare Helped Raise Doctors' Fees," *Transaction,* 5:14–19, 1968.

Mechanic, David. "The Poor State of Health," *Science,* 172(3984):701–702, 1971.

Melcher, George W. "Statement made at the Hearings Before the Subcommittee on Finance." Washington, D.C.: U.S. Government Printing Office, 1970.

Monteiro, Lois A. "Expense Is No Object: Income and Physician Visits Reconsidered," *Journal of Health and Social Behavior,* 14(2): 99–145, 1973.

Myers, Beverlee A. "The Unequal Burdens of Paying for Health Care," *Civil Rights Digest,* 10(9):12–18, 1977.

Myers, Robert J. *Medicare.* Homewood, Ill.: R. D. Irwin, 1970.

National Center for Health Services Research, HEW. *Health-US 1978.* Dept. of Health, Education, and Welfare Publication Number (PHS) 78-1232. Washington, D.C.: U.S. Government Printing Office, December 1978.

Richmond, Julius B. "The Needs of Children," in John H. Knowles (ed.), *Doing Better and Feeling Worse: Health in the U.S.* New York: W. W. Norton, 1977.

Rogers David E. "The Challenge of Primary Care," in John H. Knowles (ed.), *Doing Better and Feeling Worse: Health in the U.S.* New York: W. W. Norton, 1977.

Schechter, Mal. "Medicare on Its Fourth Birthday: Alive But Not Well," *New Republic,* 163(2):15–17, 1970.

Schwartz, Harry. "Plop, Plop. Fizz, Fizz: What Government Should and Shouldn't Do About Medical Costs," *The Alternative: An American Spectator,* 10(8):7–9, 1977.

Scitovsky, Anne A., and Nelda M. Snyder. *Medical Care Use by a Group of Elderly Insured Aged: A Case Study.* Washington, D.C.: U.S. Department of Health, Education and Welfare, 1975.

Scott, Austin. "Medical Care for Non-Whites Assailed: More Vigorous Affirmative Action Programs Urged in Congress Report," *Los Angeles Times,* November 26, 1977, Part I, p. 1.

Shapley, Deborah. "National Health Insurance, Will It Promote Costly Technology?" *Science,* 186(4162):423–25, 1974.

Social Security Administration. *Social Security Handbook.* Washington, D.C.: U.S. Department of Health, Education and Welfare, 1969.

Social Security Information Items. "Medicare Deductible Is $160 Starting Jan. 1, 1979," No. 25:1, 1978.

Staff, Ways and Means Committee, U.S. House of Representatives. *National Health Insurance Resources Book.* Washington, D.C.: U.S. Government Printing Office, 1974.

Sudovar, Stephen G., Jr., and Kathleen Sullivan. *National Health Insurance Issues: The Unprotected Population.* Washington, D.C.: Hoffman-La Roche, 1977.

Szasz, Thomas. *The Theology of Medicine.* New York: Harper, 1977.

Taylor, D. Garth, Lu Ann Aday, and Ronald Andersen. "Social Indicators of Access to Medical Care," *Journal of Health and Social Behavior*, 16(1):39–49, 1975.

U.S. Bureau of the Census. *Current Population Reports.* Series P–6, No. 107, 1977.

Welfeld, Irving. "American Housing Policy: Perverse Programs by Prudent People," *Public Interest*, 48:128–44, 1977.

Wildavsky, Aaron. "Doing Better and Feeling Worse: The Political Pathology of Health Policy," in John H. Knowles (ed.), *Doing Better and Feeling Worse: Health in the U.S.* New York: W. W. Norton, 1977.

Housing for the Poor

BECAUSE slums have been strongly associated with poverty, reformers have traditionally chosen housing as their first step in solving the poverty problem. To remake the slum into a more aesthetic and attractive place was, in many minds, equivalent to solving poverty. The provision of a clean and aesthetically pleasing housing environment would motivate the poor to work to improve themselves and their life condition. It was also presumed that the residents would respect such a housing environment and would maintain it in the same condition. This was the belief of such social reformers as Jane Addams, Lillian Wald, and Jacob Riis (Bellush and Hausknecht, p. 1). Better housing, they believed, "was the best way to solve all [the] social problems of an urban community." This position has been described as environmental determinism. These reformers led movements to pass tenement laws which would establish standards for conditions permitted in large commercial housing units. Lawrence Veiller developed a series of model housing laws in this connection (Lubove). The belief that improved housing, by clearing the slums and providing low-rent housing, will bring about improved social conditions and improved prosocietal behavior has been accepted without supporting data by authorities, community leaders, and community planners for many years. Levy, Lewis, and Martin (pp. 992–93) report that twenty-three states have relied "either directly or indirectly or vicariously by citation, that slum clearance and the provision of sanitary low rent housing decrease danger of epidemics, raise general public health, reduce crime, cut juvenile delinquency, reduce immorality, lower economic waste by reducing health, police and fire protection costs, make better citizens . . . and prevent the cancerous spread of slums" (p. 992 as quoted from McDougal and Mueller, 1942). (See Levy, Lewis, and Martin.) In *Thomas* v. *Housing Authority*, Judge Jensen, speaking for the court without calling for evidence, concluded that "if families of low income can be removed from the slums and placed in safe, sanitary and decent housing, they will be motivated and enabled to lead better, healthier and more productive lives" (Levy, Lewis, and Martin, p. 1234).

Dean disagrees. He believes that it is quite naive to assume that cleaning up and dressing up the slums and replacing tenements with new buildings will solve poverty. He presents data which generally criticize what he calls the myths of housing reform. Schorr (1963) also indicates that any correlation between slum housing and a social ill does not necessarily demonstrate that one causes the other. Burns states that the "causal correlation between housing quality and various social or medical effects [cannot be supported] by firm conclusions" (pp. 20–23). Wilner, Walkley, Pinkerton, and Tayback, in a study of two generally identical groups in improved public and private slum housing, respectively, found no significant change in the families in the newer housing.

Although physical renovation effects a temporary improvement and occasionally a temporary gain in family health, little is gained in the long run as long as the causes of residual poverty remain. There is a strong possibility that the surface manifestations of both bad housing and social ills are caused by a common underlying factor.

Housing has long been related to poverty problems for reasons other than simplistic reform impulses or aesthetics. Sociologists have been particularly alert to the effect of housing, and housing location, on health, educational opportunities, employment opportunities, physical safety, mental health, security from violence and crime, and, finally, on life opportunities for upward socioeconomic movement. Slum housing has a negative effect on health, especially the health of children (1971 report of the Select Committee on Nutrition). The lack of quiet bedrooms with adequate privacy may lead to inadequate or unrestful sleep. The presence of old-fashioned lead-based paint, which is common in old tenements, may cause lead poisoning if the paint enters the systems of the inhabitants. To dwell in a slum neighborhood usually relegates the children to a less effective school, endangering their physical safety, their opportunities for socioeconomic progress, and perhaps their emotional stability. Freedman believes that crowding, especially in high-rise buildings that do not provide for small-group clustering of tenants, leads to increased social tensions and destructive behavior.

To live in a slum is to live in an area where people are considered untrustworthy. Even the shopping centers in and near slums have automatic fences to prevent the loss of shopping carts. Surveillance for shoplifting is much more thorough in ghetto stores than elsewhere. To live in a slum is to be more of an inmate and less of an autonomous, responsible resident. This is apparent in almost every relationship and activity. To the extent that residents are not trusted in a slum area, a self-fulfilling prophesy is installed in the slum dweller.

For most Americans, housing is a personal investment representing a major portion of the family savings and much family effort. Except for the beneficiaries of certain veterans' programs, a purchaser must make a sizable downpayment, usually representing 20 to 30 percent of the purchase price. Because a mortgage is required for the balance, borrowers must have good credit ratings. Hence, their debts must be manageable within their income, their income must be reasonably stable, and their performance as earners must be proven. The family's ability to manage its income must have been demonstrated.

The financial investment which a family makes in a house has a built-in motivational effect upon the family's use of the house. In time, the fact that the family has money invested in the house gives them the assurance that it belongs to them. This idea may be illusory when the family owns less of the house than the bank or mortgage company does, but whether illusion or not, most family homes are added to, improved on, and altered to fit the family's particular needs. As the family invests more money, time, and personal interest in the house, it becomes a basis of family protection and preservation. It is known that personally owned homes receive better maintenance and protection than rented homes and apartments. A house or apartment that is rented without a financial or other personal investment by the inhabitants is associated with housing deterioration and lack of resident and visitor respect for the housing. A personally owned home lends security and stability to family life and provides the family with important components of family and individual identity.

Personal homeownership and maintenance is a common pattern of the middle-class style of life. The possession of a house in a particular neighborhood becomes a factor in keeping up property values in that neighborhood. Thus, those who own a house in a specific geographical area are automatically concerned about the quality of schools, parks, and other services and facilities in that neighborhood. They accordingly resist the intrusion of industry, slums, inappropriate commercial enterprises, and other factors that lower the value of the neighborhood.

Whether homeownership motivates middle-class behavior or vice versa cannot be ascertained from contemporary research on the general population. Experiments in self-help housing with migrant agricultural workers during the late 1960s showed that those who elected to participate did exhibit stable homeownership behavior. What could not be determined, however, is whether this was a potential behavioral pattern of all migrant workers or merely of those who chose to participate in that program.

Federal involvement in housing can be traced back to 1894, according to the 1968 Housing Supply report of the League of Women Voters. At that time, the secretary of Labor was empowered to investigate slums in large cities, especially in Baltimore, Chicago, New York, and Philadelphia where hundreds of thousands of European immigrants had congregated. The investigation was occasioned by concern over health and fire safety issues rather than over the housing conditions of the poor. The targets of the investigation were landlords of tenements who had crowded families into the limited spaces available in the densely populated cities. The government sought to control the landlords without concurrently interfering with the housing market and free enterprise among realty interests.

Housing Programs

In 1918, the federal government again became involved in housing, but only to a limited extent. This effort was to provide housing for war workers in defense impacted areas because workers were not available without the provision of housing. Congress approved funds to provide temporarily for 9,000 houses, 1,000 apartments, and 19 dormitories in twenty-four localities where they were required for shipyard and other war workers. Again, this effort was not designed to interfere with the housing market. It was merely a special wartime effort to supply housing that was not otherwise available and that was intended for national purposes rather than for service to people generally in need of housing.

Governmental housing policy during the pre-Depression years tended to focus primarily on people in poverty who would not have been able to own their own homes. For such persons a limited quantity of public housing was developed. It was assumed that all public housing tenants were potential homeowners and, in the meanwhile, they were viewed as potential renters of private housing. Prior to the Depression, housing was considered a matter of economic supply and demand, except in the case of the limited public housing programs which were viewed as an alternative to urban slums. Congress may have been interested in housing for the poor, but it was not considered appropriate for the government to get involved.

The National Housing Act established the Federal Housing Administration (FHA) in 1934 (Bellush and Hausknecht, pp. 4–7), which marked the government's first involvement in housing policy. Housing conditions were unusually difficult at that time. Because of the Depression, many middle-class families who owned their homes suddenly found they could not meet their mortgage payments and they were foreclosed upon or threatened with foreclosure. Many renters of homes and apartments, both the poverty population and middle class, could not pay their rents and were evicted or threatened with eviction. Many apartment house owners were themselves foreclosed on by banks when rent payments dried up.

The federal government first became directly involved in housing in 1932 with the creation of the Federal Home Loan Bank, which established a system of regional home loan banks. Their function was to make advances secured by first mortgages, principally to savings and loan associations. By the end of the 1960s, the consolidated resources of this bank amounted to about $10 billion. In 1933, the Home Owners Loan Corporation (HOLC) was established to provide refinancing of mortgages for homeowners. By the third year of its establishment, the HOLC had financed approximately one out of five nonfarm home mortgages. The HOLC was so successful that by 1937 the threat of poor people's mortgages being foreclosed was relieved, and the government was able to liquidate the HOLC at a small profit. Congress established two major housing programs under the Housing Act of 1937 and the Federal National Mortgage Association in 1938 because by then it had been demonstrated that the federal government would have to be involved if the housing industry was to be kept in operation and if housing was to be within the reach of most American families. This concept was no different than the policies in other industries, such as agriculture which had succumbed to repetitive periods of feast and famine when the agricultural marketplace failed.

Under the general provisions of the act, National Home Mortgage Insurance (NHMI) was made available to low- and middle-income families. Thus, if a family wished to buy a house but could not because it presented too much of a credit risk for banks to provide the loan, then the federal government would guarantee the banks that any potential loss from making the loan would be reimbursed. The government added a one-half percent insurance fee to the charges made to the home purchaser, and payment of losses was drawn from this fund. In the four decades during which this program operated, the fund was never overdrawn. In a sense, then, we can view the NHMI program as a mechanism of social insurance. Because every FHA purchaser pays the premium of one-half of a percent to provide additional security to the banks, the banks are able (although they do not always do so) to provide mortgage money at a lower rate of interest than would be available with conventional loans.

Without question, the FHA program was a poverty-preventative mechanism, especially during the early post-Depression years. Families that had lost their conventional mortgages were able to switch to FHA mortgages and thereby keep their homes. During the pre-World-War II years and the recession years, the FHA program provided a mechanism for extra employment in the economy by enabling homeowners to finance repairs and alterations for their homes. The FHA did not, however, have a sizable effect on the poverty population, primarily because the program was designed for homeowners, not for home renters, and homeowners were not usually in the poverty population. Another reason for the FHA's lack of impact on the problem of poverty derives from the organization's policies and personnel. Because many of the FHA personnel were former realtors and bankers, its policies tended to encourage applications from good mortgage risks. The program was designed to move people from the status of bad credit risks to marginal or good credit risks. Because of these policies as well as the creaming process followed by banks and FHA personnel, however, it provided greater assurances to banks and did little to move people up and out of poverty. Thus, the poor, who could not borrow money at lower interest rates through FHA, could not become qualified to buy homes. Homeownership as a method of generating socioeconomic upward mobility was certainly not available through FHA.

The League of Women Voters' report on Housing Supply states that the FHA has provided an opportunity for middle-class families to become "homeowners, contributing simultaneously to the movement from core cities to the suburbs as families chose sites with more space than their incomes could obtain on more expensive land in the central city; (p. 5). The original FHA loan provisions have been liberalized and amortization periods lengthened. The FHA later developed programs to focus on service for low- and moderate-income families (Levy, Lewis, and Martin, pp. 1136–40).

Currently, three agencies administer programs designed directly to stimulate homeownership by middle- and low-income families: the Federal Housing Administration of the Department of Housing and Urban Development (HUD), the Farmers Home Administration of the Department of Agriculture, and the Veterans Administration (VA) (Madway, p. 159). All seek to accomplish this purpose by loaning money directly to the home buyer (Farmers Home Administration); by making it easy for the buyer to obtain financing through guaranteed mortgages (Veterans Administration); by making interest subsidy payments to mortgage lenders on behalf of buyers; and by insuring the mortgage lender against any loss in the event of default, foreclosure, or inability to satisfy the outstanding obligation from the proceeds of a foreclosure sale (Federal Housing Administration). The last-mentioned program substantially reduces monthly payments by the interest subsidy.

In addition, the federal government has created a variety of programs, agencies, boards, and corporations to stimulate mortgage financing and to level out the cyclical peaks and valleys of the mortgage market. The Federal National Mortgage Association and the Government National Mortgage Association (GNMA) are among the most important entities involved in stimulating the mortgage market and in controlling the extremes of mortgage availability. GNMA guarantees the timely payment of principal and interest to holders of securities issued by private lenders and backed by pools of HUD- and VA-insured mortgages. As of November 1977, GNMA had insured over $49 billion in such securities. In addition, it provides direct, special assistance mortgages on FHA-approved homes where these would otherwise not be available. A total of $20.5 billion in commitments to purchase below market interest rate mortgages was reported as of September 30, 1977. These sums are over and beyond the FHA commitments reported later in this chapter.

A number of the FHA programs are important to students of social policy. Section 203 of the 1934 Housing Act, the oldest of the mortgage insurance programs, provides authority for insurance of mortgage loans to finance the purchase of one- to four-family new or existing homes. This program was most responsible for the building of American suburbia. It was the principal housing device used to promote recovery from the depression, and it was designed to restore the confidence of mortgage lenders by insuring them against the losses of default. It sought to stimulate residential construction by relatively low downpayments and by extended loan periods. Because the interest rate cannot exceed certain regulatory ceilings, the availability of such loans is usually reduced during periods of high inflation and heavy competition for capital. This program was designed to be self-sufficient. It provided for the insurance of loans up to thirty years for up to 97 percent of the property value. By 1974, over 9 million home mortgages had been insured under the program, and $1.5 billion had been accumulated through an excess of insurance premium incomes charged to borrowers over administrative expenses and mortgage claim payments (defaults and the like). Through September 19, 1977, over 10.2 million units were insured under Section 203(b) for mortgage insurance with a value of over $125 billion. Under 203 (i), close to 80,000 units in outlying areas were insured for over $600 million. Under a related section (Section 2, Title I), 32 million home improvement loans were insured for a value of over $26 billion through October 1977. Because Section 203 provides that "no mortgage shall be accepted for insurance unless . . . economically sound," the program has been administered in such a way as to avoid the risks of mortgages on properties in urban areas where neighborhoods are declining or where mortgagors have low and undependable incomes. It is because of this provision that Section 203 has done relatively little to effect housing improvement for the poor of the cities of America.

Another section of the Federal Housing Administration operates under Section 221 (d)2. This section was added in 1954 to help private industry provide low- and moderate-income housing, particularly for families displaced by the urban redevelopment programs that were then underway in most American cities under subsidies from the federal government. This legislation authorized the insurance of lenders against mortgage purchases for home purchases, with minimum downpayments of $200 financed by mortgages provided under Section 221 (d)2. These mortgages could be written with a maturity of up to forty years, instead of the thirty-year limit set under Section 203. There was no economic soundness criterion under this provision, such as was established under Section 203, although it became the administrator's responsibility to specify the standards by which property would be considered acceptable for mortgage insurance. Thus, the concept of acceptable risk rather than economic soundness became the basis for mortgage approval. This criterion appears to be less rigorous than the one specified in Section 203.

The original intent of Section 203 was to provide mortgages for those income groups that were too unattractive a risk for mortgage entrepreneurs. Section 203 was administered so conservatively, however, that federally guaranteed funds were preserved at the expense of refusing the risks of mortgages for the housing of the less financially secure components of the population. Each FHA mortgage has a charge of one-half percent per year, which is added to the costs laid on the borrower. This mortgage insurance fee pays for FHA administrative costs as well as for reimbursements to lenders for any losses sustained when mortgages are defaulted. As previously indicated, so few losses have been experienced over the years that the FHA's assets have grown.

A program designed to take risks when other lenders would not take them was therefore administered in a manner that merely supplemented the regular operation of lenders and reinforced their conservative lending policies. What was meant to be a mechanism to provide more housing for the poor instead became more of the same. It is important to understand the reasons for this development because they demonstrate one of the ways in which social legislation often fails to fulfill its intended purposes. When the FHA was established, many of the personnel installed in the program came from lending institutions, and these administrators, now transformed into civil servants, still managed their work in accordance with their original training. The original purpose of the program—to provide more housing for the marginally mortgageable—was frequently ignored in carrying out routines that protected the lenders and the financing underwriters rather than fulfilled the purpose of the program. Part of the problem, of course, also lay in the large downpayment requirement, but the major responsibility lay with the personnel and the plethora of regulations established by the administrators to implement the legislation.

Section 221 (d)(2) was subsequently designed to fulfill the purpose which had not been satisfied by Section 203. It was hoped that the lower downpayment would solve much of the problem of making housing available to the poor, but the establishment of such a low downpayment might not be adequate to give the poor the sense of investment and ownership that motivates careful maintenance, upkeep, and protection of property. Economic incentive theory posits that the smaller the investment, the less the residents will feel they are in control of the property, and that only if they believe they are in control will they seek to protect and develop it.

Under this provision, the maximum insurable loan for an owner-occupant of a single-family home is $31,000, or $36,000 in a high-cost area. For larger families (five or more people), the limits are $36,000 to $42,000. Higher mortgage limits apply to duplex and quadruplex family housing. As of September 1977, about 837,000 loans were issued for a total of over $11 billion.

Like Section 203, Section 221 (d)(2) failed to effectively stimulate the provision of housing for the poor. By 1968, during the War on Poverty launched by the Johnson administration, it was decided that a new program would be necessary because 221 (d)(2) and 203 had not created enough suitable low-cost housing. The new program, Section 235, attempted to assist low-income families in securing the ownership of new, rehabilitated, or existing houses by providing subsidies to reduce the current mortgage interest rate and to provide mortgage insurance to low-income families. Assistance in the form of periodic payments to the mortgagee was intended to reduce the interest costs of market-rate home mortgages. These FHA assistance payments are made on behalf of the homeowner to the lending institution in an amount necessary to make up the difference between 20 percent of the family's monthly income and the monthly payment required under the mortgage. Thus, a family with the requisite credit rating could secure a mortgage which, with the subsidy, could reduce the interest rate to as low as 1 percent. Other requirements of the program are that the family must make a minimum downpayment which usually does not exceed $200. The family may not have an income greater than 135 percent of the income of a similarly situated family eligible for public housing. The purpose of this provision is to prevent Section 235 from competing with conventional loan institutions and to reserve as much of the 235 funds for the families for whom it was designed. Because the family income limits set by local public housing programs are tailored to local incomes and living costs, the use of this criterion was chosen primarily as a convenience. The subsidy paid by FHA to the mortgagee in behalf of the mortgagor is periodically adjusted to reflect changes in the mortgagor's income. As in 221 (d)(2), the 235 program has no economic soundness provision requirement for mortgages, and such programs need only meet the acceptable risk provisions of 221 (d)(2).

Under the 235 program, HUD insures mortgages and makes monthly payments to lenders to reduce interest to as low as 4 percent. The homeowner must contribute 20 percent of his adjusted income to monthly mortgage payments and must make a downpayment of 3 percent of the cost of acquisition. Mortgage limits are $32,000, or $38,000 for families of five or more persons. In high-cost areas, the limits are $38,000 and $44,000. The income limit for a family to be eligible is 95 percent of the median area income. Through September 1977, about 478,500 units were insured with a value of about $8.6 billion.

While the 235 program seeks to solve the problems of the high down-payments and high monthly payments required of the owner with limited income, it does not resolve the problem of the requisite credit rating. Good credit ratings are quite rare among the poor, whose economic stability does not usually meet the standards of mortgage lenders and of their FHA bureaucratic counterparts. The problem of a credit rating is not easily solved by families with only marginal employment. Because of a variety of factors (described in Chapter 8 on employment), the chronic poor are usually the lowest paid, the last hired and first laid off, the least job-conditioned, and among the least successful financial managers. The poor tend to pay more than others do for the same objects, to pay late, and to pay in other costs. They have few charge accounts that could be accepted as credit references. They tend to keep few records. The poor move frequently from unpaid rental to unpaid rental and from job to job. Only the occasional poverty family can show a history of prompt, dependable payments of obligations and a consistent pattern of logical economic behavior. Such a history is even more rare among poverty families with children (and it is the poor families with children for whom home-ownership is a necessary social policy goal).

In addition to these barriers to effectiveness, no reported structural or staff changes were carried out in 1977 to focus the program on the intended population sector. Thus, the administration of the program was again given over to the people whose orientation was toward protecting funds rather than taking appropriate risks for the purpose of installing major sectors of the poor in adequate housing.

Special efforts were made to provide for adequate servicing by the lending institutions of the high-risk mortgagees; special forebearance procedures when the mortgagor's regular mortgage payment is delayed; adequate monitoring of the lending institutions dealing with low-income mortgagees; the means of educating borrowers regarding their rights and responsibilities; avoidance of foreclosure whenever possible; and, generally, some degree of flexibility in the lending institution procedures more appropriate for low-income mortgagors. It is not apparent what effect, if any, these provisions and changes had on the process. It must be stated that until 221 (d)(2) and 235, relationships between FHA personnel and lender institutions on the one hand and low-income families on the other were rare.

The business incentive of lending institutions when issuing mortgages is obviously to seek out the best credit risks and to issue the largest mortgages acceptable, at the highest interest rates (or, better yet, at the highest subsidized interest rates). If the government can guarantee the mortgage so that the lender will not suffer any chance of a loss, all the better. The most profitable way of doing business is to choose the mortgagors carefully so that the most return will be forthcoming with the least service and the least risk. There was no built-in incentive for lenders to take risks, which meant that lenders also sought the least risk among properties as well as among mortgagors. Houses in less desirable interracial, semicommercial, and semi-industrial neighborhoods are less easily resold and therefore provide less security for the lender. No lender would make a specialty of seeking out a clientele believed to have a high proportion of slow payers, defaulters, and problem cases among them. One loans more money to those one knows and is fairly sure of. The cultural gap between the affluent and the poor was never so apparent as between the bankers and the poor in search of housing. Similarly, the lenders' contention that the poor make bad mortgagors was also generally upheld, with the poor usually behaving in a manner expected of them by the lenders.

Sections 221 (d)(2) and 235 did prove effective among the stable, working poor, most of whom would have been equally eligible for and as well served by other FHA provisions or by conventional loans. Neither of the two programs effectively reached into the population of low-income, intermittently employed families with children.

A somewhat similar program was developed under Section 502, which is operated by the Farmers Home Administration. Under this section, which was passed in 1968, borrowers may use loan funds from FHA to construct, repair, or replace dwellings, or to buy houses or a building site. Until 1974, the emphasis of this program was on construction. In recent years, the Farmers Home Administration has been urged to emphasize financing the purchase of existing housing. The loan provisions require that a dwelling be modest in size and cost. Unfortunately, according to the Madway report, this program has been similarly unable to serve poverty-level families, in this instance in rural areas.

The Conference Board Housing report of September 1974 provides a picture of developments in housing construction and financing. The average price of new one-family houses in the United States ranged from a bit below $20,000 in 1963 to almost $36,000 in 1973. Between 1963 and 1973, an annual average of 500,000 and 600,000 new one-family homes were constructed. In 1963, about 300,000 new homes were purchased with conventional loans; this total had grown to 400,000 in 1973. FHA loans totaled about 125,000 in 1963, 200,000 in 1971, and only about 50,000 in 1973. The total of VA loans for housing ranged from 65,000 in 1963 to about 75,000 in 1971 and about 55,000 in 1974. Thus, FHA and VA had remained junior partners in the housing finance industry. If we examine the policies of FHA, VA, and the lender institutions holistically, we will probably find that this is not an accidental result. By and large, FHA and

VA policy, when viewed in relationship to lender policy and to interlocking relationships, shows evidences of the equivalent of the sweetheart contracts which exist between certain unions and management. (Under such contract arrangements, the union and management benefit at the expense of the consumer, merely by pursuing their own joint interests.) Only the consumer suffers. Similarly, in the housing industry, FHA, VA, and the lender institutions maintain a peaceful cooperation for mutual benefit, at the expense of the consumer, especially the low-income housing purchaser. In this respect, FHA and VA "make no waves" but in the process, they generally fail to produce the effect on the housing market which was the intent of Congress, namely, to provide sizable amounts of low-income housing. If housing ownership were a solution for the condition of poverty, and there is no evidence that it is, it would still be unattainable under the available FHA and VA structural relationships in the housing industry.

Housing Policy

The mortgage loan insurance efforts of the federal government generally represent the social insurance thrust of the program. The public assistance thrust of the federal housing program is represented by the public housing projects of America. This aspect of the housing derives from the housing policy of the 1930s. Public housing is supposed to be an in-kind program provided at reduced rates for those unable to purchase or rent their own quarters because they do not qualify for homeownership, because their families are too large for available private rental housing, or because they cannot afford to pay private housing rents.

Parallels have been drawn between public housing and food stamps as income transfer programs. Until the food stamp rules were changed in 1978, the poor person who could not afford what he needed would pay a small part of the actual cost, and the balance would be made by federal subsidy (Steiner, Chapter 4). If he could not afford any payment (as is the current practice), he was provided with the food of his choice at no charge. Williamson, et al., (1975) discuss conventional public housing, leased housing, rent supplements, and 235 homeownership subsidies as a form of income in kind or relief in kind.

The housing policy, including public housing for the poor and federally guaranteed loans for the middle class and working poor, reflects a categorical policy of public assistance for the poor and social insurance for others who can fund their needs if government mechanisms are provided. Steiner (Chapter 4) describes public housing as a "means test relief program," which increases the availability of a necessary commodity not adequately available from private enterprise.

Bellush and Hausknecht (p. 4) report on some early small-scale model housing projects for slum dwellers which were entirely experimental in the early 1900s. Because "housing is perceived by the poor as their basic problem" (Williamson, et al., p. 128) and because many others accepted this view of the causes of poverty, the building of public housing became a major project of the anti-Depression efforts of the first Franklin D. Roosevelt administration. In 1932, the Reconstruction Finance Corporation, which was itself a child of the New Deal, made loans to corporations to finance low-income housing and slum reconstruction. Two loans were made: one for $8 million for Knickerbocker Village in New York and a smaller sum for a rural project in Kansas.

The National Industrial Recovery Act (NIRA), which was another entity of the Roosevelt New Deal, also became involved in building public housing in 1933. Here, too, the primary purpose was not low-income housing, but the creation of employment opportunities for the unemployed. The NIRA authorized federal funding of low-cost public housing and slum clearance. In a few years, it provided for the construction of 40,000 low-rent housing units. By 1937, the U.S. Congress had passed the first National Housing Act which established a housing authority to furnish loans and contributions for low-rent housing to local public housing agencies. These agencies would own and operate the projects. This was the first joint venture between federal and local governments in housing, a cooperative pattern that had been developed between those entities already in the field of public assistance. The federal entity involved is now the Housing Assistance Administration of HUD.

The National Housing Act has been amended many times. In 1947, it was permitted to allow local housing agencies to exceed the established cost limitations for such projects if the local agencies provided the difference between costs and statutory limits. The 1947 amendments also prohibited the eviction of project tenants whose income had risen over the allowable limit, if such eviction would create undue hardship. Because this question was such a burning issue between the proponents of free enterprise who opposed public competition for profitmaking landlords and others who sought improved housing for all without concern for the survival of the profit system, this matter was fought again in Congress in 1948 and was reversed. By 1961, the issue was compromised in the housing act of that year, permitting overincome families to remain in housing projects by paying rent related to the size of their incomes, while the local housing agencies looked into the availability of appropriate equivalent private housing at rates related to the families' incomes. In this way, the interests of competitive private housing funds were preserved while preventing the unnecessary removal of overincome families from projects.

Another legislative act, the Lanham Act of 1940, provided public housing funds during World War II—again not for the sake of improving housing conditions but to help the war effort. After the war, these housing units were distributed to educational and state and local bodies in order to provide housing for verterans. This effort, too, was related more to post-war readjustment than to a concern for the quality of housing for low-income families. The Housing Act of 1949 was again concerned with the construction of public housing. It called for about 810,000 units, but only 10,000 such units were completed in that year, primarily because of the advent of the Korean War, which interfered with available resources.

The Housing Act of 1949 also contained provisions that created a considerable shift in public policy. Until 1949, public housing authorities served primarily intact family units made up of the working poor who usually fulfilled the expectation that they would use public housing only until they could purchase their own home or rent more expensive commercial housing. Only a small percentage (generally never above 10 percent) of the units were rented to welfare families, and particular care was given to select those welfare families most likely to move themselves out of their welfare status within two to three years. Few one-parent, female-headed families were accepted except where the mother was able to show that she was fully in control of her situation and her children and that she was likely to be a responsible tenant. A high level of discretion was permitted the managerial staff in the selection and retention of tenants, and in the establishment of project regulations. The authorities and the administration viewed the housing projects as public assets, to be conserved and protected from misuses. President Dwight D. Eisenhower, for example, spoke out for public housing as adding public wealth to the community and nation, an asset that can be "liquidated and recaptured when the need disappears" (Welfeld, 1977, p. 137, and Schorr, 1963).

A serious housing shortage existed in the United States after World War II. The housing needs of the middle class and war veterans were largely being served by the FHA and GI home mortgage programs, but the housing needs of the poor remained unsolved. As a result of this situation, Congress acted to focus on public housing as the vehicle by which to serve the poor. Welfeld contends that other motives also occasioned this policy shift, including a desire to remove public competition from private (single-home ownership and commercial rentals) enterprise and to direct those families without stable wage-earners to public housing "without cutting into the private enterprise market."

New policies for public housing were established. First preference was given to families that had been displaced by public slum clearance, redevelopment, or low-rent housing construction. A 20-percent rent gap was established between the top rent of public housing in each geographical area where public housing was located and the bottom rent of governmentally unassisted decent housing in the same area. Because the new 20 percent of income rates for public housing were now lower, these produced lower income ceilings on who might be eligible for public housing. Maximum income limits were established for admission and continued occupancy, with the requirement of mandatory removal if the tenant earned more than the limits as set. Finally, discrimination against welfare families was henceforth prohibited. Despite the fact that Senator Allen Ellender predicted, in 1948, that if the greatest need became the standard for eligibility public housing would become a poohouse (see Welfeld, p. 137), members of Congress and welfare authorities pressed for a more accessbile policy for the poor to enter public housing.

By 1950, many members of Congress, the administration, as well as individual communities had become unhappy with public housing. By then, court rulings had further weakened the housing program. Judge J. Smith Henley, for example, ruled that the unwed mother exclusion, which was utilized by many public housing programs as a section of admission policy, could not be automatically exercised except to the degree that some direct connection between that condition and bad tenancy could be established. (See *Thomas* v. *Housing Authority*, p. 1235, in Levy, Lewis, and Martin.) Because this rule could no longer be prima facie enforced and because discretion would now be required, most public housing projects discontinued any exclusion on the basis of unwed motherhood. Similarly, Judge Gavagan ruled in *Sanders* v. *Cruise* that eviction of a family with one or more members who are drug addicts "exceeds any reasonable requirement for the peaceful occupancy and preservation of property of a project." (See *Sanders* v. *Cruise*, p. 1308, in Levy, Lewis, and Martin.) Only if a project manager could prove that the tenant had committed illegal acts against the tenants and property, presumably in the support of a habit, could an eviction be instigated. (Other court restraints on public housing abound.) Thus, the public housing projects were required to change their policies from social control by selection and management to social control by police enforcement. In the process, thousands of extra housing police were hired, and in some instances, special police forces were established, as in the case of the New York Housing Authority Police. A sharp increase in vandalism, in crimes against tenants and others, and in operating costs was soon evident, according to the Conference Report on Housing (as reported by Levy, Lewis, and Martin, p. 1309).

Bechtel reports a loss of individuality by residents "because an individual's alternatives are narrowed by [acceptance of public housing]." Public housing is not the high-turnover, unstable market which some claim it to be. The average length of residence reported by Bechtel was eight years and three months. Complaints about vandalism are numerous, but most vandalism is done by resident children and teenagers. According to Bechtel, more than two-thirds of the residents' important decisions are made by the housing authority or by a related official. As a result, he concludes that "there is some doubt as to whether persons under these conditions can think of themselves as adults." His complaint of dehumanization is based on delays in repairs which are often experienced in commensurate private housing, but which are viewed as substandard maintenance in a public housing program. His report also complains of a paternalistic management and bureaucratic handling of resident problems.

A 1969 report on public housing in Cambridge, Massachusetts, entitled "Public Housing: The Idea Seems to Be That If the Government Subsidizes Your Rent, You Should Be Grateful for Whatever You Get," lists the residents complaints against the project. They objected to fines for families whose children were involved in vandalism on the project or for families that had not cleaned their own hall-landing area. They complained about the drab, institutional design of the project with its barracks-like fences and walls so like prisons. The residents also voiced complaints against the paving of courts or fenced-in grass and trees. It seems, however, that the paving and fencing were done because lawns and trees on the project had been destroyed. Residents also complained, "There are few lights on the grounds and people live in constant fear of muggings. . . . People are constantly harassed by gangs of boys" (p. 26).

Poor maintenance leaves apartments with warped floors, sagging ceilings, and filth from previous residents and vandals. Poor maintenance, in turn, is partly the result of rising expenses without increasing rents. A high level of destructive activity and abnormal wear and tear caused by residents and visitors is uncommon in private housing but quite common in public housing. Residents of public housing who complain are degraded by project managers and are labeled troublemakers. According to the 1969 report, "the usual system of all powerful agency versus malcontent tenant creates housing problems rather than solving them."

Hartman and Carr, in their appraisal of local public housing administration, conclude that "the system of quasi-independent authorities presumably devoted to the 'general good' as opposed to strong proponents of specific programs, interest and objectives, is ill-suited to the housing needs . . . of the nation's poor" (p. 24). They have found that the public housing field is less professional than necessary, especially in the smaller projects. It is unrealistic, however, to expect poorly paid and part-time project administrators to be fully knowledgeable, and their commitment to "larger and better programs is only half-hearted or non-existent." A high proportion of project directors, even in large projects, have little enthusiasm for the public housing program and "have little inclination to make necessary changes" (p. 24). According to Hartman and Carr, commissioners and directors of public housing programs share considerable de facto decision-making power. Both tend to be white, middle-aged, and conservative, unlike the residents of public housing projects. A high proportion of directors "express a lack of respect for their tenants and an unwillingness to give them any significant voice in running their affairs" (p. 25).

This situation gains significance when one considers that local public housing authorities represent the nation's largest class of landlords (Rosen). Rosen portrays the public housing resident as a second-class citizen who must deal with authority personnel who often act arbitrarily, and even illegally, in their dealings with residents. In his view, the authority's pattern in admissions, control, and evictions works to reward some groups and to discourage others. Rosen complains that "the reaction of local authorities . . . has been to exclude those 'undesirable' families which are . . . most in need of decent, safe and sanitary low-rent housing. Housing authorities see [themselves as] protecting society rather than rehabilitating families" (p. 156). He believes that housing authorities judge the personal morality of families and admit only those which meet their own standards. Since these decisions are not made openly, the families affected cannot argue against their exclusion. In his opinion, such administration is arbitrary and unacceptable in a democratic society. According to Rosen's analysis, one theme which runs through social welfare programs specifies a distinction between rights and privileges, and he cites numbers of references to support this conclusion. In public housing, he states that "this distinction emerges . . . [with] the government as landlord [with] all of the powers and rights of arbitrary action possessed by a private landlord."

Rosen's report can be criticized on several grounds. His claim that, by their policies, housing authorities eliminate from their programs the undesirable families that are most in need of "decent, safe and sanitary low-rent housing" is contradicted by the experience of authorities. Those projects that have opened their doors to undesirables have found that their projects were no longer "decent, safe, sanitary or [even] low-rent" because of the increased costs of maintenance, repair, and extra policing made necessary by the inclusion of large numbers of such families. Rosen criticizes the housing authorities as if they were private landlords in their dealings with tenants and prospective tenants. Starr has examined this issue carefully and has found that if the housing authority dealt with tenants in the same manner as private landlords and used due process in recourse to the courts before eviction (as private landlords do), then the resident would be guaranteed the same rights as other Americans.

Another error in Rosen's report is his association of public housing with public welfare. In public welfare, only two parties are involved: the client and the public welfare authority. If the public welfare decision goes against the client, he has no legal recourse. Hence, "fair hearings" have been built into the public welfare decision-making system at every step to protect the client. In contrast, in public housing, more than two parties are involved: not only the housing authority and the tenant, but also all the other tenants whose rights have been violated by an undesirable whose teenage children have been pushing drugs in the halls, have organized destructive, antisocial gangs, have caused such vandalistic behavior as defecation and urination in the halls, and removal of safety devices from elevators, or have conducted mugging blackmail programs on housing project grounds. To call for full-blown legalistic hearings before any action is taken against a tenant would require the use of neighbors as witnesses. Such witnesses, after testimony, could not go home safely; they would not be protected against retaliation at the hands of offending families or their friends.

The costs of such hearings and litigation must be borne by the authority who, in turn, must pass them on to the residents in the form of increased rentals. Protecting the rights of the violators always represents an extra cost to others, especially to the victims. The provision of public legal hearings at every level of application, management, and eviction for every case probably would mean that tenant complaints would be discouraged and that the managers' interest in maintaining an adequate quality of life in the projects would be further dampened. As vandalism, muggings, filth, and disrepair increase in projects as a result of a legalistic tenant-authority relationship, the tipping point will soon be reached and the project will go the way of Pruit-Igoe in St. Louis, where even the residual undesirables eventually left because of project deterioration.

Starr indicates that in the 1960s only in New York City had public housing been successful (when judged by the criterion that more people want to get into the projects than are willing to move out of them). This was not the case in St. Louis, Jersey City, Chicago, Washington, D.C., and other cities where vacancies exist on a large scale and where some projects have actually been abandoned. Public housing may work in New York City partly because its housing authority's policies on admissions and evictions have been quite unlike those of most other city authorities. In New York, the housing projects focus more on the working poor, while in most other cities, the emphasis has been on housing the nonworking, dependent poor. New York City has a long history of voter-conscious administrations, in which the working class has been very influential. In a sense, the working class has made New York City a metropolis, and it is understandable that New York would consider the working poor rather than the dependent poor to be its first responsibility. At times, the New York City authority has had a waiting list of over 100,000 names. This is an important fact in a city where public housing has historically provided a major source of housing for the working poor.

The Downs report (1970) of the Committee for Economic Development revealed that about one-third of those in urban poverty belong to households in which the head of the household is male and working, although not earning enough to keep the family out of poverty. Downs found that the elderly represent about 18 percent of the urban poverty population and that about 10 percent of the urban poor are in households headed by disabled or unemployed males whom Downs believes can be viewed as working-class families. Thus, we can see that almost two-thirds of the urban poor are quite unlike what Downs describes as the dependent poor. The dependent poor are mainly female-headed families who generally lack a working-class ethos and maintain a pattern of dependent behavior. Among these families, 60 percent of the female household heads do not work at all and are presumably supported by AFDC. In this population category, even if they were freed of child-care responsibilities during working hours, 70 percent of the mothers would be unable to earn more money than they are receiving on welfare and "their low skills and job motivation mark . . . them as being outside the working class."

The New York Housing Authority tenant admission standards of 1961 are listed in Dorsen and Zimmerman (pp. 251–59). These standards were set up according to two categories: clear and present danger, and conditions indicative of potential problems. Under the first category are listed such items as contagious diseases which create a hazard to other tenants; past or present engagement in illegal occupations; evidence that an individual in the household is prone to violence; confirmed drug addiction; rape or sexual deviation; grossly unacceptable housekeeping; record of unreasonable disturbance of neighbors or destruction of property; and other evidence of behavior which endangers life, safety, or morals. Under the second category are listed the following conditions: alcoholism; use of narcotics; record of antisocial behavior; membership in a violent teenage gang; record of poor rent payment or eviction for nonpayment; highly irregular work history; frequent separation of husband and wife; husband or wife under eighteen years of age; placement of children (not necessitated by such circumstances as illness or death of a parent); out-of-wedlock children (except where this condition has been changed by marriage and where the couple has lived continuously as a family for the last two years); common-law relationship where there is no impediment to marriage; presence of one or more children who are not the offspring of the applicant (except where legally adopted or placed in the family); family with minor children which does not include both parents, except where one of the parents is absent because of military service, hospitalization, institutionalization, or death; lack of parental control; mental illness which required hospitalization within the past five years; unusually frequent changes in place of residence (four or more addresses in the preceding three years); poor housekeeping standards, including lack of furniture and gross overcrowding (recently married couples and others who have experienced furniture losses beyond their control, such as in a fire, are, of course, an exception); elderly persons who cannot adequately care for themselves or for the premises, where their family cannot see to their care (such persons have been instead assigned to special residential projects for the elderly); apparent mental retardation (where special care is required and the family cannot provide it); obnoxious conduct during the processing of the application (for example, intoxication, filthy language, or grossly belligerent attitude); other than honorable discharge from military service; and other conditions indicating nondesirability.

If any conditions under the first category are present, the applicant is ineligible; if any conditions under the second category are found, the application is flagged for study. In such cases, the family's eligibility is determined after careful examination. All rejected applicants may appeal to the Tenant Review Board, and even after that, they have the usual opportunity to seek legal reversal through the courts. Tenants who have received notices of eviction are told the reasons (after having been cautioned one or more times for the possible eviction and reasons) and may appeal to the Tenant Review Board and the courts (Starr, p. 118).

Since 1961, many of the criteria established by the New York Public Housing Authority have been amended to fit changing social conditions, court decisions, and cultural traditions. Admission standards have also been changed because of political pressure and of the need to find urgently needed housing for AFDC families at rational rentals. The admission rate for public welfare families to the public housing projects has risen to 56 percent, of whom half are broken families. Starr points out that this rate is near the critical tipping point, in that the only variable associated with substandard housing in urban buildings is the presence of welfare families, especially female-headed families in which the children are out of control. Under such conditions, increases in crime and vandalism usually follow and the voluntary "moveouts" by nonwelfare families rise perceptibly. In such instances, Starr predicts that more of the working poor and others will move out of the city entirely, leaving the city to the welfare poor and the underworld.

The possibility should be considered that separation is needed in public housing just as it is required in corrections. In the field of corrections, first offenders are separated from hardened criminals who see no way of life other than crime for themselves and for anyone else with whom they come in contact. The children of the working poor and their parents who aspire to succeed in the society legitimately should not be forced to share their lives and surroundings with others for whom dependency, despair, and crime are a way of life. It is probably impossible to help the dependent poor move from the housing project to self-sufficiency and homeownership in one, or even two, generations, but with more time this change can be accomplished. Many of the working poor who have been in the more effective housing projects have already made the move. It might be feasible to provide heavy-duty projects for problem families who might be supplied with supportive social programs focusing on the multiple special problems of the female-headed, welfare-dependent family. But such projects should be separate and apart from the working poor who have no more tolerance for the life-patterns of the dependent poor than do most other sectors of the population.

Glazer examines the general question of why public housing has failed. He believes that the dissatisfaction with public housing has arisen from several problems. First, public housing has been limited to the poorest families. Inevitably, large proportions of these families are made up of those on relief, as well as broken families without wage-earners and without the ability to earn money and be self-sufficient. When the concentration of the unfortunate and miserable becomes too large, others shun the project and an excessively high vacancy rate develops. In addition, because the income limits are checked annually, the more productive, ambitious people with leadership potential are evicted.

Second, administration of public housing has been more restrictive and intrusive than that of private housing. As a result, both the number and type of applicants and residents have been limited, and considerable alienation has developed among those who have remained. Only the helpless, fatherless families on welfare consistently stay on in the projects. A third problem is that the architecture, locations, regulations, and clientele of public housing have been marked off from other housing as separate, institutional, and deviant. Nonetheless, Glazer finds little evidence that the architecture as such has had unpleasant consequences. In his view, "the jungle" is created not by the twenty-story apartment house, but by the social circumstances of the families that live in them.

Finally, public housing projects are built in old and delapidated neighborhoods and are cut off from contacts with middle-class areas and life. The residents need these contacts if they are to be socially mobile. In this regard, Schorr (1963) reports:

[N]ot only are the families [in public housing] isolated, many receive public assistance and [are] . . . in broken families. . . . They cannot be abandoned to their problems; they must be served. . . . When they are not served, buildings deteriorate, delinquencies occur and deprived youngsters grow into disabled adults . . . neglect is expensive (p. 116).

Welfeld (1977) maintains that public housing, in its post-1949 form, has led to further ghettoization of the city and to a common tenancy of the very low-income families. Such concentrations of the poor do not make for an environment in which appropriate socialization in terms of the middle-class value systems is feasible or practical (p. 138). Hartman comments on the undesirable aspects of public housing: "[T]he words 'public housing' are now anathema to many, including the program's clientele . . . images of massive, ugly projects, located in the most undesirable parts of the city teeming with problem families . . . people are simply turned off to the notion of public housing" (p. 709).

The Failure of Public Housing

Public housing as it is currently constituted has failed for several reasons. For one thing, the residual poor who now reside in public housing are not the same clientele as the previous residents, who more closely resembled the transitory poor or the immigrant poor models. Unlike the residual poor, the immigrant or transitory poor viewed "home ownership as a symbol of civic virtue—a prerequisite for the integrity of the social system" (Bellush and Hausknecht, p. 453). The tenants of the pre-1949 projects worked hard, saved their money, and sought to move up and out of the projects. While residing in the projects, they behaved in ways that would help them get ahead. Getting ahead required cooperative residential behavior, avoidance of violations of other people's persons or property, and the reporting of destructive behavior by others to the management. It also required close supervision of their children's actions in order to prevent damage to others, to avoid costly involvement with the courts, and to preserve the family's reputation, so necessary to building a respectable credit rating and employment record. Thus, in order to maintain a functional housing program without excessive control and maintenance costs, a project must necessarily retain a preponderance of families whose behavior would serve as a model and as a social constraint on the limited number of multiproblem families who might have been admitted into the project. After 1949, when the residual families became predominant in the projects, the upwardly mobile families either left as quickly as they could or no longer considered using public housing for themselves.

The second reason why public housing has failed is the restriction on overincome families. As the upwardly mobile families who would otherwise have provided leadership to the project tenants left, they were fast replaced by the nonleadership, nonupwardly mobile welfare families. Another reason was probably architectural in nature. High-rise buildings with centrally located large elevators and long, dark, impersonal hallways make for what Newman describes as indefensible space. Smaller projects, with neighborly clustering and with concierge-like locations neighbors to become acquainted with each other for their mutual protection were more appropriate but the planners rejected them on economic grounds.

Pierce believes that public housing projects can work, but only if they are kept small, located outside the ghetto area, put in the hands of a no nonsense manager backed by a strong tenant council, and provided with adequate maintenance funds. Pierce states that the projects can remain functional only if the project managers are given broad authority over tenant selection, with "an informal (termed 'benign') quota to create a healthy mixture of family types, income levels and races." A successful project would require a reasonable limit on public welfare recipients and on female-headed households, below what he describes as a "tipping point" which would otherwise drive out the other tenants. Managers have to have the right to evict socially intractable families or those with destructive children who, Pierce says, would otherwise "foul the nest for other tenants." He maintains that "concentrating problem families in projects is a sure prescription for the proven disasters of past [housing programs] which have become mere extensions of segregation, misery and crime at public expense" (p. 5). Pierce provides examples of projects that have followed his guidelines. These projects remain functional and are still serving the purposes for which they were established.

The failure of public housing could probably be basically attributed to the lack of adequate research and development time given to the problem after it was realized that public housing was not serving the interests of the residual poor. Instead of quickly switching policy, which in effect delegated maximum spaces for the residual poor, it might have been much more advisable to test the feasibility of serving so many residual poor through public housing. A small research project might have determined that this approach was impossible without also risking the loss of public housing as a viable concept for the working and transitory poor. It probably would have been advisable to retain public housing on a 90/10 percent proportion of working poor and residual poor, respectively, which would at least have provided standard quality housing for 10 percent rather than 100 percent of substandard housing for the residual poor, which is the present situation. It must be remembered that the 90/10 benign quota proportion has been proved operational and generally useful to the rehabilitation of the residual poor, while the 100 percent residual poor condition has been found to be generally destructive to the residual poor as well as to property and society.

Welfeld (1970) suggests that the provision of new housing in public housing units is the most expensive strategy possible for increasing the nation's housing supply. In his view, the total cost of new public housing units is approximately 150 percent of the amount that "decent second-hand units rent for on the open market." Welfeld believes strongly in the turnover process because it "makes sound housing possible to income groups which cannot afford new construction" (p. 34). In his view (1977) new housing "is just too expensive for even a fairly drastic redistribution of income to help the very poor unless one wishes to favor them over others with average incomes, which is politically impossible" (p. 133). Such favoritism would also require a redefinition of American concepts of justice. Welfeld believes, therefore, that "the question of housing production must be divorced from the question of housing assistance to low-income families."

Welfeld's (1970) view is that the federal government should adopt a dual policy, seeking to increase the housing supply "by subsidizing middle-income households and by subsidizing low-income families." He believes that this policy would increase housing turnover and thereby free a sizable portion of the existing housing stock for subsidized poor families. Such a policy would eliminate the need to build further public housing projects. Therefore, Welfeld actually supports the FHA and related middle-class housing mortgage programs, and suggests that these programs be enlarged and expanded. He also suggests a rent supplement program to help the poor secure rental housing as it becomes vacated by the middle-class in an expanding housing market.

Downs (1974) criticizes the "trickle-down" theory of housing provision for the poor. He believes that "reducing the poverty concentrations [which are] produced by the 'trickle-down' process is essential either to upgrading existing inner-city populations or redeveloping the neighborhoods with 'balanced mixtures' " (p. 144). He seeks voluntary dispersal and a reduced concentration of the poor in the inner cities, with balanced housing dispersed through the suburbs. Thus, Downs advocates improved income maintenance and job opportunities for the poor rather than direct involvement of the government in housing. Accordingly, he discourages the development of both further public housing and rent supplements for the poor.

Just as FHA serves to bolster the segregation of the middle class from the very poor by means of credit restrictions and high housing costs, so public housing tends to further segregate the troubled poor, keeping them from contact with, and escape to, the rest of society. In a sense, each of these programs (just as public assistance) has boundary maintenance functions that help perpetuate a specifically defined consensus society. Recent requirements that new federally aided housing provide for low and middle-income housing amidst high-cost housing have not met with much success.

One alternative for improving public housing has frequently been suggested. That is to scatter the poor in the suburbs, so that they will be closer to employment opportunities and to people whom they need to get to know if they are to learn about opportunities for upward mobility. Residence in the suburbs would also provide a better quality of schooling and would solve problems of segregation. Life in the suburbs would provide the residual poor with models of upward mobility and of mainstream behavior without which upward mobility is impossible. On the basis of this theory, the Chicago branch of the American Civil Liberties Union initiated a class-action suit against the Chicago Housing Authority (CHA) and the U.S. Department of Housing and Urban Affairs. In the first case (1966), the plaintiffs claimed discrimination against the poor people of Chicago, especially the black poor, in locating the public housing projects in neighborhoods that were predominantly black and clustered around ghetto areas (Austin).

In the Gautreux decision,* the court forbade the CHA to build any new housing projects in the city areas where black families make up more than 30 percent of the population until at least 700 units of new public housing were built in the mostly white "general areas," and in no case closer than a mile from any predominantly black area. The court also held that no project could be built for more than 120 persons (approximately thirty families), nor could any buildings be over three stories in height if they were to include children, and the sites were to be scattered throughout the city. Consequently, the CHA did nothing more for family housing for some ten years, contending that there were no suitable sites available in the general areas, (Fuerst). During this same period, however, ten projects for the elderly, containing several thousand units, were completed, notably in the general areas. The attorneys for the plaintiffs then shifted their attacks to the suburbs and pressed the Department of Housing and Urban Affairs and Judge Austin to press for an expansion of the ruling. Although Judge Austin refused to do so, the issue was reversed on appeal. The CHA can now validly claim that no suburb will agree to locate a CHA family project within their boundaries, and the CHA has no power over the suburbs to force them to accept such a project. Consequently, the CHA is free to do nothing about housing the poor of Chicago beyond continuing to operate the concentrated collection of massive high-rise projects already in operation.

The solution to housing problems for poor families as selected by the attorneys for the plaintiffs does not necessarily represent the interests and

---

*Gautreux v. Chicago Housing Authority, 296 F. Supp. 907 (N.D. Ill., 1969) subsequently affirmed in Hills v. Gautreux, 425 U.S. 284 (1976). The federal district court for the northern district of Illinois sitting in Chicago held hearings before Judge Richard B. Austin between 1967 and 1969 with a decision rendered in 1969. The issues presented related to discriminatory location of public housing projects in black neighborhoods, thus denying poor blacks the opportunity to live elsewhere. A unanimous Supreme Court of the United States affirmed the district court's decision in 1976.

desires of the Chicago poor. Fuerst and Petty report that no public family housing program in the suburbs, even if accepted by those areas, can be expected to succeed. The facts are that the residual poor who are the persons most in need of housing do not want to be located in the suburbs, in an area where they would be unable to continue to maintain the life-style they currently practice. The middle-income and low-income black families that have moved to the suburbs in sizable numbers are most unlike the black families of the inner city, both in their interests and their readiness to move. Of 40,000 families interviewed by Leadership Council relocation workers (and reported by Fuerst and Petty, p. 17), about 1 percent expressed interest in suburban living.

The action by the plaintiffs' attorneys and the appellate courts has therefore brought further public housing for poor families in Chicago to a standstill. The probability of pressing for the development of small family projects in the general areas of Chicago is now quite minimal, and the opportunity to provide a mix of predominantly working poor families with some residual poor in small projects is now no longer available. It is ironic that this dismal outlook for public housing in Chicago was brought about by pressure from the liberal establishment (the American Civil Liberties Union and proponents of desegregation). The effect of this action is borne out by Hartman, who states that efforts to resolve segregation problems concurrently with slum problems will inevitably result in failure for both (p. 704).

The stasis condition of public family housing, as presented in Chicago, is reflected in many ways throughout the United States. Because of the poor image of such housing and its expected effect on area land values and police, fire protection, and other costs, the number of middle-class areas reporting rejection of low-income family projects has grown stead-ily. This condition, however, is not the case for public housing projects for the aged (and disabled).

In 1956, Congress authorized the Public Housing Administration (PHA) to aid in building new housing or in remodeling existing low-rent housing for elderly families and low-income individuals. The 1956 act did not focus on housing for all low-income people, but only for the elderly who seemed to suffer most in large public projects. In 1961, the PHA was permitted to spend funds appropriated by the 1949 act and to complete approximately 100,000 units over the following three years.

By 1965, under the Housing and Urban Development Act, some new approaches to public and subsidized housing concepts were introduced. A new cabinet-level department was established which was supposed to be primarily concerned with housing and urban problems. The federal mort-gage guarantee agencies were absorbed into this new department. The act also made it possible to use privately owned housing in low-rent, publicly sponsored housing programs, up to a limit of 10 percent of funds available. In such instances, the tenant would use a rent certificate to pay for leased private housing at a low-rent rate and with the federal government providing the difference between the low-rent rate and the market price. This provision was added to permit the dispersal of low-income families and hence to alleviate some of the problems encountered in public housing projects.

The 1965 act also provided for the turnkey method of providing low-rent public housing. This method allows a commercial developer with a site to contract with a local housing authority to build housing based on his own plans. If the proposal is approved, the local public housing authority purchases the completed building. HUD provides the financial commitment which makes possible completion of the housing. This provision is so flexible as to permit rehabilitation of rundown or abandoned property for transfer to local housing programs.

Still another alternative plan for housing the poor was the rental supplement program. This program was established in 1965 but was either stillborn or starved at an early age by inadequate funding. This program would provide rent supplements for lodging made available by nonprofit groups such as churches, labor unions, social agencies, and community groups. These agencies would be paid on behalf of tenants whose incomes were low enough for them to qualify for public housing but who were unable to secure adequate housing at the level they were judged to be able to afford. Under this plan, the landlord would charge a fair market price for the space so that he could recover his costs. The tenant would contribute a fourth of his income (a rule of thumb proportion established by the government), and the federal government would make up the rest. As the resident's income rose, he would pay more of the rent and the government less. If the tenant became financially able to pay full rent, he could continue to live in the unit by doing so.

This program would solve the problem of overincome evictions, but not the myriad problems of the multiproblem tenant who needs to be controlled rather than evicted. The hope, however, is that a nonprofit service-oriented agency would be more energetic and innovative as landlord in working with the multiproblem family residents than a public housing authority bureaucracy.

Rent supplements for the poor were developed under the provisions of the 1965 Housing and Urban Development Act (League of Women Voters). Under this plan, funds from Section 22 (d)(3) are used to build new housing or to rehabilitate old housing where the property is owned by private, nonprofit, limited dividend, or cooperative owners. A below-market interest rate of 3 percent was established, as a method of federally subsidizing the program. Rent supplement contracts between the housing owner and the HUD secretary are made for periods of up to forty years. The tenant is therefore provided with opportunities to rent decent housing and is free to leave if he can find other owners with similar federal contracts.

Under the 1968 Housing and Urban Development Act, a new title was developed for rental housing for lower income families, under Section 236. This title provided for periodic payments to the mortgagee who is financing rental or cooperative housing for low-income families, so that the mortgagor's interest on a market-rate, FHA-insured mortgage is subsidized. Such interest readjustment payments reduce rentals to a basic charge, which the tenant pays, or to a greater amount representing 25 percent of his income (but not in excess of charges necessary to pay off the mortgage). Generally, the 1968 provisions do not change the rent supplement pattern.

David Stern objects to rent supplements and housing allowances. He points to the likelihood of long-term inefficiency because a program which provides more housing money to poor families usually induces landlords to raise rents without raising quality. This effect was observed in the Medicare program, when funds were provided for the elderly to secure medical care without increasing the supply of physicians. The result was an inflation of medical rates for all and a general, and less obvious, lowering of the time spent by physicians with individual patients. Stern believes that housing allowances alone will have a similar counterproductive effect unless some efforts are also made to enlarge housing supply. His second point is the danger that families may merely substitute housing allowances for their own housing expenditures. This, he maintains, would also be counterproductive.

Frieden (1977) criticizes housing allowances because of the large number of intermediaries who divert a high proportion of federal funds away from low-income families. This housing allowance distorts the allocation of aid, prevents programs from operating in the suburbs, and restricts the choices open to low-income families. In his view, the rent supplement program needs a number of changes. For one thing, the requirement for local government approval of rent supplements as well as public housing leasing programs should be removed. Second, where there are suitable vacancies in local housing markets, federal policy should encourage the use of public housing leasing of private facilities by local government. Where housing supplies are tight, federal policy would encourage the contracting of private management projects to provide housing for the poor. Frieden (1977) also suggests a number of proposals other than the rent supplement program to improve federal housing assistance.

When rental supplements are applied to approved housing programs, the government is assured that it is not subsidizing slum rentals. The ostensibly superior supervision provided in such projects may make them somewhat less stigmatized and more socially acceptable to others in society. The program does not, however, solve the problem of providing families with motivations and mechanisms to move up and out of poverty. At best, rental supplements are a more palatable form of in-kind housing aid, which is as much a palliative for poverty housing as public assistance is for the social-psychological-economic syndrome of residual poverty.

In October 1973, HUD concluded that not enough housing was being made available to low-income families. One problem was that Sections 235 and 236 (a similar program providing for rental and cooperative housing) were not providing enough housing to the poor (Welfeld, p. 1289). Section 236, as of June 1977, has covered only 4,217 rental or co-op projects serving 460,000 units insured for $7.9 billion (programs of HUD). Another reason given for dissatisfaction with 235 and 236 was that the programs were neither efficient nor fair in that only one of every fifteen eligible families benefited from them. HUD therefore proposed a new program, Section 8. This program represented a new approach to construction in that it offered developers opportunities to make newly constructed units available, not on a purchase-ownership basis which did not attract an adequate number of poor families, but on a special rent basis. The government would pay the developer the difference between the rents paid by the poor and the fair market price. The Section 8 leasing program was passed in August 1974. It included not only new construction but also existing rental apartments that meet standards. Unfortunately, in the writing of the regulations for the new law, the definition of the new lower income level for applicants proved to be higher than the income already set under the predecessor laws. However, a subsection in the law sets aside 30 percent of the units created under Section 8 to be used for very low-income families. Another barrier to effectiveness of Section 8 is the fact that Congress did not match the law with appropriations to provide housing for the large population under the low-income definition. Thus, Section 8, like other rent supplement laws, unfairly provides for a select few, or more likely a lucky few, while ignoring many others (Welfeld, 1978, p. 133).

The 1979 budget requests housing assistance to an additional 400,000 low-income families. As of June 4, 1977, Section 236 provides housing assistance to 4,217 projects with 460,000 units, insuring the loans for rental units at a total of $7.9 billion. As of September 30, 1977, Section 8 provides assistance to 169,000 new construction or rehabilitation units and 162,000 existing units. The budget also provides for homeownership assistance to an additional 50,000 moderate-income families. In 1977, 2.6 million families were given housing assistance, a total that was projected to rise to 3.1 million families in 1979. The 1979 budget also proposes the provision for another 56,000 units of public housing requiring $6.8 billion, plus another $400 million to amend previous public housing contracts, and another $750 million to modernize existing public housing projects.

In recent years, a series of housing assistance supply experiments have also been undertaken. One experiment covering selections of Wisconsin and Indiana (Staff Housing Supply Experiment) covered between eighteen and twenty-seven months, respectively, in two communities, providing average allowance payments of $75 per month. The report indicates that in neither site has the program disturbed neighborhood settlement or market patterns and that the programs were generally approved by officials and citizens. In both areas, approximately 8 percent of all households were enrolled. Lowry (1977) states that the experiment served a variety of families, including the unemployed and aged, and welfare mothers do not predominate in the program. Experience shows that about 80 percent of the enrollees of these projects eventually find acceptable housing and qualify for the assistance payments. About 45 percent were already in acceptable dwellings and thus eligible for the assistance payments. About 25 percent repaired their homes to meet acceptance standards. Lowry also reports that the experiment has not seriously disturbed the housing market. A later report by Lowry (1978) shows that modest housing improvements for sizable numbers of people have been achieved at less cost to the public than would have been the case with public housing. Lowry concludes that, compared with the alternatives, housing allowances are "a plausible instrument of national housing policy."

Another suggested experimental program relates to rental certificates. Olsen proposes a program that allows a set of families to purchase rent certificates for an amount less than the face value of the certificates. Sellers of housing service may redeem these certificates at face value from the city government, which would in turn be reimbursed with federal aid to cover the difference between face value and purchase price. This program operates in a manner similar to the way the federal food stamp served marginally poor families until 1978 when the policy was changed. Under this procedure the recipient was given a proportionate amount of aid based on his income level. In an earlier paper on the subject, Lowry (1971) points out that neither new housing nor major rehabilitation is appropriate or economical for low-income families. The most critical problem, Lowry indicates, is that there is too little effective demand for adequate maintenance of older buildings. Thus, he supports the rent certificate plan which allows eligible families to find their own housing, dealing directly with the landlord. Certificates would be applicable only with continued certification of housing quality, and would thus preclude use of the plan for subsidy of nonstandard units. The plan would therefore create incentive for both tenant and landlord to cooperate in housing maintenance and improvement.

Another related proposal concerns the payment method of rentals by AFDC welfare clients. Moynihan has noted the relationship between welfare tenancy and the inability of building owners to collect rents. This problem has a direct causal relationship with the thousands of apartment houses abandoned by owners because they cannot collect rents and are unable to maintain them. In New York City, Moynihan reports that for a time two-party checks were issued to welfare clients for their rent in instances where the welfare client had fallen in arrears in his rental payments and had experienced evictions. Under this system, the check was made out to the welfare client and the landlord but was given to the client. If the client was satisfied that the rent was due and if the conditions he required were met, he would then sign the check and give it to the landlord. This system prevented the client from spending rent money on some other item, while retaining some control of the payment. Because of federal requirements late in 1975, this program was drastically reduced. Subsequently, about two-thirds of these welfare clients were again in arrears for rent.

Moynihan reports that nonpayment of rent by welfare clients is a serious problem. For almost any landlord, a welfare clientele is a low-level choice as a housing tenant. Having once accepted a sizable number of such tenants, a landlord probably finds it impossible to reverse the trend by renting to nonwelfare tenants. This situation is often aggravated when nonwelfare tenants also stop paying their rent, once the word is out that welfare tenants are not paying. The usual reason for withholding rent payment is a grievance against the landlord because of inadequate services or repairs, but such services and repairs cannot be made once a sizable number of tenants stop paying. Hence, the landlord is forced to abandon services and repairs, and eventually taxes and principal payments as well. Finally, the building dies with the disappearance of the landlord, discontinuance of utilities, and condemnation of the property as unsafe by city authorities. Tenants are then forced to move out, and the house is boarded up and left to deteriorate and to be surreptitiously used by drug addicts, gangs, and illegal squatters. Thus, as a result of the disorganized use of welfare grants by clients, another house for welfare clients is struck off the available list.

In 1977 the New York City Welfare Department proposed to the Senate Committee on Finance that the two-party check system be established as a voluntary arrangement between welfare tenant and landlord, revokable at any time, in order to prevent problems for welfare clients who sought help in keeping up with their rent. This proposal had the support of several congressmen of the Black Caucus and other prominent persons concerned with welfare problems. According to Moynihan, it failed because of the opposition of the professional welfare constituency, consisting of HEW officials, federally financed poverty attorneys, state and local welfare personnel, and others who had consulted neither with the Black Caucus nor with the clients themselves. The opponents' view was that any restriction on client use of welfare, even if voluntary, smacked of coercion and therefore violated the sense of values of the professional welfare constituency.

Despite the professional welfare constituency and their sense of values, the continued deterioration of available welfare housing may ultimately require provision for two-party checks, rent certificates, or some other means of assuring that rent-designated welfare dollars become payments for housing for residual welfare families. The choice may have to be between such a mechanism and homelessness for such families, despite the anticoercive sensibilities of "the friends of the poor." The two-party check fiasco in Congress thus resembles the *Gautreux* v. *Chicago Housing Authority* fiasco, another instance of housing removal by "friends of the poor." Chapter 8 reports that the friends of the poor created a similar condition in connection with the minimum wage, as a result of which hundreds of thousands of minority youth are unable to find a "first" job in their lives.

At this point, it is helpful to review the different philosophical approaches to housing policy. Schussheim examines four different philosophies which attempt to explain the problems of low-income and other housing. The first school of housing policy holds that the housing shortage, especially for poor and middle-income families, is caused by a recurrent drought in mortgage credit. In this view, if ample financing, rental supplements, or other subsidies are provided, then everyone can be adequately housed. This is the position taken by many housing functionaries in government, in the home-building industry, and in other industry groups.

The second school believes that housing costs are too high because of the nature of the current patterns of building and building codes. These can be lowered only by mass production techniques and by revamping municipal restrictions and environmental constraints.

The third school maintains that people live in bad housing because they are poor and disadvantaged, and are victims of racial discrimination. The solution is to stress not housing, but job training, income maintenance, education, and the elimination of artificial barriers to mobility. If these are provided, the problem of housing for the poor will be resolved.

The fourth school argues that slums and ghettos reflect the inability of disorganized and politically impotent segments as well as the disorganized life-style of the affected population which makes them unable to control their own destiny. The solution lies in academic and political education, community and neighborhood organization, and careful guidance and direction.

It is obvious, then, that the problems of housing for the poor, just as the problems of residual poverty, can be understood only if one understands the basic societal theories on which the definitions of the problems depend.

A conflict view of society (see Chapter 1) brings one quickly to the third school of housing policy, and the consensus view of society leads the analyst directly to the fourth school. An objective analyst may well conclude, however, that a combination of factors, an interaction between tenant and housing system, leaves the low-income group with less adequate housing.

From a general view, probably all of the schools of housing policy require consideration. Price inflation relating to housing and lack of mortgage credit, adequate efficiency in housing planning and construction, adequate funds for rent in the hands of the poor, informed political power, and organization of the tenant's own life and family operations, all contribute to the housing shortage and to housing problems of the poor.

Housing for the poor seems to hold a dominant place in the dynamics of transgenerational poverty. Observers of the poor are initially more impressed by their dreary surroundings than by their behavior or emotional interactions. Just as the package often obscures the contents, so does the location of poverty often obscure the nature of poverty as a syndrome. Bad housing does have a direct and destructive effect on people, as is apparent from observations of the poor. Glazer suggests that crowded housing creates excessive sexual stimulation, devastating attitudes toward privacy and self, uneasy intrafamily relations, and diversion away from activities related to upward mobility. These problems may be the result of a simple shortage of space, but they are often mitigated by cultural factors.

As a mechanism for resolving or preventing poverty, housing seems to be important only among the working poor and the lower middle class. As a solution for the problem of transgenerational poverty, improved housing provides little that is lasting or effective.

Housing for the poor is being complicated still further by the precipitate rise of housing costs which began in 1977. The price of a house should be no more than double the family's annual income. According to this standard, in 1977 less than three out of ten American families could afford to buy a medium-priced used house. Couples who wish both a family and a house often have to opt for one or the other. The majority of purchasers are able to buy homes only because there are two salaries in the household. Land prices, spurred on by inflation and a de facto devaluation of the dollar, have multiplied six times in twenty years. Robert Ellickson, a housing and land-use law professor, reports that the cost rise in housing is unprecedented in recent history. Both Ellickson and Frieden state that the postwar baby-boom adults now entering the housing market are making a high demand for housing. Congress will likely be under increasing pressure to make housing available for this population group. If so, one can expect competition between this population and the growing residual poor population for their share of governmental support—during a period when governmental expenditures are being strongly questioned and cut back. In a cost-benefit analysis comparison between housing supports for the poor and for the new baby-boom adults, the latter will win because, unlike the one-parent, residually poor family, this population is employed, pays taxes, and will be able to liquidate any costs incurred in their housing over time.

Alternative Housing Plan

How shall the poor be housed then? As was suggested in the section on welfare, we propose a categorical, step-by-step orientation. Just as one segment of the poor has been redirected into SSI programs and just as others can be directed, once they move away from residual poverty patterns, a similar plan can be devised with housing. The aged poor and disabled poor have already been directed into desirable housing programs which they can support and utilize without damage to themselves and the programs. Others have been drawn off to self-help housing purchase programs where their efforts and work have served to become part of their home equity. Still others can be drawn out of the residual poverty population into projects similar to those provided the aged, if they demonstrate responsible tenancy patterns. Just as the automobile insurance companies permit lower premiums only to those who have had no moving motor vehicle violations for three years, so prospective tenants for preferred housing might be required to show a clear arrest record for the family, a record of adequate school progress, a lack of illegitimate births and child abuse or neglect over the period under consideration, no record of drug addiction, alcoholism, juvenile offenses, and police- or neighbor-involved family discord, and a record of consistent payment of rent and other regular obligations. Provision of such preferred housing might encourage others among the residual poor to follow a similar behavior pattern.

Where one lives is important in the choice of schools for one's children, in the people one gets to know, and in the opportunities one encounters. Where one lives also, to some extent, constitutes evidence of one's past achievement and behavior. The problem of providing housing for the poor, the near-poor, and now the new adults of our society requires serious analysis and planning.

References

Austin, R. *Gautreux v. Chicago Housing Authority.* Pp. 1207–24, in Robert J. Levy, Thomas P. Lewis, and Peter W. Martin (eds.), *Social Welfare and the Individual: Cases and Materials.* Mineola: Foundation Press, 1971.

Bechtel, Robert. "Deficiencies in Public Housing," as reported by Howard Schwartz in *American Psychological Association Monitor,* 2(11):10, 1971.

Bellush, Jewel, and Murray Hausknecht. "Urban Renewal: An Historical Overview." Pp. 3–16, in Jewel Bellush and Murray Hausknecht (eds.), *Urban Renewal: People, Politics and Planning.* Garden City, N.Y.: Doubleday, 1967.

———. "Public Housing, the Contexts of Failure." Pp. 451–61, in Jewel Bellush and Murray Hausknecht (eds.), *Urban Renewal: People, Politics and Planning.* Garden City, N.Y.: Doubleday, 1967.

Burns, S. "Housing as Social Overhead Capital." P. 992 (footnote 19), in Robert J. Levy, Thomas P. Lewis, and Peter W. Martin (eds.), *Social Welfare and the Individual: Cases and Materials.* Mineola: Foundation Press, 1971.

Conference Board. *Trends in Housing Costs.* New York: Conference Board, 1975.

Dean, John P. "The Myths of Housing Reform," *American Sociological Review,* 14:281–88, 1949.

Dorsen, Norman, and Stanley Zimmerman. *Housing for the Poor: Rights and Remedies.* New York: New York University School of Law, 1967.

Downs, Anthony. *Who Are the Urban Poor?* Supplementary Paper No. 26. New York: Committee for Economic Development, 1970.

———. "The Successes and Failures of Federal Housing Policy," *Public Interest,* 34:124–45, 1974.

Ellickson, Robert C. "Why Housing Prices Went Through the Roof," *Los Angeles Times,* July 24, 1978, Part II, p. 5.

Freedman, Jonathan L. *Crowding and Behavior.* San Francisco: Freeman, 1975.

Frieden, Bernard J. *Improving Federal Housing Subsidies.* Summary Report, Working Paper No. 1, Joint Institute for Urban Studies. Cambridge, Mass: Massachusetts Institute of Technology and Harvard, 1971.

———. "The New Housing Cost Problem," *Public Interest,* 49:70–87, 1977.

Fuerst, J. S., and Roy Petty. "Bleak Housing in Chicago," *Public Interest*, 52:103–10, 1978.

Judge J. Gavagan, *Sanders v. Cruise*, 10 Misc. 2d 533, 173 N.Y.S. 2d 871 (1958).

Gavagan, J. *Sanders v. Cruise.* Pp. 1305–10, in Robert J. Levy, Thomas P. Lewis, and Peter W. Martin (eds.), *Social Welfare and the Individual: Cases and Materials.* Mineola: Foundation Press, 1971.

Glazer, Nathan. "Housing Problems and Housing Policies," *Public Interest*, 7:21–51, 1967.

Hartman, Chester W. "The Politics of Housing," *Dissent*, 14(6):701–14, 1967.

————, and Gregg Carr. *Local Public Housing Administration: An Appraisal.* Working Paper No. 137, Berkeley Center for Planning and Development Research, Institute for Urban and Regional Development. Berkeley: University of California, 1970.

Judge J. Smith Henley, *Thomas v. Housing Authority*, 282 F. Supp. 575 (E.D. Ark., 1967).

Henley, J. *Thomas v. Housing Authority.* Pp. 1232–49, in Robert J. Levy, Thomas P. Lewis, and Peter W. Martin (eds.), *Social Welfare and the Individual: Cases and Materials.* Mineola: Foundation Press, 1971.

League of Women Voters. "Housing Supply," *Current Review of Human Resources.* Washington, D.C.: League of Women Voters, 1968.

Levy, Robert J., Thomas P. Lewis, and Peter W. Martin. *Social Welfare and the Individual: Cases and Materials.* Mineola: Foundation Press, 1971.

Lowry, I. S. *Housing Assistance for Low Income Urban Families, A Fresh Approach*, P–4665. Santa Monica: Rand, 1971.

————. *An Overview of the Housing Assistance Supply Experiment*, P–5967. Santa Monica: Rand, 1977.

————. *Early Findings of the Housing Assistance Supply Experiment*, P–6075. Santa Monica: Rand, 1978.

Lubove, Roy. "The Progressives and the Slums," Pp. 17–24, in Jewel Bellush and Murray Hausknecht (eds.), *Urban Renewal: People, Politics and Planning.* Garden City, N.Y.: Doubleday, 1967.

McDougal and Muller. "Public Purpose in Public Housing: An Anachronism Revisited," *Yale Law Journal* 52:42, 47–48, 1942.

Madway, David M. "A Mortgage Foreclosure Primer," *Clearinghouse Review*, 8:146–84, 1974.

Moynihan, Daniel Patrick. "The Rocky Road to Welfare Reform," *Journal of the Institute for Socio-Economic Studies*, 3(1):1–10, 1978.

Newman, Oscar. *Defensible Space, Crime Protection Through Urban Design.* New York: Macmillan, 1972.

Olsen, E. O. *An Efficient Method of Improving the Housing of Low Income Families*, P–4258. Santa Monica: Rand, 1969.

Pierce, Neal R. "Public Housing Projects Can Be Livable," *Los Angeles Times*, October 30, 1977, Part IV, p. 5.

Rosen, Michael B. "Tenant Rights in Public Housing." Pp. 154–261, in N. Dorsen and S. Zimmerman (eds.), *Housing for the Poor: Rights and Remedies*. New York: New York University School of Law, 1967.

Schorr, Alvin. *Slums and Social Security*. Washington, D.C.: U.S. Government Printing Office, 1963.

Schussheim, Morton J. "Housing in Perspective," *Public Interest*, 19:18–30, 1970.

Select Committee on Nutrition and Human Needs, U.S. Senate. *Promises to Keep: Housing Need and Federal Failure in Rural America*. Washington, D.C.: U.S. Government Printing Office, 1971.

Staff Housing Supply Experiment. *Third Annual Report of the Housing Assistance Supply Experiment*, R–2151–HUD. Santa Monica: Rand, 1977.

————. *Fourth Annual Report of the Housing Assistance Supply Experiment*, R–2302–HUD. Santa Monica: Rand, 1978.

Staff Report, Office of Economic Opportunity. "Public Housing: The Idea Seems to Be That If the Government Subsidizes Your Rent, You Should Be Grateful for Whatever You Get" (Cambridge, Mass.). Washington, D.C., Office of Economic Opportunity, 1969.

Starr, Paul. "Which of the Poor Shall Live in Housing?" *Public Interest*, 20:116–24, 1970.

Steiner, Gilbert Y. *The State of Welfare*. Washington, D.C.: Brookings, 1971.

Stern, David. *Housing Allowances: Some Considerations of Efficiency and Equity*. Working Paper No. 6, Joint Center for Urban Studies. Cambridge, Mass.: Massachusetts Institute of Technology and Harvard, 1972.

Stewart, Potter. *Hills* v. *Gautreux*. Pp. 638–47, in Donald Brieland and John Lemmon (eds.), *Social Work and the Law*. St. Paul, Minn.: West, 1977.

Time Magazine. "Housing: It's Outasight," *Time*, 110(11):50–57, 1977.

U.S. Department of Housing and Urban Development. *Programs of HUD*. Washington, D.C.: Department of Housing and Urban Development, 1978.

Welfeld, Irving H. "Toward a New Federal Housing Project," *Public Interest*, 19:31–43, 1970.

————. "American Housing Policy: Perverse Programs by Prudent People," *Public Interest*, 48:128–44, 1977.

Williamson, John B., et al. *Strategies Against Poverty in America.* New York: Wiley, 1975.

Wilner, D., R. Walkley, T. Pinkerton, and M. Tayback. "The Housing Environment and Family Life: A Longitudinal Study of the Effects of Housing on Morbidity and Mental Health." P. 993 (footnote 24), in Robert J. Levy, Thomas P. Lewis, and Peter W. Martin (eds.), *Social Welfare and the Individual: Cases and Materials.* Mineola: Foundation Press, 1971.

WORK, EDUCATION, AND POVERTY IN AMERICA   **8**

EMPLOYMENT placement has long been viewed as a method of helping individual families in poverty. In early family casework programs, such as were developed under the New York Association for Improving the Condition of the Poor (NYAIP), the worker was usually encouraged to find a job for his client (Trattner, Chapter 2). This placement was often effected through informal channels, with the worker soliciting jobs for his clients among those employers known to him through his social circle (the NYAIP workers were usually upper class volunteers). The process of fitting the job to the client and vice versa was usually done in a pro forma manner. The purpose of such job placement was to get the family on a financially independent basis. Clients received little or no training or orientation for such employment. Such job placement usually involved unskilled employees, and the job required few skills and little education.

Only in recent years has employment been downgraded as a means of resolving poverty. Steiner, in his comprehensive work on welfare, deals thoroughly with a variety of relief systems, including public housing, food stamps, and reform strategies but makes no reference to employment, even in the index. Trattner, in his comprehensive history of social welfare in America, also omits all reference to employment as a mechanism for resolving poverty. Charles A. Reich, in his popular work *Greening of America*, takes the position that increasingly sophisticated, self-regulating machinery will expand to such a degree that an increasing proportion of working-age people will be unable to find a need for their services. Thus, in Reich's view, concern for economic security or for material goods is becoming less of a motivation for work effort, and the distribution of security and rewards will eventually be carried out without regard for individual efforts. Accordingly, conventional definitions of work and employment will lose much of their relevance. A growing majority of the population will relate to the economy primarily as consumers. Reich and many other social reformers believe that this process has already begun in the creation of a sizable nonworking consuming population which includes those on welfare. Johnston labels this position on the future of work as the "Green Work Scenario." In Reich's proposal, the life-styles of most people will be directed toward diversified forms of expressive behavior. Drucker also elaborates some of the antiwork ethic views presented by the counterculture protagonists. Despite the fact that the counterculture and the youth rebellion are no longer in evidence, it must be understood that the antiwork ethic is still strongly imbedded in a sizable proportion of the population (*Socio-Economic Newsletter*, 1979).

Reich's work views have been attacked by a number of critics in Philip Noble's edited collection, *The Con III Controversy*, in which, among other things, it is contended that an increase in cybernation and automation does not, in reality, lead to less jobs but rather to a shift in the distribution of jobs from unskilled to skilled persons in the society. Automation may lead to less time for workers on the job, but not to less employment or smaller total payrolls.

According to Johnston, over one-third of the jobs in the Green Work Scenario could be expected to be ego-involving and intrinsically and personally valuable to the worker. Johnston believes that the remainder would be society-maintaining, from which many of the workers would derive not only a wage but also a contribution to their identity. Hence, the Green Work Scenario, if fulfilled, would become a mechanism for an employed elitist class which would plan, direct, and distribute the benefits of the society. It would also become a mechanism for a residual dependent class to be systematically excluded from meaningful interaction with productivity and relegated to the object role of consumer. Obviously, the welfare reformists who view the society as a limitless cornucopia from which expanding income transfers to the poor shall be distributed with few constraints or requirements can be criticized in a variety of aspects. The American economy and its resources are limited and finite, and the affluent life has been directly associated with a series of inevitable trade-offs of social costs, pollution, and a lowered quality of life for everyone.

A major fault in income transfer plans, which do not require valid exchanges from the beneficiaries, is lodged in the culture of rich and poor, most of whom view work as a necessary and satisfying activity (Goodwin and Kaplan and Tausky). Johnston states that "work is likely to retain its traditional position as a major factor in orienting the individual in the society" for the forseeable future (p. 6). Eastburn, in his *Economic Man vs. Social Man*, concludes that social problems cannot be solved without a strong and growing economy, and that is not possible unless man is economically motivated for work. Liebow, who has studied black street-corner men, states that "no man can live with the terrible knowledge that he is not needed," even though he may be otherwise well provided for (1970, p. 14). Work is so closely tied in with the social and psychological development of man that "it is almost impossible to think of what it means to be human without thinking of work." Without work a person has little on which to base his identity or to identify how he fits into the society, if at all. Liebow's concern is not with the elimination of work for all but rather with ensuring that all who belong to the society become full and valued participants in it (1970). Miller and Riessman also express a concern for employment as an acceptable route to economic improvement and social advancement in the society. Not to provide for realistic work opportunities for the poor is equivalent to relegating the poor to an eternal population category of exclusion in every sense except as consumers. Any plan that does not provide for employment opportunities for the poor is a time bomb which can eventually be expected to explode.

Sociological and social-psychological theory and research support the pro-work view. Gordon Allport, in his short volume *Becoming,* states that "salvation comes only to him who ceaselessly bestirs himself in the pursuit of objectives that in the end are not fully attained." A daily job presumably falls into such a category. Levenstein, in his explanation of *Why People Work,* maintains that "individuality itself simply cannot exist without a structured community" in which work and jobs have an important role. He defines work as creative production and labor as work for the sake of survival. He indicates that "our freedom to be ourselves depends on our freedom to compose our own balance among the four possible choices: work, labor, play and creative leisure" (p. 270). Levenstein believes that if people in a society have no basis for their labor, they become "kept," and thus increasingly powerless and inbued with no life-purpose. In his view, "work is the process by which man refuses to acknowledge that life is vanity. By working, despite all the obstacles imposed by nature and his own human institutions, he rises above the sense of impotence even while it continues to assail him" (pp. 270, 271).

Other scenarios beyond the Green Scenario have been posited for the role of work in the society. In the "Blue Scenario" described by Johnston, two basic assumptions are made. One is that the pace and direction of technological change can be modified and channeled by measures that can ensure a high level of demand for workers. The other is that such demand can be matched by a supply of appropriately trained persons desiring to work. The Blue Scenario also derives from the experience that automation has provided a continued expansion in the number and variety of professional, technical, and service work opportunities that are geared to the operation of automated equipment. The attempts to cut costs in production may also require substantial investment of labor-intensive work rather than increased automation, especially when antipollution measures preclude further automation and require more labor-intensive activity. Efforts to increase production in less developed countries may require more, rather than less, employment in the United States in future years. Finally, the general cultural demand for work and income in the society is so pervasive as to force government to provide work when able and willing job-seekers cannot find work through their private efforts. Lecht finds that the spread of automation does not portend the redundancy of millions of American workers. Johnston is convinced that continued demand for labor by business and increased governmental activity as an employer of the first resort to deal with mounting social and environmental needs implies a long-range increased demand for labor as well as an increased, rather than decreased, importance of work in American society. The Blue Scenario can therefore be geared to provide employment not only for the general population, but also for the welfare population who can work if the special factors encountered in that population are dealt with. If work is to be done in the society and if rewards and status are to be related to that work, the exclusion of welfare populations from such activity may be an injustice to them.

Johnston offers still another scenario, the "Turquoise Scenario." In this scenario, continued improvement and application of automation and technology are expected. Economic security and material wealth are increasingly supported by the cybernated technology. To maintain and further develop this technology, a core of highly trained engineers and technicians is supported. A growing corps of personnel is involved in the distribution processes fed by automated production. Increasing numbers of public and personal service workers are related to the economy. Because of their individualistic work, a growing number of craftsman and artisans are also supported in the economy. Employment is also expanded by the growth of the experience industries, including recreation and education. In this conceptualization, work retains much of its economic and social-psychological significance. The proportion of workers involved in basic production and distribution tasks is expected to shrink, and that involved in slower productivity employment is expected to grow. Thus, in the Turquoise Scenario, economic and noneconomic factors such as changes in life-styles are more closely linked. In this scenario, we see a gradual reunification of work and leisure, although such leisure may be manifested in longer and more frequent coffee breaks, increased concern for personnel in work settings, increased humanization of the work structure, and the like. In this scenario, as in the Blue Scenario, work remains important in terms of social status, personal identity, and the earning of rewards.

Obviously, the Green Scenario is highly improbable. Either the Blue or the Turquoise Scenario is to be expected as a development in the 1980 decade. If the Green Scenario were to be adopted, its economic viability would be of limited duration. In any event, work is apparently here to stay not only as an ego-involved activity, but also as an activity that provides for increased rewards and status for the individual.

Occupations are social roles (Pavalko, pp. 3–5) providing a person with a place in a social matrix. Through one's work, a person gains standing for himself in the society. In pluralist America, occupational roles are achieved, so that the awarding of an occupational role to a person is proof of his successful effort in making something of himself. Occupational roles also allow the person to interact with the incumbents of other occupational roles. Thus, they provide the worker with a ready-made package of ways of relating to others and to the organized social structure. In earlier forms of social organization, such as in the preindustrial society, the locale and extended family functioned as the major sources of the individual's identity. In such ascriptive societies, one's locality or tribe defined who one was. In contemporary industrial society, there are few viable organic communities in the locales, and the extended family has little viability. If one does not have a job, one has a real problem in answering the question "Who am I?" Not to have a job is to be dependent on the society, a position parallel to that of the child, and to be without an occupational role and identity.

Work is also a predictor of the person's behavior in his nonwork life. What a person does on his work tells others not only what to expect in terms of his behavior off the job, but also the degree to which one can depend upon him to support the norms of the society and of the social setting. Thus, work is also a factor in social control in that a person will behave responsibly in the society if he has an emotional and experiential investment in his work and the benefits it brings him.

Work also structures the person's life. It provides a place for a person to go to every work day (when others who are part of the society also go to their work), and it provides a place to come from in a return to one's home or leisure activity. As many unemployed have noted, work provides a preventative process without which a sense of purposelessness can ensue.

The lack of employment has been related to many other symptoms of dysfunctionality: the high mortality rate among the recently retired (Pavalko, p. 220–21), the high incidence of mental illness among the unemployed and the less employed (Srole and Hollingshead and Redlich), the high rate of suicide among unemployed white males (Powell), the high divorce and marital maladjustment rate among the unemployed and underemployed (Kephart), the low level of political involvement on the part of the unemployed and underemployed (Selznick and Steinberg), and the low level of involvement of the unemployed and underemployed in voluntary organizations (Hagedorn and Labovitz). These and other evidences of dysfunctionality and social isolation are proof of the human costs of unemployment. Even a person's physical health is known to be negatively affected by the lack of purposeful employment, but because of the complexity of the question, there are few conclusive data on the question.

Hence, the picture of the nonworkers of the society is one of isolation from the rest of society, of self-defeating activities, and of physical and mental disturbances.

To accept the condition of nonwork as a given in the society, no matter how well intentioned the effort, is to relegate a sizable group of men, women, and children to a complexity of unproductive physical and social depression. As Everett Hughes puts it, work is a person's calling card and price tag in the society. Not to be employable is the equivalent in the culture of becoming a nobody and worthless. Raspberry states that joblessness erodes self-respect, "even when social welfare programs see to it that no-one freezes or starves to death." It harshly "limits the dreams and aspirations." It "creates an underclass of non-contributors [and] it is inheritable" (1978, p. 5). "Children of the jobless get such a poor start, in opportunity and self-respect that [they] are likely to end up jobless as well" (1977, p. 7).

Dolgoff agrees with Pavalko and others that work is the major means by which a person develops his identity, self-concept, and self-esteem. Work provides us with job-related messages about ourselves, which are then reflected in the way we perform our other nonwork roles. These messages include such items as salary, grade classifications, job assignments, and status and work conditions. A person without positive messages or cues as to his worthiness may take on patterns of self-hatred or self-denigration, often hidden, of course, by a person of aggression, hostility, or resentment. Even when the person is well provided for, as in the case of a rich woman's husband, the inevitable sense of unworthiness is apparent both from the way the culture deals with such a person and from the way such a person usually deals with himself.

Dolgoff also lays great stress on the life agendas provided by work. The sense of purpose, which he indicates is often provided by work, often serves to hold the personality together. In his view, the loss of work can undermine the structure of an individual's personality. On the basis of these considerations, the social-psychological assumptions of a minimum guaranteed income (as discussed in Chapter 5) can be challenged. A program that offers everyone the incentive of life-long economic security can hardly expect many to opt to become workers. In the process, many will defer the serious and difficult undertaking of work and career preparation to find and make a place for themselves in the society. Without such work, major population components can be expected to be patterned as proles in a nightmarish dystropia.*

---

*A dystropia or katatopia is the opposite of a utopia. In a utopia everyone is free to choose his own life activity, residence, and the like, and necessities are not hard to secure. In a dystropia (such as in George Orwell's 1984) people trade in their freedom for a limited subsistence and security level. A prole is what George Orwell called members of the proletariat.

Kaplan and Tausky, who have developed a typology of the meaning of work, indicate that there is a range of instrumental and expressive meanings. At best, work provides a high level of expressiveness as a satisfying activity, as a status and prestige-bestowing activity, as a morally correct activity, or as a source of satisfying interpersonal experiences. At the instrumental level, work provides both an economic means of survival and a scheduled or routinized activity that keeps the person occupied. Kaplan and Tausky do not, however, suggest that work also provides a mechanism by which one can move from instrumental levels to the more purposeful, satisfying, responsible, and self-benefiting expressive levels. Just as the beginning student of the violin must expect considerable pain, dystony, and little satisfaction, so the beginning worker must necessarily not expect immediate and expansive satisfaction. This same problem permeates Liebow's street corner men as well as the relationship of work among the residually poor. The more socially distant the poor are from the world of work the more difficult this dilemma becomes. If employment is therefore a necessity for the individual, and society is concerned that the individual have the opportunity to find employment, then it is important for us to examine the mechanisms for relating individuals to jobs and jobs to individuals.

Employment Programs

Employment programs can be categorized as public or governmental and private or nongovernmental. Most private employment programs operate within the context of commercial employment agencies. These agencies operate on a generally sophisticated basis and are usually available to people who can afford to pay the fee for such service. They solicit listings from employers and seek to place registered clients in these listings (Wilcox, pp. 314–15). Their primary dealings are with positions for which specific skills and education are required. Their focus is on service to the client and employer in a process that might be analogous to that of the marriage broker. Of the two (client and employer), the employer will usually be better served, especially in periods of employment shortages. The employer is offered the best of the available agency clientele, and the fee is paid by the employee or employer. Few of the poverty population have recourse to commercial employment agencies because they lack both the skills and education for these positions and the knowledge of how to use these agencies; moreover, they usually cannot afford the fees (Wilcox, pp. 314–15).

Most people, including the poor, learn of employment openings through public employment placement programs administered by the states (which are coordinated by the U.S. Employment Service of the U.S. Department of Labor), newspaper ads, information from friends, or the indirect and relatively random solicitation of employers (Bradshaw). The state employment services are usually in direct interaction with the state's unemployment compensation office. Hence, the prospective employee has one single address for securing both his unemployment benefits and knowledge about a new job. Ideally, state employment services would serve those most in need of employment as a priority group.

The state employment services operate in all fifty states and various territories. Each state maintains offices in major towns and cities where employers list their employment requirements. Employers may also use other channels for seeking workers, such as newspaper want ads and commercial employment agencies. People who are out of work and who seek employment may register at the employment service and, hopefully, be referred to jobs. At the same time, employees who have been laid off from jobs covered by employment insurance are required to register with the employment service and to be interviewed for available jobs. In recent years, this process has become perfunctory in many states.

When a person on unemployment compensation secures a job, the unemployment benefits are, of course, discontinued. The state employment service requires that people receiving unemployment benefits register in order to minimize the benefit expenditures of the unemployment compensation fund. By and large, factors in the system tend to direct those covered by unemployment benefits to job openings more frequently than those who are not covered (Munts). Whether this situation occurs because state administrators strive to keep unemployment compensation expenditures to a minimum is not clear. It may be that people who have had a recent employment history make better job placement prospects. It may also be that people who have greater access to and acquaintanceship with the employment system, including job insurance and placement offices, are more likely to secure job referrals. Another possible explanation is that the routine services of employment agencies (rather than special programs of job conditioning and work orientation) are adequate for reemployment referral but not for placement of candidates who have not worked in a long time or who have never worked.

State employment services are therefore tied to quick reemployment of those receiving unemployment benefits. They are also necessarily tied to a policy of orientation to employer interests. Because state agencies must necessarily compete with commercial agencies for the same job listings, the state agencies send their very best prospects for each position so that the employers will call on them again when openings occur. Thus, the state agencies, which were presumably established to aid those most in need of work, instead expend most of their efforts on influencing employers. Although the Wagner-Peyser Act of 1933 established the U.S. Employment Service to serve all unemployed persons legally qualified to work, the state agency related to the service focuses on those workers who have a good and recent work history, the desired qualifications and skills, and the best chances for placement. The Lawyers Committee and Urban Coalition report, entitled *Falling Down on the Job: The United States Employment Service and the Disadvantaged*, indicates that the service has, by and large, paid little attention to the employment needs of the handicapped, veterans, farmworkers, disadvantaged, unskilled, and others with special employment placement problems. Thus, it is clear that even in times of economic growth, both commercial agency and U.S. Employment Service placement provide only a limited mechanism for helping the poor unemployed into employment and out of poverty.

Other factors have aggravated the problem for the poor. The record indicates that a steady 5-percent unemployment rate is probably not a severe hardship in a population if it is spread evenly. Teenagers and the never-employed have an unemployment rate which is two times, and often three times, that rate during summer periods (Ferguson, pp. 65–66). Thus, the major employment placement programs of America are quite able to place the working poor and the middle class when unemployment occurs, but do not adequately serve the residual poor, the unskilled, the inadequately educated, and those with no or a poor work history. The unemployment rate in itself is a generally fictive statistic in that it is composed primarily of those who are on unemployment insurance or who are actively seeking employment (*New Republic*, February 26, 1972, p. 8, and Ferguson, pp. 24–25). It does not include those who have given up the search, even if they still want to work. Automation, mechanization, and cybernation increase in the society at a steady rate related to the direct and hidden costs involved in human employment. Except for periods of recession and depression, the total number of people employed may remain relatively constant. The shift in employment occurs in the release of the unskilled, the uneducated, the undereducated, the nonjob-conditioned, the nontechnician, the less flexible, and the inexperienced. Those who are hired and retained are the dependable servants and public contacts of the machines. Their numbers grow, as does the number of those relegated to the limbo category of nonworkers (Zagoria and Michael).

Many poor families do not have a viable potential wage-earner. The aged, the blind, and the severely disabled have been relegated to the SSI program and are, by and large, almost completely out of the employment market. The potential primary wage-earner of families in the AFDC program is also almost entirely listed in the "father missing" category. The mothers in such families are supposedly unable to accept employment because they must stay home with their children. When AFDC women do secure employment, the pay is often so low that the welfare budget exceeds it and makes AFDC preferable. Those women who do accept regular housework jobs put together a multiple of a one-day-per-week arrangements in different homes to form regular employment.

Little is known about the number of AFDC mothers who pool their children in each others' homes and who regularly accept unreported household employment. (Nor do public welfare administrators conduct vigorous inquiries into the question.)

The effect of not having a respected wage-earner in a family is often transgenerational. Children grow up with the impression that life is one endless bout with idleness, purposelessness, and welfare experience. Schooling, rather than being viewed as a preparation for a job or career, is considered a required imposition upon the young until they can escape. In a sense, schooling for the children of the poor is seen much as the draft was among the middle class during the Vietnam War—as an unnecessary evil to be avoided (Stone and Schlamp).

Employment placement programs and unemployment insurance are generally symbiotic. Similarly, employers and employment placement programs are symbiotic in the sense that employers represent a politically important element in the society vital to the continuance of employment placement agencies and the agencies provide a necessary service for employers. The agencies therefore serve the needs of employers (and the more likely employment candidates) rather than those of the utterly jobless. The politically and economically important employers and their interests have become entrenched in the governance and policies of public placement agencies in many of the states. In general, it can be concluded that employment placement services are not in themselves a primary resolution for poverty.

The question may be raised, "What about full employment?" If our economy were to create more jobs and provide wages for services that are needed in the society, would employment placement then become an effective mechanism for the resolution of poverty? If the unemployed among the poor were to be given employment orientation, special training, and more thorough placement services, would that, plus the extra jobs added to the employment system, make poverty resolution possible? Under this model, the government would become the employer of the last resort. When jobs were scarce or when too few jobs met set standards, the government would create employment as appropriate. Similarly, persons most in need of employment, employment orientation, training, and placement would be sought out, motivated for their chosen goal, given literacy preparation, job reconditioning, and placement, along with the necessary coordinative and supportive services.

The problems presented by these two proposals can be viewed in terms of their effect upon the economy as well as in terms of the internally contained program difficulties. Any government can probably afford only a limited number of less productive or nonproductive crusades in each generation. Each hot war, each cold war, each space program, and each war on poverty presents a cost on the future (along with the cyclical inflationary effect of paying interest for the mortgage on the present), a governmental bankruptcy, a sale of presently held resources, or a combination of the three. Because of recent American experience which included a hot war, a cold war, a space race, an extensive funding of medical care, and an aborted war on poverty, it is apparent that a crusade to provide employment for all may be beyond American financial capability in this age. From a macro-viewpoint, such a program may not be a viable alternative.

From an operational point of view, a program that creates employment usually provides jobs that are little more than deadends. Jobs that are created by a society in which labor unions and civil servants play a dominant implementive part and where such functionaries seek to defend their status are usually supplemental and tangential to regular acceptable employment (Levitan). Thus, the nurse's aide who can never become a nurse, the teacher's aide who can never become a teacher, and the like predominate in make-work projects. Such employment can hardly be expected to provide the status and respect, let alone the income, upon which a wage-earner in a poverty family can build a career, plan to remain at home with his wife and children, and become a model for the children on their way upward in society.

An employer of the last resort program also presents the need for considerable technical backup if it is to be effective, and it is doubtful that such technical backup could be, or would be, provided by organized labor and civil service groups who are quite logically threatened by an influx of extra hands. What happens to an established bureaucratic work-group which has traditionally emphasized work-group boundary maintenance and procedures rather than task performance when extra hands are offered to it? Would the work-group accept higher performance goals and permit the extras to fit in among the regulars? Or would it seek renewed ways of filling the time allotted to the work? Suppose, for example, that the post office were offered an extra work force for the sorting and delivery of mail. Would it increase deliveries to twice daily and speed up the delivery process? Would the extras be accepted, trained, and integrated into the work force? Would the work force generously share the job security, employee benefits, and the like? Or would the work force seek to hold off the extras at arm's length, providing as little training as possible and integrating none or very few into the work group (Miller and Riessman)?

The matter of intensified job orientation and training, focused primarily on the poverty population, also presents problems in implementation. The problem is chiefly one of job availability. There are too few jobs for which the not-quite-literate can be quickly trained, if we accept the constraint that such jobs must pay more than a welfare budget. A parallel problem derives from financial support of the work candidate's family during the training period. Training, along with literacy preparation, can be a time-consuming process and may therefore require years of financial support for the family. Motivation is also a problem, especially if the program does not cream but accepts those who most need the service rather than those who would probably move upward on their own. With the least motivated, an intensive skilled type of social-psychological-emotional support is required, which is not easily found or secured among training personnel.

Still another important aspect of career or job training must be considered, especially in the case of children or young adults. Ellis's research indicates that "the upward impetus for mobility has its roots in the nuclear family." The decision of a member of a lower class family to enter into training or education is made with the approval of the family's adults. Ellis has also found that there is "a readily discernable [*sic*] pattern of maternal influence [which] characterizes the family structure of the upwardly mobile." Such a family must have a mother with at least some beginning educational attainment and the continued presence of the father which provides necessary stability in the family during the lean training years. Obviously, the residual poor are much less equipped for retraining in that the mother's educational attainments are usually limited, her interest in retraining and education are depressed by continued welfare incentives, and the father is usually long gone.

Ellis also suggests that certain specifiable functions must be carried out on a dependable basis if upward mobility decisions and efforts are to be undertaken and maintained. For such trainees or students, Ellis has identified a necessary pattern of roles which some person in the family, neighborhood, or program must be committed to if the trainee or student is to become successfully and upwardly mobile. These roles include (1) "The goad . . . who prompts the [person] to want to achieve a position in which he will be respected and looked up to." (2) "The coach . . . who trains [the individual] in the social and behavioral skills needed for meeting the demands of the [employment] world and gives him the knowledge needed for effectively shaping and directing his life goals." Without the coach, the individual cannot adequately experience the necessary anticipatory socialization related in upward mobility. (3) "The incentor who can give the sympathetic encouragement needed for continuing . . . despite [encountered setbacks and obstacles]." Without this encouragement, many students and trainees lose heart and drop out early in the experience. (4) "The sponsor . . . who can open the door to partially closed systems" (necessary to upward mobility) (p. 17).

It is obvious that most residual poor families do not provide a built-in goad, coach, incentor, and sponsor. Neither do many training programs or educational systems provide anything more than counselors (if at all) who are equipped with more than rudimentary knowledge and skills, let alone the kind of intensive capabilities and dedication needed for members of residual poor families.

Finally, the problems of timing and logistics need consideration. We cannot train people for openings that will be filled by others long before the candidates are trained. Training needs to be planned for future openings which are expected to occur concurrently with the completion of training. This kind of planning has not been evident in social welfare services in the past.

Training programs in the United States have generally been fragmented rather than unitary and cohesive. Under the Manpower Development and Training Act, in most states job identification for training purposes fell under one bureau; adult literacy education fell under another agency; job training was placed under still another; and family and supportive services were drawn from another yet unrelated agency. The job placement was conducted by another bureau, and followup on the placement was generally omitted. Generally, no coordinative process was built into the fragmented programs. Thus, the loyalty of each professional was usually located in his agency rather than in getting people trained and placed. Similar fragmentation occurred in the Work Incentives program of the AFDC. In some programs, for every 100 trainees accepted, only one person was placed. The costs per successful placement become prohibitive. The usual product of training programs is not a successfully placed person; rather, it is a professional trainee who goes from project to project seeking satisfying training program experiences. In general, then, job creation, job training, and job placement are in reality of little realistic value in planning for the resolution of poverty, unless a number of barriers to effectiveness are resolved and controlled.

The first of the barriers to effectiveness in job creation and training is a factor that occurs in the society rather than in the job program. This factor is the degree of attraction which antisocial activities in the deviant culture hold for the unemployed youth. It is impossible to attract young men into training programs for positions that will eventually pay them less than the profits made from street activity along with the support of an AFDC mother or girl friend—all without training and with less effort. The youngster who joins a training program that provides him with a limited stipend would be the laughing-stock of his neighborhood when the more exciting antisocial activities promise much greater and immediate rewards. Thus, the provision of a more effective criminal apprehension and a more rapid justice system is one hidden assumption of an effective job creation and training program. Generally, youth employment programs are effective only in low-crime neighborhoods where middle-class standards of lawful adherence prevail. Any job creation program established in a geographical area where such standards do not prevail is probably doomed to ineffectiveness before it opens its doors. For a job creation program to succeed in areas of high crime, youth must perceive that criminal activity has a high probability of personal danger, is assured of punishment, and is relatively less remunerative than legitimate employment.

Another hidden assumption for a successful job creation and training program relates to the degree and amount of welfare benefits for those who can work but do not. A welfare family budget which is based solely upon the relative needs of a family, without regard for comparable employment pay rates, can actually discourage job training efforts in a community. The inner-city youth may be undereducated and undersocialized in relation to the norms of the mainstream, but they are generally not dumb. Why should a youngster willingly submit to the discipline of obtaining literacy and job conditioning when he can retain his comfortable homeostasis in a family supported by a combination of welfare assistance, public housing, food stamps, and other benefits? The existence of others in the neighborhood who are not employed but who manage a comfortable living probably serves as a constant deterrent for job training and personal upgrading. The visible presence of illegal but remunerative activities and of welfare benefits also discourages the development of employment aspirations in children and, in turn, leads to a downgrading of the importance of education among such children and a high dropout rate from school.

The employment program must meet a number of conditions in order to be effective. One of the most important of these is that the employment opportunity structure must be permeable and not blocked to poverty populations. Even if permeability is available to the poverty population, the poor must also have role models, who were once in their situation and who worked their way up the socioeconomic ladder by individual and legitimate effort. If a person makes it by manipulative activities or by ethnic politics, such as is provided in many affirmative action programs, he is probably less effective than if he makes it on his own and by use of established educational and employment mechanisms. The mechanisms for movement up the employment opportunity structure must therefore be available to all rather than to only a select and token few.

Another factor in the effectiveness of job training programs is the nature of the jobs for which the poor are to be trained. Liebow points out that an effective manpower policy must upgrade not only the person but the position as well. Just as the airlines have upgraded the airline attendant from what is essentially a waiter or waitress by adroit public relations, smartly designed uniforms, standardization of performance standards, and a decent salary, so Liebow maintains that most menial jobs could be upgraded into respectable and desirable positions. Liebow also makes the point that many dead end jobs exist in the society without being devalued. As long as the position provides an adequate salary and a sense of respected social usefulness, people hold on to the job and enjoy relative satisfaction in it. A wide range of job skills and aspirations can be attached to "tasks which are clearly of a high order of social usefulness." In this category, Liebow lists "public and low-cost housing, restoration of cities, expansion and improvement of mail service and a host of other programs and projects directed at the unmet public need in . . . health, education, child care, urban, mass transit, conservation, pollution and so on" (1970, p. 16).

In its review of employment and the poor, the League of Women Voters reports that jobs can be found if the society makes such a search a priority. Harrison, Sheppard, and Spring, in their article "Public Jobs, Public Needs," support the League's position that meaningful, worthwhile jobs can be found by the government as an employer of last resort. They maintain that the government should act as the employer of first resort in order to provide private industry with a competitor for potential employees. Such an employment structure would constitute a built-in impetus both to improve the status and wages of less desirable positions on the part of employers and to accept job-related education and training on the part of the poor.

These authors and others raise the additional issue of job creation sponsorship. Under the Carter administration's policy, job creation funds are distributed to local cities, counties, and states to be used generally under their discretion. This approach provides a built-in incentive for city hall to distribute jobs in such a manner that a maximum short-range political impact will be derived from each grant. Thus, city hall tends to hire people for temporary, rather than permanent, positions that will eventually have to be funded with local monies. These jobs are necessarily short term and provide little of the employment security which is considered valuable in trainee upgrading. Many such city hall jobs are devoid of meaningful in-service training programs precisely because they are designed to be temporary and are added on to the bureaucratic structure rather than made an integral part of the city's work force. Few or no city halls are ready to tackle the problem of credentialization presented by civil services, professional organizations, and labor unions. As a result, most such positions are little more than a way station from one spell of unemployment to another. When the federal government was involved as more than a mere fund distributor, interested persons and groups could exert influence in terms of installation and maintenance of employment upgrading standards. This is not the case under the revenue-sharing model of employment creation. The Works Progress Administration (WPA) model, as described by Barnes, was a model in its time both in terms of creating public services, facilities, and resources, and in terms of human resource development. Under the WPA model, local governments and agencies served as subcontractors or project managers for the federal government. Just as husband and wife serve to correct one another in the successfully functional family, so the federal government and the local project sponsors interacted to check for the quality and depth of program effectiveness. This condition is not found in programs that are operated locally and whose only federal constraints relate to financial accountability.

The degree of stability and hopefulness for upgrading in jobs created for the poor is an important factor in long-range poverty resolutions. Only if such jobs are secure and hold promise for the future will the worker be attracted to stay on the job and at the same time be enabled to enter responsibly into building and maintaining a family. The presence of hundreds of thousands of female-headed households on welfare is a product of conditions of insecure, unstable, intermittent, undependable, and meaningless employment. Lack of payoff in terms of security, upgrading, and hopefulness leads to increased irresponsibility, large female-headed families, and geometrically increasing unemployed and unemployable generations.

Still another factor in the insurance of effectiveness of job creation and training as a mechanism for poverty resolution relates to the degree to which such projects provide a broadening of life experiences and "life space" for the beneficiaries. A job and training that bring an individual and, through him, his family into contact with expanding life experiences help to develop and expand their career expectations and interests. If the employment provided gives the beneficiaries an opportunity to broaden their life space sufficiently to raise their own or their children's aspirations and expectations, the project's effectiveness will be enhanced.

Similarly, if the schools and other preparatory institutions relate the employment projects to the learning provided by them and vice versa, the value of school learning for the beneficiaries will be increased. If the schools relate career counseling of the children of beneficiaries to careers upwardly articulated with the opportunities offered to the parents, this service, too, will raise the level of project effectiveness.

The provision of family counseling, training stipends, and day-care services for children of trainees is also important to the success of job creation and training projects. Many training project directors report that the spouses of trainees are often unable to endure the privations of a limited stipend and the pressure of having to support a trainee emotionally during the learning process. Increased stress occurs within the family that must be managed or the training program fails for the individual. If the program is to be effective, family counseling on a basis that goes beyond mere availability is often required. In addition, a day-care program for the younger children lessens the demands on the trainee and, at the same time, can provide the children with a head start in terms of aspirations, interest, language, and other skills necessary for their own eventual escape from continuing poverty. Bronfenbrenner maintains that employability and unemployability are determined at a very early age in relation to the quality and degree of symbolic feeding provided to children. Adequate day-care centers can often make the difference for children in poverty. Through the schools and day-care centers, children do "feed" their parents in terms of what is expected. The influence of project on parent and schools and day-care centers on children can operate in a cyclical manner in reinforcing an employment and career-directed lifestyle. Through this means, the family views the parent's work or training as desirable and worthy of emulation.

If the above conditions are not brought about and maintained, the training programs will become shortlived, meaningless experiences for trainees taken on in spring and dropped the day after each local election. Such programs tend to perpetuate the growing credibility gap among the poor who tend to discount any project promises of upgrading and economic improvement. Without safeguards, training projects will not produce graduates who move into other employment, but rather a permanent class of trainees who live on stipends and learn nothing. The Subcommittee on Fiscal Policy of the Congressional Joint Economic Committee made a study in 1971 of manpower training programs evaluating their effectiveness with employment placement of the poor. The committee concluded that without safeguards, such as have been described above, manpower training programs cannot be expected to succeed.

Despite the arguments against such an approach, proposals for public employment to supply entry-level opportunities for special groups deserve careful consideration. Ginsburg documents these arguments for general job creation (pp. 122–26). She contends that the private sector persistently comes up short in providing jobs for the total population in need of jobs. Therefore, she states, "the federal government should create a *large* and *permanent* public service program [even] in good times." (Italics in original.) She specifies that these jobs should provide "decent wages," "offer a chance for advancement," and "would replicate outside conditions." Ginsburg ties the establishment of training and supportive services in with her recommendations. She contends that training alone merely produces more chronic trainees or holders of low-level or marginal employment. The massive public service program should not be limited to the poor because to do so would "isolate the disadvantaged from the mainstream of American life." As models, Ginsburg uses the Depression era's Civil Works Agency (CWA) and WPA, which employed 4 million and 3 million persons, respectively, building roads, bridges, viaducts, public buildings, parks, playgrounds, and athletic fields, draining malarial swamps, exterminating rats in slums, organizing nursery schools, teaching illiterate adults, sponsoring dramatic productions, creating public orchestras, providing public murals, sculptures, and paintings, and researching and publishing governmental histories. The difference between Ginsburg's proposal and the employment policy of the 1930s is that she seeks expanded public employment at a period of relatively low unemployment and in a period of inflation. The CWA and WPA operated at a time of relatively high unemployment and in a period of severe deflation. Thus, what may have been salutary for the economy in the 1930s may have drastic results in the 1980s.

Ginsburg disputes the argument of the Phillips curve (pp. 19–20), which observes that prices and wages are inversely related. She claims that, although higher prices lead to higher wages, higher wages do not necessarily lead to higher prices because other costs, such as profits, rent, interest, and materials, are also to be considered. Ginsburg disputes the inflationary effect of wages and therefore justifies expanded employment policy as noninflationary, if controls were to be exerted on other market forces.

Gans is also concerned with the worsening plight of teenagers and nonwhite untrained women in search of employment. He is particularly concerned with the loss of jobs in the American economy brought about by mechanization, by export of manufacturing to overseas labor markets, and by other factors. He believes that the emphasis of public policy should be on the preservation and creation of jobs, especially in private industry, and away from issues of worker productivity. He therefore seeks a labor-intensive economy rather than a capital-intensive economy. Gans proposes the restriction of export of jobs, particularly by multinational corporations, the elimination of depreciation allowances on machines that eliminate jobs, a tax on automation (except in the case of "dirty" stigmatized jobs), and a federal subsidy of private industries which create new "decent" (Gans' term) and permanent jobs. Gans also suggests subsidy of projects that enrich boring jobs. He proposes government aid to industries that seek to create markets for crafted consumer goods and labor-intensive products, including home-grown agricultural products. Gans seeks to cut back on the use of the defense industry as a work-creating mechanism because most defense work is capital-intensive. He also recommends government-created jobs related to marketable services, services which people want and would buy on the private market if they could afford them. He does not specify what these services should be, but he recommends market research for that purpose. He does list people-oriented hospitals, low-cost mental health clinics, nursery schools, jitney (nickel) cab services, weekend hotels for children, schools with smaller classes, neighborhood children's libraries, traveling circuses, small music halls, neighborhood post offices, subsidized "social" coffeeshops in neighborhoods, and even paid volunteer organizational jobs for PTAs.

Gans realizes that his proposal means even higher labor costs than now exist, increased taxes, and a high inflation rate that would make it unacceptable to many. In any case, he expresses a vote against government support by dole rather than by employment.

The contemporary version of publicly sponsored job creation began with the 1973 Comprehensive Employment and Training Act (CETA) (Young and *Congressional Digest*, June/July 1976). This act replaced the Manpower Development and Training Act of 1962, the manpower portions of the Economic Opportunity Act of 1964, and the Emergency Employment Act of 1971. Since its inception, CETA has eliminated a number of regulatory problems inherent in its predecessor organizations. In the process, it has created its own set of complex rules and regulations, which, in Young's opinion, has undermined the "compatability and aggregate effectiveness" of the component programs. The intent of CETA was to transfer decision-making from the federal to local level, a purpose which paralleled the federal revenue-sharing program; to permit local authorities to assess their manpower needs and plan accordingly; and to enable the localities to design their own job and service programs.

Title I provides for grants to state and local governments for recruitment, testing, placement service, classroom and on-the-job training, and supportive services for persons in training or in transitional employment placement. Title II establishes grants to state and local governments in areas that experience an unemployment rate of 6.5 percent or higher for three months or more. With these grants, local and state units create public service jobs which may pay up to $10,000 per year plus fringe benefits. Participants must be underemployed or jobless for at least thirty days. Title III sets up nationally sponsored and supervised training and job placement programs for special populations-at-risk of chronic unemployment, including youth, criminal law offenders, older workers, and people with limited English language ability. This title also provides for nationally operated research and development programs, labor market information projects, and job banks.

Title IV provides for the Job Corps which was created under the War on Poverty. It offers residential programs of intensive education and counseling to young people of both sexes ages sixteen to twenty-one. Title V sets up a National Commission for Manpower Policy, established by the president, to identify manpower needs and goals and to evaluate federal manpower efforts. Title VI, a successor to the 1971 Emergency Employment Act, provides grants for emergency public employment programs to augment the locally administered jobs under Title II. The Title II requirements are somewhat modified under Title VI and VII.

A new Title VIII has been proposed in Congress, aimed specifically at youth employment efforts. The CETA Titles II and VI represented large thrusts in the Carter administration program for economic stimulation in the spring of 1978. Title VI was a particular success in putting people to work in the winter of 1977. With the economic stimulation accomplished and with the growing concern for inflation, funding for Titles II and VI was scheduled to be cut back for fiscal 1978–1979. The Carter Better Jobs and Income program included a plan for 725,000 public service jobs in 1978 under the two titles (a concurrent action with the welfare reform plan). Under this plan, the two titles were to grow to 1.4 million jobs and to be subsumed under a new CETA Title IX, with other CETA projects. Training, summer employment, the Job Corps, and the like would continue independently and unaffected by the welfare reform changes.

The original intent of Title II was to place the economically deprived in public and civil service jobs. According to Young, however, its primary effect is that it allows municipalities to hire supplemental public service employees from the ranks of the unemployed. In many instances where municipal budgets have had to be cut back, Title II has enabled localities to rehire or retain regular employees. As such, Title II is not so much a poverty employment program but a hidden subsidy for local government. Young cites sixty-five American cities in which this use has been documented.

Title VI, on the other hand, has created a variety of local recreational programs, programs for the disabled and ill, programs of specially needed traffic control, supplementation of understaffed hospital emergency rooms, and other necessary community services. It has not, however, succeeded in hiring a sizable proportion of the chronically unemployed and less placeable job-seekers or job-aspirants. In effect, CETA has become another form of revenue sharing, with all of the connotations that make revenue sharing both a blessing and a problem to the community and with few of the intended benefits for those most in need of created jobs. According to Young, 60 to 90 percent of CETA employees are simply stand-ins for normal municipal job-holders.

The congressional mandate of 1977 regarding Title VI required that a greater percentage of all new vacancies be filled by long-time unemployed, by AFDC recipients, or by those who had exhausted their unemployment compensation. Nevertheless, it is doubtful that much change can be expected in the makeup of the CETA employee group. The January 1978 report on manpower research indicated that most CETA partici-pants gained little in terms of increased earnings ability or later job stabil-ity. Thus, a program that was intended to help the poor has, in effect, helped cities keep their tax rates down and has provided jobs for the temporarily unemployed. Those who have suffered under chronic trans-generational unemployment and those with little training, literacy, and few job readiness skills have been relatively unaffected by CETA. As such, CETA, like the U.S. Employment Service, best serves those who need its services least and least serves those in greatest need. If job creation is an answer to the problems of the residual poor, CETA is probably not the appropriate form for effective change.

Employment and the Poor

The Humphrey-Hawkins proposals for full employment go beyond the limited scope of CETA efforts. These proposals are based on the Employ-ment Act of 1946, which embodied a broad policy statement committing the federal government to use its resources and facilities in order to maintain full employment. The act served as the basic rationale for much of the employment legislation of the post-World War II years. The Hum-phrey-Hawkins Bill proposes a broader and expanded policy than the 1946 policy, to the point that 3 percent would be the maximum allowable unemployment level. If unemployment went beyond that level, an auto-matic series of governmental actions would go into effect until that level were attained. The bill establishes the right of every American above sixteen years of age to have "useful paid employment at fair rates of compensation" (*Congressional Digest*). A permanent institutional frame-work would be set up for achieving the goals of the proposal, while constantly monitoring the economy to prevent an increase of inflation through anti-unemployment measures. The bill provides for long-range economic planning, job creation, establishment of an advisory committee for "full employment and balanced growth," training, placement, and utilization of public and private sector opportunities for employment. Special attention would be given to geographically depressed areas, inner cities, and appropriate economic sectors. Where necessary, the federal government would provide an alternate source of capital funds for local and state governments to finance public facilities. Special youth employ-ment provisions are included to provide a smoother transition from school to work, to prepare youths with employment handicaps for self-sustaining employment through education, training, and supporting ser-vices, and to provide special youth employment opportunities through public services, city rehabilitation, conservation, and other useful job assignments. The bill does not claim that it can meet all of the problems of dealing with unemployment. It does provide for additional programs to be devised by the Department of Labor to deal with whatever problems are encountered in attempting to meet the goals of the proposed legislation.

J. Charles Partee of the Federal Reserve Board (*Congressional Digest*) has criticized the bill on the basis that it is too rigid in disallowing unemployment over 3 percent and too inflationary in its effect on the economy and on the price structure. In his view, the anti-inflationary provisions of the bill are vague and weak. The emphasis of support on one national goal must necessarily be considered at the expense of other equally important goals, and, in Pardee's opinion, a goal of 3 percent unemployment is too great an emphasis on one national priority. Another of his criticisms is that the program would encourage workers in the private sector to press for even larger wage gains or to transfer to governmental jobs. The bill would create more unemployment than it cures by inflationary market upheaval.

With regard to the bill, the Council of Economic Advisors has testified (*Congressional Digest*) that "putting people on a public payroll in an unproductive job is not much different than unemployment insurance [in effect] because the activity contributes relatively little to the total national product." The council also believes that the huge mechanism created by the bill would be fundamentally ineffective because of the political considerations that must inevitably become part of such a program. Similarly, the council holds that public jobs programs do not ultimately create significantly more jobs than any other type of current policy. The heavy budget costs for funding such a program might well interfere with the flow of capital investment to the private sector from which most permanent employment emanates. Finally, the council states that the administration of such a law would so increase government employment as to place it far out of proportion to the private job market.

Ulmer believes that the Humphrey-Hawkins Bill "contains the seeds of its own frustration." He asserts that it does not confront the central economic problem it has set out to solve, namely, the fundamental conflict between full employment and price stability. The bill would generate a large economic expansion by huge expenditures on public employment "superimposed on an economy already established on a fairly firm expansion." This would be the equivalent of "feeding children three course meals of ice-cream, cake and candy," and the economy, like the children, would become sick on such a diet. Ulmer believes that premature inflation derives from three decades of oligopolistic industry and labor unions, for whom temporary recessions seem to be no inducement to lower prices and wages in order to maintain volume. The second reason for premature inflation lies in a structural imbalance in the supply and demand for labor.

A large portion of the labor force remains virtually unaffected by recessions; these are the skilled workers, professionals, administrators, technicians, and government employees, a labor group sometimes referred to as the first labor market. When a recession occurs, it is the unskilled and semiskilled who suffer from the rising unemployment rates. (These and the chronically unemployed have sometimes been referred to as the second labor market.)

To expand demand and employment in the contemporary two-labor market is to create overful employment for the first labor market while affecting the second labor market only slightly or not at all. To create as much public employment as proposed under the Humphrey-Hawkins Bill would "unleash a flood of spending in the private business markets with an inflationary impact that could not be contained [even] with price-wage controls." The reason it could not be contained is that the bill for public employment specifies such high rates that they might even "induce as many as ten million men and women to leave private jobs for public work." Only with mandatory selective price controls and appropriate tax policy, Ulmer believes, will it be possible to have full employment without counterproductive runaway inflation.

A symbolic version of the Humphrey-Hawkins Bill was passed in the Ninety-fifth Congress and signed by the president on October 27, 1978. This law commits the government, at least in theory, to an unemployment rate of 4 percent (or less) by 1983 and an inflation rate of 3 percent or less. If the inflation rate is higher than the 3 percent figure, then the government will not be committed to the full employment measures of the law. With a contemporary inflation rate of at least 12 percent and rising and with few measures in effect to control inflation, it is doubtful whether the Humphrey-Hawkins Bill can be expected to be anything more than a statement of unattainable intent.

Ulmer's comments on the two labor markets in relation to public jobs is already apparent in the CETA program. Community action labor specialists interviewed in July 1978 in San Francisco have indicated that on the West Coast, at least, CETA has had little or no impact on the second labor market, and particularly not on the problem of youth unemployment. These same specialists reported that the training provisions of CETA were little used, probably because most CETA workers were already trained and ready for employment.

Faltermayer offers a more logical approach to the unemployment problem than CETA. He suggests that the unemployment problem may be solved by ignoring the overall rate and by concentrating on some particular groups with special problems. The unemployed, he maintains, include many people who have not been laid off or fired; they also include the "voluntary" jobless, (perhaps those taking a sabbatical while on unemployment compensation), those who have unofficially quit their jobs, those looking for first jobs, and those who have decided to reenter the labor force. In this connection, Faltermayer believes that at least half of all unemployment that occurs among the young and among women involves those looking for first jobs, reentries, and the "voluntary" jobless. Unemployment compensation, he says, may be boosting total joblessness by as much as 1 percent, while people are awaiting the right job. Faltermayer does not disparage this activity because it improves the match between workers and jobs and thereby raises overall national productivity.

Faltermayer suggests a special focus on specific populations-at-risk in the unemployment scene. These include youth, workers who have given up trying, those who are socially distant from employment (welfare mothers), and other women who demonstrate a desire for jobs. He believes that special employment services and necessary supporting services should be established for these population groups, providing to each the different kinds of services each would require for employment placement. After each group is served, then other priority groups might be chosen. This approach, he believes, is critically needed in the long-range solution of the present chronic welfare population problem.

From a review of the difficulties in providing employment opportunities for those most in need of them, one must conclude that a massive, unfocused job creation program primarily in the public sector would probably be ineffective and inflationary. Several arguments can be offered in support of such a conclusion. First, a dual employment system exists today. We have a shortage of workers in the skilled sector, coupled with an excess of candidates seeking the few openings for the unskilled jobs which business and government offer at rates of pay comparable to those of the skilled. Second, there is an excess of marginal, low-status jobs which would be attractive to the unskilled if extended unemployment compensation without adequate controls and public assistance did not prove even more attractive to them. Laffer has found that a family of four receives more from public assistance than from employment at standard rates, minus, of course, withholding taxes. Finally, a great number of illegal immigrants in the United States are filling the marginal and beginning positions that would otherwise be the entry-level positions used by the secondary employment force. The number is estimated at 8 to 12 million (*Time*), with an annual increase of 1 million and an unlimited supply from Mexico and other nations. Under such conditions, a massive jobs program further heats up the economy without providing beginning opportunities and a mechanism for upward movement. A jobs program cannot therefore be conceived of in a vacuum. If it is to be effective, a variety of concurrent constraints must be established. These might include:

(1) Tax incentives to encourage labor-intensive rather than capital-intensive plant development and redesign.

(2) Welfare reform which requires acceptance of available employment and/or training for continued eligibility for assistance, along with the reinstatement of the principle of lesser eligibility.

(3) Supportive services (utilizing the job creation process). These services would provide quality day-care centers and transportation to work. The centers would be located in neighborhoods where the welfare clientele resides and would be available at low costs so that employment would be profitable for the welfare clientele and their children. These services would be preceded by training programs of day-care personnel, utilizing the chronically unemployed in great part.

(4) Occupational and literacy training for the chronically unemployed in depth and design similar to the Workmen's Institutes of England and other such successful programs. The job creation process would largely be used to staff these programs, which would be located mostly in neighborhoods where the chronically unemployed live. These institutes would concentrate not only on skills and literacy training, but also on the development of job readiness, on learning mainstream roles necessary for employment, and on resolving the chronically unemployed's defeatist attitude as well as unwillingness to take a risk. There would be a training program for institute personnel, utilizing in great part the pool of unskilled unemployed.

(5) The creation of entry-level jobs for specific target groups—the welfare mother, minority teenager, and so forth—with projects to be established utilizing local voluntary organizations rather than political units. The requirements would be to provide permanent employment in the private sector and upgrade skills within specified periods of time, each to be standardized to the person's beginning level of skills and the particular career track.

(6) Use of the job creation process to double the number of teachers and teachers' aides in ghetto schools, so as to ensure more literacy among job applicants at the entry level. Annual testing would measure success in learning and teaching the mainstream language.

(7) Use of the job creation process to train and install employment career coordinators. These coordinators would be required to work with school attendants, their parents, potential employers, and employment training institutions, so that each student would have his own employment goal, as well as viable and realistic plans for its achievement. Each coordinator would follow up on each graduate to assure his transition

from high school to entry-level work or further training and would also work with potential dropouts. The job of the coordinator would not be based on school attendance hours. Much of the work would be done on weekends, afternoons, and evenings.

(8) A concerted effort to upgrade marginal employment in status, pay rate, and job benefits. Low-level aide jobs in hospitals could be redesigned in a manner similar to the warrant-officer track of the military, providing for greater security on the job, upward mobility, increased job benefits, and status. Employers offering marginal employment could be partially subsidized in order to offer increased benefits and pay to the unskilled. Appropriate safeguards would be added to ensure that the employer would not use the subsidy as a means of saving money on labor costs and that the employer would offer on-the-job training opportunities for the employee. Similar mechanisms can be developed for hundreds of thousands of household employment slots by establishing thousands of neighborhood home service companies, with uniforms, status, and benefits to provide household maintenance on a monthly or weekly basis. These jobs are currently unfilled or are served by underground employment arrangements whereby housewives on welfare, illegal immigrants, or unemployment compensation beneficiaries contract secretly and illegally without either withholding tax or Social Security taxes. This type of black-market employee would no longer be available with a jobs requirement attached to AFDC and with more thorough supervision of unemployment compensation payments. This market is currently estimated at $6 billion (Lawrence). At the same time, stricter enforcement of household employment deductions and payments might be instituted in the tax mechanisms.

(9) A lowering, or even elimination, of federal and state income taxes (and withholding taxes) at the lower earning levels, so that the chronically unemployed could accept employment as a way of having more money than on public assistance.

(10) At least a selective relaxation of the minimum wage for specific target groups, so that employers might find it economically feasible to employ unskilled applicants for beginning-level positions.

(11) Discouragement of the United States as a market for illegal immigrants by installing a sizable fine for employers for each offense in the hiring of employees without proof of citizenship or legal admission, as proposed by the Carter administration (*Congressional Digest*, October 1977).

An argument could be made that these proposals would cost too much. Such an argument holds up only if the current and growing costs of chronic unemployment and welfare are considered. It could also be argued that the proposals are inflationary in effect, but such inflation is limited in time in that it provides for increased productivity and lessened payment of unproductive income transfers. But it is our position that only through such a multithrust approach can the employment problem be effectively resolved.

Killingsworth emphasizes that, although employment will never be the entire answer to the welfare problem, the lack of it has a significant bearing on the erosion of human resources in the poverty and welfare populations. Ferguson underscores the interaction between ineffective schooling, slum housing, discrimination, miscellaneous other social ills, and chronic unemployment. Faltermayer recommends that specific re-training and reemployment efforts be focused on those population subcategories with high levels of unemployment and that such efforts be designed around their needs, interests, and special problems.

Sheppard indicates that the antipoverty efforts of 1959–1966 improved the condition of only male-headed families and that the number of poor in female-headed families actually increased during this period. In the seven years since his study, this condition has worsened. It is apparently difficult to provide employment to females who are heads of families with young children. Studies of these clients over the past ten years have shown them to be unavailable for employment because of child-care needs, illness, and general unavailability because of home duties (Califano).

Thus, the only contribution job creation and training can make in resolving poverty and welfare problems is in terms of preventing the condition of unemployment which creates female-headed families in poverty. To carry this objective out, the government must necessarily focus on unemployed young men. Only if these males are provided with opportunities to build whole families will the society avoid the creation of yet another welfare generation, multiplied in number and knowing no other way of life but welfare.

The Minimum Wage

The minimum wage made its first appearance on the American scene in Massachusetts in 1912, and a number of states soon followed suit. Such wage floors were originally established to cover women and children in industry. The intent was not so much to raise the income level of workers directly as to protect the employment of men whose jobs were threatened by the low-wage competition of women and children (*Congressional Digest*). This matter was a particular concern of organized labor.

Early state wage and hour restrictions were hampered by a number of adverse court rulings, especially during the decade immediately preceding the enactment of the first federal minimum wage law in 1938. By the time that law took effect, sizable pressure for federal legislation had built up, and already a third of the states had enacted legislation on the minimum wage. Since that time, the minimum wage rate has been raised continually in an attempt to enable the lowest paid employee, working forty hours per week, to earn enough to provide basic subsistence for himself and his family.

The minimum wage at the state level was not too successful in achieving a minimal family subsistence for the lowest paid full-time worker. Competition from other states where minimum wages were not enacted prevented the expansion of the program to other states and the raising of the minimum wage for fear of outpricing employment opportunities for many states. This defect in the minimum wage was eliminated with the passage of the federal minimum wage legislation in 1938.

A second flaw in the minimum wage as a floor for the level of basic family subsistence for the lowest paid workers was not met by federal minimum wage legislation as originally enacted. The national minimum wage regulation necessarily permitted the exemption of a number of marginal employees and industries. It was thought that many of these industries and establishments would not be able to survive if they were required to meet the federal minimum wage regulations. These included certain retail or service establishments, gasoline stations, construction or reconstruction, contractors, laundry and cleaning firms, hospitals and nursing homes, and agriculture. Over the years, most of the exemptions have been eliminated or restricted.

In the history of poor law and social policy, there is little general discussion of the minimum wage as a mechanism for poverty resolution. The exceptions are the juxtaposed economic writings of Alfred Marshall and John Stuart Mill. Marshall proposed a legal minimum wage as a method of increasing the incentive of labor for productivity, which would lead to raising the share of benefits accruing to employees, employers, and consumers. Marshall viewed the low level of wages paid to marginal workers as an extravagance of the economy and a negligence of the valuable resource of human labor. Mill considered any effort to influence workers' incomes as ineffectual. In his opinion, minimum wages were in the same category as wage subsidies, guaranteed employment, and agricultural allotments: all interfered with the process by which wages and prices find their own level, and thus they disturbed the process of normative market control.

According to this economic theory, wages when uncontrolled by law are set, as are other prices, at a rate at which supply and demand are brought into equilibrium. When the wages fall too low, too few workers will apply for or stay on the job. When the wages go too high, more workers seek employment and so the wages fall. The employer will hire as many workers as he needs to make a profit. If he can hire more workers and thereby produce more goods for the market at a profit, he will do so. If he hires too many, his profits will fall, and he will discharge the less productive workers (or the more expensive from a productivity viewpoint). After a specific point is reached, as more workers are taken on, the additional rate of increased output declines as does the employer's income. If an employer is restricted from hiring people below a specific wage, he will be motivated to discharge the least productive workers (or hire fewer workers) until a point of equilibrium is reached where marginal employer profits match marginal employer losses. A minimum wage in a competitive market for labor and goods therefore results in unemployment (Von Mises).

Wilcox (pp. 219–20) points out that in a competitive market the employer cannot rig the wage level or control the market by hiring or firing employees. His only choice is to determine how many workers he will hire. The minimum wage is thus seen not as a safeguard against inhumane employers, but rather as a mechanism to prevent the employment market from falling so low that workers will be hired at less than a bare subsistence wage.

An increase in the minimum wage does not create a proportionate decrease in employment when the labor cost is only a small part of the total cost of the product. In like manner, where the demand for the product is so inelastic that the cost can be passed on to the consumer, unemployment is not a result. When an employer cannot substitute machinery for labor without severe short-run losses, the level of employment is not affected. Another instance in which the minimum wage has no effect on employment occurs in industries that have been operating at a loss which is either subsidized by government or drawn from capital resources. Where these conditions do not prevail, most economists agree that the minimum wage does increase unemployment.

In Australia and New Zealand, when the minimum wage was first introduced, the cost of labor was small compared to other costs of production. Hence, the institution of the minimum wage at that time did not cut employment, and the net effect of that experiment in social legislation was to raise the level of living standards for the lowest paid workers. Examples of inelastic demand for a product whose added costs can be passed on to the consumers are various utilities. Their products (water, gas, electricity, and the like) are essential, and increases in prices are paid without too much consumer resistance.

An example of the short-run indispensability of labor is found in the fruit and produce industry which often pays increased wages during the harvest season. The long-run pattern in this industry has resulted in a technology that provides planting, harvesting, and other machines for almost every type of fruit and vegetable. Except for marginal companies that are insufficiently capitalized, most of this industry can be expected to be fully mechanized in the coming decades.

Despite numerous empirical studies of the effects of the minimum wage, many problems in deriving a fair test of the minimum wage remain. These problems are compounded by a variety of extraneous factors. The first is the differential enforcement of minimum wage laws. In some localities, these laws are fully enforced, and in others, not at all. Some industries enforce the laws stringently, and others do not. The problem of enforcement is compounded by the nature of various industries, which makes the minimum wage less enforceable in some industries than in others.

Difficulty in enforcement is often built into particular industries and services. In some settings, the employer avoids the minimum wage by classifying many jobs as piece work. On such jobs, the employee is paid for the number of items he produces or processes. It is in the interest of the employer not to set the rate so high that he will take a loss on the production. By setting the rate at a particular figure, he can demonstrate that his skilled employees are paid at a rate that is above the minimum wage. Such a wage mechanism also aids the employer in avoiding the high cost of supervision since it is in the interest of the employee to work responsibly for maximum payment. The employer needs merely to check the quality of the products to preserve his interests. This method of payment discourages the unskilled worker from such employment and, to all intents and purposes, limits such employment to skilled workers. Learners can be paid less than a minimum wage by indicating that they have been paid what they earned. Piece work is therefore an effective mechanism for eliminating the less productive worker from the marketplace. The minimum wage law has little or no effect on such industries.

Another mechanism for avoiding the effect of the minimum wage is common to the restaurant industry. Here the employer is required to pay a minimum wage, but he is permitted to credit to that minimum a percentage of the tips which his employees receive. When the minimum wage was raised in California in recent years, many employers concurrently announced an increase in the percentage of tips calculated as credited in the minimum wage. In the process, the employees did not measurably benefit from the established raise in minimum rates.

Still another mechanism in the restaurant industry is one concerning the meals served to employees as part of their remuneration. Because the rate for such meals is less for employees than that charged to customers, employers merely raise the employee meal rates to cover the difference between the new minimum wage and the prior minimum wage. The employee cannot avoid this rate increase by eating elsewhere because the meal is a required deduction on his wage. A raise in the minimum does not usually benefit the employee in such instances.

Every time the minimum wage is raised, the restaurant industry also has the option of either paying the increased wage and cutting costs elsewhere, or restructuring its service to eliminate a massive number of services that require labor. An increase in self-service restaurants in locations that were previously full service became quite visible after a recent minimum wage increase. Restaurants discovered how to retain a status atmosphere while becoming self-service cafeterias where the customers did most of the fetching and carrying. In such instances the minimum wage increase eliminated marginal, and even some skilled, restaurant employment without benefit to the employees who are the presumed target population for the minimum wage.

The restaurant industry is only one of many which have been able to avoid the effect of the minimum wage on their establishment. The supermarkets, both food and other merchandise, are now operable with a minimum of employees, in great part as a result of a rising minimum wage structure. A mass of grocery clerks, drug, hardware, and sundry salesmen and saleswomen have been entirely eliminated from industry, partly as a result of a law which sought to raise wages for the unskilled.

Factors other than the minimum wage also have an effect on the employment rate. Business cycles create expansion and contraction of employment for reasons unaffected by the minimum wage. The exemption of a sizable number of occupations from the minimum wage provisions has made it difficult to measure the effect of such legislation. If, for example, workers are displaced by employment covered by the minimum wage and are thus forced to enter other more marginal, noncovered occupations, this changeover is not reflected in the employment rate. Marginal workers who drop out of the employment market after having been laid off because of a rising minimum wage are not reflected in the statistics.

There is serious concern for the effect of the minimum wage on the level of employment in the society. Workers who are most harmed by the minimum wage are those whose productivity is low and whose skills and indispensability are limited (Friedman and Welch and Kosters). The aged, many of whom found partial employment in the past, have been generally excluded from the labor market in recent years. With the exception of those who have a skill that is in great demand, the physically handicapped have also found it more difficult in recent years to secure employment. Those blacks, Chicanos, and Puerto Ricans who have not provided themselves with adequate literacy, job competency, desired skills, and job readiness are among those displaced by increases in the minimum wage. Unskilled women, who in the past may have been utilized as surplus workers in industries that could afford to keep them available for special work needs at low rates, have been priced out of the employment market. (Increasing numbers of skilled women, however, are being hired to service machines that have been introduced to replace hundreds of other workers.) Finally, those who are most grievously affected by the minimum wage increases are the youngsters who have never been employed. When the general unemployment rate is 9 percent, the unemployment rate for the still youthful, never meaningfully employed often approaches 18 percent. The rate for black, Chicano, and Puerto Rican unskilled, inexperienced youth is often double that. The problems for society encompassed in such a high minority-youth unemployment rate can be appreciated when one realizes that the geographical location of violent youth gangs can be predicted by such data. The lack of meaningful employment for young minority members, especially young men, is reflected in the low level of family stability among the urban poor and probably in the high rates of unmarried motherhood. Regularly employed men tend to settle into stable and responsible familial relationships. Unemployment and lack of hope for stable male employment is probably reflected in various indices of urban instability and unrest.

When enforced, the minimum wage does raise the hourly wage received by workers, and to that extent it does increase the incomes of those who are retained in employment. This effect is often circumvented, at least to some extent, by employers in marginal industries where the lowest paid workers abound.

Levy, Lewis, and Martin's (pp. 788–89) review of the data deriving from the research on the minimum wage over recent decades shows that the minimum wage raises the hourly wage received, and to that extent it increases income. But the minimum wage, they find, cannot and does not increase the hours of work available. Neither does the minimum wage do anything to resolve the problem of inadequate family income. They believe that only an increase in total family income or a decrease in family size will help in such an instance, and the minimum wage does neither. If the minimum wage were to be assigned the task of increasing total family income, the required hourly wage would have to be set so high as to price most products out of the market. Thus, they maintain, the minimum wage is not a social policy tool oriented to family size.

Lichtenstein and Friedman and Brozen have found that high minimum wage rates do more harm than good in the battle against poverty. This effect is clearly evident in the fact that over one-third of the working poor have families of six or more members. Reliance on the minimum wage to eliminate poverty would require family-size wage differentials. Two employees doing the same work would be paid wages that would be so disparate as to cause conflict between the employees and the employees and the employer. Even if the workers with few or no children were to accept such a program, its workability would still be in doubt because employers would be tempted to hire the employees they could secure at the lowest cost, and these would be the ones without children. A minimum wage with a family-size differential would, in effect eliminate employment for the intended beneficiaries of the measure.

Gans (1967) points out that the lowest wages in the society are tied to jobs that are less prestigious, physically dirty, and deadend. He believes that a raise in the minimum wage might be acceptable if it eliminates jobs no one should be asked to perform. If possible, a job should be automated rather than have the marginal worker subsidize the products for the consumer by having him accept a substandard wage. If a job cannot be automated and the product is dropped from the market, Gans believes no real harm is done. He does maintain that a number of other low-paying jobs which are necessary for the public good, such as the jobs of orderlies in hospitals, should be subsidized by the society if they cannot be funded by the employer. In this way, the cost of such services would not have to be subsidized by marginal workers or financially pressed consumers. Gans' proposal (1967) raises questions which relate more to income subsidies than to the minimum wage. (See Chapter 5.)

The minimum wage has been found to be responsible for pricing unskilled workers and low-paying jobs out of the market. It also has inflationary effects which fall most heavily on the poor and the lower middle class. As the minimum wage is raised in various industries, professional and skilled employees and employees covered by union protection and civil service become disturbed that they are paid little more than the lowest paid employees. By negotiation, job changes, and union pressure, these wages are periodically raised to provide an adequate differential between the unskilled and the skilled. The result is the encouragement of a general wage spiral which is soon reflected in an increased cost of living. Persons who are on fixed incomes such as the aged on retirement, civil servants, and persons on public assistance suffer most from inflated costs, while persons with sizable disposable incomes are less affected. Hence, the minimum wage, which was intended to improve conditions for the poor, has the reverse effect of tightening the problems of economic survival for the poor.

An increase in the minimum wage has a particularly devastating effect on minority teenage employment. When the minimum wage is set at a figure beyond which an employer can possibly gain profitable employment from teenagers, such individuals are completely shut out of entry-level employment openings. When this situation occurs, and it does occur very frequently, the result is the creation of an entire population sector which is almost entirely secluded from interaction with most others for most of their lifetimes. Ultimately, we have a form of social dynamite and problems of social control not originally intended by supporters of the minimum wage.

Meyerson accepts the Rand Corporation findings that increases in the minimum wage from 1956 to 1968 have cumulatively reduced the absorption of teenagers into the employment marketplace by 15 percent. Canada and Japan, which have also encountered this phenomenon, have adopted a lower minimum wage for teenagers in order to enable their entry into employment. Adults who have had no prior experience are usually unemployable. Only if teenage experience is possible can individuals be employable as young adults. A lower, rather than a higher, minimum wage might have been a more appropriate gift to the minority teenage youngsters in poverty.

Wilcox (p. 227) concludes that poverty is less effectively attacked by excluding workers from employment. We may add that poverty is not resolved by increasing the poverty of the poverty population. The minimum wage may be highly effective in a low labor-cost economy, but not in a high labor-cost economy. In Welch's opinion (1978), the minimum wage is "perverse, transferring income from some have nots to other have nots." He believes that "the idea was misguided in 1938, and after 40 years of evidence of adversity, its time has passed."

The minimum wage is only one of a number of social policy mechanisms which have been instituted with the best intentions but which have been based on simplistic conventional wisdom rather than on sociological analysis and an examination of societal processes. In the effort to "do good," such attempts at humane social legislation have ignored the realities of the marketplace and, in the process, have done great harm to the intended beneficiaries.

Education and Mobility

The history of the United States is replete with examples of the upward movement of the immigrant and the poor within the societal pyramid. In a New York City elementary school, the cast of characters might include a German principal, an Irish teacher, and Jewish students in one era who would be succeeded in the next era by a Jewish principal, a black teacher, and Puerto Rican students. The history of the United States is the story of a nation of successive immigrants who made the most of their educational opportunities and who used the occupations of teaching, law, business, and other professions to attain financial security and middle-class status.

The fact that schooling does make a difference in upward mobility is revealed by the comparative jobless rates of school leavers at eight years, twelve years, and sixteen or more years of schooling. (See Table 8.1.) The facts are that for each educational achievement group, a smaller percen-

TABLE 8.1   **Unemployment among Young Workers Ages Sixteen to**
Twenty-four in 1977, by Educational Achievement (*Percentage*)

EDUCATIONAL ACHIEVEMENT	HISPANICS	BLACKS	WHITES	MEN	WOMEN
Elementary					
Less than 8 years	11.1	*	18.3	14.1	28.4
8 years	*	*	29.2	30.1	32.7
High School					
1-3 years	25.6	41.3	19.6	21.5	22.6
4 years	15.6	27.8	11.1	14.1	12.6
College					
1-3 years	10.8	18.4	8.1	8.8	9.3
4 years or more	*	19.8	7.4	8.2	8.4

*The researchers did not reveal a percent where the base was less than 75,000.
SOURCE: Michelotti, Table 2.

tage of workers are unemployed at the higher educational levels. Thus, 92 percent of young men with a college education and 78 percent of high school graduates are employed. Similarly, almost all Hispanics with a college education are employed, and among high school graduates nearly 74 percent are employed. Blacks who have a college degree have a 93 or so percent assurance of employment, and those with a high school education, a 63 or so percent assurance. Women with a college degree have over a 90 percent assurance of employment, and those with a high school diploma, a 70 percent assurance.

To drop out before one has completed one's education is therefore the equivalent of opting for unemployment. This situation becomes even more critical with each increase in the technological requirements of the contemporary employment setting. The viewpoint that schooling does make a difference is supported by Avereh, et al., Bowles, and Summers and Wolfe.

Education as a means of achieving upward mobility is based on a number of assumptions:

That the educational process will be carried out under conditions which will maximize the child's learning. The content of learning will presumably include the language and conceptual competencies necessary to enable the learner to become a self-sufficient, fully responsible member of society. When the child's self-concept increases as a result of his learning successes, as recognized by himself, his parents, and his teacher, he will have a greater readiness to participate in the society. It is also presumed that the students will be universally respected by teachers and school personnel so that their self-image and confidence are not traumatized. In the symbolic interaction view effective learning occurs when the teacher clearly reports the validation of learning successes and failures to the learner. It is important that the teacher's expectations for the learner's achievements not be biased by irrelevant stereotypes which might ultimately create a self-fulfilling prophesy fallacy. If biased, the teacher expects less achievement from the student than is appropriate.

That the child's background will be such that his learning of mainstream competencies will be maximized. For such maximized learning, the child's homelife would provide

- A minimum of social-psychological strains within the family which might otherwise serve as a handicap in the focusing of the child's full attention on the learning process.
- An adequate provision of nutritional, medical, and physical accommodations for the child, so that physical debilitation would not serve as a barrier to learning.
- A cultural atmosphere in the home which serves as a bridge to the child's learning in the school. Despite the fact that the home may derive from a culture different from that of the mainstream and the school, it is assumed that the competencies taught in the school will have been introduced as valued learning in the home. It is also assumed that events in the home will have some relevancy to the learning at school and vice versa. Thus, success in life as defined by school learning will not be contradicted in the home.
- A value system in the home which is in consonance with the value system in the school. Thus, if honesty, truth, self-reliance, and responsibility are values of the school, these will be at least supported as values in the home.
- An atmosphere in the home and in the nonschool life space of the child which is not in severe competition with the school for the child's time and attention. If the street life of the child is full of activity and if the home and community do not support the school's demand for the primacy of school learning as a basic preparation for life, the child may be accepting the message that success in school is less important than making it on the street.
- A family structure and cohesion which will retain control of the child until he has become adequately socialized to adherence to mainstream norms of behavior. For an examination of the differential school-home conditions of children in middle-class suburban neighborhoods and poverty-level urban neighborhoods, see Table 8.2.

While much has been written about the failure of the schools in poverty areas, little has been written about the role of the home and neighborhood in providing the necessary support without which school learning cannot be effective. Whereas the middle-class home prepares the child, serves as his trainer and cheering section in the competition for success in school, and ensures his continued focus on school rather than on other child-like or adult pursuits, the poverty home and community provide little or no school supportive services.

TABLE 8.2 Differences in the School-Home Conditions of Children in Middle-Class Suburban Neighborhoods and Poverty-Level Urban Neighborhoods

	MIDDLE-CLASS SUBURBAN NEIGHBOORHOODS	POVERTY-LEVEL URBAN NEIGHBORHOODS
Context of learning taught	Primarily preparation for high school and college. High level of mainstream learning competency achieved.	Much less emphasis on college. Much more time spent on trying to keep order. Thus, lower level of mainstream competency achieved.
Self-concept deriving from learning competencies and successes	High	Low
Readiness to participate in mainstream activities derived from school learning	High	Low
Teacher and principal expectations of child's learning potentials	High	Low
Degree of social-psychological strains in family of learners	Believed to be low generally. Family makes a special attempt to keep child in a state of readiness for school learning.	Believed to be high among poverty families. Inability of family to plan ahead leaves family in crisis as a steady condition.
Nutritional, medical, and physical conditions	Watched constantly in regard to medical, nutritional, and physical needs. Most have an exclusive place to study, to rest, and so forth. Children undergo frequent medical and dental supervision.	Little or no regular medical or nutritional supervision. When such supervision is provided in school, it is at the expense of learning time. Poverty children live in crowded homes without spaces designated for their study and rest.
Cultural atmosphere of home as related to school	Usually an adequate number and variety of role-models available for whom schooling and learning are important. Such models emphasize to the child the need to succeed in school for the purpose of life-goals. Role-models are related to mainstream patterns and expectations.	Usually an inadequate number and variety of role-models who are in any way concerned with school success and are knowledgeable how it can be a basis for life-goals. In many cases, role-models are antagonistic to school.

Table 8.2—*Continued*

	MIDDLE-CLASS SUBURBAN NEIGHBORHOODS	POVERTY-LEVEL URBAN NEIGHBORHOODS
Value system of home as related to school	Congruent value systems. Home values support school values generally.	Highly noncongruent value systems. Home emphasis is on making it through the day or week. Home priorities are so different from those of the school as to make the successful school learning seem to be highly out of place at home.
Adherence to school and learning as a first priority for the child	Home and community highly supportive of school as a priority for child. Nonschool activities during school day are nonexistent. Child labor during school day is discouraged. Children are redirected to school when found out of it during school day.	Home activities usually unplanned. School is often a lesser priority if someone is needed to stay with younger children. If family is in dire straits, child is often encouraged to go out and "scrounge." Generally, the street and its activities operate throughout the school day, and children are not turned away from spectating or participating.

In calling attention to the parent's critical role in socializing the child for education and in sustaining the child's interest in and motivation for educational and later occupational success, we do not intend to lay all the blame on the parent when a child drops out or does not learn. A successful educational experience requires both parent preparation of the child and competent teaching at the school. We hypothesize that if A represents the parents' activity and if B represents the school's function, and if C represents successful learning, then $A + B = C$. But no matter how hard the parent tries, if the school fails to perform well, $2A$ will not equal C. In addition, no matter how hard the school tries, if the parent fails the child, $2B$ will not equal C. The true state of urban education is that, for many ghetto children, a too weak parental socialization for education and a too weak school teaching process do not yield an adequate learning experience.

A paradoxical discussion can be entered into if we seek to apportion blame for the failure of the poverty child in school. William Ryan in *Blaming the Victim* holds the schools fully accountable for their successes and failures, and completely disregards the differential degree of readiness for learning and support of learning provided by the homes, families, and communities of the putative learners. A counterpart argument can be made, putting the onus of responsibility on the families of the putative learners. Both positions could be supported with considerable data, both could be considered correct positions, and both could be deemed faulty, depending upon the evaluator's use of crisis or consensus societal models.

A parallel paradox can be found in a study of the causes of poverty. Utilizing the consensual model of society (discussed in Chapter 1), one may conclude that those who fall between the cracks of the societal structure are less competent than others or in some way are less able to make their way. We may therefore conclude that people in poverty have failed in some way. The counterpart argument is that people fall out of the society because there are holes in the structure that are unsafe and that represent a failure of the planners and maintainers. Thus, we should be blaming not the victim but the careless system and its administrators. Still another, more plausible, argument can be made. In constructing this argument, one may ask, why do some people fall through the holes in the system and others do not? The answer is that some people are careful and others are not. Thus, the third argument views the fallout problem as carelessness on the part of both the designers and users of the system. This is the interaction argument—that such accidents are the result of an interaction between system design failures and individual carelessness. In a discussion of how people fall into poverty and then remain in poverty, we soon arrive at the conclusion that such a condition is a result of the continued interaction of systemic and individual factors. (These factors are discussed in Chapter 3.)

The interactive process is very evident in the learning successes of the schools. Children who have learned to learn early in life and who respect learning because of parental and other influences enter the schools with a desire to succeed. The families service their children in terms of continued learning readiness and learning support. The schools are constantly consulted by the families on ways and means of providing familial and community support to child learning. The schools call the family's attention to any deviation by the child from adherence to the norms of school operation which might interfere with the child's or another's learning progress. The family will punish such infractions. In general, the school expects high levels of performance from the child, as does the family. The child is constantly motivated to learn by family emphasis, interest, and activity.

Without seeking to apportion blame or responsibility between parents and school, it should be noted that such cooperation between home and school seldom exists in poverty families. Generally, the poverty families cannot match the sophisticated support of the school provided by many middle-class families. Poverty families have to devote more time and energy to economic survival as well as to physical survival in the ghetto. Accordingly, they have little time and energy to concern themselves with child success in school, even if they have the skills and equipment to do so. Pressure from schools to provide such support will often meet with familial resentment or avoidance. Similarly, the low expectations for children held by the teachers in ghetto schools will seldom, if ever, be connected by the families with the lack of familial preparation for learning and support of learning.

The quality of the schools in urban ghettos must also be considered in any study of the failure of education with poverty children. Such schools usually have less experienced teachers and a greater proportion of substitutes who are assigned on such a short-term basis that lesson planning is difficult or impossible. In some of the schools, the teachers may tend to label poverty children as unteachable, although this effect is often offset by the assignment of new teachers who are young, idealistic, and unencumbered with stereotypes. (These teachers usually do not have adequate seniority to elect assignment to the suburban, middle-class schools.) As Steele shows, the effectiveness of negative labeling is itself an uncertain issue. He points out that labeling takes hold only if the child is vulnerable —and that depends upon how much preparation, socialization, and orientation to learning tasks the child has previously received (primarily at home).

Why do so many ghetto children drop out early from school? The dropout is a pushout as well, and vice versa. Such early leavers and their counterparts—the social graduates, those who complete school without the necessary competencies—are probably the result of an interactive process in which both the families and schools are responsible. (This discussion excludes children with learning problems caused by genetic or somatic reasons.) In many cases, the families and the schools are themselves unable to provide adequate participation in the child's learning. In the case of the ghetto schools, there are problems of inadequate budgets, less competent teachers as a result of low budgets, or school location in high crime and violence neighborhoods, teachers with prejudicial attitudes toward ghetto children, and general administrative inadequacies deriving from the school's marginality. In the case of the families, there is a high proportion of female-headed families who cannot provide the variety of role-models related to school success, who have a low level of family income and continued financial, medical, and legal crises which make the family less functional as a school support. In the case of transgenerational poverty families, this situation is aggravated by sheer lack of understanding of the relevance of schooling to a possible upgrading from the poverty level. Such families often provide negative role-models, such as is the case with many teenage mothers in welfare families.

In resolving this dilemma, the issue must not devolve on apportioning blame to school and family. On the contrary, the issue is one of better understanding the inadequacies of ghetto schools and families so that legislative interventions may be planned and a positive interactive process for maximized school learning may be established.

The inadequacies of ghetto schools can probably be largely resolved by obtaining increased resources and competent personnel for them. Competent personnel would, of course, have to be motivated to move to and remain in ghetto schools. Such an incentive could be in the form of a differential salary scale and increased benefits for teaching. It is doubtful that busing ghetto children out of the ghetto or suburban children into the ghetto has much effect on the ghetto child's learning. The better approach lies in improving the family's contribution to the learning situation.

Among the more effective contributions of the War on Poverty were the Head Start and Follow Through programs which sought to build the family's involvement in the schooling of poverty children. These programs attempted to provide a high level of parental involvement by means of parents' advisory and administrative committees related to their children's early schooling. They also focused on learning goals and methods that parents of poverty children could understand and that could be translated into mainstream learning competencies. An attempt was made to involve a limited number of middle-class children and parents (no more than 10 percent) in order to bridge the gap between middle-class mainstream and poverty cultures.

Head Start was designed primarily as a preschool experience; Follow Through was developed later to provide continued parental involvement and advanced learning for poverty children in the early grades. Head Start sought to provide poverty children with an in-depth preparation for school learning to match some of the preparation given middle-class children by their families. Some of the Head Start Programs were located in voluntary agencies and nonschool institutions, and others were operated by and located in regular public schools. When the auspices of Head Start classes occurred outside the traditional school system methodology, the children often learned rapidly and developed a sense of self-competence. Their newfound skills became a problem when they entered public schools and met teachers who were unused to such "knowing" children. In areas where Head Start was conducted in traditional school settings, the programs were geared to fit into the expectancy patterns of public school teachers in the ghetto.

By and large, Head Start suffered from a number of problems which were built into the programs. First, it was difficult to involve parents when the predominant family pattern was that of female-headed families and when the mother was either employed full time or overloaded with other family responsibilities or concerns. A second problem was the conflict of cultures between the schools and poverty families which had been kept on the back-burners for decades and which suddenly confronted the personnel of the programs. Another was how to meaningfully involve ghetto parents without launching a parallel adult education program in depth to orient the parents to the mainstream's goals of education. Still another problem related to the need to develop mechanisms to introduce role-models into the lives of Head Start children other than those of the welfare mother, the working (and overworked mother), the unidentified man who "visits" the mother, and the female teachers who represent another culture and society. A continuing problem involves providing adequately innovative learning relevant to the life of the Head Start child within a school system at a local, state, and federal level which is highly professionalized and which maintains strong boundary defenses. A final problem is how to help Head Start children retain their sense of self-confidence at early grade levels within teacher and student cultures that devalue learning precocity.

The costs of Head Start and Follow Through are not negligible. With so few controlled studies of Head Start programs under differential auspices, teaching modalities, and conditions, it is impossible to predict which conditions and auspices can provide the most significant learning competency results at the most favorable cost/benefit ratio. Nevertheless, it is important that Head Start and Follow Through be continued, providing controlled studies are conducted concurrently. (See Barnow).

Even if Head Start were refined, redesigned, and developed for maximum cost effectiveness, it is doubtful that it could be very useful in resolving poverty unless other aspects of the problem were dealt with. For example, some sort of stable financial support of the family would be needed while children are in school. In addition, some sort of legislative intervention which would make learning a desired condition for poverty parents to support would be desirable. Some means would also have to be developed to perpetuate whatever gains Head Start made, so that they could continue in grade and high school. Some programs might be developed to produce similar learning gains for poverty children in high school. Finally, the problem of how to serve children whose parents are either uninterested in their children's schooling or ineffective influences over their children's activities is yet to be resolved.

In any case, it should be noted that learning failures tend to perpetuate cyclical poverty. These failures cannot be traced only to schools or families or communities. They are also a product of interactive dysfunctionality, and they can be solved only if an objective viewpoint is retained and plans to tackle these problems are developed within the society.

In an article written during the heat of the War on Poverty, John Hersey listed ten major points about the schools in relation to poverty. His first point is that education, by itself, cannot wipe out the manifold causes of poverty, even if education were applied with maximal effectiveness over a series of generations. Hersey uses the example of one city with changing neighborhoods which found that its schools were required to deal with "a swirling and eddying mass of humanity." New minority families were forever moving in, "staying a while, being evicted, moving up and down the social ladder" and many moving horizontally (p. 157). The middle-income and professional people were moving out to the suburbs, technical workers were shifting with changing jobs, and people were being ousted by slum clearance programs. Few in the city were staying put long enough for the schools to have any lasting effect on the children, and for reasons unrelated to the schools.

Hersey's second point is that, in the last analysis, the poor themselves have the task of climbing out of poverty. Any action by the schools to help the poor move their children out of poverty will require the action and involvement of the poor. The initiative must come from the parents and cannot be paternalistic pseudo-involvement in which the poor are objects rather than actors. Hersey's third point is that new educational conditions are required if education is to be effective with the poor. These conditions must necessarily be the product of cooperation among all the agencies and interests involved with the schools. Such a working alliance of political elements, local, state, and federal entities, and others can be achieved only if these elements and the society in general desire more effective ghetto schools. Without such support, education remains a concern primarily of professional educators and middle-class parents whose children have something to gain from education.

Hersey's emphasis on the school as an arena of cooperation among political elements, local parents, and educational professionals is important if public education is to play an effective role in providing upward mobility for the underclass, let alone to continue to serve as the major socialization mechanism for the democratic mainstream society. The facts are that public education is currently "facing a loss of public confidence which could prove fatal [to it]." As a result of court orders spurred by desegregationist forces, which have often had more concern for equalizing education than for maintaining its quality, public education has undergone severe changes. Participation by whites and middle-class minorities has diminished as forced busing has influenced sizable numbers of families to flee further out into the suburbs. The unwillingness of the public to support educational budgets and construction has left public education with less money to deal with children who, with each generation, are even less prepared for schooling, regardless of their socioeconomic stratum. The result has been an increasingly less effective educational process for all. The 1970 study by the United Nations (released by

Senator George McGovern) indicates that at that time illiteracy in the United States was three times that of the Soviet Union. At least 2 million Americans of normal intelligence were functionally illiterate, and U.S. students scored an average in mathematics of 31 points below British students, 25.5 points below Japanese students, and 21.1 points below West German students. Thus, public education, even if supported by the necessary family socialization for mainstream purposes, is even less able now to resolve the educational problems of the residual poor than it was in previous decades.

Hersey's fourth point is that a massive assault in education is required if it is to become an effective mechanism for resolving poverty. Smaller classes in problem neighborhoods with even individual tutoring by teachers for special problem children is just one of the very expensive but necessary approaches to the problem. Special bonuses for teachers who accept assignments to ghetto schools might also be expensive, but they would assure a higher quality and more experienced kind of teacher in such schools. Very small classes with experienced teachers can also make possible the separation of children in such schools according to their differential levels of readiness for learning, so that class discipline concerns and social-learner problems will not slow down those who are most ready to learn. With very small classes, teachers are better able to reach out to the families and get them involved in their children's education.

Hersey's fifth point was that a massive assault in education might also make possible a very close involvement between teachers of children in the lower grades and parents, which might set a pattern for continued parent-school relations for upper grades as well. If such an effective parent-school interaction could be developed, it would serve as a strong counterforce to the dropout problem of the upper elementary years. A new educational approach might make possible the highly structured classrooms for children whose delayed socialization cannot be solved in the ordinary classroom and whose presence in the regular classroom serves as a negative role-model for other children. Finally, a massive assault might provide education beginning at earlier ages in ghetto neighborhoods and thus an earlier educational value influence on children before the crucial years when parental influence on children wanes in the ghetto.

Hersey's sixth point is that school organization might need considerable change if it is to be effective. He suggests getting to the poor children when they are younger and instituting both a longer school day and longer school year. He suggests that for schools to become effective in the ghetto, they may have to take on responsibilities for children that are ordinarily carried out by parents.

Hersey's seventh point is that teachers and principals might have to develop new attitudes about the capabilities of ghetto children. He lists the classical deficiencies of the children of the ghetto: "Verbal awkwardness, poor auditory attention, anti-intellectualism, and very weak reading ability" which lead to "intensified alienation, . . . rebellion and finally apathy" (p. 159). Ghetto children, he says, have the benefit of freedom from overprotection and inner guilt, and a physical mode of existence which is displayed in enjoyment of sports, games, and the like. Where his examination of the poor falters is in his eighth point, his description of the closeness and warmth of the extended family of the poor, and of the degree of humor, easiness, and fluidity of feeling found among them. The very fluidity of feeling and "delight in doing" which Hersey so values as an educational asset is usually manifested in violence. His point, however, is well made. If the poor are to be reached by education, then educators must understand the limited responses of the poor to new and disturbing situations.

Hersey's concern for the alienation of the poor who have been rejected (or at least seemingly so) by the schools is also well placed. His view that the poor have lost their ability to communicate might better be seen as their never having attained it except for the limited verbal interactions between individuals in a highly isolated and simplistic setting, when compared to the complex mainstream. Middle-class professionals often perceive the external shell of the poor as a form of nihilism; as Hersey says, it is quite thick, tough, and durable. But this shell can be punctured and the poor reached if education can demonstrate to parents early enough in the life of their children that it offers them hope and tradable skills.

This brings us to Hersey's ninth point. Because the poor are incapable of becoming involved in future-oriented behavior and planning, schools can offer very little to the children of the poor unless the end product of a school program is either a job or further education that is related to a better job. Such employment "must be clearly visible to the child from his first years in the classroom." In Hersey's view, "the skill of reading . . . can be seen from the start not as an aspect of the culture of 'nice people' but . . . as a real work skill" (p. 159).

Hersey's last point relates to a revamping of vocational education. He believes that the vocational schools have to be overhauled so that they will no longer be what he calls "the junkyard of public schooling" (p. 160). The vocational schools, he maintains, serve more as a place of detention for the academic failures than as an alternate and equally important learning route. According to Hersey, the vocational schools teach now obsolete skills and are not adequately tuned into the many middle-level skills of a technological and consumer society. He does not deal with the so-called continuation school which permits underage students with work permits to avoid regular or vocational school as long as they attend a weekly half-day technical class. Many of these students are not employed but use the continuation school as a means of dropping out of the learning process without undergoing any hassle with parents and teachers. The continuation school was originally supported by craft labor unions to cut down on youthful competition to the limited jobs available during depressed times. Youths who could not work a full week were less competition for full-time jobs than youths who had no school obligation. The same influence of labor unions which helped create continuation schools has prevented the development of meaningful craft skill programs in many vocational and continuation schools. In a sense, meaningless vocational and continuation schools inoculate youths against schooling attendance constraints and thus ensure that their learning and preparation will be minimal.

Hersey and others put much of the onus of learning failure on the schools, either by outright statement or by inference. In 1964, Kenneth B. Clark made a number of statements about ghetto education which he has continued to express today. He maintains that by not gaining a minimum qualification in basic subjects such as reading or arithmetic, the vast bulk of disadvantaged youngsters are unable to meet minimal standards for other than menial, lower status employment. The gap between the performance of such youth and national norms consistently widens from year to year, so that they fall more securely in the morass of what Clark describes as "the cycle of poor education, broken homes . . . unstable family life, and a general pattern of social pathology." Clark objects to job training programs that do not also provide compensatory basic education. He states that the schools need to be goaded into greater effectiveness with black students, and in the process he infers that the primary blame must necessarily fall on the schools. Gordon also takes the position that poverty youth have been let down by the institutions of American society rather than by their own familial structures.

It is important to examine the syndrome of social pathology described by Clark. Among the therapeutic professions, the set of requirements for change in a client commonly includes three factors: capacity, opportunity, and motivation. It is interesting to examine why it is that the middle-class student in the suburban school usually makes it academically and the lower class child in the ghetto school does not.

Franz Boas, a leader in American anthropology, has promoted the concept of historicalism which holds that each man's and woman's feelings and thoughts are tied to the culture which that man or woman uses as a reference base. This view conflicts severely with those of other anthropologists such as William Henry Morgan and Sir Edward Taylor, who propounded a theory of cultural evolution (Torrey, p. 19). According to the evolutionary theory, all men are really the same in feelings, responses, and thoughts. They theorized that as the Bushmen and Aborigines moved up the evolutionary scale, they in turn would think exactly as do all of the more highly evolved cultures. In their view, the Western cultures are at the top of the evolutionary scale.

Many American anthropologists vigorously support the Boas position. Its theoretical base correlates strongly with cultural relativity (Horton and Leslie, p. 29), a position that is generally accepted in American sociology. This view indicates that no aspect of human life can be judged meaningfully outside of the context of the specific society, culture, and time, of which the aspect is a functional part.

From the meanings which a person identifies with a particular aspect of his life have come the behavioral actions and reactions which affect his performance and acceptance (or rejection) in a particular society. Thus, a Bushman or Aborigine may be viewed as a behavior problem and as a retarded student in an American middle-class schoolroom, even though he might be considered a promising and successful young leader in his tribe. By the same token, an American middle-class youth would probably be viewed as a failure in a tribe of Aborigines or Bushmen. The child who is a successful performer in a ghetto gang, in a culture of poverty family, or in an organized lower class criminal syndicate would have few or none of the daily life symbols meaningful to middle-class children and school officials, and vice versa. The view of the cultural evolutionists, humanitarian romanticists, and advocates of the poor notwithstanding, people from different cultures are not the same in their meanings, feelings, reactions, and behavioral responses to symbols that are common to each. The reactions of a person to the same symbol might provoke hostility and violence or acquiescence and cooperation, depending on that person's cultural context for the symbol.

If American education were concerned with two accepted, functioning, and nonconflicting cultures, such as exists in the Quebec Province of Canada, Belgium, and Switzerland, the problem of the cultural gap for symbols would be less difficult to resolve. Children would be brought up in one or the other cultural milieu, and the state would have to develop bridges between the cultures. Accordingly, the children would be provided with bilingual curricula, intercultural education, and other mechanisms established to build crosscultural cooperation. When the cultures cannot be reconciled, as in Northern Ireland, conflict becomes constant and pervasive.

In the interaction between the culture of the mainstream of the American society and that of the outer cultures (the ghetto, the drug culture, the world of organized crime, and the poverty populations), resolution of cultural differences is quite impossible. None of the rules and operational patterns that make the mainstream society functional is reconcilable with the rules and operational patterns of the outer cultures. It is true that some people succeed in living across the cultures, but at best their performance is usually marginal in one or both. For some of the important symbols that both cultures use but with different meanings, see Table 8.3.

If some view authority as security and protection and others as something to be hated and avoided, how can the differences in meaning be resolved? Should the meaning be compromised, pressing some to be less accepting of it and others to be more accepting of it? Or should we accept a "bilingual view" of authority and allow everyone to respond to authority according to his own cultural meaning? If the society and its authorities were foolish enough to seek such a dilution of the meaning of the term, the result would be chaos and disorder. Similarly, the differential meanings held for such key symbols as education, delinquency, violence, and sex are so disparate as to require the superimposition of one of the cultures over the other. If the two societies (the mainstream and the outer cultures) held reasonably congruent views regarding many of the key symbols, and if both societies were mutually productive and perhaps symbiotic, as is the case in many bicultural countries, there would be no irreconcilable conflicts. But when one culture provides all of the goods and services for both societies, when the societies are more competitive than symbiotic in regard to those goods and services, and when the people of one society are required to fund and control both societies if the people of both are to survive, then the mainstream, as the supporting society, seeks to legitimate its symbols. The realistic viewpoint about any culture is that attempts to seek equal acceptance of its symbols in a multicultural society can be legitimated only to the extent that it can back up its demands with performance in the production of goods, services, and funding for the shared societal complex.

Only a grasp of the legitimated meanings for symbols can assure a child of success in the mainstream culture, which is equivalent to describing success in the society generally. Because there can be no legitimated authority in the outer culture, there can be no outer culture education which can hold any promise for a child of the society. The child of the ghetto has only one hope of success in the society and that is through the mainstream and its schools. This is not to mean that the child must abandon his entire cultural heritage. In the choice of mainstream values versus outer culture values, however, the child must either choose the mainstream or so successfully develop a bicultural repertoire of meanings that he can differentially apply them appropriately in both mainstream and outer culture life. Thus, the schools of the mainstream become the vehicle of logical choice for all of society's children. The middle-class children usually fall into the use of this mechanism without question. Eventually, the society hopes, the parents of the children of the ghetto will also behave reasonably in opting for mainstream education after exhausting all of the alternatives.

The schools of the ghetto should not relate to ghetto children on a take

TABLE 8.3 **The Cultural Chasm Reconsidered: The Ideals Espoused, the Middle-Class Realities, and the View from Beneath**

CONCEPT	THE IDEAL MEANING	THE MIDDLE-CLASS REALITY MEANING	THE LOWER-CLASS REALITY MEANING
Authority (courts, police, school principal)	Someone we helped choose and whose activities we are responsible for.	Security—to be taken for granted, wooed, and used for personal benefit.	Something to be hated and avoided.
Education	A means of learning more about the world God gave us.	The road to better things for one's children and one's self.	An obstacle course to be surmounted until children can go to work.
Joining a church	To recharge our spiritual and ethical batteries and motivations.	Affiliation for social acceptance and activity.	An emotional release.
Ideal goal	To be a better person.	Money, property; to be accepted by the successful.	"Coolness"; to make out without attracting the attention of the authorities.
Society	Something we all are responsible for and from which we cannot stand idly by.	The pattern one conforms to in the interests of security and being "popular."	"The Man"—an enemy to be resisted and suspected.
Delinquency	An act of injustice to someone or one's self.	An evil originating outside the middle-class home.	One of life's inevitable events to be ignored unless the police get into the act.
The Future	Something which we make for ourselves (subject to supernatural cancellation).	A rosy horizon.	Nonexistent, so we live each moment fully.
"The Street"	A road for which we are responsible and which we need to use responsibly.	A path for the auto—somewhere to throw our used beer cans and cigarette wrappers.	A meeting place; an escape from a crowded home; the place where the "action" is.

Table 8.3—*Continued*

CONCEPT	THE IDEAL MEANING	THE MIDDLE-CLASS REALITY MEANING	THE LOWER-CLASS REALITY MEANING
Liquor	Something to be used with caution and for fulfillment.	Sociability; cocktail parties.	A means to welcome oblivion.
Violence	Something to be abhorred as destructive to humans.	A last resort of authorities for protecting the law-abiding; is acceptable when used.	A tool for living and getting on; a way of getting the attention of those who won't listen.
Sex	Only a part (but an important part) of a deeper mutual intertwining of two lives.	An adventure and a binding force for the family, creating problems of birth control.	One of life's few remaining "free" pleasures: usually short in time and "body-centered."
Money	Something to be used for personal growth and participation in further support and improvement of society.	A resource to be cautiously spent and saved for the future.	Something to be used quickly before it disappears.

SOURCE: Segalman (October 1969): 1-4.

it or leave it basis. If the schools are to become effective in the ghetto, they must necessarily start where the children are, using as many identically held meanings as possible, represented by the children's own symbols. Through the educational process, the schools need to bring the children into contact with more and more of the mainstream meanings and language, and less and less of the ghetto terminology and meanings. The ultimate hope is that ghetto children will finally catch up to the level of mainstream understanding held by middle-class children. Only in this way can the ghetto child's hopes of making it in the society be enhanced. At no time is it to be contemplated that the cultural norms of the outer culture will be adopted or legitimated by the ghetto schools. To do that would be the equivalent of giving ghetto children the double bind messages which can lead to cultural schizophrenia.

It is helpful to examine a child's capacity, motivation, and opportunity with regard to an educational experience. A utopian model of these factors would probably include the following:

Capacity Factors for Mainstream Education

(1) Genetic inheritance. (See discussion below.)

(2) Somatic inheritance, including adequate brain development, physical and nutritional health, and physical and neurological capability to attend and participate in regular school classes.

(3) Adequate experience in a culture where learning and school progress are valued more highly than the diversions and comforts of school activities, street activity, leisure, and the like.

(4) Socialization and preparation for norm adherence in an atmosphere of mainstream school or one similar to mainstream school.

(5) Socialization and preparation for learning roles where the learner is responsive to the teacher.

(6) Socialization and preparation for communication utilizing mainstream meanings attached to commonly required symbols.

(7) Pre-installment of a set of mainstream career aspirations and expectations which can be related to the school as ends and means.

(8) A set of internalized adult role-models which equip the child with idealized modes of behavior that can be adapted to the mainstream school setting.

(9) Some beginning skills in the use of human conceptual communication which have been taught to the child by social interactive methods.

(10) A self-concept related to beginning problem-solving skills which have been appropriately validated (praised) by the child's significant others, particularly adults. For such a child, learning is a major mechanism of gaining positive feedback to his sense of self and his sense of familial belonging.

(11) A sense of belonging to a set of adults whom the child perceives to be acceptable persons to the teacher and school authorities.

(12) A sense of the importance of school learning which the child perceives his significant adults to hold.

Motivation Factors for Mainstream Education

(1) A personal choice by the child of role-models related to school learning as means.

(2) A personal choice of school activity as equally attractive (or more attractive) than other activities available to the child.

(3) A personal desire to learn whatever the school has to offer (learning as an end in itself).

Opportunity Factors for Mainstream Education

(1) A chance to attend a well-staffed and equipped school. (An ill-staffed school cannot serve both the social control and teaching functions.)

(2) A chance to attend a school where mainstream learning is a priority not obscured by necessary absorption with child control, social diversions, and so forth.

(3) A chance to attend school at a time in life when physical health needs are fully attended to, so that the child is free to focus on learning.

(4) A chance to attend a school where teachers and staff have learning expecta-

tions for the child that are neither pessimistic nor unrealistically optimistic.

(5) A chance to attend a school which is not so overcrowded that each child's learning needs cannot be carefully and individually understood and served.

(6) A place to study at home (or in some other setting), so that the child can adequately order and integrate each day's learning in preparation for the next day.

(7) A chance to attend a school which is not too distant from his home either in terms of walking or schoolbus time (not too onerous a travel time and energy demand on the child's day).

(8) A chance to study without being overwhelmed with outside employment, family chores, and other responsibilities which are overly debilitating or time consuming.

Among the factors listed under *Capacity*, note that only the genetic factors have received much attention in the literature. Much of the discussion of genetic factors has centered around the differential learning capabilities of black versus white children without adequate consideration of whether such capability was related to genetic inheritance, somatic capacity, or early life experiences (*Harvard Educational Review*, Eysenck and Herrnstein). Much of the genetic argument is based on the assumption that IQ is a highly heritable characteristic, but this assumption has never been tested. It is quite conceivable that two twins with equal genetic equipment will perform unequally if fulfillment of their physical needs or preschool socialization preparation is unequal, even though both have equal opportunity to learn once they reach school age.

In connection with the genetic discussion, the appropriateness of using IQ tests to measure differential levels of learning ability of children has also been much debated. This argument becomes largely irrelevant when we recall the purpose of the measurement: to determine the degree of preparation which a particular child exhibits for the mainstream learning assignments that await him if he is to succeed in the society.

The long list of capabilities which a child needs in order to proceed successfully into mainstream success shows that most poverty children are ill equipped for school learning while most middle-class children are well prepared for learning. It is in the congeries of factors, as stated above, rather than in the school opportunity category that the poverty child's chances for success in education are lost. No revision of the ghetto schools alone can help a child who has lost out in capacity preparation. If education is to be seriously viewed as a mechanism for poverty resolution, then the society must be mobilized to go beyond school enrichment in providing effective education for the poor. Thus, the families of ghetto children would have to receive guidance with regard to their children's nutrition and health long before the child was ready to enter any type of school. They would also need help in raising their own valuations of a school experience for their children. Ghetto parents and very young children would need early help in the development of socialization techniques and goals needed to better prepare the children for later school involvement. Career orientations would have to be discussed with ghetto parents and children. Both would need help in learning the mainstream communications skills basic to the classroom. Parents in the ghetto would need help in developing adequate self-concepts for themselves, so that they might be able to build adequate self-concepts in their children. Accordingly, parents in the ghetto might have to be helped to secure meaningful employment which would in turn justify their absorption of meaningful self-concepts. Finally, parents in the ghetto might have to learn the realities of their own limits: that they cannot adequately help a child make a success of his life if they (and he) are surrounded with so many siblings that neither the parents' presence nor the family resources can make a sufficient impact.

The factors of opportunity for mainstream education are probably of less importance than the above in terms of educational effectiveness. A child who is prepared to want to learn and who has the capacity to learn will use his schooling opportunities to the utmost and will improvise when they fall short. In his description of the "good boy," Hartung indicates that the prepared child will proceed even against odds of peer opposition, overwork, severe poverty, and institutional antagonism. (His question about delinquency is not why there are so many delinquents among the poor but why there are not more.) Even in relation to opportunity, there is much that society can do in providing more accessible and amenable schooling to the ghetto child with additional supports and aids. Similarly, the motivation of ghetto children to school learning can be enhanced considerably by eliminating illegitimate opportunities to ends (such as criminal activity) and by providing meaningful, school-related employment opportunities and postschool careers.

The provision of special avenues for motivated children to escape from failure-ridden settings is important in building upward educational opportunities. Unlike mandatory busing which merely creates an enforced mix of residual children after others have escaped into private schools and suburban enclaves, voluntary busing makes it possible for motivated children to attend schools that have more to offer them than the discipline-focused inner-city school or the lowest common denominator residual city school. The provision of magnet schools that encourage excellence in learning along with voluntary busing to such schools gives the educational system and the society the permeability needed for the democratic ethic to survive. Such magnet schools can also encourage the retention of middle-class motivated students who would otherwise leave the public school system, thus lowering the potential learning level for all. As such, the provision of such schools is critical in maintaining a viable public education system tied to the democratic process.

Still another method that might be undertaken to improve the effectiveness of public education relates to the mechanisms and regulations for school leaving. In a number of developing countries, children are not moved from grade to grade until they pass a proficiency test specified for each grade. In addition, no child, except for the brain damaged, the diagnosed mentally disturbed and retarded, or with similar conditions, is permitted to leave school until he has achieved a specified level of proficiency in those subjects deemed necessary for his self-sufficiency and his functioning as a citizen. In those countries, the proficiency level is raised each year, so that eventually no child is permitted to leave school without a secondary education. This requirement is clearly set out for parents, children, teachers, and school administrators. Safeguards are installed to ensure that no special exams are provided which might ease some children out of the system without adequate proficiency.

This policy of school leaving, if carefully enforced, motivates children and parents to proceed with the required learning even if it is not highly regarded at home. It also motivates teachers and schools to maximize their efforts with all children. By setting out learning goals that must be met before a child is permitted to leave, more efforts are directed toward learning and less effort toward disciplinary controls and nonlearning activity. Under present conditions the child is often under pressure from his peers, who are often his only effective role models, to leave school and join them. His parents may also be concerned that he be able to help in support of the family as soon as possible. If he is to help earn money he has to leave school. If he leaves school before he has completed his education, his younger siblings will also view school as something to get done with as soon as possible. Under the present system the pressure on children to leave school is considerable. A revised school learning policy, such as was discussed above, might serve to take such pressures off the children if it were generally adopted. In addition to the learning gains, this policy teaches those in the poverty culture the methods and advantages of postponed gratifications for the sake of improved and increased rewards.

A school leaving policy such as is described above may not be successful unless other policies and actions are carried out. No school system could carry out such a policy unless all other school systems adopted it. Otherwise, some children would be transferred from one school district to another by systems seeking to evade the impact of the policy, and some parents might move to the less restrictive systems. Other supportive policies would relate to truancy laws and continuation school laws. The school leaving policy would be useless if the schools were not provided with the necessary resources to make such schools effective with the slow learners particularly, and with special facilities for teenage mothers and their babies.

Another innovation for public education involves the differential degree of difficulty in teaching in various schools and districts. In the urban schools where reading levels are lowest, schools, through subsidies, might have very small classes with higher paid master teachers. In other schools where proficiency levels are achieved according to standards, the size of classes might remain at the standard numbers of twenty-eight to thirty-five students. Thus, parents in urban settings would not be as strongly motivated as they are now to secure a suburban quality type of education for their children. Funds would be allocated to schools on the cumulative preparation levels of their children rather than on the school-district property tax base, or on only the number of children served. Such an arrangement might lessen parental interest in school desegregation and busing because parents are increasingly focusing on the quality of education as delivered.

All of the above efforts would require a societal mobilization and funding probably equal to that necessary for the early space program. It may even take as long as the Vietnam War did to turn education in a more effective direction. In any case, to seek to improve the ghetto schools without adequate prior preparation of the children they serve may well be an exercise in futility equal to the waste of the Vietnam War.

Because in our society all advancement begins in the schools (Schrag), it is clear that the society can remain permeable, and thus stable, only if the schools are made equally effective. And schools cannot be made equally effective unless the parental preschool preparation for schooling is made equally effective, and that means going beyond the schools into the homes and families of the ghetto. To do less than that is to choose inequality in the guise of egalitarianism. From a legal-realist viewpoint, justice to all children may require special treatment for some parents.

REFERENCES

Allport, Gordon W. *Becoming.* New York: Yale Press, 1955.

Avereh, Harvey A., Stephen J. Carroll, Theodore S. Donaldson, Herbert J. Kiesling, and John Pincus. *How Effective Is Schooling? A Critical Review and Synthesis of Research Findings.* Englewood Cliffs, N.J.: Educational Technology Publications, 1974.

Barnes, Peter. "Bringing Back the WPA: Fringe Benefits of a Depression," *New Republic,* 172(11):19–21, 1975.

Barnow, Burt, "Evaluating Project Head Start," Institute for Research on Poverty Discussion Papers, nos. 189–93. Madison: Institute for Research on Poverty of the University of Wisconsin, 1973.

Bednarzik, Robert W., and Stephen M. St Marie. "Employment and Unemployment in 1976," *Monthly Labor Review,* 100(2):3–13, 1977.

Boas, Franz. "On Grammatical Categories." Pp. 121–23, in Dell Hymes (ed.), *Language in Culture and Society: A Reader in Linguistics and Anthropology.* New York: Harper, 1964.

Bobrow, S. B. *Reasonable Expectations: Limits on the Promise of Community Councils,* P–5824. Santa Monica: Rand, 1977.

Bowles, S. "Toward an Educational Production Function," *Studies in Income and Wealth,* 35:11–60, 1970.

Bradshaw, Thomas F. "Job Seeking Methods Used by Unemployed Workers," *Monthly Labor Review,* 96(2):35–40, 1973.

Bronfenbrenner, Urie. "Damping the Unemployability Explosion," *Saturday Review,* 52(1):108–10, 1969.

Califano, Joseph A. "Special HEW Report on Welfare Reform." *Hearings Before the Subcommittee on Public Assistance and Unemployment Compensation of the Committee on Ways and Means,* Ninety-fifth Congress. Washington, D.C.: U.S. Government Printing Office, 1977.

Clark, Kenneth B. *Social and Economic Implications of Integration in the Public Schools.* Washington, D.C.: U.S. Department of Labor, 1965.

Committee for Economic Development. *Improving the Public Welfare System.* New York: Committee for Economic Development, 1971.

Congressional Digest. "Proposed Revision of the Federal Minimum Wage Law," 51(4):98–100, 102–104, 128, 1972.

———. "Congress and the Humphrey-Hawkins Employment Bill," 55(6–7):162–92, June/July 1976.

———. "Controversy in Congress over Proposed Amnesty for Illegal Aliens," 56(10):225–55, 1977.

Dolgoff, Thomas. "The Psychological Meaning of Work," *Menninger Perspective:* 5–9, Summer 1976.

Drucker, Peter F. "Beyond Stick and Carrot: Hysteria Over the Work Ethic," *Psychology Today* 7(6):86–96, November 1973.

Duncan, O. D., D. L. Featherman, and B. Duncan. *Socio-economic Background and Achievement.* London: Seminar Press, 1972.

Eastburn, David P. *Economic Man vs. Social Man.* New York: *New York Times,* 1970.

Ellis, Robert A. "Some New Perspectives on Upward Mobility," *Urban and Social Change Review* 4(1): 15–17, Fall 1970.

Eysenck, H. J. *The I.Q. Argument: Race, Intelligence and Education.* New York: Library Press, 1971.

Faltermayer, Edmund. "A Better Way to Deal with Unemployment," *Fortune* Magazine 87(6):146–49, 236, 238, 241–42, 1973.

Ferguson, Robert H. *Unemployment: Its Scope, Measurement and Effect on Poverty.* Bulletin 53–2 Revised. Ithaca, N.Y.: Cornell University, 1971.

Friedman, Milton. "Friedman Calls Minimum Wage 'Anti-Negro'," *Socio-Economic Newsletter,* 3(3):3, 1978.

———, and Yale Brozen. *The Minimum Wage: Who Pays?* Pamphlet. Washington, D.C.: Free Society of America, 1966.

Gans, Herbert J. "Jobs and Services: Toward a Labor-Intensive Economy," New York: Center for Policy Research, Columbia University, 1976.

———. "Income Grants and 'Dirty Work'." *The Public Interest,* 6:110–13, Winter 1967.

Ginsburg, Helen. *Unemployment, Sub-Employment and Public Policy.* New York: New York University, School of Social Work, 1975.

Goodwin, Leonard. "The Work Ethic Among the Poor," *Los Angeles Times,* September 28, 1972, Part II, p. 7.

Gordon, Margaret S. (ed.). *Poverty in America.* San Francisco: Chandler, 1965.

Hagedorn, Robert, and Sanford Labovitz. "Occupational Characteristics and Participation in Voluntary Associations," *Social Forces,* 47(1):16–27, 1968.

Harrison, Bennett, Harold L. Sheppard, and William J. Spring. "Public Jobs. Public Needs: Government as the Employer of First Resort," *New Republic,* 167(17):18–21, 1972.

Hartung, Frank. *Crime, Law and Society.* Detroit: Wayne State Press, 1966.

Harvard Educational Review. Environment, Heredity and Intelligence. Reprint Series No. 2, 1969.

Hayakawa, S. I. "Remarks by U.S. Senator S. I. Hayakawa, R-California, at National Press Club Luncheon," May 4, 1977.

Herrnstein, Richard. "I.Q.," *Atlantic Monthly,* 228(3):44–64, 1971.

Hersey, John. "Education, An Antidote to Poverty," *American Association of University Women Journal,* 58(4):157–60, 1965.

Hollingshead, August B., and Frederick C. Redlich. *Social Class and Mental Illness.* New York: Wiley, 1958.

Horton, Paul B., and Gerald R. Leslie. *The Sociology of Social Problems.* 3d ed. New York: Appleton, 1965.

Hughes, Everett. "Work and Self." Pp. 313–14, in John H. Rohrer and Muzafer Sherif (eds.), *Social Psychology at the Crossroads.* New York: Harpers, 1951.

Johnston, Denis F. "The Future of Work: Three Possible Alternatives," *Monthly Labor Review,* 95(5):3–11, 1972.

Kaplan, Roy H., and Curt Tausky. "The Meaning of Work Among the Hard Core Unemployed," *Pacific Sociological Review,* 17(2):185–98, 1974.

Kephart, William M. "Occupational Level and Marital Disruption," *American Sociological Review,* 20:456–65, 1955.

Killingsworth, Charles C. "Employment as an Alternative to Welfare." Paper presented at UCLA Conference on National Welfare Policy, September 29, 1972.

Laffer, Arthur. "The Disincentive Factor," *Time* Magazine, 112 (14):55, 1978.

Lawrence, John F. "Household Help Laws Discourage Hiring, Encourage Cheating," *Los Angeles Times,* September 17, 1978, Part V, p. 3.

Lawyers Committee for Civil Rights Under the Law and the National Urban Coalition. *Falling Down on the Job: The United States Employment Service and the Disadvantaged.* Washington, D.C.: National Urban Coalition, 1971.

League of Women Voters. "Jobs and Hard Cash." Mimeographed, 1967.

Lecht, Leonard A. *Manpower Needs for National Goals in the 1970's.* New York: Praeger, 1969.

Levenstein, Aaron. *Why People Work: Changing Incentives in a Troubled World.* New York: Collier, 1964.

Levitan, Sar. *Anti-Poverty Work and Training Efforts: Goals and Reality.* Washington, D.C.: National Manpower Policy Task Force, 1967.

Levy, Robert J., Thomas P. Lewis, and Peter M. Martin. *Social Welfare and the Individual: Cases and Materials.* Mineola: Foundation Press, 1971.

Lichtenstein, Charles. "On the Minimum Wage," *Public Interest,* 6:113–15, 1967.

Liebow, Elliot. *Tally's Corner: A Study of Negro Streetcorner Men.* Boston: Little, Brown, 1967.

————. "No Man Can Live with the Terrible Knowledge That He Is Not Needed," *Social Service Outlook,* 5(9):1–3, 14–16, 1970.

McCormack, Patricia. "A Report on Children Bearing Children: Lifelong Handicap Predicted," *International Herald Tribune,* August 22, 1978, p. 6.

McGovern, George. "McGovern Says Illiteracy Increase Is Alarming," *Los Angeles Times,* September 8, 1978, Part 1, p. 20.

Manpower Research Office. "Longitudinal Manpower Survey." Washington, D.C.: U.S. Department of Labor, 1978.

Marshall, Alfred. *Principles of Economics.* New York: Macmillan, 1920.

Meyerson, Adam. "The Public Policy: On Raising the Minimum Wage," *The Alternative: An American Spectator,* 8(8):32–33, 1975.

Michael, Donald W. *Cybernation: The Silent Conquest.* Santa Barbara: Center for the Study of Democratic Institutions, 1962.

Michelotti, Kopp. "Educational Attainment of Workers, March 1977," Special Labor Force Report No. 209. Washington, D.C.: U.S. Department of Labor, 1978.

Mill, John Stuart. *Principles of Political Economy.* London: Longmans, 1917.

Miller, S. M., and Frank Riessman. "The Credentials Trap," *Social Service Outlook,* 5(5):1–4, 1970.

Munts, Raymond. "Objectives for Today's Economy," *Manpower,* 1(7):18–21, 1969.

New Republic, The. "Invisible Unemployed" (editorial), 166(9): 8, 1972.

Noble, Philip (ed.). *The Con III Controversy.* New York: Pocket Books, 1971.

Pavalko, Ronald M. *Sociology of Occupations and Professions.* Itaska, N.Y.: Peacock, 1971.

Powell, Elwin H. "Occupation, Status and Suicide: Toward a Redefinition of Anomie," *American Sociological Review,* 23:131–38, 1958.

Rainwater, Lee. "Crucible of Identity: The Negro Lower Class Family," *Daedalus,* 95(1):172–216, 1966.

Raspberry, William. "A Generation of Kids Who Don't Know What Work Is," *Los Angeles Times,* December 6, 1977, Part II, p. 7.

———. " 'Joblessness Isn't Really So Bad' Oh, No?" *Los Angeles Times,* January 10, 1978, Part II, p. 5.

Reich, Charles A. *The Greening of America.* New York: Random House, 1970.

Ryan, William. *Blaming the Victim.* New York: Vintage, 1971.

Schrag, Peter. "End of the Impossible Dream," *Saturday Review,* 53(38):68–70, 92–94, 1970.

Segalman, Ralph. "The Cultural Chasm Reconsidered," *Rocky Mountain Social Science Journal,* 6(2):143–45, 1969.

Selznick, Gertrude J., and Stephen Steinberg. "Social Class, Ideology and Voting Preference." Pp. 216–26, in Celia S. Heller (ed.), *Structural Social Inequality.* New York: Macmillan, 1969.

Sheppard, Harold L. *A Search for New Directions in the War Against Poverty.* Washington, D.C.: Upjohn Institute for Employment Research, 1968.

Socioeconomic Newsletter. "Major Inflation Cause: Waning Work Ethic," 4(6): 3, 1979.

Srole, Leo, Thomas S. Langner, Stanley T. Michael, Marvin K. Opler, and Thomas A. C. Rennie. *Mental Health in the Metropolis.* New York: McGraw-Hill, 1962.

Steele, Paul D. "Exploration of the Labelling Systems in a Mental Health Rehabilitation Program." Paper given at the Midwest Sociological Society, Chicago, April 8, 1975.

Steiner, Gilbert. *The State of Welfare.* Washington, D.C.: Brookings Institution, 1971.

Stone, Robert C., and Frederic H. Schlamp. *Family Life Styles Below the Poverty Line.* San Francisco: Institute for Social Science Research, San Francisco State University, 1967.

Subcommittee on Fiscal Policy of the Joint Economic Committee, U.S.

Congress. *The Effectiveness of Manpower Training Programs: A Review of Research on the Impact on the Poor.* Washington, D.C.: U.S. Government Printing Office. 1972.

Summers, Anita, A., and Barbara L. Wolfe. "Do Schools Make a Difference?" *American Economic Review,* 67(4):639–52, 1977.

Time Magazine. "It's Your Turn in the Sun. Now 19 Million, and Growing Fast, Hispanics Are Becoming a Power," 112(16):48–52, 55, 58, 61, 1978.

Timnich, Lois. "Escaping the Welfare Rolls a Giant Step," *Los Angeles Times,* September 12, 1978, Part I, pp. 1, 17, 19.

Torrey, Fuller E. *The Mind Game: Witch Doctors and Psychiatrists.* New York: Bantam, 1973.

Ulmer, Melville J. "Taking a Dim View of Humphrey-Hawkins," *New Republic,* 174(24):17–19, 1976.

U.S. Bureau of Labor Statistics. *Employment in Perspective: Working Women.* No. 2, Report No. 544. Washington, D.C.: U.S. Department of Labor, 1978.

Urkowitz, Allen. "Danger: Not Enough Young at Work," *Time* Magazine, 109(22):64–65, 1977.

Vogl, Frank. "Can America Solve Its Jobs Problem?" *London Times,* August 24, 1978, p. 17.

Von Mises, Ludwig. *Planned Chaos.* New York: Irvington on Hudson Foundation for Economic Education, Inc., 1947, reprinted 1972.

Watts, Harold W., and Felicity Skidmore. "The Implications for Changing Family Patterns and Behavior for Labor Force and Hardship Management." Madison, Wis.: Institute for Research on Poverty, University of Wisconsin, 1978.

Welch, F. R. *Minimum Wage Legislation in the U.S.,* P5145. Santa Monica: Rand, 1973.

———. *Effects of Minimum Wages on the Age Composition of Youth Employment,* P5468. Santa Monica: Rand, 1975.

———. *Minimum Wages: Issues and Evidence,* P5999. Santa Monica: Rand, 1978.

———, and M. Kosters. *The Effects of Minimum Wages on the Distribution of Changes in Aggregate Employment,* RM–6273–OEO. Santa Monica: Rand, 1970.

Wilcox, Claire. *Toward Social Welfare.* Homewood, Ill.: Irwin, 1969.

Young, Ned. "Work and Welfare," *Journal of the Institute for Socio-Economic Studies,* 3(1):40–51, 1978.

Zagoria, Sam. *Working with Automation.* Seminar on Manpower Policy and Program Series. Washington, D.C.: U.S. Government Printing Office, 1967.

Zigler, Edward. *Project Head Start: A Legacy of the War on Poverty.* New York: Free Press, 1979.

POSTSCRIPT

POVERTY in America has changed in both structure and context. Structurally, value transformations in the meaning of poverty have become institutionalized. The status of the poor has come to be viewed as a function of socioeconomic imbalance. Historically, man strove to maximize long-range security and life satisfaction for himself and his family. He viewed institutionalized guidelines and social prescriptions as a means of upgrading status and the right to control his own life through productivity in society. The most widely sanctioned goal was that of being in the mainstream of societal activities. The current attitude, particularly with respect to the residual poor, is the reverse of this picture. Welfare measures, largely directed to ameliorate poverty, have created transgenerational poverty. They have engendered a situation in which governmental policies have helped to perpetuate a status immobility of hopelessness and alienation. The blame for this seemingly persistent and intractable condition has been placed on the structural forces of our government and, finally, the "power elite."

Contextually, the incentives of motivation and normative guidelines have been replaced by increased subsidies, guaranteed security, and, now, the rhetoric of some social scientists who plan to homogenize welfare by merging public assistance with social insurance benefits. We maintain that the self-reliant and self-supporting population is best served by separating social insurance from public assistance programs. Such a measure will ensure the constraints appropriate to the poverty population, which also needs to be provided with a meaningful chance of entry into mainstream society. As argued in Chapter 8, a multistep pattern of assistance and services needs to be formulated for welfare, housing, education, and employment. Services and constraints should be commensurate with the readiness of that segment of the population to utilize both to their own and society's advantage.

The gap between the growing residual poor and mainstream America is becoming wider both qualitatively and quantitatively. Since taxpayer resistance has become a strong contemporary political force, welfare grants cannot be expected to keep pace with inflationary trends. In time, pressures to select out and better serve the more responsible population among the welfare poor may yet lead to a graduated rehabilitation program.

Welfare, Ideology, and Social Structure

Work and education are inexorably connected to the discussion of poverty in industrialized America. Any discussion of manpower policy in the amelioration of poverty in America should take into account the burgeoning techno-industrial premise of the American economy. Meaningful entry into mainstream occupational activity is almost entirely conditioned upon development of work skills preceded by appropriate educational training. Economist Jan Pen addresses himself to the social dimension of this issue:

Statistically, the greater part of income inequality is attributable to the inequality of incomes from work, and psychologically the comparison of these remunerations summons up at least as much frustration. And therefore an important question is what fundamental changes can be achieved in the wage and salary structure. That is to say, not by adjusting pay relations without an alteration in the underlying factors, but by a different arrangement of productive contributions. Human relations interact with income relations (p. 402).

Pen makes a number of policy recommendations. He maintains that a sound employment policy is based on the factor of full employment. A decent job should be available to all. In an earlier paper, Johnson (pp. 168–69) succinctly outlined three sources of poverty: "inadequate provision of jobs by governmental economic management," "immobility of labor," and "discrimination." Johnson argues that the second and third factors contributing to poverty are in large part dependent upon the first. He concludes that "the really effective solution to the problem of poverty lies in raising the level of demand for goods and services—and therefore for labor—to the point where poverty, instead of being part of the natural order of things, becomes a signal of economic waste, so that it will pay someone to take steps to eliminate it" (Johnson, p. 169). Full employment would enhance a broad demand for labor.

Pen also argues that lack of employment through deflation must be avoided. Temporary adjustments such as government expenditures, tax rates, and monetary policy should be provided for, and a massive tax reduction may have to be effected. With regard to unemployment, Pen states that "unemployment through deflation is not enough." A regional policy directly initiated by the policy planners should be considered. In American terms, the current high statistics of unemployment in the central-city cores should be considered in relation to this regional scheme.

Mechanization does not necessarily result in technological unemployment. Pen contends that an active manpower policy may help equalize the supply and demand. However, herein we surmise that a common failure of nerve in initiating and implementing these policies (in the 1960s, for example) has been evident in the absence of a mutual working relationship between the private and public sectors. Even if public sectors were to train and maintain training programs, in the final analysis, jobs have to be located in the private sector. Government-sponsored work programs have recently instituted tax incentives for the private sector. As elaborated in Chapter 5, income maintenance plans are no panacea. The socioeconomic constraints of these proposals have come under serious scrutiny. Furthermore, current socialist regimes which have maintained income guarantee plans to retrain their workers are able to do so only when the overall economic health of the nation is sound. A good example is Sweden in 1978. The Swedish social welfare system, under a long-standing bourgeoise-socialist premise, has been committed to an income redistribution policy through direct benefit and retraining elements of the program. Current strains on such a solely public-based policy can be attributed to two factors. First, the promise of such a program has been directly related to Sweden's steady economic growth; now that the growth rate is slowing down (*The Socio-Economic Newsletter,* p. 4), the economic system is under stress. Second, in the final analysis the success of any government-sponsored welfare measures is equally dependent upon the programs' acceptability to the public. The ideological receptivity of the public will have to match the government's policies. The broad contour of this issue lies with the discussion of class character and the creedal values of a nation. (This point is elaborated later in this section.) We believe that in Sweden and elsewhere, the electorate is beginning to question public-sponsored programs without private cooperation.

Finally, Pen argues the cause of education. He suggests that the lack of education has been attributed to "the failure of democracy, violence, juvenile delinquency, the lack of tolerance, the unsatisfactory place of art in the community, the shortage of creative activities, egotism, and problems of war and peace" (p. 404). Furthermore, in American terms, Lipset (1960, Chapter 2) has equated education with political stability and industrialization. In brief, democratic societies need an educated cadre. The literature on inequality has completely missed the point here (Kolko). Education has provided the human capital in the industrial nations (Harbison and Myers). It is precisely the lack of education which produces unequal sociopolitical choices. Political equality, thus stability, is inexorably related to a nation's ability to open the doors of learning to all rather than to a selected few. Economic development varies indirectly with the class inequality of a nation.

Any discussion of education is related directly to class distinctions and the poor (Miller, 1962). In industrialized America, where technical skills are important, a comprehensive, pragmatically oriented educational program for the able poor is urgently needed. Any manpower policy must take this fundamental fact into account. Here again, educational institutions, much like government-sponsored programs, have worked in isolation. Both educational institutions and technical firms would do well to join in developing a program of comprehensive training. Unfortunately, only recently have some of these joint private-public programs been initiated. It is hoped that the overall product will be the development in the individual of cohesion, obligation, and a sense of social belonging which promises to upgrade the individual's own social/family status.

Upward mobility is related to work and education (Blau and Duncon, pp. 152–61). The discussion of social mobility in the industrialized societies is concomitantly related to occupation (Lipset and Zetterberg, p. 562). An occupation (or lack of one) is perhaps the major indicator of poverty. As argued in Chapter 8, a job provides a meaningful entry into the society. Finally, it becomes the question of self-evaluation. As Lipset and Zetterberg put it: "The evaluation (rank, class) a person receives from his society determines in large measure his self-evaluation." "A person's actions are guided, in part at least, by an insatiable desire to maximize a favorable self-evaluation" (p. 566).

The inequality and welfare literature (Titmuss and Miller, et al., p. 566) argues this point in reverse. Their argument may be stated as follows: "Class structure [is] in the social consciousness" (Ossowski). Commitment to welfare only represents the "partial dis-services for social costs and social insecurities which are part of the price we pay to some for bearing part of the costs of other people's progress" (Titmuss, 133). At the core of the argument is the contradiction between liberalism and egalitarianism. Friedman underscores this dilemma well:

[T]he heart of the liberal philosophy is a belief in the dignity of the individual, in his freedom to make the most of his capacities and opportunities according to his own lights. . . . [T]he liberal will therefore distinguish sharply between equality of rights and equality of opportunity, on the one hand, and material equality and equality of outcome on the other. . . . [T]he egalitarian will go this far, too. But he will want to go further. He will defend taking from some to give to others, not as a more effective means whereby the "some" can achieve an objective they want to achieve, but on the grounds of "justice". *At this point, equality comes sharply into conflict with freedom;* one must choose. One cannot be both an egalitarian, in this sense, and a liberal (Friedman, p. 195). [Emphasis added.]

The advanced industrial society, especially the United States, with its primary emphasis on achieved goal orientation, finds itself in turmoil when it seeks traditional ascriptive solutions in order to equalize social conditions. The contradiction is largely reflected and permeated within the occupational structure. No other planned social instrument is more ascriptive than the present rush to affirmative action. Earl Raab has delineated the underlying premises of a democratic society succinctly:

One of the marks of the free society is the ascendance of performance over ancestry—or, to put it more comprehensively, the ascendance of achieved status over ascribed status. Aristocracies and racist societies confer status on the basis of heredity. A democratic society begins with the cutting of the ancestral cord. This by itself does not yet make a humanistic society or even properly a democratic one. There is, for example, the not inconsiderable question of distributive justice in rewarding performance. But achieved versus ascribed status is *one* inexorable dividing line between a democratic and an undemocratic society. This is the aspect of democracy which represents the primacy of the individual, and of individual freedom (p. 42).

The term civil rights has come to mean civil outcome. Such an outcome proposes to react to traditional forms of inequality by circumventing the formal legal-rational structure where gratifications are mainly achieved. American universities and colleges are a case in point. The Carnegie Council on Policy Studies in Higher Education, in its report "Making Affirmative Action Work in Higher Education" released August 10, 1975, states that as a result of federal requirements the nation's campuses are "confused [and] even chaotic." The right to articulate such policies often boils down to multiple federal agencies working at cross purposes. In this instance, three different agencies have vied for authority: the U.S. Department of Labor, the U.S. Department of Health, Education and Welfare, and, finally, the Equal Employment Opportunity Commission (*San Francisco Chronicle*, p. 10).

In Western democracies, occupation has served as the pivotal transformer in the social structure. The empirical data are much too abundant to document here; let it suffice here to say that bargainable, pluralist politics has enunciated an end to ascription. Thus, while a democratic and hence a rational system can constitutionally confer on each citizen an equal opportunity, it cannot guarantee equal achievement. Axiomatically, any attempt to equate the two is bound to produce rancor. This discussion boils down to a basic proposition which might very well continue to haunt us throughout the coming postindustrial generations. How does an avowedly democratic nation-state legitimize opportunity? The burden of social proof is in the presumption of equality (Bedeau, p. 19). Special preference to some is the denial of opportunity to all.

The historical-empirical evidence in America suggests that the overall effect of stratification (mobility) has been towards greater equality. The economic component of this issue can be derived by plotting a Lorenz curve (Schnitzer, p. 37). Schnitzer, documenting the personal income distribution data in America since 1929, observes that there exists a considerable income equality (pp. 32–33). U.S. Bureau of Census data report that in terms of the constant dollar, the standard of living has increased steadily from 1935–1971. This socioeconomic status mobility is further enhanced by a growth in median income (*Historical Statistics of the United States*). An influential rise in overall economic growth in America and among the industrialized nations has also been demonstrated by Kuznets. During the same period of socioeconomic growth, Janowitz demonstrates that "welfare expenditures have come to consume the bulk of the economic surplus" (p. 22). Total social welfare cost as a percentage of gross national product since 1935 has risen steadily (Janowitz, p. 21). The inference is an important one. Social welfare expenditures and economic growth are directly correlated. Moreover, as the socioeconomic status of the overall population has risen steadily, these citizens have paid higher tax dollars for the welfare programs. The question is, why has the relative percentage of population under poverty remained the same, while a greater income distribution is being achieved as measured in constant dollars?

Throughout this book, it is argued that social choices are an integral part of understanding poverty. Differential allocation of social-structural and motivational factors have played an important role in class differentiation. Compare our earlier examination of the social basis of the immigrant and the residual poor. Is the argument that increased mobility (by the immigrant poor, for example) has in part been achieved at the cost of residual poor tenable? We do not think so. We contend that the structural and motivational ability via institutional resources has increasingly become pluralistic. Exponents of disservices need to examine the social roots of achievement rather than inequality. Viewed in such a way, cost may become profit.

Finally, the American class character, the Puritan pursuit of work ethic notwithstanding, views welfare and poverty programs as a social cost. American creedal value is opposed to a continued and a rapid welfare growth, particularly when the overall health of the national economy is in jeopardy. The American electorate's continued desire for a change in welfare institutions to provide work incentives has been documented by opinion polls. In short, the American welfare crisis is a deep-seated creedal challenge. Tropman (p. 64) summarizes these value commitments as follows:

VALUE DIMENSION	VALUES
1. Independence	Inner versus other direction
2. Mobility	Contest versus sponsorship
3. Status	Achievement versus equality
4. Occupation/Activity	Private regardingness versus public regardingness

5. Moralism	Freedom versus control
6. Integrity	Self-reliance versus dependency
7. Ascription	Performance versus quality

Tropman proceeds to compare these values with the "subdominant" welfare values, and he concludes that "we thus can expect programs aimed at helping the poor to be in a state of constant crisis and perpetual perplexity, primarily because the poor are continually threatening dominant values in America" (p. 80).

Glazer (p. 12) sees the role of the sociologist as falling somewhere between that of the economist and reformer. Much of the reformist tradition has recently come to mean the transformation of various social programs into a collectivized welfare package. This mistaken liberal tradition has indeed confused the sources of equality, for the notion that equates liberty with equality is a false one. In providing a milieu of free choice, America promulgates a liberal ideology that will define and seek to solve the problem of poverty in the context of a struggle for egalitarianism. A plethora of welfare measures to attack poverty will be of no avail if we choose to misread the social basis of democracy. The history of this nation amply demonstrates that social choices are at the heart of individual liberty. Government-initiated programs can and must enhance, through structural measures, the individual's choices to seek socioeconomic upgrading, thus alleviating poverty. It can do no more. Our choice is a right to liberty, not a justification of equality. Tocqueville's insight into the cardinal premises of liberty still stands today as a benchmark for the American democracy. Welfare programs directed specifically at coping with poverty should be mindful of this nation's fundamental premise.

References

Bedeau, Hugo Adam. "Egalitarianism and the Idea of Equality." Pp. 16–25, in Roland Pennock and John W. Chapman (eds.), *Equality*. New York: Atherton, 1967.

Blau, Peter, and Otis Dudley Duncan. *The American Occupational Structure*. New York: Wiley, 1967.

Friedman, Milton. *Capitalism and Freedom*. Chicago: University Press, 1963.

Glazer, Nathan. "A Sociologist's View of Poverty." Pp. 12–26, in Margaret S. Gordon (ed.), *Poverty in America*. San Francisco: Chandler, 1965.

Harbison, F., and C. A. Myers. *Education, Manpower, and Economic Growth: Strategies of Human Resource Development*. New York: McGraw-Hill, 1964.

Janowitz, Morris. "Social Control of the Welfare State." Mimeographed, n.d.

Johnson, Harry G. "Poverty and Unemployment." Pp. 166–70, in Burton A. Weisbrod (ed.), *The Economics of Poverty*. Englewood Cliffs, N.J.: Prentiss-Hall, 1965.

Kolko, Gabriel. *Wealth and Power in America: An Analysis of Social Class and Income Distribution*. New York: Praeger, 1962.

Kuznets, Simon. *Economic Growth of Nations*. Cambridge, Mass.: Harvard Press, 1971.

Lipset, Seymour Martin. *Political Man: The Social Bases of Politics*. New York: Doubleday, 1960.

————, and Hans Zetterberg. "A Theory of Social Mobility." Pp. 561–73, in R. Bendix and S. M. Lipset (Eds.), *Class, Status and Power*. 2d ed. New York: Free Press, 1966.

Miller, Herman P. "Income and Education: Does Education Pay Off?" Pp. 129–46, in Selma J. Mushkin (Ed.), *Economics of Higher Education*. Washington, D.C.: U.S. Department of Health, Education and Welfare, 1962.

Miller, S. M., M. Rein, P. Roby, and B. Gross. "Poverty, Inequality and Conflict," *The Annals*, 373:16–52, 1967.

Ossowski, S. *Class Structure in the Social Consciousness*. London: Routledge, 1963.

Pen, Jan. *Income Distribution: Facts, Theories, Policies*. Trevor S. Preston (trans.). New York: Praeger, 1971.

Raab, Earl. "Quotas by Any Other Name," *Commentary*, 53(1):41–45, 1972.

San Francisco Chronicle. "Making Affirmative Action Work in Higher Education," August 11, 1975, p. 10.

Schnitzer, Martin. *Income Distribution*. New York: Praeger, 1974.

Socioeconomic Newsletter. "Social Welfare Abroad: Swedish Welfare System Under Stress," *Socioeconomic Newsletter*, 3(8):4–5, 1978.

Titmuss, Richard M. *Commitment to Welfare*. New York: Pantheon, 1968.

Tocqueville, Alexis de. *Democracy in America*. Vols. 1 and 2. New York: Vintage, 1954.

Tropman, John E. "The Constant Crisis: Social Welfare and the American Cultural Structure," *California Sociologist*, 1(1):61–88.

U.S. Bureau of the Census. *Historical Statistics of the United States—Colonial Times to 1970*. Washington, D.C.: U.S. Department of Commerce, 1975.

BIBLIOGRAPHY

Aaron, Henry. "Financing Welfare Reform and Income Distribution." Speech (and oral response to audience questions), UCLA Conference on National Welfare Policy, September 29, 1972.

Abel-Smith, Brian. "Value for Money in Health Services," *Social Security Bulletin* 17–19, July 1974.

Abrahamse, Allan F., David M. de Ferranti, Patricia D. Fleischauer, and Albert Lipson. *AFDC Caseload and the Job Market in California: Selected Issues*, R–2115–CDOBP. Santa Monica: Rand, 1977.

Adams, Julius J. *The Challenge: A Study in Negro Leadership*. New York: Malliet, 1949.

Albrecht, James W., "Negative Income Taxation and Divorce in SIME/DIME," *Journal of the Institute for Socio–Economic Studies*, 4(3):75–82, Autumn 1979.

Allen, Henry L. "A Radical Critique of Federal Work and Manpower Programs, 1933–1974." Pp. 23–38, in Betty Reid Mandell (ed.), *Welfare in America: Controlling the "Dangerous Classes."* Englewood Cliffs, N.J.: Prentice-Hall, 1975.

Allen, Vernon. "Introduction" in Vernon Allen (ed.), *Psychological Factors in Poverty*. Chicago: Markham Publishing, 1970.

Allport, Gordon W. *Becoming*. New York: Yale Press, 1955.

American Conservative Union. "An Alternative Approach to Welfare Reform." Memorandum to Congress, 1969.

Andersen, Ronald and Odin W. Anderson "Trends in the Use of Health Services" in Howard E. Freeman, Sol Levin, and Leo G. Reeder (eds). *Handbook in Medical Sociology*. Englewood Cliffs, N.J.: Prentice Hall, 1979, pp. 317–91.

Anderson, Martin. *Welfare: The Political Economy of Welfare Reform in the U.S.* Stanford, Calif.: Hoover Institution Press, 1978.

Anderson, Ordin M., Ronald Andersen, Joan Daley, and Johanna Kravitz. *Expenditures for Personal Health Services: National Trends and Variations, 1953–1970*. Washington, D.C.: U.S. Department of Health, Education and Welfare, 1973.

———, Ronald Andersen, Rachael McGreely, and Johanna Kravitz. *Health Services Use: National Trends and Variations*. Washington, D.C.: U.S. Department of Health, Education and Welfare, 1973.

Angrow, Webster. "Formula for Explosion," *Frontier*, 16(12):7–9, October 1965.

Austin, R. *Gautreux v. Chicago Housing Authority*. Pp. 1207–24, in Robert J. Levy, Thomas P. Lewis, and Peter W. Martin (eds.), *Social Welfare and the Individual: Cases and Materials* Mineola: Foundation Press, 1971.

Avereh, Harvey A., Stephen J. Carroll, Theodore S. Donaldson, Herbert J. Kiesling, and John Pincus. *How Effective Is Schooling? A Critical Review and Synthesis of Research Findings*. Englewood Cliffs, N.J.: Educational Technology Publications, 1974.

Axinn, June, and Herman Levin. *Social Welfare— A History of the American Response to Need.* New York: Dodd, Mead, 1975.

Bagdikan, Ben H. "The Invisible Americans," *Saturday Evening Post,* 236(45):28–33, 37–38, 1963.

Bailyn, Bernard. *The Ideological Origins of the American Revolution.* Cambridge, Mass.: Harvard University Press, 1967.

Ball, Robert M. "Principles of Representative Payment," *Oasis,* August 1967.

Bandler, Louise S. *Casework with Multi-Problem Families.* New York: Columbia University Press, 1964.

Banfield, Edward C. "Welfare: A Crisis Without Solutions," *Public Interest,* 16:89–101, 1969.

Barnes, Peter. "Bringing Back the WPA: Fringe Benefits of a Depression," *New Republic,* 172(11):19–21, 1975.

Battle, Esther S., and Julian B. Rotter. "Children's Feelings of Personal Control as Related to Social Class and Ethnic Group," *Journal of Personality,* 31:482–90, 1963.

Bechtel, Robert. "Deficiencies in Public Housing," *American Psychological Association Monitor,* 2(11):10, 1971.

Bedeau, Hugo Adam. "Egalitarianism and the Idea of Equality." Pp. 3–27, in Roland Pennock and John W. Chapman (eds.), *Equality.* New York: Atherton, 1967.

Bednarzik, Robert W., and Stephen M. St Marie. "Employment and Unemployment in 1976," *Monthly Labor Review,* 100(2):3–13, 1977.

Bell, Carolyn Shaw. "The Carter Bill— Is It Welfare Reform?" *Journal of the Institute for Socio-Economic Studies,* 3(2):9–19, 1978.

Bell, Winifred, and Charles T. O'Reilly. "What About the Manpower Crisis in Social Welfare:" *Public Welfare,* 27(4):348–52, 1969.

Bellin, Lowell E. "Statement before the Subcommittee on Medicare-Medicaid of the Committee on Finance." Pp. 511–38, in *Hearings Before the Subcommittee on Medicare-Medicaid,* Part Two, June 2. Washington, D.C.: U.S. Government Printing Office, 1970.

Bellush, Jewel, and Murray Hausknecht. "Urban Renewal: An Historical Overview." Pp. 3–16, in Jewel Bellush and Murray Hausknecht (eds.), *Urban Renewal: People, Politics and Planning.* Garden City, N.Y.: Doubleday, 1967.

———— "Public Housing, the Contexts of Failure." Pp. 451–61, in Jewel Bellush and Murray Hausknecht (eds.), *Urban Renewal: People, Politics and Planning.* Garden City. N.Y.: Doubleday, 1967.

Bennet, Berkeley V. "Statement Before the Subcommittee on Finance." Pp. 565–617, in *Hearings Before the Subcommittee on Medicare-Medicaid,* Part Two, June 3. Washington, D.C.: U.S. Government Printing Office, 1970.

Berger, Peter, and Thomas Luckmann. *The Social Construction of Reality.* New York: Doubleday, 1966.

Bertrand, Alvin L. "The Stress-Strain Element of Social Systems: A Micro-Theory of Conflict and Change," *Social Forces,* 42(1):1–9, 1963.

Beveridge, William H. *Full Employment in a Free Society.* New York: W.W. Norton, 1945.

Bishop, John. "Jobs, Cash Transfer and Marital Instability: A Review of the Evidence." Written testimony to the Welfare Reform Subcommittee of the Committees on Agriculture, Education and Labor, Ways and Means of the U.S. House of Representatives, October 14, 1977.

Blau, Peter M. "Critical Remarks on Weber's Theory of Authority," *American Political Science Review,* 57(2):305–16, 1963.

———— . *Exchange and Power in Social Life.* New York: Wiley, 1964.

————, and Otis Dudley Dunncan. *The American Occupational Structure*. New York: Wiley, 1967.

Blumer, Herbert. "Society as Symbolic Interaction." Pp. 139–48, in Jerome G. Manis and Bernard N. Meltzer (eds.), *Symbolic Interaction: A Reader in Social Psychology*. Boston: Bacon, 1967.

————. *Symbolic Interactionism: Perspectives and Methods*. Englewood Cliffs, N.J.: Prentice-Hall, 1969.

Boas, Franz. "On Grammatical Categories." Pp. 121–23, in Dell Hymes (ed.), *Language in Culture and Society: A Reader in Linguistics and Anthropology*. New York: Harper, 1964.

Bobrow, S. B. *Reasonable Expectations: Limits on the Promise of Community Councils*, P-5824. Santa Monica: Rand, 1977.

Booth, Charles. *Life and Labor of the People of London*. 10 vols. London: Longmans, 1900–1911.

Bowles, S. "Toward an Educational Production Function," *Studies in Income and Wealth*, 35:11–60, 1970.

Bradshaw, Thomas F. "Job Seeking Methods Used by Unemployed Workers," *Monthly Labor Review*, 96(2):35–40, 1973.

Bremner, Robert H. *American Philanthropy*. Chicago: University of Chicago Press, 1960.

Breslin, Jimmy. "Why a 15 Year-Old Girl Wants to Have a Baby." *San Francisco Chronicle*, April 27, 1978, p. 36.

Brieland, Donald, and John Lemmon (eds.). *Social Work and the Law*. St. Paul, Minn.: West, 1977.

Briggs, John Walker. *An Italian Passage: Immigrants to Three American Cities, 1890–1930*. New Haven, Conn.: Yale Press, 1978.

Bronfenbrenner, Urie. "Damping the Unemployability Explosion," *Saturday Review*, 52(1):108–10, 1969.

Brooke, R. H., and K. M. Williams. *Evaluating Quality of Health Care for the Disadvantaged: A Literature Review*. Santa Monica: Rand, 1975.

Buckley, Walter. *Sociology and Modern Systems Theory*. Englewood Cliffs, N.J.: Prentice-Hall, 1967.

Budget of the United States Government. *Fiscal Year 1979*. Washington, D.C.: U.S. Government Printing Office, 1978.

Burns, S. "Housing as Social Overhead Capital." P. 992 (footnote 19), in Robert J. Levy, Thomas P. Lewis, and Peter W. Martin (eds.), *Social Welfare and the Individual: Cases and Materials*. Mineola: Foundation Press, 1971.

Califano, Joseph A. "Special HEW Report on Welfare Reform." *Hearings Before the Subcommitte and Public Assistance and Unemployment Compensation of the Committee on Ways and Means*—Ninety-fifth Congress. Washington, D.C.: U.S. Government Printing Office, 1977.

————. "Putting the Public into Public Policy Development," *Journal of the Institute for Socio-Economic Studies*, 3(2):1–8, 1978.

Caplovitz, David. *The Poor Pay More*. N.Y.: Free Press, 1967.

Cassell, Eric J. "In Sickness and Health," *Commentary*, 49:59–66, 1970.

————. "Disease as a Way of Life," *Commentary*, 55 (2): 80–83, February 1973.

Chapman, William. "The Welfare Enigma: Despite All the Programs, Reforms and Billions, the Poor and Their Problems Will Not Go Away," *Manchester Guardian*, June 5, 1977, pp. 1, 17–18.

Chilman, Catherine S. "Child-rearing and Family Relations: Patterns of the Very Poor," *Welfare in Review*, 3:9–19, 1965.

Christmas, June Jackson. "How Our Health System Fails Minorities: Systemic Defects and

Systemic Discrimination," *Civil Rights Digest,* 10(1):2–11, 1977.

Clairborne, Robert. "The Great Health Care Rip-Off," *Saturday Review,* 5:10–13, 16, 50, January 7, 1978.

Clark, Kenneth B. *Social and Economic Implications of Integration in the Public Schools.* Washington, D.C.: U.S. Department of Labor, 1965.

Cloward, Richard, and Irwin Epstein. "Private Social Welfare's Disengagement from the Poor." Mimeographed, n.d.

Cohen, Nathan E. "Reduction of Welfare Dependency." Pp. 292–93, in Margaret S. Gordon (ed.), *Poverty in America.* San Francisco: Chandler, 1965.

Coles, Robert. "The Poor Don't Want to Be Middle Class," *New York Times Magazine,* December 19, 1965, pp. 7, 54–56, 58.

Coll, Blanche D. "Perspectives in Public Welfare: The English Heritage," *Welfare in Review,* 4(3):1–12, 1966.

————. *Perspectives in Public Welfare.* Washington, D.C.: U.S. Government Printing Office, 1969.

Colombotus, John. "Physicians and Medicare: A Before-After Study of the Effects of Legislation Attitudes," *American Sociological Review,* 34(3):318–34, 1969.

Committee for Economic Development. *Improving the Public Welfare System.* New York: Committee for Economic Development, 1971.

————. *Building a National Health Care System: A Statement by the Research and Policy Committee.* Washington, D.C.: Committee for Economic Development, 1973.

Comptroller General's Office. *Questionable Claims Under the Medicaid Program for the Care of Persons in State Institutions for the Mentally Retarded in California.* Washington, D.C.: Comptroller General's Office, 1970.

————. *Improved Controls Needed Over Extent of Care Provided by Hospitals and Other Facilities to Medicare Patients.* Washington, D.C.: Comptroller General's Office, 1971.

————. *Ineffective Controls Over Program Requirements Relating to Medically Needy Persons Covered by Medicaid.* Washington, D.C.: Comptroller General's Office, 1971.

————. *Report to the Committee on Finance, U.S. Senate: Comparison of the Simplified and Traditional Methods of Determining Eligibility for AFDC.* Washington, D.C.: Comptroller General's Office, 1971.

Comrie, Keith. "Statement by Keith Comrie, Director, Los Angeles County, Department of Public Social Services," Testimony to the Subcommittee on Social Services and Welfare, California Legislature, December 11, 1978, mimeographed.

Conference Board, *Trends in Housing Costs.* New York: Conference Board, 1975.

Congressional Budget Office. "Poverty Status of Families Under Alternative Definitions of Income." Background Paper No. 17. Washington, D.C.: Congressional Budget Office, 1977.

Congressional Digest. "Proposed Revision of the Federal Minimum Wage Law," 51(4):98–100, 102–104, 128, 1972.

————. "Congress and the Humphrey-Hawkins Employment Bill," 55(6–7):162–92, June/July 1976.

————. "Controversy in Congress over Proposed Amnesty for Illegal Aliens," 56(10):225–55, 1977.

————. "Main Health Insurance Proposals Pending in the 95th Congress," 198–99, 224, August-September 1977.

Cooper, Maudine. "Comment over National Public Radio," January 30, 1975.

Coser, Lewis. *Functions of Social Conflict.* Glencoe, Ill.: Free Press, 1956.

————. *Political Sociology: Selected Essays.* New York: Harper, 1967.

Cronkhite, Leonard. "Control and Regulation of the Health Industry," *Journal of Medical Education,* 49(1):14–18, 1974.

Culliton, Barbara. "Caspar Weinberger: Beware of an 'All-Pervasive' Federal Government," *Science*, 189(4203):617–19, 1975.

Dahl, Robert A. "The Concept of Power," *Behavioral Science*, 2:201–15, 1957.

Dahrendorf, Rolf. *Essays in the Theory of Society*. Stanford, Calif.: University Press, 1958.

――――. "Toward a Theory of Social Conflict," *Journal of Conflict Resolution*, 2(1):170–83, 1958.

Danziger, Sheldon. "Can Welfare Reform Eliminate Poverty?" Paper presented at the Annual Meeting of the American Sociological Association, San Francisco, 1978.

――――, Robert Haveman, and Eugene Smolensky. *The Program for Better Jobs and Income: A Guide and Critique*. Washington, D.C.: U.S. Government Printing Office, 1977.

――――, and Robert J. Lampman. "Getting and Spending," *Annals of the American Academy of Political and Social Science*, 435:23–39, 1978.

――――, and Robert Plotnick. "Poverty Today: Does It Persist or Has It Been Eliminated?" Paper prepared for the Center for the Study of Democratic Institutions, 1977.

Davie, Maurice R. *Refugees in America*. New York: Harper, 1947.

Davis, Karen, and Cathy Schoen. *Health and the War on Poverty: A Ten Year Proposal*. Washington, D.C.: Brookings, 1978.

Dean, John P. "The Myths of Housing Reform," *American Sociological Review*, 14:281–88, 1949.

Decker, Peter R. *Fortunes and Failures: White Collar Mobility in Nineteenth Century San Francisco*. Cambridge, Mass.: Harvard Press, 1978.

Deutsch, M. "The Disadvantaged Child and the Learning Process," Pp. 163–79 in A. H. Passow (ed.), *Education in Depressed Areas*. New York: Bureau of Publications, Teachers College, Columbia University, 1963.

Dolgoff, Thomas. "The Psychological Meaning of Work," *Menninger Perspective* 5–9, Summer 1976.

Doolittle, Frederick, Frank Levy, and Michael Wiseman. "The Mirage of Welfare Reform," *Public Interest*, 47:62–87, 1977.

Dorsen, Norman, and Stanley Zimmerman. *Housing for the Poor: Rights and Remedies*. Project on Social Welfare Law, Supplement No. 1. New York: New York University School of Law, 1967.

Downs, Anthony. *Who Are the Urban Poor?* Committee for Economic Development, Supplementary Paper No. 26. New York: Committee for Economic Development, 1970.

――――. "The Successes and Failures of Federal Housing Policy," *Public Interest*, 34:124–45, 1974.

Dreitzel, Hans Peter. *Recent Sociology, Patterns of Communicative Behavior*. New York: Macmillan, 1970.

Drucker, Peter F., "Beyond Stick and Carrot: Hysteria Over the Work Ethic." *Psychology Today*, 7(6):86–96, November 1973.

Dubos, Rene. *Mirage of Health, Utopias, Progress and Biological Change*. Garden City, N.Y.: Doubleday-Anchor, 1959.

Dugan, Dennis and William H. Leaky. "Poverty Reconsidered," in Dennis Dugan and William H. Leaky (eds.), *Perspectives on Poverty*. New York: Praeger, 1973.

Duncan, O. D., D. L. Fetherman, and B. Duncan. *Socio-economic Background and Achievement*. London: Seminar Press, 1972.

Durbon, Elizabeth. *Welfare and Employment*. New York: Praeger, 1969.

Durham, Eugene. "Have the Poor Been Regulated? Toward a Multivariate Understanding of Welfare Growth," *Social Service Review*, 47(3):339–59, 1973.

Durkheim, Emile. *Division of Labor in Society*. Glencoe, Ill.: Free Press, 1933.

Duval, Melvin K. "The Population, The Government, and the Consumer" in John H.

Knowles (ed.), *Doing Better and Feeling Worse: Health in the U.S.* New York: W.W. Norton, 1977, pp. 185–92.

Eastburn, David P. *Economic Man vs. Social Man.* New York: *New York Times,* 1970.

Eitzen, D. Stanley, *Social Problems.* Boston: Allyn and Bacon, 1980.

Ellickson, Robert C. "Why Housing Prices Went Through the Roof," *Los Angeles Times,* July 24, 1978, Part II, p. 5.

Ellis, Robert A. "Some New Perspectives on Upward Mobility," *Urban and Social Change Review,* 4(1):15–17, 1970.

Ellison, Ralph. "Harlem Is Nowhere," *Harpers,* 229(1371):53–57, 1964.

Enos, Darryl D., and Paul Sultan. *The Sociology of Health Care: Social, Economic and Political Perspectives.* New York: Praeger, 1977.

Erikson, Kai Ti. *Wayward Puritans: A Study in the Sociology of Deviance.* New York: Wiley, 1966.

Eysenck, H. J. *The I.Q. Argument: Race, Intelligence and Education.* New York: Library Press, 1971.

Faltermayer, Edmund. "A Better Way to Deal with Unemployment," *Fortune* Magazine, 87(6):146–49, 236, 238, 241–42, 1973.

Faris, Robert E. L. *Social Disorganization.* New York: The Ronald Press, 1948.

Feagin, Joe R. "Poverty: We Still Believe That God Helps Those Who Help Themselves," *Psychology Today,* 6:101–129, November, 1972.

Ferguson, Robert H. *Unemployment: Its Scope, Measurement and Effect on Poverty.* Bulletin 53–2 Revised. Ithaca, N.Y.: Cornell University, 1971.

Fink, Arthur E. *The Field of Social Work.* New York: Holt, 1974.

Fishbein, Bette K. "The Food Stamp Program," *Journal of the Institute for Socio-Economic Studies:* Special Supplement, July 1977.

Forman, Lewis, Joyce Kornbluth, and Alan Forman, *Poverty in America.* Ann Arbor: University of Michigan Press, 1965.

Fox, Peter D. "Options for National Health Insurance: An Overview," *Policy Analysis,* 3(1):3–24, Winter 1977.

Frazier, E. Franklin. *The Negro Family in the United States,* Chicago, Illinois: The University of Chicago Press, 1937.

Freedman, Jonathan L. *Crowding and Behavior.* San Francisco: Freeman, 1975.

Freeman, Roger A. *Welfare Reform and the Family Assistance Plan.* Statement Before the Committee on Finance, U.S. Senate, January 27, 1972. Washington, D.C.: U.S. Government Printing Office, 1972.

Freymann, John Gordon. *The American Health Care System: Its Genesis and Trajectory.* New York: Med Comm Press, 1974.

Frieden, Bernard J. *Improving Federal Housing Subsidies.* Summary Report, Working Paper No. 1. Cambridge, Mass.: Joint Institute for Urban Studies, 1971.

———. "The New Housing Cost Problem," *Public Interest,* 49:70–87, 1977.

Friedlander, Walter A. and Robert Z. Apte. *Introduction to Social Welfare.* Englewood Cliffs, N.J.: Prentice-Hall, 1974.

Friedman, Milton. *Capitalism and Freedom.* Chicago: University Press, 1963.

———. "Friedman Calls Minimum Wage 'Anti-Negro'," *Socio-Economic Newsletter,* 3(3):3, 1978.

———, and Yale Brozen. *The Minimum Wage: Who Pays?* Pamphlet. Washington, D.C.: Free Society of America, 1966.

Friedson, Elliott. *Profession of Medicine.* New York: Dodd, Mead, 1970.

———. "Professionalism: The Doctor's Dilemma," *Social Policy,* 1(5):35–40, January-February 1971.

Fuerst, J. S., and Roy Petty. "Black Housing in Chicago," *Public Interest,* 52:103–10, 1978.

Gans, Herbert J. "Income Grants and 'Dirty Work'." *Public Interest,* 6:110–13, Winter 1967.

———. "Jobs and Services: Toward a Labor-Intensive Economy," New York: Center for Policy Research, Columbia University, 1976.

Garfinkel, Irwin. "Universal vs. Income Tested Debate Focuses on Income Maintenance Programs," *Socio-Economic Newsletter,* 3(9):1–2, 1978.

Garmzey, Norman. "Vulnerability Research and the Issue of Primary Prevention," *American Journal of Orthopsychiatry,* 41(1):101–16, 1971.

———. *Vulnerable and Invulnerable Children, Theory, Research and Intervention.* Washington, D.C.: American Psychological Association, 1976.

Gavagan, J. *Sanders v. Cruise.* Pp. 1305–10, in Robert J. Levy, Thomas P. Lewis, and Peter W. Martin (eds.), *Social Welfare and the Individual: Cases and Materials.* Mineola: Foundation Press, 1971.

———. *Sanders v. Cruise,* 10 Misc 2d, 533–173 NYS 2d 871 (1958).

Gilbert, N., and H. Specht. *Dimensions of Social Welfare Policy.* Englewood Cliffs, N.J.: Prentice-Hall, 1974.

Gilsinian, James F. "Symbolic Interaction and Ethnomethodology: A Comparison." Paper presented at Rocky Mountain Social Sciences Association, Salt Lake City, Utah, 1972.

Ginsberg, Eli. *The Limits of Health Reform.* New York: Basic Books, 1977.

———. "Health Service, Power Centers and Decision-Making Mechanisms" in John H. Knowles (ed.), *Doing Better and Feeling Worse: Health in the U.S.* New York: W.W. Norton, 1977, pp. 203–13.

Ginsburg, Helen. *Unemployment, Subemployment and Public Policy.* New York: New York University, School of Social Work, 1975.

Glasser, Paul, and Elizabeth Naverre. "Structural Problems of the One Parent Family," *Journal of Social Issues,* 21:98–109, 1965.

———. "The Problems of Families in the AFDC Program," *Children,* 12:151–156, July/August 1965.

Glazer, Nathan. "A Sociologist's View of Poverty." Pp. 12–26, in Margaret S. Gordon (ed.), *Poverty in America.* San Francisco: Chandler, 1965.

———, and Daniel P. Moynihan. *Beyond the Melting Pot: The Negroes, Puerto Ricans, Jews, Italians and Irish of New York City.* Cambridge, Mass.: MIT Press, 1963.

Glazer, Nona and Carol Creedon. *Children and Poverty: Some Sociological and Psychological Perspectives.* (Chicago: Rand McNally, 1968).

Godmere, Richard C. "Medicaid Management Information System," *Social and Rehabilitation Record,* 1(3):30–33, 1974.

Goffman, Erving. *Stigma, Notes on the Management of Spoiled Identity.* Englewood Cliffs, N.J.: Prentice-Hall, 1963.

Goldstein, Aaron H. *Interviewing for Eligibility Determination: A Management Aid for Enhancing Agency-Recipient Communication.* Washington, D.C.: U.S. Department of Health, Education and Welfare, 1975.

Gonzalez, Nancie L. *The Spanish-Americans of New Mexico.* Albuquerque: University of New Mexico Press, 1967.

Goodwin, Leonard. *Do the Poor Want to Work? A Social-Psychological Study of Work Orientations.* Washington, D.C.: Brookings, 1972.

———. "Welfare Mothers and the Work Ethic," *Monthly Labor Review,* 95(8): 35–37, 1972.

———. "The Work Ethic Among the Poor," *Los Angeles Times,* September 28, 1972, Part II, p. 7.

Gordon, Chad, and Kenneth J. Gergen. *The Self in Social Interaction.* New York: Wiley, 1968.

Gordon, Margaret S. (ed.). *Poverty in America*. San Francisco: Chandler, 1965.

Gordon, Milton M. *Assimilation in American Life*. New York: Oxford University Press, 1964.

Gould, Julius, and William L. Kolb. *A Dictionary of the Social Sciences*. Glencoe, Ill.: Free Press, 1964.

Greenberg, D. H. *Income Guarantees and the Working Poor in New York City: The Effect of Income Maintenance Programs on the Hours of Work of Male Family Heads*, R–658–NYC. Santa Monica: Rand, 1971.

———, and M. Kosters. *Income Guarantees and the Working Poor: The Effect of Income Maintenance Programs on the Hours of Work of Male Family Heads*, R–579–OEO. Santa Monica: Rand, 1970.

Greene, Leonard M. *A Plan for a Demogrant Financed by a Value-Added Tax*. White Plains, N.Y.: Institute for Socio-Economic Studies, 1976.

Griffen, Clyde, and Sally Griffen. *Natives and Newcomers: The Ordering of Opportunity in Mid-Nineteenth Century Poughkeepsie*. Cambridge, Mass.: Harvard Press, 1977.

Griffiths, Martha. "Conference (With)," *Journal of the Institute for Socio-Economic Studies*, 1(2):40–67, 1976.

Hagedorn, Robert, and Sanford Labovitz. "Occupational Characteristics and Participation in Voluntary Associations," *Social Forces*, 47:16–27, 1968.

Haggstrom, Warren C. "The Power of the Poor," in Sneden, Lawrence E., II (ed.), *Poverty: A Psychosocial Analysis*. Berkeley: McCutchan, 1970.

Hamilton, John A. "Will 'Work' Work?" *Saturday Review*, 53(21):24–27,1970.

Handler, Joel F. *The Coercive Social Worker, British Lessons for American Social Services*. Chicago: Markham Press, 1973.

Handlin, Oscar. *The Uprooted*. New York: Brown, 1951.

Harbison, F., and C. A. Myers. *Education, Manpower, and Economic Growth: Strategies of Human Resource Development*. New York: McGraw-Hill, 1964.

Harrington, Michael. *The Other America*. Baltimore: Penguin, 1963.

———, "Is There a Culture of Poverty?" New York: National Social Welfare Assembly, Occasional Papers, Poverty No. 1, May 12, 1964.

———, "Introduction," in Susan Sheehan, *A Welfare Mother*. New York: Mentor-New American Library, 1976.

Harris, Louis. *Living Sick: How the Poor View Their Health Sources*. New York: Blue Cross Association, 1969.

Harrison, Bennett. *Education, Training and the Urban Ghetto*. Baltimore: Johns Hopkins Press, 1972.

———, Harold L. Shepard, and William J. Spring. "Public Jobs, Public Needs: Government as the Employer of First Resort," *New Republic*, 167(17):18–21, 1972.

Hartman, Chester W. "The Politics of Housing," *Dissent*, 14(6):701–14, 1967.

———, and Gregg Carr. *Local Public Housing Administration: An Appraisal*. Working Paper No. 137. Institute for Urban and Regional Development. Berkeley: University of California, 1970.

Hartung, Frank. *Crime, Law and Society*. Detroit: Wayne State Press, 1966.

Harvard Educational Review. Environment, Heredity, and Intelligence. Reprint Series No. 2, 1969.

Hausman, Leonard. "The Potential for Financial Self-Support Among AFDC and AFDC-UP Families," *Southern Economic Journal*, 36(1):63, 1969.

Hayakawa, S. I. "Remarks by U.S. Senator S. I. Hayakawa, R–California, at National Press Club Luncheon," May 4, 1977.

Hearings before the Committee on Ways and Means of the House of Representatives, Ninety-First Congress on the Subject of Social Security and Welfare Proposals. Washington, D.C.: U.S. Government Printing Office, 1969.

Heffernan, Joseph. "Public Assistance and Social Services." Pp. 109–20, in Joint Economic Committee of the U.S. Congress, *Studies in Public Welfare: Issues in Welfare Administration: Inter-Governmental Relationships.* Washington, D.C.: U.S. Government Printing Office, 1973.

Henley, J. *Thomas v. Housing Authority.* Pp. 1232–49, in Robert J. Levy, Thomas P. Lewis, and Peter W. Martin (eds.), *Social Welfare and the Individual: Cases and Materials.* Mineola: Foundation Press, 1971.

——, *Thomas vs. Housing Authority* 282 F Supp 575, E.D. Ark. 1967.

Hernstein, Richard. "I.Q." *Atlantic Monthly,* 228(3):44–64, 1971.

Hersey, John. "Education, An Antidote to Poverty," *American Association of University Women Journal,* 58(4):157–60, 1965.

Hess, Robert D. "Educability and Rehabilitation: The Future of the Welfare Class." Paper presented at the Thirteenth Groves Conference on Marriage and the Family, Knoxville, Tenn., 1964.

——, Virginia Shipman, Brophy Jeref, and Roberta Meyer Baer. "The Cognitive Environments of Urban Pre-School Children, Summary of the Completed Project." Graduate School of Education, University of Chicago, 1969.

Hogan, John D., and Francis A.J. Ianni. *American Social Legislation.* New York: Harper, 1956.

Holden, Constance. "Teen Age Pregnancies Out of Control," *Science,* 204(4393):597, May 11, 1979.

Hollingshead, August B., and Frederick C. Redlich. *Social Class and Mental Illness.* New York: Wiley, 1958.

Horowitz, Irving Louis. "Consensus, Conflict and Cooperation: A Sociological Inventory," *Social Forces,* 41(2):177–88, 1962.

Horton, John. "Order and Conflict Theories of Social Problems as Competing Ideologies," *American Journal of Sociology,* 71(6):701–13, 1966.

Horton, Paul B., and Gerald R. Leslie. *The Sociology of Social Problems.* 3d ed. New York: Appleton, 1965.

Hoult, Thomas Ford. *Dictionary of Modern Sociology.* Totowa, N.J.: Littlefield, 1969.

Howe, Louisa P. "Some Sociological Aspects of Identification." Pp. 61–79, in Warner Muensterberger and Sidney Axelrad (eds.), *Psycho-Analysis and the Social Sciences,* Vol. 4. New York: International Universities Press, 1955.

Hughes, Everett. "Work and Self." Pp. 313–14, in John H. Rohrer and Muzafer Sherif (eds.), *Social Psychology at the Crossroads.* New York: Harpers, 1951.

Hurvitz, Nathan. "Symbolic Interactionism: A Social Psychological Theory for Marriage and Family Counseling." Pp. 853–54, in Proceedings of the Eightieth Annual American Psychological Association. Washington, D.C.: American Psychological Association, 1972.

Hyman, Herbert H. "The Value Systems of Different Classes," in Reinhard Bendix and Seymour Martin Lipset (eds.), *Class, Status and Power.* Glencoe: Free Press, 1953.

Isaccson, Peter. "There's Only So Much That a Doctor Can Do: Poverty and Health," *New Republic,* 171(24):15–17, 1974.

Jackson, Jacqueline J. "Where Are the Black Men? Scarcity of Males Upsets the Life Styles of [Black] Women," *Ebony,* 27(5):99–102, 104, 106, 1972.

Janowitz, Morris. "Social Control of the Welfare State." Mimeographed, n.d.

Johnson, Alexander. *The Almshouses.* New York: Charities Publication Committee, 1911.

Johnson, Beverly L. "Women Who Head Families 1970–1977; Their Number Rose, Income Lagged," *Monthly Labor Review,* 101(2):32–37, 1978.

Johnson, Harry G. "Poverty and Unemployment." Pp. 166–70, in Burton A. Weisbrod (ed.), *The Economics of Poverty.* Englewood Cliffs, N.J.: Prentice-Hall, 1965.

Johnston, Denis F. "The Future of Work: Three Possible Alternatives," *Monthly Labor Review*, 95(5):3–11, 1972.

Jones, Brian J. "Change for Money? An Analysis of Welfare Failure." Paper presented at the Annual Meeting of the Society for the Study of Social Problems, San Francisco, 1978.

Jordan, Bill. *Poor Parents: Social Policy and The Cycle of Deprivation*. London: Routledge and Kegan Paul, 1974.

Kaplan, Roy H., and Curt Tausky. "The Meaning of Work Among the Hard Core Unemployed," *Pacific Sociological Review*, 17(2):185–98, 1974.

Kardiner, Abram. *The Individual and His Society*. New York: Columbia Press, 1974.

———, and Lionel Ovesey. *The Mark of Oppression: Explorations in the Personality of the American Negro*. New York: Meridian, 1964.

Karp, Abraham J. *Golden Door to America: The Jewish Immigrant Experience*. N.Y.: Penguin, 1977.

Kephart, William M. "Occupational Level and Marital Disruption," *American Sociological Review*, 20:456–65, 1955.

Killingsworth, Charles C. "Employment as an Alternative to Welfare." Paper presented at UCLA Conference on National Welfare Policy, September 29, 1972.

Klarman, Herbert F. "Major Initiatives in Health Care," *Public Interest*, 34:106–23, 1974.

Klausner, Samuel Z. *Six Years in the Lives of the Impoverished: An Examination of the WIN Thesis*. Philadelphia: Center for Research of the Acts of Man, 1978.

Kluckhorn, Florence. "Family Diagnosis: Variations in the Basic Values of Family Systems," *Social Casework*, 1958.

Knowles, John H. "The Responsibility of the Individual" in John H. Knowles (ed.). *Doing Better and Feeling Worse: Health in the U.S.* New York: W.W. Norton, 1977, pp. 57–80.

Kolko, Gabriel. *Wealth and Power in America: An Analysis of Social Class and Income Distribution*. New York: Praeger, 1962.

Kotelchuk, David, "The Health Status of Americans" in David Kotelchuk (ed.). *Prognosis Negative: Crisis in the Health Care System*. New York: Vintage, 1976, pp. 5–19.

Kristol, Irving. "Welfare: The Best of Intentions, The Worst of Results," *Atlantic Monthly*, 228(2):45–47, 1971.

Kuhn, Manford H. "Major Trends in Symbolic Interaction Theory in One Past 25 Years," *Sociological Quarterly*, 5(1):61–84, 1964.

Kurzman, Paul A. "Poor Relief in Medieval England: The Forgotten Chapter in the History of Social Welfare," *Child Welfare*, 49:495–501, 1970.

Kuznets, Simon. *Economic Growth of Nations*. Cambridge, Mass.: Harvard Press, 1971.

Laffer, Arthur. "The Disincentive Factor," *Time* Magazine, 112(14):55, 1978.

Laing, R. D. *The Politics of Experience*. New York: Pantheon, 1967.

Lane, Lionel C. "The Identity of the Public Social Service Worker," *Public Welfare*, 27(4):311–17, 1969.

Langer, Elinor. "The Shame of Medicine," *New York Review of Books*, 6(9):6, 8–11, 1966.

———, "The Shame of Medicine" in Rose Giallombardo (ed.). *Contemporary Social Issues*. Santa Barbara: Hamilton, 1975, pp. 330–38.

Lawrence, John F. "Household Help Laws Discourage Hiring, Encourage Cheating," *Los Angeles Times*, September 17, 1978, Part V, p. 3.

Lawrence, William J., and Stephen Leeds. *An Inventory of Federal Income Transfer Programs, Fiscal Year 1977*. White Plains, N.Y.: Institute for Socio-Economic Studies, 1978.

Lawyers Committee for Civil Rights Under the Law and the National Urban Coalition. *Falling Down on the Job: The United States Employment Service and the Disadvantaged*. Washington, D.C.: National Urban Coalition, 1971.

League of Women Voters. "Jobs and Hard Cash." Mimeographed, 1967.

———. "Housing Supply," *Current Review of Human Resources*. Washington, D.C.: League of Women Voters, 1968.

Lecht, Leonard A. *Manpower Needs for National Goals in the 1970's*. New York: Praeger, 1969.

Lefkowitz, Myron J. *Poverty and Health*. Discussion Paper 71–70. Madison, Wis.: Institute for Research on Poverty, 1970.

———. "Poverty and Health: A Re-examination," *Inquiry*, 16(1):3–13, 1973.

Leonard, E. M. *The Early History of the English Poor Relief*. New York: Barnes and Noble, 1965.

Levenstein, Aaron. *Why People Work: Changing Incentives in a Troubled World*. New York: Collier, 1964.

Leveson, I. *The Demand for Neighborhood Medical Care*. Santa Monica: Rand, 1968.

Levin, Tom. *American Health: Professional Privilege Versus Public Need*. New York: Praeger, 1974.

Levine, Sol, and Paul E. White. "Exchange as a Conceptual Framework for Study of Interorganizational Relationships." Pp. 117–32, in Amitai Etzioni (ed.), *A Sociological Reader on Complex Organizations*. New York: Holt, 1969.

Levinson, Perry. "How Employable Are AFDC Mothers?" *Welfare in Review*, 8:19, 1970.

Levitan, Sar. *Anti-Poverty Work and Training Efforts: Goals and Reality*. Washington, D.C.: National Manpower Policy Task Force, 1967.

Levy, Frank. "Poverty by the Numbers, "*The American Spectator*, 2(7):24–26, May 1978.

Levy, Robert J., Thomas P. Lewis, and Peter M. Martin (eds.), *Social Welfare and the Individual: Cases and Materials*. Mineola: Foundation Press, 1971.

Lewis, Oscar. *La Vida: A Puerto Rican Family in the Culture of Poverty, San Juan and New York*. New York: Random House, 1956.

———. *Five Families*. New York: Basic Books, 1959.

———. "The Culture of Poverty," *Scientific American*, 215(4):19–25, October 1966.

———. *A Study of Slum Culture: Backgrounds for La Vida*. New York: Random House, 1968.

———. *La Vida*. London: Panther Press, 1968.

Lichtenstein, Charles. "On the Minimum Wage," *Public Interest*, 6:113–15, 1967.

Liebow, Elliot. "Fathers Without Children," *Public Interest*, 5:13–25, 1966.

———. *Tally's Corner: A Study of Negro Streetcorner Men*. Boston: Little, Brown, 1967.

———. "No Man Can Live with the Terrible Knowledge That He Is Not Needed," *Social Service Outlook*, 5(9):1–3, 14–16, 1970.

Lipset, Seymour Martin. *Political Man: The Social Bases of Politics*. New York: Doubleday, 1960.

———, and Hans Zetterberg. "A Theory of Social Mobility." Pp. 561–73, in R. Bendix and S. M. Lipset (eds.), *Class, Status, and Power*. 2d ed. New York: Free Press, 1966.

Loch, Sir Charles S. *Charity and Social Life: A Short Study of Religious and Social Thought in Relation to Charitable Methods and Literature*. London: Macmillan, 1910.

Lockridge, Kenneth A. *A New England Town: The First Hundred Years*. New York: W.W. Norton, 1970.

Loomis, Charles P. "In Praise of Conflict and Its Resolution," *American Sociological Review*, 32(6):875–90, 1967.

Lowry, I. S. *Housing Assistance for Low Income Urban Families, A Fresh Approach*, P–4665. Santa Monica: Rand, 1971.

———. *An Overview of the Housing Assistance Supply Experiment*, P–5967. Santa Monica: Rand, 1977.

———. *Early Findings of the Housing Assistance Supply Experiment*, P–6075. Santa Monica: Rand, 1978.

Lubove, Roy. "The Progressives and the Slums." Pp. 17–24, in Jewel Bellush and Murray Hausknecht (eds.), *Urban Renewal: People, Politics and Planning.* Garden City, N.Y.: Doubleday, 1967.

Lyon, D. W., P. A. Armstrong, J. R. Hosek, and J. J. McCall. *Multiple Benefits in New York City,* R–2002–HEW. Santa Monica: Rand, 1976.

———, C. P. Rydell, and M. D. Menchik. *Welfare Policy Research: Findings on the Dynamics of Dependency,* P5566. Santa Monica: Rand, 1975.

McClure, Ethel. *More Than Poor: The Development of Minnesota Poor Farms and Homes for the Aged.* St. Paul, Minn.: Minnesota Historical Society, 1968.

McCord, Joan, and William McCord. "The Effects of Parental Role on Criminality," *Journal of Social Issues,* 14:66–75, 1958.

McCormack, Patricia. "A Report on Children Bearing Children: Lifelong Handicap Predicted," *International Herald Tribune,* August 22, 1978, p. 6.

McCormick, Harvey L. *Medicare and Medicaid: Claims and Procedures.* St. Paul, Minn.: West, 1977.

Macdonald, Dwight. *Our Invisible Poor.* New York: Sidney Hillman Foundation, n.d.

Macdonald, Maurice. "Food Stamps: An Analytical History," *Social Service Review,* 51(4):642–58, 1977.

McDougal and Muller. "Public Purpose in Public Housing: An Anachronism Revisited" *Yale Law Journal,* 52(42):47–48, 1942.

McGovern, George. "McGovern Says Illiteracy Increase Is Alarming," *Los Angeles Times,* September 8, 1978, Part I, p. 20.

McIntosh, Donald. "Weber and Freud: On the Nature and Sources of Authority," *American Sociological Review,* 35(5):901–11, 1970.

MacIver, R. M. *The Ramparts We Watch.* New York: Macmillan, 1950.

Mack, Raymond W., and Richard C. Snyder. "The Analysis of Social Conflict—Toward an Overview and Synthesis," *Journal of Conflict Resolution,* 1(1):212–48, 1957.

McKinney, Edward A. "Health Crisis for Whom?" *Health and Social Work,* 1(1):101–16, 1976.

MacLatchie, Elizabeth B. *Simplifying Application and Investigation Processes.* Chicago: American Public Welfare Association, 1968.

Madway, David M. "A Mortgage Foreclosure Primer," *Clearinghouse Review,* 8:146–84, 1974.

Magnum, Garth L. "The Why, How and Whence of Manpower Programs," in Lawrence Sneden, II (ed.). *Poverty a Psychosocial Analysis.* Berkeley: McCutchan, 1970.

Manis, Jerome, and Bernard Meltzer (eds.). *Symbolic Interaction: A Reader in Social Psychology.* Boston: Bacon, 1967.

Manpower Research Office. "Longitudinal Manpower Survey." Washington, D.C.: U.S. Department of Labor, 1978.

Marmor, Theodore R. "Why Medicare Helped Raise Doctors' Fees," *Transaction,* 5:14–19, 1968.

Marshall, Alfred. *Principles of Economics.* New York: Macmillan, 1920.

May, Edgar. *The Wasted Americans.* New York: Signet, 1964.

Maynard, Rebecca, Irwin Garfinkel, and Valerie Leach. *Analysis of Nine Month Interviews for Supported Work: Results of an Early AFDC Sample.* Institute for Research on Poverty, University of Wisconsin at Madison, 1977.

Mechanic, David. "The Poor State of Health," *Science,* 172(3984):701–702, 1971.

Melcher, George W. "Statement made at the Hearings Before the Subcommittee on Finance." Washington, D.C.: U.S. Government Printing Office, 1970.

Meltzner, Bernard N., John W. Peters, and Larry T. Reynolds. *Symbolic Interaction: Genesis, Varieties, and Criticism.* Boston: Routledge, 1975.

Mencher, Samuel. *Poor Law to Poverty Program.* Pittsburgh: University Press, 1967.

Merton, Robert K. "Social Structure and Anomie," *American Sociological Review,* 3(5): 672–82, 1938.

———. *Social Theory and Social Structure.* Glencoe, Ill.: Free Press, 1957.

Meyerson, Adam. "The Public Policy: On Raising the Minimum Wage," *The Alternative: An American Spectator,* 8(8):32–33, 1975.

Michael, Donald W. *Cybernation: The Silent Conquest.* Santa Barbara: Center for the Study of Democratic Institutions, 1962.

Michelotti, Kopp. "Educational Attainment of Workers, March 1977," Special Labor Force Report No. 209. Washington, D.C.: U.S. Department of Labor, 1978.

Middleton, Russell. "Psychological Well-being." Chapter 7 in *Final Report of the Rural Negative Income Tax Experiment.* Madison, Wis.: Institute for Research on Poverty, University of Wisconsin, 1976.

———, and Vernon Allen. "Social-Psychological Effects." Chapter 8 in H. Watts and A. Rees (eds.). *The New Jersey Income Maintenance Experiment.* New York: Academic Press, 1977.

Mill, John Stuart. *Principles of Political Economy.* London: Longmans, 1917.

Miller, Herman P. "Income and Education: Does Education Pay Off?" Pp. 129–46, in Selma J. Mushkin (ed.), *Economics of Higher Education.* Washington, D.C.: U.S. Department of Health, Education and Welfare, 1962.

Miller, S. M. "The American Lower Classes: A Typological Approach." Pp. 9–23, in Arthur B. Shostak and William Gomberg (eds.), *Blue Collar World: Studies of the American Worker.* Englewood Cliffs, N.J.: Prentice-Hall, 1964.

———, M. Rein, P. Roby, and B. Gross. "Poverty, Inequality and Conflict," *The Annals,* 373:16–52, 1967.

———, and Frank Riessman. "The Credentials Trap," *Social Service Outlook,* 5(5):1–4, 1970.

Miller, Walter B. "The Elimination of the American Lower Class as National Policy: A Critique of the Ideology of the Poverty Movement of the 1960's." Pp. 260–316, in Daniel P. Moynihan (ed.), *On Understanding Poverty.* New York: Basic Books, 1968.

Milner, Murray, Jr. "On Getting Somewhere: Notes on 'Equal Opportunity' and Other Convenient Delusions," *Columbia Forum,* 1(2):19–25, 1972.

———. *The Illusion of Equality.* San Francisco: Josey Bass, 1972.

Minuchin, Salvador, Braulio Montalvo, Bernard G. Guerney, Bernice Rosman, and Florence Shumer. *Families of the Slums, An Exploration of Their Structure and Treatment.* New York: Basic Books, 1967.

Monteiro, Lois A. "Expense Is No Object: Income and Physician Visits Reconsidered," *Journal of Health and Social Behavior,* 14(2):99–145, 1973.

Morris, Robert. "Welfare Reform, 1973: The Social Service Dimension," *Science,* 181(4099):515–22, 1973.

Moynihan, Daniel P. *The Negro Family: The Case for National Action.* Washington, D.C.: U.S. Government Printing Office, 1965.

———. "The Crisis in Welfare," *Public Interest,* 19:3–29, 1968.

———. *The Politics of a Guarranteed Income: The Nixon Administration and the Family Assistance Plan.* New York: Free Press, 1969.

———. "One Step We Must Take," *Saturday Review,* 53(21):20–23, 1970.

———. "The Rocky Road to Welfare Reform," *Journal of the Institute for Socio-Economic Studies,* 3(1):1–10, 1978.

Munnel, Alicia H. *The Future of Social Security.* Washington, D.C.: Brookings, 1977.

———. "Social Security: Public Financing for Human Needs," *The Pioneer,* October 19, 1978, pp. 6–7.

Munts, Raymond. "Objectives for Today's Economy," *Manpower,* 1(7):18–21, 1969.

Myers, Beverlee A. "The Unequal Burdens of Paying for Health Care," *Civil Rights Digest,* 10(9):12–18, 1977.

Myers, Robert J. *Medicare.* Homewood, Ill.: R. D. Irwin, 1970.

Nash, Jim. "Counter-Culture: A Bloodsucker on Our System," *Los Angeles Times,* July 26, 1978, Part II, p. 5.

National Center for Social Statistics. *Disposition of Public Assistance Cases Involving Questions of Fraud.* Washington, D.C.: U.S. Department of Health, Education and Welfare, n.d.

———. *Public Assistance Statistics.* Washington, D.C.: U.S. Department of Health, Education and Welfare, n.d.

———. *National Cross Tabulations from the 1967 and 1969 AFDC Studies.* Washington, D.C.: U.S. Department of Health, Education and Welfare, 1971.

New Republic, The. "Invisible Unemployed" (editorial), 166(9):8, 1972.

———. "Feeding a Hungry World" (editorial), 171(1–2):5–8, 1974.

Newman, Oscar. *Defensible Space: Crime Protection Through Urban Design.* New York: McMillan, 1972.

New York Times. "Goldin Audit Finds Fraud in Women on Welfare Not Reporting Marriages," October 30, 1977, Part I, p. 37.

Noble, Philip (ed.) *The Con III Controversy.* New York: Pocket Books, 1971.

Notestein, Wallace. *The English People on the Eve of Colonization, 1603–1630.* New York: Harper, 1954.

Oblata, J. R. "The Blacks of Baldwin Hills: Worthy Models for Youth," *Los Angeles Times,* June 16, 1973, Part II, p. 7.

Office of Child Support Enforcement. "Good Cause for Refusing to Cooperate." Action Transmissal to State Agencies and Local Agencies, April 5, 1978. Washington, D.C.: U.S. Department of Health, Education and Welfare, 1978.

Office of Research and Statistics. *AFDC 1975 Recipient Characteristics.* Washington, D.C.: U.S. Department of Health, Education and Welfare, 1977.

———. "Public Assistance: Comparison of Calendar Years 1975–1977." Research and Statistics Note No. 10. Washington, D.C.: U.S. Department of Health, Education and Welfare, 1978.

Office of the Secretary, U.S. Department of Health, Education and Welfare. *Better Jobs and Income Act HR 9030: A Summary and Sectional Explanation.* Washington, D.C.: U.S. Department of Health, Education and Welfare, 1977.

Olsen, E. O. *An Efficient Method of Improving the Housing of Low Income Families,* P–4258. Santa Monica: Rand, 1969.

Ornati, Oscar. *Poverty in America.* Washington, D.C.: National Policy Committee on Pockets of Poverty of the Farmers Educational Foundation, 1964.

Ossowski, S. *Class Structure in the Social Consciousness.* London: Routledge, 1963.

Parsons, Talcott. *The Social System.* Glencoe, Ill.: Free Press, 1951.

———. *Societies: Evolutionary and Comparative Purposes.* Englewood Cliffs, N.J.: Prentice-Hall, 1966.

———, and Edward A. Shils. *Toward a General Theory of Action.* Cambridge, Mass.: Harvard Press, 1951.

Pascal, A. H. *Enhancing Opportunities in Job Markets: Summary of Research and Recommendations for Policy, R 580-OEO.* Santa Monica: Rand, 1971.

Passell, Peter, and Leonard Ross. *Retreat from Riches. Affluence and Its Enemies.* New York: Viking Press, 1973.

Pavalko, Ronald M. *Sociology of Occupations and Professions.* Itaska, Ill.: Peacock, 1971.

Pen, Jan. *Income Distribution: Facts, Theories, Policies.* Trevor S. Preston (trans.). New York: Praeger, 1971.

Pierce, Neal R. "Public Housing Projects Can Be Livable," *Los Angeles Times,* October 30, 1977, Part IV, p. 5.

Piven, Frances Fox, and Richard A. Cloward. *Regulating the Poor.* New York: Random House, 1971.

Powell, Elvin H. "Occupation, Status and Suicide; Toward a Redefinition of Anomie," *American Sociological Review,* 23:131–38, 1958.

Pruitt, Walter A., and H. van de Castle. "Dependency Measures and Welfare Chronicity," *Journal of Consulting Psychology,* 26:559–60, 1962.

Raab, Earl. "Quotas by Any Other Name," *Commentary,* 53(1):41–45, 1972.

Rainwater, Lee. "Crucible of Identity: The Negro Lower Class Family," *Daedalus,* 95(1):172–216, 1966.

———. "Poverty, Living Standards and Family Well Being." Working Paper No. 10. Cambridge, Mass.: Joint Center for Urban Studies, 1972.

Raspberry, William. "A Generation of Kids Who Don't Know What Work Is," *Los Angeles Times,* December 6, 1977, Part II, p. 7.

———. " 'Joblessness Isn't So Bad' Oh, No?" *Los Angeles Times,* January 10, 1978, Part II, p. 5.

Reich, Charles A. *The Greening of America.* New York: Random House, 1970.

Rein, Martin. "The Strange Case of Public Dependency," *Transaction,* 3(3):16–23, 1966.

———, and Lee Rainwater. *Patterns of Welfare Use.* Working Paper No. 47. Cambridge, Mass.: Joint Center for Urban Studies, 1977.

———. "How Large is the Welfare Class?" *Challenge,* 20–23, September/October 1977.

Rein, Mildred, and Barbara Wishnov. "Patterns of Work and Welfare in AFDC," *Welfare in Review,* 9(6):7–12, 1971.

Ribich, Thomas I. "The Problem of Equal Opportunity: A Review Article," *Journal of Human Resources,* 7(4):518–26, 1972.

Richan, Willard. "The Two Kinds of Social Service in Public Welfare," *Public Welfare,* 27(4):307–10, 1969.

Richmond, Julius B. "The Needs of Children" in John H. Knowles (ed.), *Doing Better and Feeling Worse: Health in the U.S.* New York: W.W. Norton, 1977, pp. 247–59.

Riessman, Frank, *The Culturally Deprived Child.* New York: Harper and Row, 1962.

———. "A Portrait of the Underprivileged." Pp. 74–77, in Robert E. Will and Harold G. Vatler (eds.), *Poverty in Affluence: The Social, Political and Economic Dimensions in the U.S.* New York: Harcourt, 1965.

Roach, Jack L. "Sociological Analysis and Poverty," *American Journal of Sociology,* 71(1):68–77, 1965.

Rodgers, Brian. *The Battle Against Poverty.* Vol. 1, *From Pauperism to Human Rights,* Vol. 2 *Toward a Welfare State.* London: Routledge, 1968.

Rogers, David E. "The Challenge of Primary Care" in John H. Knowles (ed.), *Doing Better and Feeling Worse; Health in the U.S.* New York: W.W. Norton, 1977, pp. 81–103.

Rose, Arnold. *Human Behavior and Social Process.* Boston: Houghton Mifflin, 1962.

———. "Law and the Causation of Social Problems," *Social Problems,* 16(1):33–43, 1968.

Rose, Arnold M. "The Unemployables" in Irwin Deutscher and Elizabeth J. Thompson (eds.), *Among the People: Encounters with the Poor.* New York: Basic Books, 1968.

Rosen, Michael B. "Tenant Rights in Public Housing." Pp. 154–261, in N. Dorsen and S. Zimmerman (eds.), *Housing for the Poor: Rights and Remedies.* New York: New York University School of Law, 1967.

Rowntree, B. Seebohm. *Poverty, A Study of Town Life.* New York: Macmillan, 1903.

Runes, Dagobert D. *Dictionary of Philosophy*. Totowa, N.J.: Little Adams, 1962.

Ryan, William. *Blaming the Victim*. New York: Vintage, 1971.

Rycroft, Charles. *A Critical Dictionary of Psychoanalysis*. New York: Basic Books, 1968.

Rydell, C. P., T. Palmerio, G. Blais, and D. Brown. *Welfare Caseload Dynamics*, R–1441–NYC. Santa Monica: Rand, 1974.

San Francisco Chronicle. "Making Affirmative Action Work in Higher Education," August 11, 1975, p. 10.

Sarbin, Theodore R. "The Culture of Poverty, Social Identity and Cognitive Outcomes," in Vernon Allen (ed.), *Psychological Factors in Poverty*. Chicago: Markham Publishing, 1970.

Schechter, Mal. "Medicare on Its Fourth Birthday: Alive But Not Well," *New Republic*, 163(2):15–17, 1970.

Scheff, Thomas J. *Being Mentally Ill: A Sociological Theory*. Chicago: Aldine, 1966.

―――. "Toward a Sociological Model of Consensus," *American Sociological Review*, 32(1):32–46, 1967.

Schmid, Calvin F., and Charles E. Nobbe. "Socio-Economic Differentials Among Non-White Races," *American Sociological Review*, 30(6):909–22.

Schnitzer, Martin. *Income Distribution*. New York: Praeger Publishers, 1974.

Schorr, Alvin. *Slums and Social Insecurity*. Washington, D.C.: U.S. Government Printing Office, 1963.

―――. "Income Maintenance and the Birth Rate," *Social Security Bulletin*, 28:22–30, 1965.

―――. "Against a Negative Income Tax," *Public Interest*, 5:110–17, 1966.

―――. "The Family Cycle and Income Development," *Social Security Bulletin*, 29:14–25, 1966.

Schrag, Peter. "End of the Impossible Dream," *Saturday Review*, 53(38):68–70, 92–94, 1970.

Schussheim, Morton J. "Housing in Perspective," *Public Interest*, 19:18–30, 1970.

Schwartz, Harry. "Plop, Plop, Fizz, Fizz: What Government Should and Shouldn't Do About Medical Costs," *The Alternative: An American Spectator*, 10(8):7–9, 1977.

Schweinitz, Karl de. *England's Road to Social Security, 1349–1947*. 3d rev. ed. Philadelphia: University of Philadelphia Press, 1947.

Scitovsky, Anne A., and Nelda M. Snyder. *Medical Care Use by a Group of Elderly Insured Aged: A Case Study*. Washington, D.C.: U.S. Department of Health, Education and Welfare, 1975.

Scott, Austin. "Medical Care for Non-Whites Assailed: More Vigorous Affirmative Action Programs Urged in Congress Report," *Los Angeles Times*, November 26, 1977, Part I, p. 1.

Scott, Marvin B. "The Social Sources of Alienation." Pp. 239–52, in I. L. Horowitz (ed.), *The New Sociology: Essays in Social Science and Social Theory in Honor of C. Wright Mills*. New York: Oxford Press, 1965.

Seeman, Melvin. "On the Meaning of Alienation." Pp. 525–39, in Lewis A. Coser and Bernard Rosenberg (eds.), *Sociological Theory: A Book of Readings*. New York: Macmillan, 1964.

Segalman, Ralph. "The Protestant Ethic and Social Welfare," *Journal of Social Issues*, 24(2):125–41, 1968.

―――. "The Cultural Chasm Reconsidered," *Rocky Mountain Social Science Journal*, 6(2):143–45, 1969.

Select Committee on Nutrition and Human Needs, U.S. Senate, *Promises to Keep: Housing Need and Federal Failure in Rural America*. Washington, D.C.: U.S. Government Printing Office, 1971.

Selznick, Gertrude J., and Stephen Steinberg. "Social Class, Ideology and Voting Prefer-ence." Pp. 216–26, in Celia S. Heller (ed.), *Structural Social Inequality*. New York: Macmillan, 1969.

Shapley, Deborah. "National Health Insurance: Will It Promote Costly Technology?" *Science*, 186(4162):423–25, 1974.

Sheehan, Susan. *A Welfare Mother*. New York: New American Library (Mentor Books), 1976.

Sheppard, Harold L. *A Search for New Directions in the War Against Poverty*. Washington, D.C.: Upjohn Institute for Employment Research, 1968.

Shibutani, Tamotsu. *Society and Personality: An Interactionist Approach to Social Psychol-ogy*. Englewood Cliffs, N.J.: Prentice-Hall, 1961.

――――. *Human Native and Collective Behavior: Papers in Honor of Herbert Blumer*. Engle-wood Cliffs, N.J.: Prentice-Hall, 1970.

Silberman, Charles E. *Crisis in Black and White*. New York: Random House, 1964.

――――. "Beware the Day They Change Their Minds," *Fortune*: 150–53, 255, 258, 262, 267, November 1965.

Simmel, Georg. *Conflict and the Web of Group Affiliations*. Glencoe, Ill.: Free Press, 1955.

――――. "The Poor." Claire Jacobson (trans.). *Social Problems*, 13(2):118–39, February 1965.

Simmons, Ozzie G. "The Mutual Images and Expectations of Anglo-Americans and Mexi-can-Americans," in John H. Burma (ed.), *Mexican-Americans in the United States*. New York: Schenkman, 1970.

Skelly and White. "Wishing for More for Less," *Time* Magazine 112(17):26, 28, 1978.

Smith, Adam. *The Wealth of Nations*. Edwin Cannon (ed.). New York: Modern Library, 1937.

Smith, J. P. *Assets, Savings and Labor Supply*, P–5470–1. Santa Monica: Rand, November 1976.

Snee, John, and Mary Ross. "Social Security Amendments of 1977: Legislative History and Summary of Provisions," *Social Security Bulletin*, (SSA) 78–11700, March 1978.

Social Security Administration. *A Chartbook: Aid to Families with Dependent Children*. Washington, D.C.: U.S. Department of Health, Education and Welfare, 1968.

――――. *Social Security Handbook*. Washington, D.C.: U.S. Department of Health, Educa-tion and Welfare, 1969.

――――. *Social Security Program Charts*. Washington, D.C.: U.S. Department of Health, Education and Welfare, 1978.

――――. *Public Assistance Statistics: October 1978*. Washington, D.C.: U.S. Department of Health, Education and Welfare, 1979.

Social Security Information Items. "Trustees Report Social Security Financially Sound," No. 21, July 1, 1978.

――――. "Effort Made to Increase Child Support Collections," No. 23, September 1978.

――――. "Medicare Deductible Is $160 Starting Jan. 1, 1979," No. 25:1, 1978.

Socioeconomic Newsletter. "Social Welfare Abroad: Swedish Welfare System Under Stress," 3(8):4–5, 1978.

――――. "Major Inflation Cause: Waning Work Ethic," 4(6):3, 1979.

Special HEW Report on Welfare Reform in "Administrations Welfare Reform Proposal," Joint Hearings, Welfare Reform subcommittee of Committee on Agriculture, Com-mittee on Education and Labor, Committee on Ways and Means, House of Repre-sentatives, Ninety-fifth Congress. First Session on H.R. 9030, Sept. 19, 20, and 21, 1977. Serials 95–47. Washington, D.C.: U.S. Government Printing Office, 1977, pp. 11–94.

Srole, Leo, Thomas S. Langner, Stanley T. Michael, Marvin K. Opler, and Thomas A.C. Rennie. *Mental Health in the Metropolis*. New York: McGraw-Hill, 1962.

Staff Housing Supply Experiment. *Third Annual Report of the Housing Assistance Supply Experiment*, R-2151-HUD. Santa Monica: Rand, 1977.

———. *Fourth Annual Report of the Housing Assistance Supply Experiment*, R-2302-HUD. Santa Monica: Rand, 1978.

Staff Report, Office of Economic Opportunity. "Public Housing: The Idea Seems to Be That If the Government Subsidizes Your Rent, You Should Be Grateful for What You Get" (Cambridge, Mass,). Washington, D.C.: Office of Economic Opportunity, 1969.

Staff Study. *Studies in Public Welfare: Public Income Transfer Programs: The Incidence of Multiple Benefits and the Issues Raised by Their Receipts*. Paper No. 1. Washington, D.C.: U.S. Government Printing Office, 1973.

———. *Issues in Welfare Administration: Welfare an Administrative Nightmare*. Paper No. 5. Washington, D.C.: U.S. Government Printing Office, 1974.

Staff, Ways and Means Committee, U.S. House of Representatives. *National Health Insurance Resources Book*. Washington, D.C.: U.S. Government Printing Office, 1974.

Starr, Paul "Which of the Poor Shall Live in Housing," *Public Interest*, 20:116-24, 1970.

Steele, Paul D. "The Labelling Perspective of Deviance: A Critical Assessment," *Journal of Sociology*, 3:17-37, 1973.

———. "Exploration of the Labelling Perspective of Mental Illness in a Rehabilitation Situation." Ph.D. Dissertation, University of Texas at Austin, 1974.

———. "Exploration of the Labelling Systems in a Mental Health Rehabilitation Program." Paper presented at the Midwest Sociological Society, Chicago, April 8, 1975.

Steiner, Gilbert Y. *The State of Welfare*. Washington, D.C.: Brookings, 1971.

———. "Reform Follows Reality: The Growth of Welfare," *Public Interest*, 34:47-65, 1974.

Stern, David. *Housing Allowances: Some Considerations of Efficiency and Equity*. Working Paper No. 6. Cambridge, Mass.: Joint Center for Urban Studies, 1972.

Stewart, Maxwell S. *The Poor Among Us: Challenge and Opportunity*. New York: Public Affairs Pamphlet No. 22, 1972.

Stewart, Potter. *Hills v. Gautreux*. Pp. 638-47, in Donald Brieland and John Lemmon (eds.), *Social Work and the Law*. St. Paul, Minn.: West, 1977.

Stockman, David A. "Welfare Is the Problem," *Journal of the Institute for Socio-Economic Studies*, 3(3):39-50, 1978.

Stone, Robert C., and Frederic T. Schlamp. "Characteristics Associated with Receipt and Non-receipt of Financial Aid from Welfare Agencies," *Welfare in Review* 3:1-11, July 1965.

———. *Family Life Styles Below the Poverty Line*. San Francisco: Institute for Social Science Research, San Francisco State University, 1967.

Storer, Norman W. *The Social System of Science*. New York: Holt, 1966.

Stouffer, Samuel F. et al. *Studies in Social Psychology in World War II*, volume 1, *The American Soldier: Adjustment During Army Life*. Princeton, New Jersey: Princeton University Press, 1949.

Street, David. "Welfare Administration and Organization Theory." Paper presented at the Annual Meeting of the American Sociological Association, San Francisco, 1978.

Subcommittee on Fiscal Policy of the Joint Economic Committee, U.S. Congress. *The Effectiveness of Manpower Training Programs: A Review of Research on the Impact on the Poor*. Washington, D.C.: U.S. Government Printing Office, 1972.

Sudovar, Stephen G., Jr., and Kathleen Sullivan. *National Health Insurance Issues: The Unprotected Population*. Washington, D.C.: Hoffman-La Roche, 1977.

Summers, Anita A., and Barbara L. Wolfe. "Do Schools Make A Difference?" *American Economic Review*, 67(4):639-52, 1977.

Szasz, Thomas. *The Myth of Mental Illness: Foundations of a Theory of Personal Conduct.* New York: Dell, 1961.

———. *The Theology of Medicine.* New York: Harper, 1977.

Taylor, D. Garth, Lu Ann Aday, and Ronald Anderson. "Social Indicators of Access to Medical Care," *Journal of Health and Social Behavior,* 16(1):39–49, 1975.

Theobald, Robert. *The Rich and the Poor.* New York: Mentor, 1961.

Theodorson, George A., and Achilles G. Theodorson. *Modern Dictionary of Sociology.* New York: Crowell, 1969.

Thomas, Dorothea. "SSI Beneficiaries Medically Determined to Be Alcoholics or Drug Addicts." Research and Statistics Note No. 8. Washington, D.C.: Social Security Administration, 1977.

Thomas, E. J., and R. D. Carter. "Social Psychological Factors in Poverty," in M. N. Zald (ed.), *Organizing for Community Welfare.* Chicago: Quadrangle Books, 1967.

Thomas, W. I. *The Unadjusted Girl.* Boston: Little, Brown, 1931.

Thurz, Daniel. "Social Aspects of Poverty," *Public Welfare* 25(3):179–86, July 1967.

Time Magazine. "Housing: It's Outasight," 110(11):50–57, 1977.

———. "It's Your Turn in the Sun. Now 19 Million and Growing Fast, Hispanics Are Becoming a Power," 112(16):48–52, 55, 58, 61, 1978.

Timnich, Lois. "Escaping the Welfare Rolls a Giant Step," *Los Angeles Times,* September 12, 1978, Part I, pp. 1, 17, 19.

Titmuss, Richard M. *Commitment to Welfare.* New York: Pantheon, 1968.

Tocqueville, Alexis de. *Democracy in America.* Vols. 1 and 2. New York: Vintage, 1954.

Tonnies, Ferdinand. *Community and Society, Gemeinschaft and Gesellschaft.* C. P. Loomis (ed.). New York: Harper, 1963.

Torrey, Fuller E. *The Mind Game: Witch Doctors and Psychiatrists.* New York: Bantam, 1973.

Trattner, Walter I. *From Poor Law to Welfare State: A History of Social Welfare in America.* New York: Free Press, 1974.

Treitel, Ralph. "Effect of Disabled Beneficiary Rehabilitation," *Social Security Bulletin* (DHEW Publication No. 76–11703), pp. 1–12, November 1975.

Tropman, John E. "Public Welfare, Change, Appropriations, Service." Mimeographed, 1971.

———. "The Constant Crisis: Social Welfare and the American Cultural Structure," *California Sociologist,* 1(1):61–88, 1978.

Ulmer, Melville J. "Taking a Dim View of Humphrey-Hawkins," *New Republic,* 174(24):17–19, 1976.

Upman, Frances. "The Changing Roles of Welfare Employee and Client," *Public Welfare,* 27(4):318–26, 1969.

Urkowitz, Allen. "Danger: Not Enough Young at Work," *Time* Magazine, 109(22):64–65, 1977.

U.S Bureau of Labor Statistics. *Employment in Perspective: Working Women.* No. 2, Report No. 544. Washington, D.C.: U.S. Department of Labor, 1978.

U.S. Bureau of the Census. "Poor Families Headed by Women Show Rise," *Los Angeles Times,* April 5, 1974, Part 1B, p. 3.

———. *Historical Statistics of the United States—Colonial Times to 1970.* Washington, D.C.: U.S. Department of Commerce, 1975.

U.S. Bureau of the Census. *Current Population Reports.* Series P–6, No. 107, 1977.

U.S. Department of Housing and Urban Development. *Programs of HUD.* Washington, D.C.: Department of Housing and Urban Development, 1978.

U.S. Bureau of the Census, *Current Population Reports,* Series P–60, No. 115, "Characteristics of the Population below the Poverty Level: 1976," Washington, D.C.: U.S. Government Printing Office, 1978.

Valentine, Charles A. *Culture and Poverty: Critique and Counter-Proposals.* Chicago: University Press, 1968.

van den Hoag, Ernest, "Realistic Steps for 'Reforming' Welfare," *The Journal of the Institute for Socio–Economic Studies,* 4(4):73–79, Winter 1979.

Von Mises, Ludwig. *Planned Chaos.* New York: Irvington on Hudson Foundation for Economic Education, Inc., 1947, reprinted in 1972.

Vogl, Frank. "Can America Solve Its Jobs Problem?" *London Times,* August 24, 1978, p. 17.

Wildavsky, Aaron, "Doing Better and Feeling Worse: The Political Pathology of Health Policy" in John H. Knowles (ed.), *Doing Better and Feeling Worse: Health in the U.S.* New York: W.W. Norton, 1977, pp. 105–23.

Warren, R. L. "The Conflict Intersystem and the Change Agent," *Journal of Conflict Resolution,* 8(3):231–41, 1964.

Watts, Harold W. "The Measurement of Poverty: An Exploratory Exercise," Institute for Research on Poverty, University of Wisconsin at Madison, 1969.

———, and Felicity Skidmore. "The Implications for Changing Family Patterns and Behavior for Labor Force and Hardship Management." Madison, Wis.: Institute for Research on Poverty, University of Wisconsin, 1978.

Waxman, Chaim I. *The Stigma of Poverty: A Critique of Poverty Theories and Policies.* New York: Pergamon, 1977.

Ways and Means Committee, U.S. Congress. *Hearings on H.R. 10032.* Eighty-seventh Congress, Second Session. Washington, D.C.: U.S. Government Printing Office, 1962.

Webb, Beatrice (Potter), and James Sydney Webb Passfield. *English Poor Law Policy.* London: Longmans, 1910.

Webb, Sidney, and Beatrice Webb. "Report of the Royal Commission on Poor Laws and Relief of Distress: Minority Report 1909, Introduction to Part I," in Roy Lubove *Social Welfare in Transition: Selected English Documents 1834–1909.* Pittsburgh: University of Pittsburgh Press, 1966.

Weinberger, Caspar. "The Reform of Welfare: A National Necessity," *Journal of the Institute for Socio-Economic Studies,* 1(1):1–27, 1976.

Welch, F. R. *Minimum Wage Legislation in the U.S.,* P5145. Santa Monica: Rand, 1973.

———. *Effects of Minimum Wages on the Age Composition of Youth Employment,* P5468. Santa Monica: Rand, 1975.

———. *Minimum Wages: Issues and Evidence,* P5999. Santa Monica: Rand, 1978.

———, and M. Kosters. *The Effects of Minimum Wages on the Distribution of Changes in Aggregate Employment,* RM–6273–OEO. Santa Monica: Rand, 1970.

Welfeld, Irving H. "Toward a New Federal Housing Project," *Public Interest,* 19:31–43, 1970.

———. "American Housing Policy: Perverse Programs by Prudent People," *Public Interest,* 48:128–44, 1977.

Wilcox, Claire. *Toward Social Welfare.* Homewood, Ill.: Irwin, 1969.

Wilensky, Harold L., and C. N. Lebeaux. *Industrial Society and Social Welfare.* New York: Free Press, 1958.

Wilhelm, Sidney M., and Edwin H. Powell. "Who Needs the Negro?" *Transaction,* 1(6):3–6, 1964.

Williams, Kenton. "Some Implications for Services," *Public Welfare,* 27(4):327–32, 1969.

Williamson, John B. "Beliefs About Welfare Recipients." Paper presented at the American Sociological Association, 1973.

———. "Beliefs About the Welfare Poor," *Sociology and Social Research,* 58(2):163–75, 1974.

———. "National Income Insurance as an Anti-Poverty Strategy." Paper presented at the Annual Meeting of the Society for the Study of Social Problems, 1974.

———. "Social Security: Insurance or Welfare?" Paper presented at the Annual Meeting of the Society for the Study of Social Problems, 1978.

———, et al. *Strategies Against Poverty in America.* New York: Schenkman, 1975.

Wilner, D., R. Walkley, T. Pinkerton, and M. Tayback. "The Housing Environment and Family Life: A Longitudinal Study of the Effects of Housing on Morbidity and Mental Health." P. 993, (footnote 24), in Robert J. Levy, Thomas P. Lewis, and Peter W. Martin (eds.), *Social Welfare and the Individual: Cases and Materials.* Mineola: Foundation Press, 1971.

Winslow, Benjamin H. *Wage Record Clearance Systems: Colorado and Oklahoma.* Washington, D.C.: U.S. Department of Health, Education and Welfare, 1975.

Winston, M. P., and T. Forsher. *Non-support of Legitimate Children by Affluent Fathers as a Cause of Poverty and Welfare Dependence,* P4665–1. Santa Monica: Rand, 1974.

Wishnov, Barbara. *Determinants of the Work-Welfare Choice: A Study of AFDC Women.* Boston: Boston College, 1973.

Witte, Edwin E. *The Development of the Social Security Act.* Madison: University of Wisconsin Press, 1962.

Woodroofe, Kathleen. *From Charity to Social Work in England and the United States.* Toronto: University Press, 1962.

Yanis-McLaughlin, Virginia. *Family and Community: Italian Immigrants in Buffalo, 1880–1930.* Ithaca, N.Y.: Cornell Press, 1978.

Yankelovich, Daniel. "The Revolt's Deeper Roots," *Time* Magazine 112(3):59–60, 1978.

Yelaja, Shankar (ed.). *Authority and Social Work: Concept and Use.* Toronto: University Press, 1971.

Young, Ned. "Work and Welfare," *Journal of the Institute for Socio-Economic Studies,* 3(1):40–51, 1978.

Zagoria, Sam. *Working with Automation.* Seminar on Manpower Policy and Program Series. Washington, D.C.: U.S. Government Printing Office, 1967.

Zigler, Edward. *Project Head Start: A Legacy of the War on Poverty,* New York: Free Press, 1979.

INDEX

College students: as transitional poor, 11

Colombotos, John, 254

Colonial America: adoption of Elizabethan Poor Law, 73; and centralized control of assistance, 74; doctrine of lesser eligibility, 75; *gemeinschaft,* 73; poor law provisions of, 74-78

Commercial insurance, 124; compared to social insurance, 84; failings of, 84, programs, 93 (table). *See also* Social insurance

Committee for Economic Development: Downs report, 289

Commonlaw marriage, 168

Compact Between Generations Plan: compared to Prepaid Plan, 104 (table)

Comprehensive Employment and Training Act (1973) (CETA), 210-12, 327-29; impact of, 331; problems of, 329; titles within, 327-28

Comprehensive Health Care Act, 264-65

Comrie, Keith, 12

Conference Board Housing Report (1974), 281, 285

Conflict theory: and housing policy, 303; of macrosociety, 41-42; problem-solving approach of, 48; and view of poor, 46

Consumer Price Index, 208

Consumer protection law, 129

Con III Controversy, The (Noble), 310

Cooper, Maudine, 141

COS. *See* Charity Organization Society

Coser, Lewis, 42

Council of Economic Advisors: criticism of Humphrey-Hawkins Bill, 330

Credit: poor's perception of, 30

Credit income tax: features of, 198

Creedon, Carol, 12

Cronkhite, Leonard, 261

Culliton, Barbara, 257, 260

Cultural evolution: theory of, 354-55

Cultural gap: between bankers and poor, 281

Cultural theory: of lower class behavior, 7

Culture: differences within, 355-56

Culture of poverty, 5-6, 12, 14, 34; models for, 9; origins, 6. *See also* Poverty

CWA. *See* Civil Works Agency

Cybernation, 26, 317; effect of, 310. *See also* Automation

Dahl, Robert A., 42

Dahrendorf, Rolf, 42

Danziger, Sheldon, 211-13, 216, 223

Davie, Maurice R., 35

Davis, Karen, 237

Day-care centers, 219, 325

Dean, John P., 272

Decker, Peter R., 14

Deflation, 370

Dehumanization: as welfare issue, 165

Delinquency: meanings of, 357 (table)

Delivered equality: consequences of, *xi-xii*; defined, *xi*

Demogrant, 203; defined, 188-89

Deportation, 14

Depression (the), 40, 80, 274; welfare programs during, 220

Desertion: factor in public assistance, 137; as poor man's divorce, 147

Deutsch, M., 32

Disabled Workers Insurance: Social Security provisions for, 107

Discrimination: as health care obstacle, 232, 235-36; types of, 128-29

Disease: factors of, 238; as life style, 237

Divorce: factor in public assistance, 137

Dix, Dorothy, 78

Doctrine of lesser eligibility, 70-73,

(table). *See also* Commercial insurance

Social legislation: destructiveness of, 223; evolution of, 40; failures of, 278

Social mobility, 372; relation to education, 342-63

Social problem: defined, 40

Social reality: levels of, 99 (table)

Social reform: types of, 78

Social stratification: consequences of elimination, 225; effect of, 373

Social Security Act (1935), 72, 75, 79

Social Security Administration, 91

Social Security program, 84; beneficiary functions of, 105-13; expansion, 133; funding, 104-05

Social services: types, 176

Social work profession: personnel problems, 173-74

Society: democratic, 373; meanings of, 357 (table)

Society for the Improvement of the Conditions of the Poor (1840), 78

Society for the Prevention of Pauperism (1819), 78

Specht, H., 175

Speenhamland system, 68-69

Spiegelman, Robert G., 190

Spring, William J., 323

Srole, Leo, 313

SSI. *See* Supplementary Security Income

SSI-Aged. *See* Supplementary Security Income-Aid to Aged

SSI-Blind Aid. *See* Supplementary Security Income-Aid to Blind

SSI-Disabled. *See* Supplementary Security Income-Disabled Assistance

Starr, Paul, 287, 290

State (the): as provisions dispenser, *xi*

State employment service. *See* Employment programs

State Vocational Rehabilitation Agency (SVRA), 95

Status inflation, 3

Statute of Laborers: under Edward III, 62

Steele, Paul D., 138

Steinberg, Stephen, 313

Steiner, Gilbert Y., 137, 171, 282, 309

Stern, David, 298

Steward, Maxwell S., 29 (table), 30

Stigma, 57 (table), 138, 145; effect of, 147; perception of, 172; as public assistance issue, 115; public assistance versus social insurance, 87 (table), 114 (table); relation to poor law, 147; and Supplementary Security Income, 131

Stockman, David, 215-16; child payment proposal, 116

Stone, Robert C., 6, 149, 318

Storer, Norman W., 41

Stouffer, Samuel F.: *The American Soldier,* 11

Structural-functional theory: of macrosociety, 41; problem-solving approach of, 48; relation to school success, 347-48; and view of poor, 44

Student Nonviolent Committee, 136

Subcommittee on Fiscal Policy of the Congressional Joint Economic Committee: study of, 325

Success: in mainstream culture, 356; necessary capabilities for, 360

Sudovar, Stephen G., Jr., 237

Sullivan, Kathleen, 237

Sultan, Paul, 237, 242, 258

Summers, Anita A., 343

Sunday School Society, 78

Supplementary Security Income (SSI), 45, 80, 304; and Aid to Families with Dependent Children transfers, 221-22; compared to Aid to Families with Dependent Children, 99 (table); compared to General Assistance, 99 (table); effect on child, 146; provisions of, 131; recipient employment potential, 317; recipients, 117, 132; shortcomings of, 132; as social insur-

About the Authors

RALPH SEGALMAN is Professor of Sociology at California State University, Northridge. His earlier books include *Conflicting Rights: Social Legislation and Policy* and *Dynamics of Social Behavior and Development*.

ASOKE BASU is Professor of Sociology at California State University, Hayward. He is the author of *Elementary Statistical Theory in Sociology* and *Culture, Politics and Critical Academics*.